SPECIAL EDUCATION LAW

SPECIAL EDUCATION LAW

Thomas F. Guernsey
Professor of Law and Associate Dean
University of Richmond

Kathe Klare
Assistant Clinical Professor of Law
Director, Mental Disabilities Clinic
University of Richmond

CAROLINA
ACADEMIC
PRESS

700 KENT ST.
DURHAM, NC
27701

Dedication

For our children, Alison and Adam, who continue to teach us to be tolerant and understanding, and who willingly share us with the children we represent.

For Jonathan and his parents and all the other children and their parents who have received the benefit of IDEA.

International Standard Book Number: 0-89089-530-9
Library of Congress Number: 92-76162

Carolina Academic Press
700 Kent Street
Durham, North Carolina 27701
919-489-7486   FAX 919-493-5668

Printed in the United States of America

Contents

Preface

In the United States, over 4.5 million children between birth and 21 years of age have some form of disability. Four million of these children are receiving services under the Individuals with Disabilities Education Act (IDEA). That means four million individualized education programs were to be developed during that period; most of them were developed with little difficulty. A fair number of them, however, resulted in disputes between the parents of the child and the public agency responsible for educating the child.

This book is designed to take the lawyers, educators, and other professionals without prior experience through the process of providing special education services to children and, if agreement is not reached between the school and the public agency responsible for educating the child, through the process of resolving that disagreement. While the book assumes no knowledge on the part of the professional, it attempts to be more than an introduction. What we have strived to do is write a book that provides a solid background in special education law. The lawyer or other professional who seeks to do more detailed legal research should find the footnotes accompanying each section helpful.

One of the predominate themes of special education is that it should be individualized. As such, many of the cases in this area are fact-specific. While the text cannot explore each of these case-specific applications, the footnotes and appendixes should provide research leads for more particularized research.

By its very nature, this book is primarily limited to federal law in general and IDEA and Section 504 of the Rehabilitation Act of 1973 (504) in particular. One of the difficulties dealing with special education law is the interplay of several federal statutes, primarily IDEA and 504, and to a lesser extent 42 U.S.C. 1983, as well as supporting federal regulations. Further, there are often statutes and regulations affecting general education which affect special education. For example, the Education Department General Administrative Regulations (EDGAR) and the Family Educational Rights and Privacy Act (FERPA or the Buckley Amendments) play a significant role. Chapter 1 provides a general overview of IDEA and its interrelationship with 504, 1983, EDGAR and FERPA. In each of the succeeding chapters, the primary focus is on the IDEA, however, full attention is also given to the impact 504 has on the subject, as well as any additional federal statute affecting the particular area.

State law should always be checked. Each state has its own statutes and regulations implementing the IDEA. The supremacy clause prohibits states from providing less than the federal statutes and regulations. While these statutes and regulations usually mirror the federal statutes and regulations, this is not always the case. For example, federal statutes and regulations are silent on some points, and Congress has allowed states to develop independent standards in some areas. Further, some states actually provide more substantive and procedural rights than required under IDEA. The addresses where copies of state regulations can be obtained, often at no cost, are listed in Appendix 2.

Even the lawyer reading the footnotes may find some authorities with which he or she is not familiar. There are of course citations to court decisions, federal statutes and regulations. In addition, however, there are numerous citations to opinions written by the staff of two offices of the Department of Education: The Office of Civil Rights (OCR), the Office of Special Education and Rehabilitative Services (OSERS), and its Office of Special Education Programs (OSEP). OCR is responsible for monitoring compliance with 504, while OSEP is responsible for monitoring compliance with IDEA. Each office, therefore has occasion to interpret the regulations of the respective statutes.

The OCR and OSEP opinions, being the interpretation of the agency having written the regulation, are afforded, as with all agency determinations, considerable deference by the courts. In areas where there are no court decisions, they may be particularly significant.

For the non-lawyer, a brief explanation of the primary authorities used is contained in Appendix 1.

Portions of this work have appeared, often in significantly different form in the following law journals. The authors thank the journals for their permission to use the material in this book. Guernsey and Sweeney, *The Church, the State, and the EHA: Educating the Handicapped in Light of the Establishment Clause*, 73 Marquette L. Rev. 101 (1990); Guernsey, *The Education for All Handicapped Children Act, 42 U.S.C. Section 1983 and Section 504 of the Rehabilitation Act of 1973: Statutory Interaction Following the Handicapped Children's Protection Act of 1986*, 68 Nebraska Law Review 564 (1989); Guernsey, *The School Pays the Piper, But How Much? Attorneys' Fees in Special Education Cases After the Handicapped Children's Protection Act of 1986*, 23 Wake Forest Law Review 237 (1988); Guernsey, *When the Teachers and Parents Can't Agree, Who Really Decides? Burdens of Proof and Standards of Review Under the Education for All Handicapped Children Act*, 36 Cleveland State Law Review 67 (1987–1988).

We would also like to thank several people for their assistance, including Scott Fell, Christopher Royer, Diane Silverman, Debra Tedeschi and Linda Ziegler, former University of Richmond law students. M. Grey Sweeney, also a former University of Richmond law student, deserves special thanks for her work on chapters 5 and 8.

Note on Abbreviations

Special education law is replete with abbreviations beginning with the title of the act. The abbreviations are explained throughout the text. We have, however, as a matter of convenience listed below the more common:

EAHCA   Education for all Handicapped Children Act

EDGAR   Education Department General Administrative Regulations

EHA   Education for the Handicapped Act

FAPE   Free Appropriate Public Education

FERPA   Family Educational Rights and Privacy Act (Buckley Amendments)

IDEA   Individuals with Disabilities Education Act

IEE   Individualized Education Program

IFSP   Individualized Family Service Plan

ITDA   Infants and Toddlers with Disabilities Act

LEA   Local Education Authority

OCR   Office of Civil Rights (U.S. Department of Education)

OSEP   Office of Special Education Programs (U.S. Department of Education)

OSERS   Office of Special Education and Rehabilitative Services (U.S. Department of Education)

SEA   State Education Authority

Chapter 1

An Overview

1.1 Introduction

Signed into law in 1975, the Individuals with Disabilities Education Act[1] imposes significant responsibilities on the local and state educational authorities to insure that children with disabilities are receiving a free and appropriate public education (FAPE). The Act was formerly called the Education for All Handicapped Children Act. Known also as the EAHCA, EHA, or Public Law 94-142, its name was changed in December, 1990. The new acronym is IDEA (Individuals with Disabilities Education Act). To avoid confusion, we refer to the statute as IDEA or the Act, except where quotations require reference to a previously used acronym.

This landmark legislation was designed to insure not only the substantive right to the FAPE, but also to provide extensive procedural protections, including the right to file a judicial action following exhaustion of administrative remedies as a means of assuring the provision of the substantive right.

Section 504 of the Rehabilitation Act of 1973 also affects educational rights of children with disabilities.[2] Section 504 is broad and general in coverage, while IDEA is narrow and specific. Section 504 prohibits discrimination generally and covers not just educational institutions, nor simply public institutions, since it covers all people with disabilities and all programs or activities receiving federal assistance.[3] There is significant overlap between the two statutes.[4] There are, however, significant differences that will be discussed.

In addition, 42 U.S.C. § 1983 plays a role in insuring the protections afforded to children and their parents under IDEA. Further, in specific contexts, general

---

1. 20 U.S.C. §§ 1400–1485.

2. 29 U.S.C. § 794. Section 504 provides:

> No otherwise qualified handicapped individual . . . shall, solely by reason of his handicap, be excluded from participation in, be denied the benefits of, or be subjected to discrimination under any program or activity receiving federal financial assistance.

3. *Id.*

4. Indeed, New Mexico, at one time the only state to have opted out of IDEA, discovered that it would have to follow much of IDEA in order to avoid discrimination under § 504. New Mexico Association for Retarded Citizens v. New Mexico, 495 F. Supp. 391 (D.N.M. 1980) *rev'd. in part*, 678 F.2d 847 (10th Cir. 1982). The New Mexico legislature participated in IDEA funding after it became clear that § 504 would require compliance with federal requirements without the corresponding funding of IDEA. C. Salomone, **Equal Education Under Law** 149 n.46 (1986).

educational provisions also play a role. In particular, the Education Department General Administrative Regulations[5] and the Family Educational Rights and Privacy Act[6] affect delivery of educational services to children with disabilities.

1.2 Brief History

The modern legal history of education for children with disabilities began with *Brown v. Board of Education*,[7] in which the United States Supreme Court held that education, "where the state has undertaken to provide it, is a right which must be available to all on equal terms."[8] It was not, however, until 1971 that "lightning struck"[9] and significant progress was made in insuring this right to children with disabilities. In *Pennsylvania Association of Retarded Citizens (PARC) v. Pennsylvania*,[10] the state of Pennsylvania, in a consent decree, recognized the right to education for mentally retarded children. By the terms of the consent decree, parents in Pennsylvania were provided with significant procedural and substantive rights that would "set a detailed model for future advocates"[11] and would find their national application four years later in IDEA. Among the rights agreed to in the *PARC* decision were the right to a free appropriate education, individualized education planning, notice of proposed changes in educational programming, and other due process procedures, including formal due process hearings.

In a second decision of equal importance, *Mills v. Board of Education*,[12] the federal district court held that the District of Columbia's exclusion of children with disabilities from educational programming denied the children due process and equal protection of the law. Rejecting the District's argument that funds were insufficient,[13] the court ordered the District to develop a plan to provide both appropriate educational programming and due process rights to protect the substantive educational rights.

While litigation, as represented by *PARC* and *Mills*, was proceeding, Section 504 of the Rehabilitation Act of 1973 was enacted, providing that "No otherwise qualified handicapped individual...shall solely by reason of his handicap be excluded from participation in, be denied the benefits of, or be subjected to discrimination under any program or activity receiving federal assistance."[14]

---

5. 34 C.F.R. § 76.1; *see also* 20 U.S.C. §§ 1221e(a)(1), 2831(a), 3474.

6. 20 U.S.C. §§ 1230 *et seq.*; 34 C.F.R., Part 99.

7. 347 U.S. 483 (1954).

8. Id. at 493.

9. Weiner and Hume, **And Education for All** 27 (2d ed. 1987).

10. 343 F. Supp. 279 (E.D. Pa. 1972), *modifying* 334 F. Supp. 1257 (E.D. Pa. 1971).

11. Goldberg, **Special Education** 3 (1982).

12. 348 F. Supp. 866 (D.D.C. 1972).

13. "[I]f sufficient funds are not available to finance all of the services and programs that are needed and desirable in the system then the available funds must be expended equitably in such a manner that no child is entirely excluded from a publicly supported education consistent with his needs and ability to benefit there from." *Id.* at 876.

14. 29 U.S.C. § 794.

In 1974, Congress took another major step, amending the Elementary and Secondary Education Act. These amendments would be the heart of the Education for All Children Act, but did not have the specific mandate of a time table imposing on states the obligation to implement substantive and procedural rights. In 1975, however, Congress passed, and President Ford signed into law P.L. 94-142, the Education for All Handicapped Children Act of 1975.[15] The law became fully effective in 1978, and required states accepting federal special education funding to implement explicit, detailed substantive and procedural rights. By its implementation in 1978, all states, except New Mexico, had decided to accept the funds and implement the Act. New Mexico, six years later, discovered that it was subject to many of the same requirements under § 504 as it would be under IDEA, and opted to accept the federal funds and implement IDEA.[16]

Given the apparent overlap of § 504 and IDEA, actions were brought to vindicate educational rights under both acts. Several advantages were readily apparent in bringing an action under § 504 for protections that were also available under IDEA. Among the significant advantages to parents included the fact that attorneys' fees were available under § 504, but prior to late 1986, they were not available under IDEA.[17] Further, § 504 does not have the extensive administrative procedures which must be exhausted prior to bringing a lawsuit.[18]

In addition to § 504, suits were brought concurrently under 42 U.S.C. § 1983[19] on claims that were covered by IDEA.[20] Section 1983 claims were brought on the assumption that failure to provide services consistent with the requirements of IDEA was a deprivation of a right guaranteed by federal statute.[21] Section 1983, unlike § 504, has no separate implementing regulations. Section 1983, however, provided three important advantages: attorneys' fees,[22] damages,[23] and lack of an administrative remedy to exhaust.[24] The fact that violations of § 504 or § 1983 could result in the award of attorneys' fees guaranteed that suits alleging underlying violations of IDEA would also allege violations of § 504 and § 1983.[25]

---

15. 20 U.S.C. § 1401 et seq.

16. New Mexico Association for Retarded Citizens v. New Mexico (*NMARC*), 678 F.2d 847 (10th Cir. 1982).

17. Smith v. Robinson, 468 U.S. 992 (1984).

18. Miener v. State of Missouri, 673 F.2d 969 (8th Cir. 1982); Camenisch v. University of Texas, 616 F.2d 127, 135 (5th Cir. 1980) *vacated on other grounds* 451 U.S. 390 (1981); Adashunas v. Negley, 626 F.2d 600 (7th Cir. 1980); Sanders v. Marquette Pub. Schools, 561 F. Supp. 1361, 1369 (W.D. Mich. 1983). *See generally* Hyatt, *Litigating The Rights Of Handicapped Children To An Appropriate Education: Procedures And Remedies*, 29 U.C.L.A. L. Rev. 1, 35–38(1981); Smith, *Handicap Discrimination* 30 Ark. L. Rev. 1, 41–43 (1985). *But see* Smith v. United States Postal Service, 742 F.2d 257 (6th Cir. 1984) aff'd. 766 F.2d 205 (6th Cir. 1985) (requiring exhaustion under § 504).

19. 42 U.S.C. § 1983.

20. *E.g.*, Jose P. v. Ambach, 669 F.2d 865 (2d Cir. 1982).

21. *See, e.g.*, Quackenbush v. Johnson City School Dist., 716 F.2d 141 (2d Cir. 1983).

22. 42 U.S.C. § 1988.

23. *See* Hyatt, *supra* note 12, at 588.

24. *See* Patsy v. Florida Bd. of Regents, 457 U.S. 496 (1982); *see generally,* S. Nahmod, **Civil Rights and Civil Liberties Litigation** 295–298 (2d ed. 1986).

25. *See, e.g.*, Quackenbush v. Johnson City School Dist., 716 F.2d 141 (2d Cir. 1983); Colin K.

Lower courts split on the issue of whether IDEA was the exclusive remedy or whether actions covered by IDEA could be brought concurrently under § 1983 and § 504.[26] The United States Supreme Court in 1984 addressed the issue in *Smith v. Robinson*.[27] The Court held: "Congress intended the EAHCA to be the exclusive avenue through which a plaintiff may assert an equal protection claim to a publicly financed special education."[28]

In *Smith*, the Court held that IDEA and its lack of an attorneys' fees provision, as well as its detailed administrative requirements, could not be circumvented by filing suit under § 504 or § 1983. In the language of the Court:

> Even assuming that the reach of § 504 is co-extensive with that of the EAHCA, there is no doubt that the remedies, rights, and procedures Congress set out in the EAHCA are the ones it intended to apply to a handicapped child's claim to a free appropriate education. We are satisfied that Congress did not intend a handicapped child to be able to circumvent the requirements or supplement the remedies of the EAHCA by resort to the general anti-discrimination provision of § 504.[29]

Smith interestingly left open the possibility of suits under either § 1983 or § 504 where the respective statute provided protection in addition to that offered by IDEA. Considering the § 1983 action, the Court in *Smith* found the due process and equal protection claims raised by the plaintiffs to be virtually identical to IDEA claims that were raised. The Court, however, did not rule out relief under § 1983 when the violation alleged was not the substantial equivalent to an underlying IDEA claim. In fact, the Court raised, but left undecided the issue of "whether the procedural safeguards set out in the EAHCA manifest Congress' intent to preclude resort to § 1983 on a due process challenge . . . "[30]

Similarly, *Smith* recognized that where § 504 provided greater substantive protection, suit could be brought under § 504:

> We emphasize the narrowness of our holding. We do not address a situation where the EAHCA is not available or where § 504 guarantees substantive rights greater than those available under the EAHCA. We hold only that where, as here, whatever remedy might be provided under § 504 is, provided with more clarity and precision under the EAHCA, a plaintiff may not circumvent or enlarge on the remedies available under the EAHCA by resort to § 504.[31]

---

v. Schmidt, 715 F.2d 1 (1st Cir. 1983) *affirming* 536 F. Supp. 1375 (D. R.I. 1982); Department of Educ. of Hawaii v. Katherine D., 727 F.2d 809 (9th Cir. 1983); Hymes v. Harnett County Bd. of Educ., 664 F.2d 410 (4th Cir. 1981).

26. *Compare* Georgia Association of Retarded Citizens v. McDaniel, 716 F.2d 1565, 1578–1579 (11th Cir. 1983) vacated on other grounds 468 U.S. 1213 (1984); Quackenbush v. Johnson City School Dist., 716 F.2d 141 (2d Cir. 1983) (§ 1983 remedies available) *with* Department of Educ. of Hawaii v. Katherine D., 727 F.2d 809 (9th Cir.1983) (IDEA provides exclusive remedies); Anderson v. Thompson, 658 F.2d 1205 (7th Cir. 1981).

27. 468 U.S. 992 (1984).

28. *Id*. at 1009.

29. *Id*. at 1019.

30. *Smith*, 468 U.S. at 1013.

31. *Id*. at 1021.

Congress reacted quickly to *Smith* by enacting the Handicapped Children's Protection Act of 1986,[32] amending IDEA and providing for the award of attorneys' fees.[33] In addition to the award of attorneys' fees, however, Congress also provided that IDEA would not be the "exclusive avenue" and a cause of action under § 1983 and § 504 was again possible for educational rights of children with disabilities.[34]

The attorneys' fees provisions of the amendments were widely known and quickly acted upon by lawyers.[35] The reaffirmation of the role of §§ 504 and 1983, however, received little attention, with courts dismissing § 504 and § 1983 claims well after IDEA was amended.[36] More recently, however, courts have rec-

---

32. 20 U.S.C. §§ 1415(e)(4) and 1415(f).

33. For a discussion of the attorneys' fees provisions of IDEA see chapter 15.

34. 20 U.S.C. § 1415(f). The amended ACT now provides:

Nothing in this chapter shall be construed to restrict or limit the rights, procedures, and remedies available under the Constitution, Title V of the Rehabilitation Act of 1973 [§ 504], or other Federal statutes... except that before the filing of a civil action under such laws seeking relief that is also available under [IDEA], the procedures... [of this section] shall be exhausted to the same extent as would be required had the action been brought under [IDEA].

35. *E.g.*, School Bd. of Prince William County v. Malone, 662 F. Supp. 999 (E.D. Va. 1987); Burpee v. Manchester School Dist., 661 F. Supp. 731 (D.N.H. 1987).

36. The silence with which this provision was received is illustrated by numerous cases dismissing § 1983 or § 504 claims after the amendment was passed. *See, e.g.*, Kerr Center Parents Assoc. v. Charles, 842 F.2d 1052 (9th Cir. 1988); Association for Retarded Citizens of Alabama, Inc. v. Teague, 830 F.2d 158 (11th Cir. 1987); Barwacz v. Michigan Dep't. of Educ., 674 F. Supp. 1296 (W.D. Mich. 1987); DeFalco v. Deer Lake School Dist., 663 F. Supp. 1108 (W.D. Pa. 1987) (§ 1983 claims dismissed on basis of Smith v. Robinson); *see generally* Robinson v. Pinderhughes, 810 F. 2d 1270 (4th Cir. 1987).

This lack of attention is consistent with the general lack of understanding of the relationship of § 504 and IDEA. In the House Report supporting the then proposed Handicapped Children's Protection Act of 1986, in reference to the ability to file complaints under § 504 as well as IDEA, it was written "Several witnesses testified regarding the need to clarify the availability of these avenues." H.R. Rep. No. 296, 99th Cong., 1st Sess. 7 (1985).

Some of the lack of attention to the amendment itself, however, may result from confusion over the effective date of the amended IDEA. Congress specifically provided that the attorneys' fees provisions would have partial retroactive effect. Attorneys' fees were to be available in all actions brought after July 3, 1984, or were pending on July 4, 1984. P.L. 99-372, section 5. This provision allowed recovery of fees in actions that were concluded over two years prior to the amendment. The absence of such a specific provision has led courts to hold that the reinstatement of the § 504 and § 1983 claims was not to be retroactive. *E.g.*, Silano v. Tirozzi, 651 F. Supp. 1021, 1025 (D. Conn. 1987). Courts, such as *Silano*, however, have held that § 504 and § 1983 are not only unavailable for claims litigated to completion between July 4, 1984 and the amendment in August, 1986, but § 504 and § 1983 are unavailable for claims which were pending at the time of the amendment. *Id.* (absence of retroactive language in light of attorneys' fees retroactivity, congressional language that no intent to be retroactive, and manifest injustice all indicate § 1983 and § 504 inapplicable to claims pending at time of enactment); Taylor v. Board of Educ. of the Copake-Taconic Hills Central School Dist., 649 F. Supp. 1253, 1259 (N.D.N.Y. 1986).

Several other courts have held that the absence of a specific retroactivity provision does not preclude assertion of § 504 or § 1983 claims in suits which were pending at the time of the amendment. *See, e.g.*, Mrs. W. v. Tirozzi, 832 F.2d 748, 755 (2d Cir. 1987) ("a court is required to apply the law in effect when it renders a decision, absent congressional directive to the contrary."); *accord* Edward B. v. Rochester New Hampshire School Dist., 558 Educ. Handicapped L. Rep. (CRR) 176 (D.N.H. Nov. 20, 1986) (no injustice in applying amended act to pending suit).

ognized the ability to bring an action under IDEA as well as under § 504 and § 1983.[37]

There are, however, court decisions which hold, citing pre-*Smith v. Robinson* decisions, that despite Congressional action recognizing the ability to bring suit under §§ 504 and 1983, compliance with IDEA satisfies the requirements of §504.[38] Assuming, however, the rights and protections in the § 504 implementing regulations are valid,[39] it would appear that §§ 504 and 1983 do provide educational rights in addition to any rights under IDEA. It is unlikely Congress would have reaffirmed the ability to bring suit under both IDEA and §§ 504 and 1983, if it had not envisioned the ability of § 504 or § 1983 to provide additional rights. Truly independent claims that did not enlarge on the remedies available under IDEA were not precluded under *Smith* in any event.[40]

1.3 IDEA: An Overview

IDEA is a funding statute. In order to qualify to receive federal funds, commonly referred to as Part B funds,[41] a state educational authority (SEA) must assume responsibility for effecting a policy that assures a free appropriate public education (FAPE) is being provided by local agencies to all children with disabilities.[42]

Funding under IDEA is determined on a state-by-state basis, according to the number of children with disabilities served. The number of children with disabilities ages three to twenty-one, inclusive, who are receiving special education and related services is multiplied by a figure equalling forty percent of the average national per pupil expenditure in elementary and secondary schools during the second fiscal year preceding the year of computation. The figure determined by the formula represents a ceiling on the amount of funds to which a state is entitled, not the actual amount a state will receive.[43]

Each state is charged with the task of devising and implementing its own program to monitor the performance of its public schools in providing special education and related services.[44] The key provision of IDEA is that each child is entitled to a free and appropriate public education (FAPE).[45] A free appropriate education is defined as special education and related services provided in con-

---

37. *E.g.*, Mrs. C. v. Wheaton, 916 F.2d 69 (2d Cir. 1990) (failure to provide notice violated both IDEA and § 504); *see also* Howell v. Waterford Pub. Schools, 731 F. Supp. 1314 (E.D. Mich. 1990); G.C. v. Coler, 673 F. Supp. 1093 (S.D. Fla. 1987).

38. *E.g.*, Burke County Bd. of Educ. v. Denton, 895 F.2d 973 (4th Cir. 1990).

39. For a discussion of the validity of the regulations, see 1.4.1.

40. *See supra* text at note 25.

41. P.L. 94-142 is often referred to as Part B of the Education of the Handicapped Act. Part B funds, therefore, refers to monies provided under the entitlement program added to the Act by P.L. 94-142.

42. 20 U.S.C. § 1412(1).

43. Jones, A Practical Guide to Federal Special Education Law: Understanding and Implementing P.L. 94-142, 36–37 (1981). *See* 20 U.S.C. § 1411 (entitlements and allocations).

44. *See, e.g.*, 20 U.S.C. § 1413(a)(11).

45. 20 U.S.C. § 1400(c); 34 C.F.R. § 300.1; *see* 20 U.S.C. § 1401(a)(18); 34 C.F.R. § 300.8.

formity with the requirements of IDEA.[46] The centerpiece of IDEA is the requirement that the local educational agency (LEA) develop, at least annually, an individualized educational program (IEP) for each child.[47] The IEP is to state the child's present level of educational functioning and articulate both long- and short-term educational goals and objectives.[48] Placements must be in the least restrictive environment.[49]

Beyond these general principles, Congress provided very little in the way of defining the substantive right to an education. Congress was, however, very explicit when it came to the procedural protections to which the parents and child were entitled to ensure the school authorities provided those identified children with a FAPE.

The extensive procedural protections include parental consent or involvement in most decisions affecting the child's educational program.[50] Indeed, the requirement of "meaningful input into all decisions affecting their child's education …" was reaffirmed by the United States Supreme Court in *Honig v. Doe.*[51] The Court further stated:

> Envisioning the IEP as the centerpiece of the statute's education delivery system for disabled children, and aware that schools had all too often denied such children appropriate educations without in any way consulting their parents, Congress repeatedly emphasized throughout the Act the importance and indeed the necessity of parental participation in both the development of the IEP and any subsequent assessment of its effectiveness.[52]

Specific procedural protections include first that the child be identified.[53] The child is then evaluated by the multi-disciplinary team.[54] Following evaluation, a meeting is convened to determine the child's eligibility for special education.[55] After an eligibility determination, an IEP is developed, with parental participation.[56]

Following development of an IEP, a placement decision is made, based on the goals and objectives contained in the IEP.[57] The IEP must then be reviewed at least annually. In addition, the child must be re-evaluated at least every three years.[58] Congress also required multi-disciplinary and nondiscriminatory testing.[59] To insure the parents have sufficient information available to participate in

---

46. 20 U.S.C. § 1401(a)(18); 34 C.F.R. § 300.8.
47. 20 U.S.C. § 1412(4); § 1414(a)(5); 34 C.F.R. § 300.343(d).
48. 20 U.S.C. § 1401(19); 34 C.F.R. § 300.346.
49. 20 U.S.C. § 1412(5)(B); § 1414(a)(1)(C)(iv); 34 C.F.R. § 300.550–554. See 8.2.
50. 20 U.S.C § 1414(a)(1)(c)(iii); 1415(b)(1).
51. 484 U.S. 305, 311 (1988).
52. *Id.*
53. 20 U.S.C. § 1414(a)(1)(A); 34 C.F.R § 300.220.
54. 20 U.S.C. § 1412(5)(C); 34 C.F.R. § 300.531.
55. 34 C.F.R. § 300.343–.345.
56. 20 U.S.C. § 1401(19); *see* 34 C.F.R. § 300.345.
57. 34 C.F.R. § 300.552; .342(b)(1), *see also* 20 U.S.C. §§ 1412(2)(B)(4), (5)(B), (6), 1414(a)(5); 34 C.F.R. Pt. 300, App. C, Question 42.
58. 34 C.F.R. 300.534; *see also* 20 U.S.C. § 1412(5)(c).
59. 20 U.S.C. § 1412(5)(C); *see* 34 C.F.R. § 300.532.

the educational decision-making, Congress provided the parents with the right to have an independent educational evaluation (IEE) at public expense.[60] The IEE, like the school system's evaluation, is to be multi-disciplinary.[61]

If at any point in this process there is a disagreement between parents and the LEA, a due process hearing may be requested.[62] Following this administrative hearing, the state may provide a state level review.[63] Following this administrative process, suit may be filed in either state or federal court.[64]

1.4 Section 504: An Overview

Regulations promulgated by the Department of Education,[65] implementing § 504 provide procedural and substantive obligations which local educational agencies are to follow. In many instances, the regulations explicitly mirror IDEA and regulations promulgated under it.[66] In fact, the relationship of § 504 and IDEA was recognized by the United States Department of Education. In the comments to IDEA regulations, the Department stated:

> As the regulations being developed under section 504 . . . are in the process of being finalized at the same time these proposed regulations [for IDEA] are being published, every effort will be made to have the final regulations be consistent in concept, policy, and, wherever possible, consistent with the language of the final 504 regulations.[67]

1.4.1 The Validity of Section 504 Regulations and Undue Burden

Section 504 is a broad statutory prohibition. Regulations promulgated under it, however, articulate specific requirements that school systems are required to follow. Before a meaningful comparison of the requirements under § 504 and IDEA can be made, however, a preliminary question concerning the validity of the Department of Education's regulations under § 504 must be addressed: To the extent the 504 regulations require more than IDEA, do they exceed the authority Congress intended the Department of Education to exercise? This is particularly true in light of court decisions which hold that compliance with IDEA will always insure compliance with § 504.[68]

---

60. 20 U.S.C. § 1415(b)(1)(A); *see* 34 C.F.R. § 300.503.
61. 20 U.S.C. § 1415(b)(1)(A).
62. 20 U.S.C. § 1415(b)(2).
63. *Id.* § 1415(c).
64. *Id.* § 1415(e)(1).
65. 34 C.F.R. § 104.31 *et seq.*
66. *Compare, e.g.,* 34 C.F.R. § 104.33 *with* 34 C.F.R. § 300.8, both of which define a free appropriate public education.
67. 41 Fed. Reg. 56967 (1976).
68. *See* Burke County Bd. of Educ. v. Denton, 895 F.2d 973 (4th Cir. 1990).

Any discussion of the validity of § 504 regulations must begin with a discussion of the Supreme Court decision in *Southeastern Community College v. Davis*.[69] *Davis* involved the efforts of a hearing impaired woman to gain enrollment in a community college nurse training program. Frances Davis filed suit in federal court alleging the community college had violated her rights under § 504. Davis alleged the college failed to accept her into its nursing program and provide adjustments to its standard educational program which would allow her to benefit despite her disability. Ms. Davis's disability allowed her to understand normal speech only through lip reading.

In addressing Ms. Davis's claims of discrimination, the Court focused on § 504's "otherwise qualified" language, and concluded that Ms. Davis was not otherwise qualified. Focusing on her inability to hear speech, the Court stated that such an ability was "indispensable for many of the functions that a registered nurse performs."[70] Further, the Court held that the accommodations that would be required for Ms. Davis to benefit from the nursing program would require such fundamental changes in the course of study that she would not "receive even a rough equivalent of the training a nursing program normally gives."[71]

The Supreme Court placed heavy reliance on the administrative regulations in reaching its decision, holding that it "is reasonably clear that [the regulation] does not encompass the kind of curricular changes that would be necessary to accommodate respondent in the nursing program."[72] Expanding on this concern with substantive changes in the program, the Court stated:

> Moreover, an interpretation of the regulations that required extensive modifications necessary to include respondent in the nursing program would raise grave doubts about their validity. If these regulations were to require substantial adjustments in existing programs beyond those necessary to eliminate discrimination against otherwise qualified individuals, they would do more than clarify the meaning of § 504. Instead, they would constitute an unauthorized extension of obligations imposed by that statute.[73]

The Court explicitly held that even if the regulation attempted to create an affirmative obligation, the United States Department of Health Education and Welfare (HEW) lacked the authority to do so.[74] The Court, however, left open the door that some affirmative action might be required. Holding that the line

---

69. 442 U.S. 397 (1979). Numerous law review articles have been written discussing *Davis*. *See e.g.* Cook & Laski, *Beyond* Davis: *Equality of Opportunity for Higher Education for Disabled Students Under the Rehabilitation Act of 1973*, 15 Harv. C.R.-C.L. L. Rev. 415 (1980); Wegner, *The Antidiscrimination Model Reconsidered: Ensuring Equal Opportunity Without Respect To Handicap Under Section 504 Of The Rehabilitation Act of 1973*, 69 Cornell L. Rev. 401, 452–459 (1984).

70. Davis, 442 U.S. at 407.

71. *Id.* at 410. Ms. Davis suggested that she be given individual supervision whenever attending patients directly and that certain required courses be waived. *Id.* at 407–408.

72. *Id.* at 409.

73. *Id.* at 410. The Court also pointed out Congress' specific requirement for affirmative efforts on the part of the federal government under §§ 501(b) and 503(a) and the absence of such a specific affirmative action requirement under § 504 as an indication "that Congress understood accommodation of the needs of the handicapped individuals may require affirmative action and knew how to provide for it in those instances where it wished to do so." *Id.* at 411.

74. *Id* at 411–412.

between "a lawful refusal to extend affirmative action and illegal discrimination" was not clear,[75] the Court stated that under certain circumstances continuing past practices could result in discrimination against qualified individuals. For example, technology might change such that "without imposing undue financial and administrative burdens upon a state" accommodations could be made which would allow participation by otherwise qualified individuals.[76]

What *Davis* left was the rule that § 504 does not require affirmative action on the part of the recipient, unless, apparently, the requested accommodations do not impose "undue financial and administrative burdens."[77] While decisions are not consistent in determining what an undue burden is, there are decisions holding that § 504 requires a great deal.

Perhaps the most important case addressing the impact of *Davis* on the special education regulations under 504 is *New Mexico Association for Retarded Citizens v. New Mexico (NMARC)*.[78] At the time of this decision, New Mexico was the only state that had not accepted funds under IDEA. Suit, therefore, was brought alleging the state's treatment of students with disabilities violated § 504. In holding for plaintiffs, the district court found that the various therapies and diagnostic services offered by the state were insufficient and that the state inadequately funded special education programs.

The United States Tenth Circuit Court of Appeals held that the Supreme Court's suggestion in *Davis* that refusal to modify an existing program might become discriminatory was applicable where "the entity's practices preclude the handicapped from obtaining system benefits realized by the non-handicapped."[79] Before such a finding, however, the district court must determine whether the State's existing program precludes people with a disability from enjoying benefits realized by the non-disabled; would the program modifications allow the person with a disability to benefit; and finally, whether the program modification would "jeopardize the overall viability of the state's educational system."[80] *NMARC*, estab-

---

75. *Id.* at 412.

76. *Id.* at 412. The Supreme Court's use of the phrase "affirmative action" was criticized by many commentators. The Court subsequently stated, "Regardless of the aptness of our choice of words in *Davis*, it is clear from the context ... that the term 'affirmative action' referred to those 'changes,' 'adjustments,' or modifications to existing programs that would be 'substantial' ... or that would constitute 'fundamental, alteration[s] in the nature of the program ...' " Alexander v. Choate, 469 U.S. 287, 301 n.20 (1985).

77. Davis, 442 U.S. at 412.

78. 678 F.2d 847 (10th Cir. 1982); *see also*, *e.g.*, S-1 v. Turlington, 635 F.2d 342 (5th Cir. 1981) (§ 504 requires educational services and procedural protections); Lora v. Board of Educ. of New York City, 456 F. Supp. 1211 (E.D.N.Y. 1978) (inadequate educational programming for emotionally disturbed children); Howard v. Friendswood Independent School Dist., 454 F. Supp. 634 (S.D. Tex. 1978) (failure to provide educational programming and procedural protections to brain damaged, emotionally disturbed child).

79. NMARC, 678 F.2d at 853. The court drew an analogy to two cases arising under Title VI of the Civil Rights Act of 1964, in which it was held that failure to provide educational programs for non-English speaking students discriminated against those students. *See* Lau v. Nichols, 414 U.S. 563(1974); Serna v. Portales Municipal Schools, 499 F.2d 1147 (10th Cir. 1974).

80. NMARC, 678 F.2d at 855. This three part test, occasioned by the special circumstances involving affirmative action on the part of the recipient, would apparently be in addition to the standard analysis of a regulations validity.

lished the general validity of the regulations, conditioned most significantly on the financial impact to the school system.

But, perhaps the best argument that § 504 regulations do not exceed what Congress intended, and hence are valid, is Congressional reaffirmation of § 504's application to the education of children with disabilities. Although courts vary widely in relying on subsequent legislation to infer congressional intent, it is generally recognized that subsequent legislation is probative. In *Zemel v. Rusk*,[81] for example, addressing the validity of regulations promulgated under passport legislation, the United States Supreme Court said that "Congress' failure to repeal or revise . . . administrative interpretation has been held to be persuasive evidence that interpretation is the one intended by Congress."[82]

The history of the promulgation of the regulations was tortured.[83] The Supreme Court in *Davis* used this history to point out that the deference normally due the administrative agency was diminished.[84] It further pointed out that "isolated statements by individual Members of Congress or its committees, all made after the enactment of the statute under consideration, cannot substitute for a clear expression of legislative intent at the time of enactment."[85] The Court stated, "these comments, none of which represents the will of Congress as a whole, constitute subsequent 'legislation' such as this Court might weigh in construing the meaning of an earlier enactment."[86]

"Subsequent legislation," however, has been passed. Congressional action in reaffirming the applicability of § 504 to education of children with disabilities is itself a reflection of Congress' view that § 504 regulations are valid. Rather than mere isolated comments that existed at the time *Davis* was decided, this provision provides a logical inference that Congress intended to affirm the regulations promulgated under § 504.

Congress was aware of existing regulations when it reinstated 504's full impact on educating children with disabilities.[87] The level of Congress' knowledge of the regulations, is the fact that rather than simply reaffirm the applicability of § 504, aware that there was no obligation to exhaust administrative remedies under 504, Congress provided that if there is a cause under both IDEA and 504, then IDEA

---

81. 381 U.S. 1 (1965).

82. *Id.* at 11; *see also* Allstate Construction Co. v. Durkin, 345 U.S. 13, 16–17 (1953) (explicit enactment that administration interpretation would remain in effect); United States v. Bergh, 352 U.S. 40 (1956) (failure of Congress to repeal regulations is evidence of Congressional intent).

83. When originally passed, § 504 was silent as to the power of federal agencies to promulgate implementing regulations. The Department of Health Education and Welfare implemented regulations in 1977 only after being ordered to by the executive as well as by court order. *See* Wegner, *The-Antidiscrimination Model Reconsidered: Ensuring Equal Opportunity Without Respect To Handicap Under Section 504 of The Rehabilitation Act of 1973*, 69 Cornell L. Rev. 401, 411–413 (1984).

84. Davis, 442 U.S. at 412 n.11.

85. Davis, 442 U.S. at 411 n.11.

86. *Id.* at 412 n.11.

87. The House report supporting the then proposed amendment stated:

The section 504 regulations were the result of extensive consideration in the regulatory process. . . . Congress had the opportunity to review these regulations during oversight hearings in 1977. . . . At that time, Congress explicitly approved the section 504 regulations.

H.R. Rep. No. 296, 99th Cong., 1st Sess. 8 (1985).

administrative proceedings must be exhausted. Congress was enacting legislation that affected both the interpretation of § 504 and IDEA. It is reasonable to assume that had it disagreed with the administrative interpretation of § 504, it had the perfect opportunity to express that disagreement.[88]

The counterbalancing argument, however, is that it is unlikely that Congress intended a broad brush statute like § 504 would impose a greater duty on the local and state education agency than the highly specific IDEA. Even assuming the death of *Smith*, courts may so hold. In *St. Louis Developmental Disabilities Treatment Center Parents Association v. Mallory*,[89] although post-*Smith v. Robinson*, the court assumed the *inapplicability* of *Smith* to an allegation under § 504. The court held that "The Education Act sets the outer limits on what is required of a state in the area of educating the handicapped."[90]

The *Mallory* decision is the functional equivalent of the *Smith* holding. If Congress intended IDEA to provide the outer limit, why did it feel compelled to reinstate the applicability of § 504 as a cause of action? Congress, it is logical to assume, saw in § 504 additional protection of some type.[91] Holding that IDEA provides the outer limit, therefore, would make the Congressional reaffirmation of § 504 superfluous. Congress must have intended more or it would simply have enacted the attorneys' fees provisions.

1.4.2 Section 504 Undue Burden— Case Examples

Whether a specific educational requirement would be an undue burden has been considered a factual question to be determined on a case-by-case basis. In *Sanders v. Marquette Public Schools*,[92] suit was brought under § 1983, IDEA,

---

88. Despite the questions raised in *Davis* concerning the validity of § 504 regulations, the United States Supreme Court has repeatedly relied on the regulations:

> As we have previously recognized, these regulations were drafted with the oversight of Congress, see *Consolidated Rail Corporation v. Darrone*, 465 U.S. 624, 634–635 and nn. 14–16.... (1984); they provide 'an important source of guidance on the meaning of 504.' *Alexander v. Choate*, 469 U.S. 287, 304 n.24 ... (1985). School Bd. of Nassau County, Florida v. Arline, 480 U.S. 273, 279 (1987). *See also* South Carolina v. Baker, 485 U.S. 505, 517 n.10 (1988).

89. 591 F. Supp. 1416 (W.D. Mo. 1984) *aff'd* 767 F. 2d 518 (8th Cir. 1985).

90. *Id.* at 1470; *see also* Darlene L. v. Illinois State Bd. of Educ., 568 F. Supp. 1340 (N.D. Ill. 1983).

91. It would be possible to argue that Congress intended § 504 to retain validity in the field as a means of filling in gaps in IDEA. That § 504 would provide the mechanism to insure, for example, that architectural barriers did not inhibit educational programming. The problem with this argument, however, is that even after *Smith* § 504 could be relied upon for an allegation that fell beyond IDEA. The Supreme Court in *Smith* was very explicit in stating:

> We emphasize the narrowness of our holding. We do not address a situation where the EAHCA is not available or where § 504 guarantees substantive rights greater than those available under the EAHCA. We hold only that where, as here, whatever remedy might be provided under § 504 is provided with more clarity and precision under the EAHCA, a plaintiff may not circumvent to enlarge on the remedies available under the EAHCA by resort to § 504.

468 U.S. at 1021.

92. 561 F. Supp. 1361 (W.D. Mich. 1983).

and § 504 alleging the school system failed to identify and place a child in special education programming. Addressing the § 504 claim the court stated that *Davis* allowed the school system to establish that the failure to provide special education services was the result of the burden such services would cause. "Such evidence might be data showing that funding was simply unavailable, or that the program requested by plaintiff could not have been provided without great expense and detriment to the system."[93] The reader should be quickly reminded that this language only concerns a § 504 claim. Under IDEA, unavailability of resources has generally not been a justification for refusing to provide specific types of services, and is clearly not a justification for denying all services.[94]

A few courts appear to take the position that an undue burden exists *per se* if the requested educational programing requires creation of a completely new service. In *Turilio v. Tyson*,[95] the district court held that although § 504 might require modification of an existing program, "it never compels a school system to finance a private educational placement."[96] If modification of an existing program is requested, then apparently, an individual determination as in *Sanders* is made to decide whether the requested service will provide an undue financial or administrative burden.

Georgia Association of Retarded Citizens v. McDaniel[97] addressed the 180 day limitation in a suit brought under IDEA and § 504. Although ultimately modified as a result of *Smith v. Robinson*, it held that a policy precluding educational programming for more than 180 days violated both acts. Indeed, citing one of its own earlier decisions, the Eleventh Circuit held "The Supreme Court's decision in *Southeastern Community College* says only that § 504 does not require a school to provide services to a handicapped individual for a program for which the individual's handicap precludes him from ever realizing the benefit of the training."[98]

A broad reading of *Davis*, as in *McDaniel*, of course, makes increased rights under § 504 much more likely. In *Yaris v. Special School District of St.Louis*,[99] for example, suit was brought under both IDEA and § 504 concerning the school system's failure to provide children with disabilities with more than the standard 180 days of instruction. The court held that the plain meaning of the statute

---

93. *Id.* at 1371.

94. Clevenger v. Oak Ridge School Bd., 744 F.2d 514 (6th Cir 1984) (cost is legitimate factor only when choosing between several appropriate options). See § 3.5.

95. 535 F. Supp. 577 (D. R.I. 1982).

96. *Id.* at 588.; *see also* Rollison v. Biggs, 567 F. Supp. 964 (D. Del. 1983); Darlene L. v. Illinois State Bd. of Educ., 568 F. Supp. 1340 (N.D. Ill. 1983); *see generally* Kruelle v. New Castle County School Dist., 642 F.2d 687, 695–696 (3d Cir. 1981).

97. 716 F.2d 1565 (11th Cir. 1983) *modified in part* 40 F.2d 902 (11th Cir. 1984).

98. *Id.* at 1580 (quoting Camenisch v. University of Texas, 616 F.2d 127, 133 (5th Cir. 1980)); *see also* Association For Retarded Citizens In Colorado v. Frazier, 517 F. Supp. 105, 122 (D. Colo. 1981) ("*Davis* is distinguishable . . . to the extent that it deals with the absence of a requirement to provide a substantial modification for a handicapped individual . . . for which that person's handicap precluded her from ever realizing the benefits of that program."); Tatro v. Texas, 625 F.2d 557, 564 (5th Cir.1980) (quoting *Camenisch*, 616 F.2d at 133) *aff'd on other grounds sub nom* Irving Independent School Dist. v. Tatro, 468 U.S. 883 (1984).

99. 558 F. Supp. 545 (E.D. Mo. 1983), *aff'd*, 728 F.2d 1055 (8th Cir. 1984).

indicated a violation if children with disabilities are precluded from receiving the same benefits realized by other children. Since children without disabilities could attend summer school, § 504 was violated by the failure to provide summer programming for children with disabilities.

The court in *Yaris* then went on to address the § 504 regulations to determine whether they also required more than the traditional 180 days. Concluding that the regulations' requirements for individualized education required the potential for greater than 180 days of instruction, the court held that § 504 regulations were violated. Addressing the validity of the regulations, the court cited *NMARC*, among other decisions, and added the interesting rationale that, since the state had already adopted virtually identical requirements under IDEA, the implementation of these regulations would not require substantial adjustments. The court specifically declined to decide whether there would be a substantial adjustment if IDEA had not been accepted by the states.

1.5 Section 1983 and IDEA

As stated before, *Smith v. Robinson*,[100] in holding that IDEA was the exclusive remedy precluded reliance on § 1983 where the action was covered by IDEA. Also as stated, the 1986 amendments[101] to the act reinstated the ability to use § 1983. As stated by the court in *Hiller v. Board of Education of Brunswick Central School District*:[102]

> The school district's contention that plaintiff is not entitled to at least plead a cause of action under section 1983 is patently absurd in light of the Second Circuit's recent decision in *Mrs. W. v. Tirozzi*, 832 F.2d 748 (2d Cir. 1987). In *Tirozzi* the Court held that section 1415(f) was enacted to overrule the Supreme court's decision in *Smith v. Robinson*, 468 U.S. 992, 104 S.Ct. 3457, 82 L.Ed.2d 746 (1984), holding that the EACHA is the exclusive remedy and section 1983 is not available except in very limited circumstances.
>
> After a thorough discussion of the legislative history, the Second Circuit concluded that after the enactment of section 1415(f), plaintiffs are entitled to assert a cause of action under section 1983 for alleged EACHA violations...[103]

When viewing the interplay of § 1983, three areas of inquiry must be addressed. First, § 1983 claims may be based on independent violations that exist outside the relief afforded by IDEA. Second it must be questioned whether § 1983 provides an independent grounds for asserting rights specifically contained in IDEA and to which relief could be granted under IDEA. Third, several practical issues of how § 1983 changes special education litigation must be addressed.

---

100. 468 U.S. 992 (1984).
101. 20 U.S.C. § 1415(f).
102. 687 F. Supp. 735, 743–744 (N.D.N.Y. 1988).
103. The court in Mrs. W. v. Tirozzi, 832 F.2d 748, 754–55 (2d Cir. 1987) stated:

Congress stated that section 1415(f) was designed to "re-establish statutory rights as repealed by *Smith v. Robinson*," and to "reaffirm, in light of this decision, the viability of ..., 42 U.S.C. 1983, and other statutes as separate vehicles for ensuring the rights of handicapped children."

Valid § 1983 claims, completely independent of the underlying IDEA claim, are illustrated by a number of court decisions which followed *Smith v. Robinson*. It will be remembered that in *Smith* the Court in dicta left open the possibility of an independent due process claim. At one point the Court stated, "On the other hand, unlike an independent equal protection claim, maintenance of an independent due process challenge to state procedures would not be inconsistent with the EAHCA's comprehensive scheme."[104] The Court, by way of example, stated:

> And, while Congress apparently has determined local and state agencies should litigants who succeed, through resort to procedures outlined in the EAHCA ... there is no indication that agencies should be exempt from a fee award where plaintiffs have had to resort to judicial relief to force the agencies to provide them the process they were constitutionally due.[105]

Following *Smith*, lower courts adopted the Supreme Court's dicta and held that various actions by local and state agencies constituted independent violations of § 1983. Not surprisingly, one of the first cases involved facts nearly identical to the example used by the Supreme Court. In *Manecke v. School Board of Pinellas County, Florida*,[106] the Eleventh Circuit Court of Appeals addressed a claim brought under § 1983 and § 504. In *Manecke*, plaintiffs filed suit alleging the school board failed to provide them with a due process hearing on the issue of an educational placement for their daughter. Plaintiffs further alleged that this failure required them unilaterally to place their daughter in a residential facility. The district court dismissed both the § 1983 and the § 504 claims. The Eleventh Circuit panel, however, after discussing *Smith*, stated:

> where the local educational agency deprives a handicapped child of due process by effectively denying that child access to the heart of the EAHCA administrative machinery, the impartial due process hearing, an action may be brought under §1983.[107]

Procedural violations other than failure of authorities to hold a due process hearing were also recognized as grounds for relief under § 1983 despite *Smith*. In *Rose v. Nebraska*,[108] plaintiff brought suit under § 1983 and § 504. Plaintiff claimed that, in violation of the Due Process Clause of the Fourteenth Amendment, the hearing procedures used by the state did not provide for an impartial hearing.

The district court in *Rose* granted an injunction and eventually awarded attorneys' fees for work done in securing the injunction. The Eighth Circuit held *Smith* should be read as recognizing independent procedural claims are subject to § 1983. Citing the Supreme Court's references in *Smith* that due process claims might appropriately be brought under § 1983, the court held "that a § 1983 suit and a fee award are appropriate when a plaintiff claims that he is being denied due process ... "[109]

---

104. Smith, 468 U.S. at 1014 n.17.
105. *Id.*
106. 762 F.2d 912 (11th Cir. 1985).
107. *Id.* at 919.
108. 748 F.2d 1258 (8th Cir. 1984); *see also* Stark v. Walter, 592 F. Supp. 785 (S.D. Ohio 1984).
109. 748 F.2d at 1263.

The Fifth Circuit also addressed the issue following *Smith*. In *Teresa P. v. Alief Independent School District*,[110] the parents alleged procedural violations "in notice, evaluation, consent, development of individualized educational plans, timing of meetings, and expulsion from services."[111] Relying on *Smith*, the Court held that "attorney's fees [premised on a violation of § 1983] may be appropriate where procedural due process claims were effectively raised and maintained."[112]

Another important protection provided by § 1983 is in the enforcement of due process hearing officer decisions. In *Reid v. Lincolnshire-Prairie View School District 103*,[113] the court held that IDEA did not provide a cause of action where the school system failed to implement an educational program ordered by the administrative hearing officer. The court held, however, that § 1983 did provide for such a cause of action.[114]

The protection afforded in actions such as these is of course critical to the ability of IDEA to function. The administrative proceedings mandated by IDEA would be ineffective protection since the LEA has precluded use of the administrative process. If failure to provide access to procedural protections were the only area where the amended IDEA allowed concurrent suits under § 1983, nothing affecting the relationship of § 1983 and IDEA would have been changed by the 1986 amendment. As indicated above, these actions could be brought under *Smith*.[115] The question becomes then, are rights under § 1983 also coextensive with the substantive protections of IDEA? In other words, may suit be brought under § 1983 on the basis that a proposed IEP will not provide a FAPE? Or, may a suit be brought under § 1983 attacking the qualifications of the evaluation team or the validity of the testing tools?

The answer would seem to be yes. A failure to provide any of the rights, either procedural or substantive under IDEA should allow suit to be brought under § 1983. Courts addressing educational claims, however, have not always so held. Numerous cases have held that for a § 1983 claim to exist, there must be a violation of state or federal law for which there is no other adequate remedy. For example, *Fee v. Herndon*,[116] involved an allegation that a student with a disability received excessive corporal punishment. The court, held that the § 1983 claim was improper because the state had reasonable restrictions on corporal punishment and provided appropriate legal remedies for violation of these restrictions.[117] Other courts have indicated a willingness to hear claims based in substantive violations of IDEA.[118]

---

110. 744 F.2d 484 (5th Cir. 1984).

111. *Id.* at 491.

112. *Id.*

113. 765 F. Supp. 965 (N.D. Ill. 1991).

114. *See also* Robinson v. Pinderhughes, 810 F.2d 1270, 1273–74 (4th Cir. 1987).

115. *See* § 1.2 at note 25.

116. 900 F.2d 804 (5th Cir. 1990); *see also* Cunnigham v. Beavers, 858 F.2d 269 (5th Cir. 1988); Brown v. Johnson, 710 F. Supp. 183 (E.D. Ky. 1989).

117. The court relied upon the United States Supreme Court decision in Ingraham v. Wright, 430 U.S. 651, 673 (1977).

118. Board of Educ. v. Diamond, 808 F.2d 987, 994–95 (3d Cir. 1986) (reversing lower court dismissal of counter claim seeking monetary damages); Fontenot v. Louisiana Bd. of Elementary

1.6 Education Department General Administrative Regulations

Education Department General Administrative Regulations (EDGAR) apply to all state administered programs of the United States Department of Education.[119] As such, EDGAR regulations apply to a wide variety of programs receiving funds from the United States Department of Education, including both regular and special education programs.[120]

In general, the requirements under IDEA and its regulations are more stringent than those under EDGAR. EDGAR, however, contains additional requirements in the area of private school students.[121]

1.7 Family Educational Rights and Privacy Act

The Family Educational Rights and Privacy Act (FERPA or the Buckley Amendments) provides general regulations on maintaining and disclosing educational records. IDEA requirements are generally more stringent than FERPA.[122]

---

and Secondary Educ., 805 F.2d 1222, 1223 (5th Cir. 1986) (approving award of attorneys fees for success on substantive merits); *see generally* Mrs. W. v. Tirozzi, 832 F.2d 748, 754–755 (2d Cir. 1987) (§ 1983 available for violations of IDEA).

119. 34 C.F.R. § 76.1; *see also* 20 U.S.C. § 1221(a)(1).

120. *See, e.g.*, 34 C.F.R. Part 76, Table 76-A.

121. 34 C.F.R. § 76.780 -.783.

122. See Chapter 16.

Chapter 2

Parties to the Process

2.1 Parents and Child As Parties

The right of the parent and child to seek relief under IDEA, of course, is the purpose of the statute. Indeed, an important element in the procedural protection afforded under the Act is the right to parental participation in most stages of the educational process. As stated by the Supreme Court in *Hendrick Hudson Board of Education v. Rowley,*[1]

> It seems to us no exaggeration to say that Congress placed every bit as much emphasis upon compliance with procedures giving parents and guardians a large measure of participation at every stage of the administrative process . . . as it did upon the measurement of the resulting IEP against a substantive standard.[2]

Federal regulations have a broad definition of parent. Under federal regulations, a parent is defined as a "a parent, a guardian [or] a person acting as a parent of a child . . ."[3] The Comment to the regulation indicates that the term parent "include[s] persons acting in the place of a parent, such as a grandmother or step parent with whom a child is living, as well as persons legally responsible for a child's welfare."[4]

Congress provided "a generous bill of rights for parents, guardians, and surrogates of handicapped children who might wish to contest the evaluation and placement policies of educational authorities."[5] Even after the child attains the age of majority, the parent may bring an action because IDEA provides rights to parent as well as child.[6] Hence, suit may be brought by the child, and the child's parents in their own right.[7]

---

1. 458 U.S. 176, 205–206 (1981).
2. 458 U.S. 176, 205–206 (1981); *see also* Honig v. Doe, 484 U.S. 305, 311 (1988) ("the Act establishes various procedural safeguards that guarantee parents . . . an opportunity for meaningful input into all decisions affecting their child's education . . ."); Devries v. Spillane, 853 F.2d 264, 266 (4th Cir. 1988) (parents to have "meaningful participation in all aspects").
3. 34 C.F.R. § 300.13; *see also* 20 U.S.C. § 1415(b)(1)(A), (B).
4. 34 C.F.R. § 300.13 Comment; *see also* 20 U.S.C. § 1415(b)(1)(A), (B).
5. Stemple v. Board of Educ., 623 F.2d 893, 898 (4th Cir. 1980).
6. Vander Malle v. Ambach, 673 F.2d 49 (2d Cir. 1982); John H. v. MacDonald, 558 Educ. Handicapped L. Rep. (CRR) 366 (D.N.H. 1987).
7. Vander Malle, 673 F.2d at 49; Tschannerl v. Dist. of Columbia Bd. of Educ., 594 F. Supp. 407 (D.D.C. 1984).

The importance the Supreme Court attached to parental involvement in the development of the IEP was well-supported in the legislative history of IDEA. As the Senate Report states, "individualized planning conferences are a way to provide parent involvement and protection to assure that appropriate services are provided to a handicapped child."[8]

Where parents are divorced, the question of which parent exercises rights under IDEA is a question of state law and judicial order in the divorce.[9] Typically, if both parents have joint custody, both parents enjoy equal rights.[10]

2.2 Effect of Termination of Parental Custody

Courts are split on the right of a parent to be involved in decision-making under IDEA after the parents have lost temporary custody of their child. Courts have held that the surrogate parent is to represent the interests of the child, and that parents have independent standing to challenge the educational placement of the child even where temporary custody was awarded to the state. In *In the Interest of J.D.*,[11] the Florida District Court stated:

> Finally, assuming proper adjudication of dependency and proper partici-
> pation by the surrogate parent, we reiterate our strong disagreement with
> appellees' position that the surrogate usurps altogether the parent's role in
> deciding the child's educational placement. Such an argument runs counter
> to the "historical recognition that freedom of personal choice in matters of
> family life is a fundamental liberty interest protected by the Fourteenth
> Amendment." Santosky v. Kramer, 455 U.S. 745, 753, 102 S.Ct. 1388, 1394,
> 71 L.Ed.2d 599, 610 (1982). As emphasized in Lassiter v. Department of
> Social Services, 452 U.S. 18, 27, 101 S.Ct. 2153, 2159, 68 L.Ed.2d 640 (1981),
> it is "plain beyond the need for multiple citation" that a natural parent's
> "desire for and right to 'the companionship, care, custody, and management
> of his or her children' " is, in the words of the Santosky opinion, "an interest
> far more precious than any property right." 455 U.S. at 758–759, 102 S.Ct.
> 1388, 71 L.Ed.2d 599. Significantly, the Supreme Court in Santosky declared
> that "[t]he fundamental liberty interest of natural parents in the care, custody,
> and management of their child does not evaporate simply because they have
> not been model parents or have lost temporary custody of their child to the
> State." *Id.*, at 753, 102 S.Ct. at 1394.[12]

This position is consistent with the position taken by courts that the parent and child each have separate, but related rights under IDEA.

In *Susan R.M. v. Northeastern Independent School District*,[13] however, the father obtained appointment of the Department of Human services as the "man-

---

8. S. Rep. No. 68, 94th Cong., 1st Sess. at 11–12, *quoted in* Rowley, 458 U.S. at 208–209.
9. Dunlap Inquiry, 211 Educ. Handicapped L. Rep. (CRR) 462 (April 30, 1987).
10. Arnold Inquiry, 211 Educ. Handicapped L. Rep. (CRR) 297 (EHA January 11, 1983).
11. In the Interest of J.D., 510 So. 2d 623 (Fla. Dist. Ct. of App. 1987).
12. *Id.* at 629.
13. 818 F.2d 455 (5th Cir. 1987).

aging conservator" of the child in order to facilitate placement in a state institution. The Fifth Circuit held that the father no longer had standing, since state law provided that only the conservator may bring suit on behalf of the child. The court also stated that when the child turned 18 and the conservatorship thereby ended, neither the father nor the state would have custody and therefore the father would not have independent standing to bring an action to protect the child's educational rights. After 18, the father's involvement would be limited to appointment as "next friend" under Federal Rule of Civil Procedure 17(c).[14]

The Fifth Circuit's decision seems ill-advised. While perhaps the result of the fact that the father was proceeding *pro se*, the opinion made reference to IDEA only to state that the underlying cause of action arose under it. No mention was made of the definition of the parent or of the special role and individual rights accorded the parent under IDEA.

2.3 Surrogate Parents in General

IDEA has as a central theme the involvement of the parents in virtually every major decision affecting the education of their child. If the child, for one reason or another, does not have a parent or the parent cannot be located, the educational agency is responsible for appointing a surrogate parent.

Specifically, the educational agency must appoint a surrogate where either no parent can be identified, the agency, after reasonable efforts cannot find the parent, or the child is, under the laws of the state, a ward of the state.[15] The surrogate's responsibilities are to represent the child in all matters relating to identification, evaluation, and educational placement, as well as matters relating to the provision of a free appropriate public education.[16]

The agency may select the surrogate in any manner allowed by state law,[17] however, the surrogate must have no interest which conflicts with that of the child, and the surrogate must have knowledge and skills to insure the child is adequately represented.[18] Further, "a surrogate may not be an employee of a public agency which is involved in the education or care of the child."[19]

---

14. Fed. R. Civ. P. 17(c) provides:

> Whenever an infant or incompetent person has a representative, such as a general guardian, committee, conservator, or other like fiduciary, the representative may sue or defend on behalf of the infant or incompetent person. An infant or incompetent person who does not have a duly appointed representative may sue by a next friend or by a guardian ad litem. The court shall appoint a guardian ad litem for an infant or incompetent person not otherwise represented in an action or shall make such other order as it deems proper for the protection of the infant or incompetent person.

15. 34 C.F.R. § 300.514(a); *see* 20 U.S.C. § 1415(b)(1)(B).

16. 34 C.F.R. § 300.514(e); *see also* 20 U.S.C. 1415(b)(1)(B); *see generally* Abney v. District of Columbia, 849 F.2d 1491 (D.C. Cir. 1988) (procedural violation where surrogate parent was not provided notice of change in programming).

17. 34 C.F.R. § 300.514(c)(1); see also 20 U.S.C. § 1415(b)(1)(B).

18. 34 C.F.R. § 300.514(c); see also 20 U.S.C. § 1415(b)(1)(B).

19. 34 C.F.R. § 300.514(d). Receiving money for acting as a surrogate does not make the surrogate an employee of the agency. *Id.; see also* 20 U.S.C. § 1415(b)(1)(B).

Section 504 and its regulations also require the appointment of surrogate parents.[20]

2.3.1 The State and its Employees As Surrogate Parents

IDEA regulations state explicitly that, "a surrogate may not be an employee of a public agency which is involved in the education or care of the child."[21] When the child is in the custody of the state, the agency responsible for the care of the child, such as the department of human services or the department of corrections, may not, therefore, appoint one of its employees as surrogate.

2.4 Foster Parents in General

A continuing problem under IDEA involves the role of foster parents. Two questions typically arise. The first question is whether the foster parents, or some employee of the state agency, is a parent within the definition of the federal regulations. If the person falls within the definition of a parent, then under the prevailing interpretation of IDEA, there is no need to appoint a surrogate, and indeed, the appointment of a surrogate parent would be improper.[22] If, however, the person is not a "parent," a second question arises whether they may be appointed as a surrogate parent.

Whether foster parents are parents for the purposes of IDEA depends in large part on the relative permanency of the foster care placement. In *Criswell v. State Department of Education*,[23] the court held that "permanent foster parents" who had been caring for a child for eight years clearly fell within the definition of parents, and therefore it was improper to appoint a surrogate parent to make educational decisions.

The United States Department of Education Office Of Special Education Programs (OSEP), following *Criswell* has opined that because it had not established limits on how long the foster care relationship had to exist, a state policy providing that placements in excess of six months were "long term," and therefore the foster care parents were IDEA parents, was within the discretion available to states.[24]

---

20. United States Department of Education Administrative Policy Manual for the Program for Exceptional Children and Youth, Bulletin No. 26, *quoted in* Alabama Dep't. of Educ. Complaint Letter of Finding (January 24, 1990) *reprinted in* 16 Educ. Handicapped L. Rep. (LRP) 475 (January 20, 1990).

21. 34 C.F.R. § 300.514(d). Receiving money for acting as a surrogate does not make the surrogate an employee of the agency. *Id.*

22. Criswell v. State Dept. of Educ., 558 Educ. Handicapped L. Rep. (CRR) 156 (M.D. Tn. 1986).

23. *Id.*

24. Hargan Inquiry, 16 Educ. Handicapped L. Rep. (LRP) 738 (March 19, 1990); Reynolds Inquiry, 211 Educ. Handicapped L. Rep. (CRR) 470 (June 11, 1987).

2.4.1 Foster Parents As Surrogate Parents

The LEA must appoint a surrogate where either no parent can be identified, the agency after reasonable efforts cannot find the parent, *or* the child is, under the laws of the state, a ward of the state.[25] The language of the regulation clearly provides, therefore, that even if there is an identifiable parent whose location is known, the LEA must appoint a surrogate when the child becomes a ward of the state. Under the prevailing interpretation of IDEA, however, if the child has a parent whose whereabouts are known, there is no need to appoint a surrogate parent, even if the child has been placed in foster care.[26]

A separate question, however, is whether foster parents whose relationship with the child does not rise to the level of IDEA parent, may be appointed by the LEA to act as a surrogate parent. OSEP has indicated that it is currently reviewing whether foster parents who are paid may serve as surrogates, if they are otherwise qualified.[27]

At first glance, it appears that it makes good sense to combine decision making by training the foster parents adequately to allow them to be surrogate parents as well. A concern exists, however, that the use of foster parents as surrogates may raise conflict of interest problems. Unlike the permanent foster parent who has a history of ties to and support of the child, shorter term foster care parents may find themselves in conflict between demands of the state agency appointing them, typically a social or human services department, and their advocacy of the child's rights.

If it is taken as given that the social or human services department itself may not act as surrogate,[28] placing someone dependent on that agency for continued support in their role as foster parent may, in some circumstances, defeat the intended isolation of the surrogate from the state agency contemplated under IDEA. Further, to the extent the foster care parent receives any compensation from the social or human services department, they might be considered an employee of the state agency charged with the care of the child, and, therefore, prohibited from acting in the capacity of surrogate parent.

The countervailing argument, of course, is that 1) permanent foster care parents may find themselves in the same position concerning pressure from the social or human services department, 2) the conflict that does exist, if any, is no greater than the inherent conflict of a LEA appointing the surrogate who then may feel pressure when it comes to deciding, for example, whether to request a due process hearing for the child.

To the extent that a surrogate fails to represent the interests of the child adequately, Federal Rule of Civil Procedure 17 would allow an interested person to seek to protect the child's interest.[29]

---

25. 34 C.F.R. § 300.514(a)(emphasis added); *see* 20 U.S.C. § 1415(b)(1)(B).

26. See § 2.4.1; *see also* 45 C.F.R. Part 121a, app. A (analysis to final regulation), 42 Fed. Reg. 42511 (August 23, 1977) (the regulations have subsequently been recodified under 34 C.F.R., Part 300). As recently as March, 1990, the OSEP has restated this position. *See* Hargan Inquiry, 16 Educ. Handicapped L. Rep. (LRP) 738, 739 (OSEP March 19, 1990).

27. Reynolds Inquiry, 211 Educ. Handicapped L. Rep. (CRR) 428 (1986).

28. See § 2.3.1.

29. See § 2.2.

2.5 The LEA As a Party

The parents may proceed against the local educational agency (LEA) responsible for the direct provision of educational services.[30] The LEA also has the right to seek administrative and judicial review of educational decision-making.[31]

2.5.1 Determining the Appropriate LEA Against Whom to Proceed (Residency)

Under both IDEA[32] and § 504,[33] the residency of the child determines which agency has responsibility for providing a FAPE. Residence requires physical presence and an intent to remain.[34] For most children, this test is easily applied and a child will be considered a resident of the district in which the child and parent reside. Further, it is clear that where a child is placed outside the district for educational reasons, either by the LEA or unilaterally by the parents, the residency remains that of the parents and does not shift to the locality of the placement.[35]

The difficulty arises when the parent and child for some non-educational reasons live in different districts. Many states have statutes which provide that the child's residence is that of the parents'. It has been argued, therefore, that when a child is placed in a district other than where the parents reside, the district in which the child is placed does not have an obligation to provide educational programming.

Statutes that mandate that a child's residence is always that of the parent are constitutionally suspect. In *Steven M. v. Gilhool*,[36] a class action was brought on constitutional grounds challenging the Pennsylvania state law which provided "A child shall be considered a resident of the school district in which his parents … reside … " The action was brought on behalf of school-age children in "children's institutions" who were being charged tuition by local school systems if their parents lived out of state. The court held that the Pennsylvania statute created an invalid, irrebuttable presumption. The court enjoined defendants from denying residency status solely on the fact that a parent's residence was outside the district where the child lived and attended school. The court held that plaintiffs must be

---

30. *But see* Tschanneral v. District of Columbia Bd. of Educ., 594 F. Supp. 407 (D.D.C. 1984) (in the District of Columbia, the proper entity is *not* the Board of Education, but any suit to recover money must be against the District of Columbia).

31. 34 C.F.R. § 300.506(a). Interestingly, 20 U.S.C. § 1415(b)(2), upon which this regulation is based, only recognizes the right of a parent or guardian to initiate a due process hearing, not the LEA.

32. 20 U.S.C. § 1414(a)(1)(A); 34 C.F.R. § 300.220.

33. 34 C.F.R. § 104.33(a).

34. Martinez v. Bynum, 461 U.S. 321, 331 (1982).

35. 34 C.F.R. § 104 app. A n.23 (under § 504 "[i]f a recipient places a child in a program other than its own, it remains financially responsible for the child, whether or not the program is operated by another recipient or educational agency"); School Dist. No. 153 Cook County v. School Dist. No. 154 ½, 54 2, 54 Ill. App. 3d 587, 370 N.E.2d 22 (1977) (under IDEA, LEA where mother resided had responsibility, not LEA where child in state institution).

36. Steven M. v. Gilhool, 700 F. Supp. 261 (E.D. Pa. 1988).

given an opportunity to establish that they are residents of the district in which they live.

The United States Supreme Court has upheld as a *bona fide* residency test whether the child's presence in the district, is for the primary purpose of attending public schools. If the presence of the child in-district is for primarily educational purposes, the district may treat the residency as that of the out-of-district parents.[37]

Where, however, a child is placed in a non-educational institution, as a general rule the locality in which the institution is situated will have responsibility for educating the child.[38] Where a child is placed in a psychiatric hospital for only a short time, however, the location of the hospital does not constitute the residence of the child.[39]

Absent a statute to the contrary, the residency of a child in the custody of a state or local agency should be based on the residence of the child's foster parents. State law should be checked. It is not uncommon for the state to assume the obligation to educate children within state facilities,[40] or specifically to identify which local agency has responsibility for educating children in the custody of social or human services departments.[41]

Where the child has been placed by the parents themselves in the care of another, the motivation for the parents placing the child in another district should be determinative. Where the natural parents place a child with "foster" parents for primarily non-educational reasons, the district in which the child is living will be considered the child's residence.[42]

If a child changes residency during the administrative or court proceedings, the action becomes moot.[43]

2.6 The State As a Party Defendant

In determining the obligation of the state to the parents, a distinction must be drawn between the ability of the parents to force the state to provide direct services and the ability of the parents to seek reimbursement or some other form

---

37. Martinez v. Bynum, 461 U.S. 321, 323 (1982).

38. Mills Inquiry, 213 Educ. Handicapped L. Rep. (CRR) 139 (May 23, 1988).

39. Hall v. Freeman, 700 F. Supp. 1106 (N.D. Ga. 1987).

40. *See, e.g.*, In re Children Residing at St. Aloysius Home, 556 A.2d 552 (RI 1989); Doe v. Sanders, 189 Ill. App. 3d 572, 545 N.E.2d 454 (1989).

41. *See, e.g.*, Brentwood Union Free School Dist. v. Ambach, 495 N.Y.S.2d 513, 115 A.D. 2d 147 (N.Y. Sup. Ct. 1985) (under New York law, agency responsible for child in custody of social services is agency in which student last resided before placement in custody of social services).

42. Rabinowitz v. New Jersey State Bd. of Educ., 550 F. Supp. 481 (D.N.J. 1982) (New York natural parents placed child with New Jersey foster parents; residence of foster parent was residence of child); *see also* Catlin v. Ambach, 644 F. Supp. 161 (N.D.N.Y. 1986) (natural parents moved out of state, paid for the costs of care, but never visited the child; residence of foster parents was residence of child), *vacated and remanded*, 820 F.2d 588 (2d Cir. 1987) (district court should abstain until determination of state law question of what constitutes "actual and only residence"); *but see* Catlin v. Sobol, 77 N.Y.2d 552, 569 N.Y.S.2d 353 (1991) (natural parents moved out of state, paid for the costs of care, but never visited the child; residence parents was residence of child).

43. Rowe v. Henry County School Bd., 718 F.2d 115 (4th Cir. 1983); Monahan v. Nebraska, 687 F.2d 1164, 1168 (8th Cir. 1982).

of damages from the state. Prospective injunctive relief is available from the state.[44] Damages are possibly available against the state.[45] For a full discussion of the ability to bring an action against the state see Chapter 14.

2.7 The State As a Plaintiff

For a discussion of the state educational agency's role see Chapter 17.

2.8 Third-Party Interests

As with any law suit, the action may be commenced only by a real party in interest who has been aggrieved. For example, an insurer lacks standing to seek reimbursement from a school system for moneys it has paid.[46] Also, since IDEA is designed to provide protection and services to parents and children, local educational agencies do not have standing to sue state agencies to compel a state agency to perform its statutory obligations.[47]

---

44. See 14.2.
45. See 14.3.
46. Gehman v. Prudential Property and Casualty Ins. Co., 702 F. Supp. 1192 (E.D. Pa. 1989); Allstate Ins. Co. v. Bethlehem Area School Dist., 678 F. Supp. 1132 (E.D. Pa. 1987) (court raised lack of standing sua sponte).
47. Andrews v. Ledbetter, 880 F.2d 1287 (11th Cir. 1989).

Chapter 3

Provision of a Free Appropriate Education

3.1 Introduction

IDEA requires a state receiving funds to demonstrate that it "has in effect a policy that assures all children with disabilities the right to a free appropriate education."[1] IDEA requires provision of educational services between the ages of five and eighteen in all cases, and between the ages of three and twenty-one in most cases. The requirement is a blanket one and affects, for example, children who are incarcerated[2] or who cannot be transported to school because of medical reasons.[3]

The meaning of the phrase "free appropriate education" was first addressed by the United States Supreme Court in *Hendrick Hudson District Board of Education v. Rowley*.[4] Any analysis of whether a school system is meeting its statutory obligation must begin with a consideration of that case. In *Rowley*, the Court identified two areas of inquiry in determining whether a state has met its requirements under IDEA:

> [A] court's inquiry in suits brought under § 1415(e)(2) is twofold. First has the State complied with the procedures set forth in the Act? And second, is the individualized educational program developed through the Act's procedures reasonably calculated to enable the child to receive educational benefits? If these requirements are met, the State has complied with the obligations imposed by Congress and the courts can require no more.[5]

It is useful, therefore to view the provision of a FAPE as both a procedural right and a substantive right. Failure to provide either right results in a violation of IDEA.

---

1. 20 U.S.C. § 1412(1).
2. Green v. Johnson, 513 F. Supp. 965 (D. Mass. 1981).
3. Abney v. District of Columbia, 849 F.2d 1491 (D.C. Cir. 1988).
4. 458 U.S. 176 (1981).
5. *Id.* at 206–207.

3.2 Provision of a FAPE as a Procedural Right in General

Congress was very explicit in articulating specific procedural protections to be afforded by IDEA. The extensive procedural protections include parental consent or involvement in most decisions affecting the child's educational program.[6] Indeed, the requirement of "meaningful input into all decisions affecting their child's education ..." was recently reaffirmed by the United States Supreme Court in *Honig v. Doe*.[7] The Court also stated:

> Envisioning the IEP as the centerpiece of the statute's education delivery system for disabled children, and aware that schools had all too often denied such children appropriate educations without in any way consulting their parents, Congress repeatedly emphasized throughout the Act the importance and indeed the necessity of parental participation in both the development of the IEP and any subsequent assessment of its effectiveness.[8]

The United States Supreme Court has recognized that these procedural rights are as important as the substantive rights accorded under IDEA:

> When the elaborate and highly specific procedural safeguards embodied in § 1415 are contrasted with the general and somewhat imprecise substantive admonitions contained in the Act, we think that the importance Congress attached to these procedural safeguards cannot be gainsaid. It seems to us no exaggeration to say that Congress placed every bit as much emphasis upon compliance with procedures giving parents and guardians a large measure of participation at every stage of the administrative process ... as it did upon the measurement of the resulting IEP against a substantive standard.[9]

3.3 Provision of a FAPE as a Substantive Right in General

On a substantive level, Congress was much less specific in defining a FAPE than it was on a procedural level. IDEA provides that a FAPE:

> means special education and related services which (A) have been provided at public expense, under public supervision and direction, and without charge, (B) meet standards of the State educational agency, (C) include an appropriate preschool, elementary, or secondary school education in the State involved, and (D) are provided in conformity with the individualized education program ...[10]

---

6. 20 U.S.C § 1414(a)(1)(c)(iii); 1415(b)(1).

7. 484 U.S. 305, 311 (1988).

8. *Id.*

9. Rowley, 458 U.S. at 207; *see also* Smith v. Robinson, 468 U.S. 992, 1011 (1984) (the procedures "effect Congress' intent that each child's individual educational needs be worked out through a process that ... includes ... detailed procedural safeguards.").

10. 20 U.S.C. § 1401(18)(C); *see also* 34 C.F.R. § 300.8.

The statutory definition of special education" is:

> specially designed instruction, at no cost to parents or guardians, to meet the unique needs of a handicapped child, including classroom instruction, instruction in physical education, home instruction, and instruction in hospitals and institutions.[11]

"Related Services" are defined as "transportation, and such developmental, corrective, and other supportive services ... as may be required to assist a handicapped child to benefit from special education."[12] Examples of related services are given in IDEA as well.[13]

3.3.1 Level of Education Required to Constitute FAPE Under IDEA

The United States Supreme Court stated in *Rowley* that: "Noticeably absent from the language of the statute is any substantive standard prescribing the level of education to be accorded handicapped children."[14] In *Rowley*, the Court rejected an argument that IDEA required the provision of educational services that would "maximize each child's potential 'commensurate with the opportunity provided other children.' "[15]

Reviewing the language of IDEA and legislative history, the Court concluded that "the 'basic floor of opportunity' provided by the EAHCA consists of access to specialized instruction and related services which are individually designed to provide educational benefit to the handicapped child."[16] While specifically disclaiming any attempt to develop "any one test for determining the adequacy of educational benefits conferred upon all children,"[17] the Court did hold that the school system satisfies this requirement by "providing personalized instruction with sufficient support services to permit the child to benefit educationally from that instruction."[18]

Lower courts and school systems were quick to recognize that, absent a contrary state provision requiring a higher standard, *Rowley* did not require provision of the "best" education, but merely one that would provide some educational benefit.[19] Lower courts have provided very little additional guidance on what meets

---

11. 20 U.S.C. § 1401(16); 34 C.F.R. § 300.17(a)(1). Regulations also indicate that "special education" includes vocational education if specially designed to meet the needs of a disabled child. 34 C.F.R. § 300.17(a)(3). Further, if "related services" have independent educational value they may constitute special education. 34 C.F.R. § 300.17(a)(2).

12. 20 U.S.C. § 1401(17).

13. *See* § 3.9.

14. Rowley, 458 U.S. at 189.

15. *Id.* at 198; *see also* Burke v. County Bd. of Educ. v. Denton, 895 F.2d 973 (4th Cir. 1990) (issue is "whether services beyond the regular school day are essential for the child to receive any educational benefit.").

16. Rowley, 458 U.S. at 201; *see also* Rettig v. Kent City School Dist., 788 F.2d 328 6th Cir. 1986) (equal opportunity with non-disabled is not the standard).

17. Rowley, 458 U.S. at 202.

18. Rowley, 458 U.S. at 203.

19. *See, e.g.*, Gallagher v. Pontiac Pub. School Dist., 807 F.2d 75 (6th Cir. 1986) (most appropriate not required); Hessler v. State Board of Educ. of Maryland, 700 F.2d 134, 139 (4th Cir. 1983).

the required level of educational programming. While it appears clear that more than some minimal, or trivial[20] educational benefit is necessary, no more precise definition has developed. Rather than identifying a prospective test of what constitutes a FAPE, lower courts have focused on a case-by-case determination of whether the program proposed by the LEA will provide educational benefit.

One objective factor that has been urged by school systems as an indication that a child's program does provide educational benefit is that the child has been promoted from grade to grade. In fact, in *Rowley* the Court found the child's academic progress "to be dispositive."[21] The Court, however, specifically stated it was not holding that every child who progresses from grade to grade is receiving a FAPE.

The United States Fourth Circuit Court of Appeals specifically addressed grade progression as an objective indicator in *Hall v. Vance County Board of Education*:[22]

> Although the *Rowley* Court considered Amy Rowley's promotions in determining that she had been afforded a FAPE, the Court limited its analysis to that one case and recognized that promotions were a fallible measure of educational benefit... The district court [in the instant case] did not err in discounting James' promotions in light of the school's policy of social promotion and James' test scores and independent evaluations. Nor is the district court compelled by a showing of minimal improvement on some test results to rule that the school had given James a FAPE.

Indeed, progression from grade to grade is an impossible measure of educational benefit where the child has a disability so severe that grade levels are irrelevant.[23]

Perhaps the clearest evidence that the educational program is not providing educational benefit is that the child is not progressing educationally, or is even actually regressing in the present educational placement.[24] If the child is unable to benefit from educational programming, however, the school system may be relieved from providing educational services.[25]

3.3.2 Higher State Standard for Level of Services

Individual state statutes and regulations must be checked to determine whether a higher level of educational benefit is required. IDEA provides the minimum

20. Polk v. Central Susquehanna Intermediate Unit 16, 853 F.2d 171 (3d Cir. 1988) (more than trivial benefit); Board of Educ. v. Diamond, 808 F.2d 987 (3d Cir. 1986) (Rowley requires plan that will allow progress, not regression or trivial educational benefit); Hall v. Vance County Bd. of Educ., 774 F.2d 629 (4th Cir. 1985) (more than trivial).

21. Rowley, 458 U.S. at 302 n.25; *see also* Bertolucci v. San Carlos Elementary School Dist., 721 F. Supp. 1150 (N.D. Cal. 1989) (progress from grade to grade and test scores showed benefit).

22. 774 F.2d 629, 635–6 (4th Cir. 1985).

23. *See* Polk v. Central Susquehanna Intermediate Unit 16, 853 F.2d 171 (3d Cir. 1988) (disability may be so severe that progress cannot be measured by grade promotion).

24. Board of Educ. v. Diamond, 808 F.2d 987 (3d Cir. 1986) (regression); Garland Independent School Dist. v. Wilks, 657 F. Supp. 1163 (N.D. Texas 1987) (failure to provide FAPE where student moved from residential to day program and regressed educationally).

25. *See* § 5.2.3.

level of educational services, it does not prohibit states from providing more. Several states establish a higher standard than articulated in *Rowley*.[26] Federal courts are not precluded under the Eleventh Amendment from enforcing these higher state standards.[27]

3.3.3 Level of Education Required to Constitute FAPE Under § 504

Section 504 arguably requires a higher level of educational benefit than IDEA. While judicial gloss provided by the United States Supreme Court in *Rowley* indicates that an appropriate education need only provide some educational benefit,[28] § 504's regulations set a standard of meeting the educational needs of the disabled "as adequately as the needs of nonhandicapped persons ..."[29] Unless a school system is willing to publicly assert the proposition that it is providing a minimal educational experience to its non-disabled students, it could be argued that reliance on § 504 circumvents *Rowley's* minimal standard in those areas where IDEA and § 504 overlap.[30] To the extent a school system professes to maximize a non-disabled child's educational benefit, or make available educational services which provide more than some minimal educational benefit, the school should be required, under § 504, to have the same educational goal for children with disabilities. No case has been found to support this argument.

3.4 Education to Be at No Cost to Parents

IDEA clearly requires the provision of a *free* appropriate education.[31] Provision of the education, therefore must be at no cost to the parents. Parents, for example,

---

26. *See, e.g.,* Cal. Code of Regs. § 3001(b) ("provide equal opportunity ... commensurate with the opportunity provided to other pupils") *discussed in* Pink v. Mt. Diablo Unified School Dist., 738 F. Supp. 345 (N.D. Cal. 1990)); Mass. Gen. L. ch. 71B, § 3 *discussed in* David D. v. Dartmouth School Committee, 615 F. Supp. 639 (D. Mass. 84) ("maximum possible development"), *aff'd*, 775 F.2d 411 (1st Cir. 1985); Mich. Comp. Laws Ann. §§ 380.1701, .1711, .1751 ("shall provide education programs and services designed to develop the maximum potential of each handicapped person.") *discussed in* Barwacz v. Michigan Dep't. of Educ., 674 F. Supp. 1296 (W.D. Mich. 1987); N.J. Admin. Code §§ 6:28–2.1, 2.2 (1978) ("best achieve") *discussed in* Lascari v. Ramapo Indian Hills Reg. H.S. Bd. of Educ., 116 N.J. 30, 560 A.2d 1180 (1989); Geis v. Board of Educ. of Parsippany-Troy Hills, 589 F. Supp. 269, 272, (D. N.J. 1984) *aff'd* 774 F.2d 575 (3d Cir. 1985); Tenn. Code Ann. § 49–10–101(a)(1) (maximize capablilities).

27. David D. v. Dartmouth School Committee, 775 F.2d 411, 420, (1st Cir. 1985); Geis v. Bd. of Educ., 774 F.2d 575, 581 (3d Cir. 1985); Barwacz v. Michigan Dep't. of Educ., 674 F. Supp. 1296 (W.D. Mich. 1987).

28. *See* Rowley, 458 U.S. at 203; Hall v. Vance County Bd. of Educ., 774 F.2d 629, 635 (4th Cir. 1985). See § 3.3.1.

29. 34 C.F.R. § 104.33(b).

30. Section 504 regulations were drafted prior to *Rowley*. It is, therefore, conceivable they were intended to have a different standard than articulated in *Rowley*.

31. 20 U.S.C. § 1412(1), 1401(18); Rowley, 458 U.S. at 188; Mahoney v. Administrative School Dist. 1, 42 Or. App. 665, 601 P.2d 826 (Ct. App. Or. 1979).

cannot be required to use personal insurance for the payment of educational programming, if it would reduce their lifetime benefits.[32] Also, the state may not require the participation of the parents in the educational program as a prerequisite to the provision of educational services.[33]

To the extent that a residential program is required in order for a child to receive a FAPE, "the program, including non-medical care and room and board, must be at no cost to the parents of the child."[34]

Incidental fees normally charged to non-disabled students may be charged to children consistent with IDEA.[35]

3.5 Cost As Factor in Providing FAPE

IDEA requires the provision of educational services to all children with disabilities, and makes no provision for refusing to provide those services because of cost. Limitations on funding, at least from the federal government, were clearly rejected in the legislative history of IDEA as justification for denying an appropriate education:

> The Committee rejects the argument that the Federal Government should only mandate services to handicapped children if, in fact, funds are appropriated in sufficient amounts to cover the full cost of this education. The Committee recognizes the State's primary responsibility to uphold the Constitution of the United States and their own State Constitutions and State laws as well as Congress' own responsibility under the 14th Amendment to assure equal protection of the law.[36]

Further, "cost considerations are only relevant when choosing between several options, all of which offer an 'appropriate' education. When only one is appropriate, then there is no choice."[37] Where for example, both a residential facility and a community group home will provide an appropriate education, the public

---

32. Seals v. Loftis, 614 F. Supp. 302 (E.D. Tenn. 1985); *see also* Shook v. Gaston County Bd. of Educ., 882 F.2d 119 (4th Cir. 1989) (parents were able to sue to seek reimbursement for depletion of $100,000 medical insurance policy of $64,200 because the education must not diminish the resources of the parent).

33. *See, e.g.,* Teresa Diane P. v. Alief Independent School Dist., 744 F.2d 484 (5th Cir. 1984) (conditioning on parental participation in group therapy violates equal protection and substantive due process).

34. 34 C.F.R. § 300.302; *see* 20 U.S.C. § 1413(a)(4)(B); *see also* Jenkins v. Florida, 556 Educ. Handicapped L. Rep. (CRR) 471 (M.D. Fla. 1985) (where residential placement is required for educational reasons, state may not charge fee for living expenses).

35. 34 C.F.R. § 300.17(b)(1).

36. Sen. Rep. No. 168, 94th Cong., 1st Sess. at 22, *reprinted in* 1975 U.S. Code Cong. & Admin. News 1425, 1446; *see also* 121 Cong. Rec. 37025 (remarks of Rep. Mink); 121 Cong. Rec. 19503 (1975) (remarks of Sen. Cranston).

37. Clevenger v. Oak Ridge School Board, 744 F.2d 514 (6th Cir. 1984); *see also* Roncker v. Walter, 700 F.2d 1058, 1063 (6th Cir. 1983); Kruelle v. New Castle County School Dist., 642 F.2d 687, 695 (3d Cir. 1981) ("comprehensive range of services...regardless of financial and administrative burdens").

agency may choose the less expensive placement.[38] Cost may also be a consideration when choosing the least restrictive placement.[39]

It is possible, of course, that the funds are simply unavailable to educate both disabled and non-disabled children to the extent desired by the school system. Congress did indeed recognize that funds could be limited:

> When a state or local educational agency, because of funding limitations, places limits on the services that may be provided handicapped children, the manner in which the financial deficit is to be adjusted is indicated by legislative history.

> > If sufficient funds are not available to finance all of the services and programs that are needed and desirable in the system then the available funds must be expended equitably in such manner that no child is excluded from publicly supported education consistent with his needs and abilities to benefit therefrom. The inadequacies of [the school system] whether occasioned by insufficient funding or administrative inefficiency, certainly cannot be permitted to bear more heavily on the 'exceptional' or handicapped child than on the normal child.

Lack of funds, therefore, may not limit the availability of "appropriate" educational services to children with disabilities more severely than it does to normal or nonhandicapped children.[40]

According to the United States Department of Education's Office of Civil Rights, cost is likewise insufficient as a defense under Section 504.[41]

---

38. Abrahamson v. Hershman, 701 F.2d 223 (1st Cir. 1983).

39. See § 8.2.

40. Crawford v. Pittman, 708 F.2d 1028, 1035 (5th Cir. 1983) *citing* S. Rep. No. 168, 94th Cong., 1st Sess. at 23, *reprinted in* 1975 U.S. Code Cong. & Admin. News at 1447. The court also pointed out: "This quotation from the legislative history first appeared in Mills v. Board of Educ., 348 F. Supp. 866, 876 (D.C. 1972). It has frequently been quoted when efforts were made to explain the substantive requirements of the Act; *see, Rowley*, 458 U.S. 178, 193 n.15 ..." 708 F.2d at 1035 n.30; *but see* Stacey G. v. Pasadena Indep. School Dist., 547 F. Supp. 61, 78, (S.D. Tx. 1982), *vacated and remanded on other grounds*, 695 F.2d 949 (5th Cir. 1983):

> It cannot be disputed that educational funding is limited. Accordingly, it necessarily follows that competing interests must be balanced to reach a reasonable and fair accommodation. On the one hand are the personal and unique needs of the individual and handicapped child; on the other hand are the realities of limited funding and the necessity of assisting in the education of all handicapped children. These competing interests must be considered by the Court in its analysis of what is a "free appropriate public education."

The court also stated:

> The fact that Congress intended or at least was acutely aware of the need to strike a balance between the competing interests ... is evidenced also by the requirement contained in the Act that the State establish "priorities for providing a free appropriate education for all handicapped children" 20 U.S.C. § 1412(3) (1978); *see also*, 34 C.F.R. §§ 300.320–300.324 (1981).

Id. at 78; Department of Educ. v. Katherine D., 727 F.2d 809, 813 (9th Cir. 1984) ("Because budgetary constraints limit resources that realistically can be committed to these special programs, the DOE is required to make only those efforts to accommodate Katherine's needs that are 'within reason.' ").

41. *See* Bremen High School Dist. No. 228, 257 Educ. Handicapped L. Rep. (CRR) 195 (OCR February 12, 1981) (§ 504 violated when refuse residential solely based on cost).

3.6 Age Coverage

IDEA requires educational programming for all children "aged three through twenty-one."[42] If the state chooses to educate two-year-old children it may receive federal money.[43] IDEA, however, also limits the obligation to three to five and nineteen to twenty-one year-old students.[44] Specifically, provision of a FAPE, consistent with IDEA, must be made for those three to five years of age and those eighteen to twenty-one years of age must be made:

- whenever state law or a court order requires the education of any portion of children with disabilities in these age groups, the entire population in these groups must be provided with the same benefit;[45]
- if any children without disabilities in these age groups are provided with educational services, at least a proportionate share of those with disabilities must be provided educational services;[46]
- if the state provides services to 50% or more of children with disabilities in these age groups, it must provide the services to all.[47]

State statutes and regulations should be consulted to determine whether a particular state has chosen to limit age coverage.

It should be kept in mind that age does not usually terminate educational opportunity for children without disabilities. For example, a child who fails a grade is given an opportunity to repeat it. That student may then graduate when she is nineteen. Since this service is provided to regular education students, it must be provided to students with disabilities.[48]

Regulations promulgated under § 504 define those qualified to receive a FAPE as those who are of an age that would receive education were they not disabled, those of an age where state law requires mandatory education, or those children covered under IDEA.[49] Education services under § 504 can be terminated on the twenty-second birthday, since nothing in the statute requires funding to continue until the end of the academic year.[50]

For a child who falls below the age limit for educational programming under IDEA or § 504, counsel should explore the recently enacted Early Intervention Program for Infants and Toddlers With Handicaps.[51] This "Infants and Toddlers" program provides for interagency coordination of services, including the development of Individual Family Service Plans for children from birth through two years of age, who "are experiencing developmental delays ... or ... have a diag-

---

42. 34 C.F.R. § 300.300(a); *see* 20 U.S.C. § 1412(2)(B).

43. 20 U.S.C. § 1419; 34 C.F.R. Part 301.

44. 34 C.F.R. § 300.300(b); *see* 20 U.S.C. § 1412(2)(B).

45. 34 C.F.R. § 300.300(b)(1); *see also* 20 U.S.C. § 1412(2)(B).

46. *Id.* at § 300.300(b)(2); *see also* 20 U.S.C. § 1412(2)(B).

47. *Id.* at § 300.300(b)(3); *see also* 20 U.S.C. § 1412(2)(B).

48. *See* Helms v. Independent School Dist. No. 3 of Broken Arrow, 750 F.2d 820 (10th Cir. 1985).

49. 34 C.F.R. § 104.3(k)(2).

50. Williamson County School Dist., 352 Educ. Handicapped L. Rep. (CRR) 514 (OCR January 7, 1988).

51. 20 U.S.C. §§ 1471-1485; 34 C.F.R. Part 303. *See* Chapter 18.

nosed physical or mental condition which has a high probability of resulting in developmental delay."[52]

3.7 The Effect of Graduation under IDEA

A special education student who graduates does not have the right to educational services under IDEA beyond graduation.[53] Where a student has successfully completed the goals and objectives of an appropriate IEP, and that completion "is analogous to successful completion of graduation requirements for non-handicapped students," the school system's obligation to educate the child ends.[54] Under IDEA, the school system is only obligated to provide post-graduation educational services "to the extent and in the same proportion that it does for non-handicapped students."[55]

Of course, if the graduation is "a sham designed to terminate the school system's responsibility at the earliest possible moment under circumstances where non-handicapped children are provided further schooling,"[56] the school system can be required to provide educational services from eighteen to twenty-one consistent with its provision to educational services to children who are non-disabled.

3.8 The Effect of Graduation under § 504

Regulations promulgated under § 504 define those qualified to receive a FAPE as those who are of an age that would receive education were they not disabled, those of an age where state law requires mandatory education, or those children covered under IDEA.[57] If, therefore, a local school system provides adult educational programming to the non-disabled, comparable adult programming should be available to the disabled. For example, there are numerous children with disabilities who could continue to receive educational benefit beyond 22 years of age. Although the school system may argue that the disabled person is not otherwise qualified to benefit from the adult educational program, once the school system has undertaken the general education of the non-disabled, the school system must provide services to the disabled.[58] Since the school system is already

---

52. 20 U.S.C. § 1472(1).

53. Gorski v. Lynchburg School Board, 441 Educ. Handicapped L. Rep. (CRR) 415 (4th Cir. 1989); Wexler v. Westfield Bd. of Educ., 784 F.2d 176, 183–184 (3d Cir. 1986).

54. Wexler v. Westfield Bd. of Educ., 784 F.2d 176, (3d Cir. 1986); see also Gorski v. Lynchburg School Board, 441 Educ. Handicapped L. Rep. (CRR) 415 (4th Cir. 1989).

55. Wexler, 784 F.2d at 183.

56. Id. (citing Helms v. Independent School Dist. No. 3 of Broken Arrow, 750 F.2d 820 (10th Cir. 1985)).

57. 34 C.F.R. § 104.3(k)(2).

58. See discussion § 1.4.2. In Georgia Association of Retarded Citizens v. McDaniel, 716 F.2d 1565, 1579 (11th Cir. 1983), a pre Smith v. Robinson decision, the court relied on the fact that § 504 does not contain specific age limitations as one of the reasons for determining that IDEA did not preclude resort to § 504.

Until overridden by Congressional action, the fact that adult education programs might not receive

providing the services "it may be logically inferred that it would not have imposed an 'undue burden' on defendants to provide a special educational program for the plaintiff."[59]

Further, if services of a particular type are already being provided to one group of people, what is being requested is a reallocation of existing resources, not an expansion of funding.[60] By the same token, these latter cases may well result in more litigation, since if there is not dual coverage with IDEA, there is no need to exhaust administrative remedies.[61]

3.9 Related Services in General

Provision of a FAPE requires "related services" as well as special education.[62] Related services are defined in IDEA as "[t]ransportation, and such developmental, corrective, and other supportive services ... as may be required to assist a disabled child to benefit from special education."[63] The regulations specifically mention speech pathology and audiology, psychological services, physical and occupational therapy, recreation, early identification and assessment, medical services for diagnostic and evaluation purposes, school health services, social work services, and parent counseling and training.[64] The list is not exhaustive and other services have been required.[65]

The related service, as is clear from the definition, must be necessary to enable the child to receive educational benefit.[66] The mere fact that the child is disabled does not entitle the child to a particular related service. For example, a hearing impaired student enrolled in a private school is not entitled to transportation as a related service, if the need for transportation is unrelated to her disability.[67]

It should also be kept in mind that *Rowley* places limits on the required provision of related services. In *Rowley*, the parents were seeking a sign-language

---

direct federal aid could have caused a serious problem in enforcing such a right. The United States Supreme Court had ruled that "an agency's authority under Title IX ... is subject to the *program-specific* limitations of §§ 901 and 902." Grove City College v. Bell, 465 U.S. 555, 570 (1984). The similarity between Title IX and § 504 led courts to adopt this program-specific approach. *See e.g.* Gallagher v. Pontiac School Dist., 807 F.2d 75 (6th Cir. 1986). Congress overturned *Grove City* March 22, 1988. 42 U.S.C. § 2000d-4a.

59. Sanders v. Marquette Pub. Schools, 561 F. Supp. 1361, 1371 (W.D. Mich. 1983).

60. It has been suggested that in cases where there is an unequal treatment of the disabled "[d]efendant will also have little success in relying upon cost-based defenses in such situations, for ... the question is primarily one of allocation of available resources in an evenhanded fashion." Wegner, *The Antidiscrimination Model Reconsidered: Ensuring Equal Opportunity Without Respect To Handicap Under Section 504 Of the Rehabilitation Act of 1973*, 69 Cornell L. Rev. 401, 499 (1984).

61. See § 13.3.

62. 20 U.S.C. § 1401(18); 34 C.F.R. § 300.8.

63. 20 U.S.C. § 1401(17).

64. 34 C.F.R. § 300.16(a); 20 U.S.C. § 1401(17).

65. *E.g.*, Espino v. Besteiro, 520 F. Supp. 905 (S.D. Tex. 1981) (air conditioning). The Comment to 34 C.F.R. § 300.13 also lists art, music and dance therapy

66. *See, e.g.*, McNair v. Oak Hills School Dist., 872 F.2d 153 (6th Cir. 1989) (transportation not required).

67. McNair, 872 F.2d 153.

interpreter as a related service. The Court held that, since the child was already receiving an adequate education under the standard that the LEA need not maximize educational benefit, the interpreter need not be provided.[68]

Parents may be reimbursed for unilateral provision of related services, when it is determined that the school has improperly withheld the services.[69]

3.9.1 Equipment Versus Services

The United States Supreme Court had occasion to address related services under IDEA in *Irving Independent School District v. Tatro*.[70] Among the criteria necessary for something to constitute a related service according to *Tatro* was that it be a service, not equipment. Specifically, the Court held: "Finally, we note that respondents are not asking petitioner to provide *equipment* that Amber needs for CIC [clean intermittent catheterization]. They seek only the services of a qualified person at the school"[71] The obligation of the LEA to provide equipment such as computers, hearing aids, and medical supplies is, therefore, thrown into question by *Tatro*. Taken to its extreme, *Tatro* could provide serious limitations on the provision of special education. In practice, *Tatro* appears not to have been taken this far. For example, it is clear that transportation services, including, of course, a large piece of equipment, are required under IDEA.[72]

Section 504 more clearly contemplates the provision of equipment. Section 504 regulations define an appropriate education as "regular or special education and related aids or services that are... designed to meet individual education needs of handicapped persons as adequately as the needs of nonhandicapped persons are met."[73] The § 504 definition differs from IDEA definition, therefore, in the inclusion of the words "aids or services" in the § 504 regulation, while IDEA merely states "related services."

---

68. Rowley, 458 U.S. at 211–212.

69. *See* Max. M. v. Illinois State Bd. of Educ., 629 F. Supp. 1504, 1519 (N.D. Ill. 1986); Seals v. Loftis, 614 F. Supp. 302, 305–306 (E.D. Tenn. 1985). For a complete discussion of reimbursement see § 14.4.

70. 468 U.S. 883 (1984). The Court did not, however, have occasion to address the issue under § 504 since on the same day it had decided IDEA was the exclusive remedy and that Section 504 did not apply. *Id*. at 895 (citing Smith v. Robinson, 468 U.S. 992 (1984)).

71. *Id*.

72. 20 U.S.C. § 1401(17); 34 C.F.R. § 300.13(b)(14); In re: Farmingdale Union Free School Dist., 503 Educ. Handicapped L. Rep. (CRR) 221 (SEA N.Y. March 1, 1982) (specially equipped minibus required); *see also* Case No. SE 85461, 507 Educ. Handicapped L. Rep. (CRR) 416 (SEA CA. October 25, 1985) (IEP required provision of computer with voice synthesizer similar to equipment used at home); Stoher, 213 Educ. Handicapped L. Rep. (CRR) 209 (OSEP February 17, 1989) (wheelchair may be related service as in transportation). The Infants and Toddlers with Disabilities Act encourages the use of "assistive technology." *See* § 18.7.

73. 34 C.F.R. § 104.33(b). It should be pointed out that § 504 is not only broader in terms of the people it covers, but also broader in terms of the services required. IDEA clearly limits application to provision of special education and related services. Section 504, however, requires provision of an appropriate education and which may simply be provision of a regular education in a regular classroom. *See, e.g.*, Elizabeth S. v. Gilhool, 558 Educ. Handicapped L. Rep. (CRR) 461 (M.D. Pa. 1987) (children with disabilities who do not require special education may require other modifications or services to obtain access to educational programming).

A sense of the types of aids contemplated under § 504 regulations is found in the postsecondary education regulations of § 504 which illustrate the types of aids required in programs governed by those regulations.[74] The types of aids recognized, and implicitly relied upon by the Court in *Southeastern Community College v. Davis*,[75] in the § 504 postsecondary education regulations, and by analogy to IDEA, is quite extensive.[76]

Under § 504 and IDEA, therefore, the question becomes where to draw the line between non-required "equipment," and required related aids/services. The Supreme Court in *Davis* relying on post secondary regulations[77] specifically indicated that there was no need to provide devices or services of a personal nature.[78] It appears the same holds true for IDEA. Take for example, a United States Department of Education's Office of Civil Rights (OCR) complaint that a local school system violated § 504 in failing to provide a homebound disabled student with a computer and adaptive headgear. The student was enrolled in a computer class which, if he had been taking the course in the regular classroom would have included access to a computer.

OCR determined that, since the student would have been provided with access to a computer had he not been disabled, the LEA's failure to provide a computer and adaptive headgear in order to allow him to use the computer for homebound instruction was a violation.[79] Critical, of course, was the LEA's provision of computers to non-disabled children at no cost.

A strict interpretation of *Tatro*, however, might lead to the conclusion that the adaptive headgear would not be mandated under IDEA because it constitutes equipment. Yet, even under *Tatro*, if the child needs the headgear in order to benefit from the instruction, it seems necessary. If the headgear is necessary to take advantage of a piece of equipment otherwise provided without charge (the computer), then in a reading class where books are provided to the students who are non-disabled why are eyeglasses not necessary to the visually impaired? Did Congress intend the schools to provide eyeglasses, or hearing aids?

In this circumstance the headgear is similar to a book. The book is a specific piece of "equipment" necessary to receive the benefit of a specific activity within the instructional program. The specific book, however, does not benefit the student outside that classroom. Equipment such as eyeglasses would likewise help that student in the reading class, but would have general utility to the student beyond the particular class and are therefore in more of a personal nature.

There is some attraction to this distinction. Hence, a school is required to provide a specially equipped van to transport a disabled child to the school, since transportation is necessary in order to allow the child to receive educational benefit.[80] The school, however, would not be required to provide a child with an

74. 34 C.F.R. § 104.44(d).

75. 442 U.S. 397 (1979). Davis is discussed more fully in § 1.4.1.

76. 45 C.F.R. § 84.44.

77. Davis, 442 U.S. at 406–407.

78. *Id.* at 409.

79. Eldon (MO) R-I School Dist., 352 Educ. Handicapped L. Rep. (CRR) 144 (January 16, 1986).

80. *See, e.g.*, Kennedy v. Board of Educ., 175 W. Va. 668, 337 S.E.2d 905 (W. Va. 1985) (purchase of vehicle required to transport over non-maintained road).

individual wheelchair which would be used in the child's activities outside the school system.[81] If, based on an individualized determination, the equipment were necessary at home in order for the child to receive educational benefit, the equipment should be provided by the school system. This position seems to be the one taken by the United States Department of Education's Office of Civil Rights.[82]

A more liberal reading of *Tatro* is consistent with this interpretation. In *Tatro* the Supreme Court's reference to equipment was to the equipment necessary to perform Clean Intermittent Catheterization (CIC). This equipment, while used during the school day, addressed a need well beyond the specific educational services the child was receiving at the time. In a sense, the equipment was more in the nature of a wheelchair than headgear. Such an interpretation would, for all practical purposes, make § 504 and IDEA coextensive regarding the provision of equipment.[83]

3.9.2 Transportation As a Related Service

Transportation is specifically mentioned as a related service under IDEA.[84] Transportation includes travel to and from school, as well as travel within the school and between schools.[85] Unless the child is on homebound or other type of residential educational program, it seems logical that transportation from home to the educational setting is necessary for any child to receive educational benefit. Transportation must be door-to-door if the child is unable to get to the bus stop.[86] If both parents are working, transportation to an after school caretaker is also required, even if the caretaker lives outside the student's school district.[87] Likewise, the LEA's transportation plan must be reasonable.[88]

The LEA's responsibility to provide transportation extends to children placed in private facilities because of the unavailability of a FAPE in the public school, though reasonable limits on the frequency of trips can be made.[89] The LEA's

---

81. If the equipment is required at home for educational purposes, the equipment should be provided for home use as well.

82. *See* Inquiry, 18 Individuals with Disabilities Educ. L. Re. (LRP) 627 (Nov. 27, 1991) (IEP meeting required to detemine whether technological device required for home use).

83. Close cases will still exist under this approach. Unlike the seriously emotionally disturbed child who may receive medication to control behavior throughout the day, a child with Attention Deficit Disorder (ADD) may require Ritalin only during the academic day. Does this mean that the school must not only administer the drug, but also pay for the drug as a related service?

84. 34 C.F.R. § 300.16(a); *see* 20 U.S.C. § 1401(17); *see also* McNair v. Oak Hills Local School Dist., 872 F.2d 153 (6th Cir. 1989).

85. 34 C.F.R. § 300.16(b)(4); *see also* 20 U.S.C. § 1401(17).

86. Hurry v. Jones, 560 F. Supp. 500 (D.R.I. 1983), *aff'd in part rev. in part*, 734 F.2d 879 (1st Cir. 1984) (reimbursement for school systems failure to provide door-to-door transportation for physically impaired student).

87. Alamo Heights Indep. School Dist. v. State Bd. of Educ., 790 F.2d 1153 (5th Cir. 1986) (absent a showing of unfair burden, substantial additional expense, disruption of efficient planning, or lengthening transportation time of other children, LEA obligated to transport child one mile out-of-district to child caretaker).

88. *See* Pinkerton v. Moye, 509 F. Supp. 107 (W.D. Va. 1981) (because of length of time required by LEA's system, parent could seek alternative transportation and receive reimbursement).

89. Cohen v. School Bd., 450 So. 2d 1238 (Fla. Dist Ct. App. 1984) (three round trips for student between home and out of state residential placement sufficient to meet IEP goals of family integration and counseling).

obligation is to transport the student to and from the residential program, not transport the parents.[90] Reimbursement for expenses of transportation to a unilateral placement by the parents ultimately determined after the due process proceedings to be appropriate is required under the Supreme Court's decision in *Town of Burlington v. Department of Education*.[91]

As discussed elsewhere, even when the LEA is able to provide a FAPE, but the parent unilaterally decides to place the child in a private program, considerable responsibility remains on the LEA to make special education and related services available.[92] Transportation from home to the private school and back, however, is not required.[93] If the publicly provided special education program of a child unilaterally placed in a private school takes place away from the private school, a split of opinion exists whether LEA must provide transportation from and back to the private school.[94]

3.9.3 Speech Pathology and Audiology As Related Services

Federal regulations provide that as a related service "audiology" includes identification, determining the range, nature and degree of loss, providing habilitative activities, creating programs to prevent hearing loss, counseling and guidance of students, parents and teachers, and providing services related to amplification.[95]

"Speech pathology" as a related service includes identification, diagnosis, referral, counseling and provision of speech and language services[96]

3.9.4 Psychological Services and Counseling As Related Services

Psychotherapy required in order for a child to receive educational benefit comes within psychological services.[97] In addition to administering tests, interpreting

---

90. Bales v. Clarke, 523 F. Supp. 1366 (E.D. Va. 1981).

91. 471 U.S. 359 (1985); *see* Taylor v. Board of Educ., 649 F. Supp. 1253 (N.D.N.Y. 1986) (citing *Burlington*). *Burlington* is discussed more fully in § 14.4.

92. See § 8.10.

93. Work v. McKenzie, 661 F. Supp. 225 (D.D.C. 1987); McNair v. Cardimone, 676 F. Supp. 1361 (S.D. Ohio 1987), *aff'd sum nom*, McNair v. Oak Hills Local School Dist., 872 F.2d 153 (6th Cir. 1989).

94. Transportation required: *see, e.g.*, Work v. McKenzie, 661 F. Supp. 225 (D.D.C. 1987); Cunningham Inquiry, 213 Educ. Handicapped L. Rep. (CRR) 125 (EHA February 1, 1988); Wheatland Unified School Dist., 508 Educ. Handicapped L. Rep. (CRR) 310 (SEA Ca. February 3, 1987); Case No. SE 85377, 507 Educ. Handicapped L. Rep. (CRR) 125 (SEA Ca. April 18, 1985). Transportation not required: Prince George's County (Md.) Pub. Schools, 352 Educ. Handicapped L. Rep. (CRR) 226 (OCR June 30, 1986).

95. 34 C.F.R. § 300.16(b)(1); *see also* 20 U.S.C. § 1401(17).

96. 34 C.F.R. § 300.16(b)(13); *see also* 20 U.S.C. § 1401(17).

97. 34 C.F.R. § 300.16(b)(8)(v) (psychological counseling); *see* Seals v. Loftis, 614 F. Supp. 302 (E.D. Tenn. 1985); T.G. v. Board of Educ., 576 F. Supp. 420 (D.N.J. 1983); Papacoda v. Connecticut, 528 F. Supp. 68 (D. Conn. 1981); Gary B. v. Cronin, 542 F. Supp. 102 (N.D. Ill. 1980); In re "A" Family, 184 Mont. 145, 602 P.2d 157 (1979); *see also* 20 U.S.C. § 1401(17).

results, planning programs and consulting with other staff,[98] psychological services include psychotherapy.[99]

An issue that has arisen is whether psychotherapy provided by a psychiatrist is a related service, or a precluded medical service. *Max. M. v. Thompson, (Max M. III)*[100] addressed this issue. Balancing the recognition of psychotherapy as a related service with the limitation of medical services to diagnosis and evaluation, the court held that IDEA "requires... cost free psychotherapy that could be carried out by psychologists, social workers, or guidance counselors."[101] The court in *Max. M. III* required the LEA to reimburse for the psychiatric services at a rate "normally and reasonably charged" by a non-physician professional of this type.

The position taken in *Max M. III* is consistent with the Supreme Court's recognition in *Irving Independent School District v. Tatro*[102] of Congressional concern with not overburdening school systems and thus requiring nursing services, but not the services of a licensed physician.[103] At least one other court, however, has held that whether the reimbursement is required depends not on who provides the service, but on nature and purpose of the services.[104]

Counseling services may overlap with psychological services since they include "services provided by qualified social workers, psychologists, guidance counselors, or other qualified personnel."[105] In fact, the requirement of counseling services has been used as an alternative justification for finding psychotherapy to be a related service.[106]

3.9.5 Physical Therapy, Occupational Therapy, Recreation, Early Identification and Assessment of Disabilities As Related Services

Physical therapy is simply defined in the regulations as "services provided by a qualified physical therapist."[107]

---

98. 34 C.F.R. § 300.16(b)(8); *see also* 20 U.S.C. § 1401(17).

99. 34 C.F.R. § 300.16(b)(8)(v); T.G. v. Board of Educ., 576 F. Supp. 420 (D.N.J. 1983) *aff'd*, 738 F.2d 420 (3d Cir. 1984); Papacoda v. Connecticut, 528 F. Supp. 68 (D. Ct. 1981); *see also* 20 U.S.C. § 1401(17).

100. 592 F. Supp. 1437 (N.D. Ill. 1984)

101. *See also* Darlene L. v. Illinois State Board of Educ., 568 F. Supp. 1340, 1345 (N.D. Ill. 1983).

102. 468 U.S. 883 (1984). The Court did not, however, have occasion to address the issue under § 504, since on the same day it had decided IDEA was the exclusive remedy and that Section 504 did not apply. *Id.* at 895 (citing Smith v. Robinson, 468 U.S. 992 (1984)).

103. Tatro, 468 U.S. 883 (1984).

104. Board of Educ. v. Department of Educ., 17 Educ. Handicapped L. Rep. (LRP) 942 (Conn. Super. Ct. May 16, 1991); see also Field v. Haddonfield Bd. of Educ., 769 F. Supp. 1313 (D.N.J. 1991) (whether drug treatment program is related service depends on purpose and nature of service, not on provider).

105. 34 C.F.R. § 300.17(b)(2); *see also* 20 U.S.C. § 1401(16).

106. *See, e.g.,* Max M. (III), 592 F. Supp. at 1444; Gary B. v. Cronin, 542 F. Supp. 102 (N.D. Ill. 1980).

107. 34 C.F.R. § 300.16(b)(7); *see also* 20 U.S.C. § 1401(17). As with all special education and

" 'Occupational therapy' includes [i]mproving, developing or restoring functions," prevention and parent counseling and training.[108]

"Recreation" as a related service includes assessment, provision of therapeutic services, recreation programs and leisure education.[109]

Recreation as a related service, and therefore mandated only as a "supportive service" and not required for all children with disabilities, should be distinguished from physical education, which is contained in the definition of "special education" and is, therefore, required for all children covered by IDEA.[110] Recreation should also be distinguished from extracurricular activities which, despite specific references in the regulations, may not be required by IDEA.[111]

Early identification means "implementation of a formal plan for identifying a disability as early as possible in a child's life."[112]

3.9.6 Medical Services As Related Services

Medical services required under IDEA are limited to those necessary for diagnostic and evaluation purposes.[113] The regulations provide that " '[m]edical services' means services provided by a licensed physician *to determine* a child's medically related *handicapping condition* which results in the child's need for special education and related services."[114]

The regulation, by its own terms, limits medical services to those necessary for diagnosis of disabilities. The United States Supreme Court recognized this limitation in *Irving Independent School District v. Tatro*,[115] where it held that the services of a licensed physician were not a related service.

The Court in *Tatro* pointed out that the regulations did provide for school health services, provided by someone other than a physician. The Court held that requiring medical services only for diagnosis, but requiring other health services by non-physicians, was a reasonable distinction. The distinction was reasonable in light of Congressional intent to avoid imposing on school systems obligations that were "unduly expensive" or beyond their competence, while at the same time recognizing that "Congress plainly required schools hire various specially trained personnel to help handicapped children ... "[116]

A distinction must also be made between medical services, as just discussed, and medical evaluations that are required to determine eligibility or to plan for an IEP. The medical evaluations are clearly contemplated for under IDEA.[117]

---

related service, the public agency's failure to provide physical therapy would be denial of a free appropriate education, Polk v. Central Susquehanna Intermediate Unit 16, 853 F.2d 171 (3d Cir. 1988), and the agency must provide physical therapy during the summer if necessary in order to receive benefit. Holmes v. Sobol, 690 F. Supp. 154 (W.D.N.Y. 1988).

108. 34 C.F.R. § 300.16(b)(5); *see also* 20 U.S.C. § 1401(17).

109. 34 C.F.R. § 300.16(b)(9); *see also* 20 U.S.C. § 1401(17).

110. 20 U.S.C. § 1401(a)(16); 34 C.F.R. § 300.306.

111. *See* § 3.12.

112. 34 C.F.R. § 300.16(b)(3); *see also* 20 U.S.C. § 1401(16).

113. 34 C.F.R. § 300.16(b)(4); *see also* 20 U.S.C. § 1401(17).

114. 34 C.F.R. § 300.16(b)(4) (emphasis added); *see also* 20 U.S.C. § 1401(17).

115. 468 U.S. 883 (1984).

116. *Id.* at 892–893.

117. Doe v. Board of Educ. of Nashville-Davidson County, 441 Educ. Handicapped L. Rep. (CRR) 106 (M.D. Tenn. 1988); Seals v. Loftis, 614 F. Supp. 302 (E.D. Tenn. 1985).

The distinction between medical services and nursing services is also critical in the area of residential programming. Where a child requires a residential program for medical as opposed to educational reasons, courts hold that the school system is not responsible for the residential portion of the placement. In these situations, usually hospitalization for a psychiatric disorder, critical to the determination is that the child is primarily receiving medical services beyond diagnosis and evaluation.[118]

Placements made primarily for medical reasons, however, must be distinguished from those cases where a child has medical problems, but the placement is necessary for educational reasons. The test to be applied to determine whether the placement is for medical or educational purposes is "are the social, emotional, medical and educational problems so intertwined 'that realistically it is not possible for the court to perform the Solomon-like task of separating them'... [T]he unseverability of such needs is the very basis for holding that the services are an essential prerequisite for learning."[119]

A issue that is of increasing concern in distinguishing between medical and other services is whether drug treatment programs can be a related service. In *Field v. Haddonfield Board of Education*,[120] the court held that whether a drug treatment program was a related service depended on the purpose and nature of the services, not on who provided the services or the mere fact that the services involved drug treatment. Holding that the program at issue was not a related service, the the court found that the particular program at issue "provided intensive therapy for Daniel's underlying psychiatric disorders, which included psychiatric counselling, numerous physical evaluations as well as medication."[121]

3.9.7 School Health Services As Related Services

As discussed in the previous section, both IDEA regulations and the United States Supreme Court in *Irving Independent School District v. Tatro*,[122] recognize a distinction between the provision of medical services and school health services. "School health services" are "services provided by a qualified school nurse or other qualified person."[123]

Tatro dealt with an 8-year-old girl, Amber, born with spina bifida:

> [S]he must be catheterized every three or four hours to avoid injury to her kidneys. In accordance with accepted medical practice, clean intermittent

118. *See* Clovis Unified School Dist. v. California Office of Admin. Hearings, 903 F.2d 635 (9th Cir. 1990); Tice v. Botetourt County School Bd., 441 Educ. Handicapped L. Rep. (CRR) 486 (W.D. Va. 1989), *aff'd in part, vac. in part, remanded*, 908 F.2d 1200 (4th Cir. 1990); Darlene L. v. Illinois State Bd. of Educ., 568 F. Supp. 1340, 1344 (N.D. Ill. 1983); McKenzie v. Jefferson, 566 F. Supp. 404 (D.D.C. 1983).

119. Kruelle v. New Castle County School Dist., 642 F.2d 687, 694 (3d Cir. 1981) (quoting North v. District of Columbia Bd. of Educ., 471 F. Supp. 136, 141 (D.D.C. 1979)). For a complete discussion of residential placements see 8.8.

120. 769, F. Supp. 1313 (D.N.J. 1991).

121. *Id.* at 1327.

122. 468 U.S. 883 (1984).

123. 34 C.F.R. § 300.16(b)(11); *see also* 20 U.S.C. § 1401(17).

catheterization (CIC), a procedure involving the insertion of a catheter into the urethra to drain the bladder, has been prescribed. The procedure is a simple one that may be performed in a few minutes by a layperson with less than an hour's training.[124]

The school system refused to place in Amber's IEP a requirement that school personnel perform CIC. Since CIC did not require a licensed physician to perform, and in fact it could be performed by a nurse or trained layperson, the Court held it constituted a required school health service.

The Court concluded with what amounts to a checklist of requirements that must be met to be eligible for related services:

1. The child must be disabled and eligible for special education;
2. The service must be "necessary to aid a handicapped child to benefit from special education ... ";
3. Nursing services may be required, but not if the service must be performed by a licensed physician;
4. Services are required to be provided, not equipment.[125]

A required health service which can be performed by a nurse, however, does not always constitute a related service. Courts have consistently held that health services must be "within reason."[126] Two similar decisions illustrate the limits. In *Detsel v. Board of Education*[127] and *Bevin H. v. Wright*[128] the courts were requested to order extensive nursing services. In both cases the child had severe mental and physical disabilities, and both had a tracheostomy and gastrostomy. "Most significantly, both children because of the tracheostomy and their inability to care for it themselves, require the constant undivided attention of a nurse."[129] In both cases, the district courts held that the level of services required exceeded those contemplated as related services: [T]he nursing services required are so varied, intensive and costly, and more in the nature of 'medical services' ... "[130]

Both *Detsel* and *Bevin H.* were severely criticized in *Macomb County Intermediate School District v. Joshua S.*[131] Further, more intermittent nursing care than in either *Detsel* or *Bevin H.* has been upheld as a related service. Thus, in *State of Hawaii Department of Education v. Katherine D.*,[132] the court held that repositioning a suction tube in a child's throat was a related service where it could be done by school personnel.[133]

124. Tatro, 468 U.S. at 885.

125. *Id.* at 894–5.

126. *See, e.g.*, Department of Educ. v. Katherine D., 727 F.2d 809, 813 (9th Cir. 1983) (requiring tracheostomy care as related service); Tokarcik v. Forest Hills School Dist., 665 F.2d 443, 455 (3d Cir. 1981) (pre-*Tatro* requiring CIC).

127. 637 F. Supp. 1022 (N.D.N.Y. 1986), *aff'd*, 820 F.2d 587 (2d Cir. 1987).

128. 666 F. Supp. 71 (W.D. Pa. 1987).

129. *Id.* at 74.

130. *Id.* at 76.

131. 715 F. Supp. 824 (E.D. Mich. 1989).

132. 727 F.2d 809 (9th Cir. 1983).

133. *See also* Hymes v. Harnett County Bd. of Educ., 664 F.2d 410 (4th Cir. 1981) (tracheostomy care assumed to be related service).

3.9.8 Social Work Services, Parent Counseling And Training As Related Services

"Parent counseling and training" as a related service "means assisting parents in understanding the special needs of their children and providing parents with information about child development."[134] For example, in *Chris D. v. Montgomery County Board of Education*,[135] the court ordered the public school to provide training and counseling to a child's parents because the services were necessary in order to implement the IEP.

"Social work services in school include preparing histories, counseling, working with problems in school, home and community, and mobilizing resources."[136]

3.9.9 Related Services without Special Education

Statutory language would indicate that eligibility for special education is a prerequisite for mandated related services. The statute requires "supportive services ... as may be required to assist a handicapped child to benefit from special education."[137] There is, therefore, a specific requirement that related services be directed to those receiving special education. The United States Supreme Court recognized this in *Tatro* when it held that the related service must be "necessary to aid a handicapped child to benefit from special education ..."[138]

It is possible, however, that what is generally considered a related service may have educational content. The definition of special education under the regulations indicates that

> [t]he term includes speech pathology, or any other related service, if the service consists of specially designed instruction ... and is considered "special education" rather than a "related service" under State standards.[139]

Individual state regulations should be checked to determine what "related services" are considered to have educational content.[140]

---

134. 34 C.F.R. § 300.16(b)(6); see also 20 U.S.C. § 1401(17).

135. 753 F. Supp. 922 (M.D. Ala. 1990).

136. 34 C.F.R. § 300.16(b)(12); see also 20 U.S.C. § 1401(17).

137. 20 U.S.C. § 1401(17).

138. Tatro, 468 U.S. at 894. See Dubois v. Connecticut State Bd. of Educ., 727 F.2d 44 (2d Cir. 1984) (eligibility for transportation costs to out-of-state placement paid for by LEA is dependent on whether placement is necessary for special education); A.A. v. Cooperman, 218 N.J. Super 32, 526 A.2d 1103 1987) (orthopedically impaired student not in need of special education, therefore related service of transportation not required under IDEA).

139. 34 C.F.R. § 300.17(2); see also 20 U.S.C. § 1401(17).

140. OSEP Memorandum 87–21 to State Directors of Special Education, reprinted 202 Educ. Handicapped L. Rep. (CRR) 372 (June 29, 1987).

3.10 Physical Education

Congress clearly intended,[141] and IDEA clearly requires, the provision of physical education to all children with disabilities.[142] The definition of "special education" found within IDEA specifically includes physical education.[143]

Physical education is defined in the regulations as including physical and motor fitness and "[s]kills in aquatics, dance, and individual and group games and sports (including intramural and life sports)."[144]

Consistent with the overriding requirement that the child be educated in the least restrictive environment, children with disabilities are to participate in regular physical education classes unless the child is enrolled in a separate facility or the child's IEP requires a specialized physical education program.[145]

3.11 Vocational Education

The definition of special education under IDEA includes vocational education.[146] It should also be known that school systems providing vocational education are subject to the United States Department of Education's anti-discrimination regulation under § 504, as well as the Guidelines for Eliminating Discrimination and Denial of Services on the Basis of Race, Color, National Origin, Sex and Handicap in Vocational Education Programs.[147]

3.12 Extracurricular Activities

Regulations promulgated under IDEA require an equal opportunity for children with disabilities to participate in nonacademic and extracurricular activities.[148] These activities "may include counseling services, athletics, transportation, health services, recreational activities, special interest groups or clubs . . . referrals . . . and employment . . ."[149] The validity of this requirement has been called into question by the United States Sixth Circuit Court of Appeals.

In one of the few judicial opinions addressing this requirement, the court in *Rettig v. Kent City School District*,[150] held that since the regulation requiring nonacademic and extracurricular activities required strict equality of opportunity it was contrary to the interpretation of IDEA as announced by the Supreme Court in *Hendrick Hudson District Board of Education v. Rowley*.[151] In *Rowley*, the

---

141. H.R. Rep. No. 332, 94th Cong., 1st Sess. 9 (1975).
142. 20 U.S.C. § 1401(16); 34 C.F.R. § 300.307.
143. 20 U.S.C. § 1401(16).
144. 34 C.F.R. § 300.17(b)(2); see also 20 U.S.C. § 1401(16).
145. 34 C.F.R. § 300.307(b); see also 20 U.S.C. §§ 1401(16), 1412(5)(B).
146. 34 C.F.R. § 300.17(b)(3); see also 20 U.S.C. § 1401(16).
147. 34 C.F.R. Part 100 app. B.
148. 34 C.F.R. § 300.306(a); see also 20 U.S.C. § 1414(a)(1)(C).
149. 34 C.F.R. § 300.306(b); see also 20 U.S.C. § 1414(a)(1)(C).
150. 788 F.2d 328 (6th Cir. 1986).
151. 458 U.S. 176 (1981).

United States Supreme Court rejected a reading of IDEA which measured level of educational services based on equal opportunity.[152] The court in *Rettig*, relying on the language in *Rowley*, stated "the applicable test under *Rowley* is whether the handicapped child's IEP, when taken in its entirety, is reasonably calculated to enable the child to receive educational benefits."[153] Since the child in *Rettig* was determined by the district court to not be able to "significantly benefit,"[154] the court held "the school district was not obligated to provide extracurricular activities from which [the child] would receive no significant educational benefit."[155]

Given the ability to bring a suit under § 504 of the Rehabilitation Act of 1974 concurrently with IDEA, (something that could not have been done when *Rettig* was decided), there is an argument that the functional equivalent of the regulation is now available by seeking relief under § 504, since § 504 does establish at least a general equal opportunity requirement.[156]

---

152. Id. at 198–199.

153. Rettig, 788 F.2d at 332.

154. Id.

155. Id. For a discussion of inability to benefit generally, see § 5.2.3.

156. Grube v. Bethlehem Area School Dist., 550 F. Supp. 418 (E.D. Pa. 1982) (exclusion from athletics based on having only one kidney improper under § 504 where medical testimony indicated slight risk of harm); but see Cavallaro v. Ambach, 575 F. Supp. 171 (W.D.N.Y. 1983) (exclusion of learning disabled student from athletics did not violate § 504 where exclusion based on age, not handicapping condition); Arlington County (Va) Pub. Schools, 16 Educ. Handicapped L. Rep. (LRP) 1188 (OCR 1990) (violation of § 504 where general day camp provided, but no therapeutic day camp); Clayton (Mo.) School Dist., 16 Educ. Handicapped L. Rep. (LRP) 766 (OCR March 16, 1990) (§ 504 requires equal and meaningful participation in recreation).

Chapter 4

Identification and Evaluation

4.1 In General

Each local education agency must establish procedures by which children in need of special education and related services are identified, located, and evaluated. The states are left to develop their own identification procedures, but the law requires an active effort to identify children in need of services.[1]

Both § 504 and IDEA provide for the evaluation of children in their regulations.[2] Although § 504 mentions that reevaluations and compliance with procedural safeguards consistent with IDEA regulations will also meet standards for compliance under § 504,[3] compliance with either IDEA or § 504 regulations does not insure compliance with the other.[4]

4.2 Identification

Typically, local school systems screen kindergarten children on an annual basis. Such efforts, however, are not alone sufficient, since disabilities may not appear until later and, of course, IDEA requires services prior to school age.[5] Further, early intervention can be critical to success.[6] In addition to kindergarten screening, therefore, schools use a variety of procedures including public education programs, public meetings, contact with day-care providers, as well as other service

---

1. 34 C.F.R. § 300.220; 20 U.S.C. § 1414(a)(1)(A).

2. *Compare* 34 C.F.R. §§ 104.35-.36 (1989) with 34 C.F.R. § 300.530-.534.

3. 34 C.F.R. §§ 104.35(d)-.36.

4. *See* Kennedy Inquiry, 16 Educ. Handicapped L. Rep. (LRP) 226 (EHA August 9, 1989). This is particularly true in the area of the need for re-evaluations based in change in placement. See § 4.5.

5. See § 3.6.

6. The need for early intervention has led to the recently enacted Early Intervention Program for Infants and Toddlers With Handicaps. 20 U.S.C. §§ 1471-1485; 34 C.F.R. Part 303. This "Infants and Toddlers" program provides for interagency coordination of services, including the development of Individual Family Service Plans for children from birth through two years of age, for children who "are experiencing developmental delays ... or ... have a diagnosed physical or mental condition which has a high probability of resulting in developmental delay." 20 U.S.C. § 1472(1).

providers, media advertising, and referrals from other sources, such as physicians, who suspect a disability.

Once an LEA is aware or has a suspicion that a child may need special education an evaluation is required.[7] Even when a parent fails to disclose a medical condition, if the LEA has knowledge of the condition it must evaluate.[8] Actions by the LEA such as excluding a child from activities or secluding him, are evidence that a problem requiring evaluation exists.[9]

Absenteeism may be sufficient to warrant evaluation if an LEA's guidelines indicate that absenteeism shall be regarded as a condition from which counseling should be initiated. If, however, the child's absences were not believed to have resulted from any psychological disorder, disability, or disruptive behavior, and no requests for evaluation were received, absenteeism may not be sufficient to indicate an evaluation is in order.[10]

There are conflicting rulings regarding an indication to evaluate based upon psychiatric hospitalization. In 1990, the United States Department of Education's Office of Civil Rights (OCR) found that a student previously in a regular education program did not require an evaluation solely because she was hospitalized, since her academic status showed no change.[11] In 1989, however, the OCR stated that any child who was hospitalized for psychiatric diagnoses of depression, dysthymic disorder, or emotional problems should be evaluated.[12] A third ruling, made in 1990, may indicate that when a change in academic performance is coupled with a history of psychiatric hospitalization an evaluation should then be triggered.[13] If a psychologist refers a child for evaluation after a psychiatric hospitalization, one must be performed.[14]

Substance abuse may be sufficient under § 504 to qualify the child as a proper candidate for evaluation.[15] Failing to identify the child's substance abuse problem, however, is not a violation of § 504, if his problem was never displayed in any perceivable manner (e.g. a change in behavior or academic performance) and there was no pattern of refusing evaluations, or ignoring the needs of substance abusers by the LEA.[16]

---

7. Auburn, Al. School Dist., 16 Educ. Handicapped L. Rep. (LRP) 177 (OCR June 15, 1989).

8. Great Valley, Pa. School Dist., 16 Educ. Handicapped L. Rep. (LRP) 101 (OCR July 6, 1989).

9. New York City Bd. of Educ., 16 Educ. Handicapped L. Rep. (LRP) 455 (OCR November 2, 1989).

10. *Compare* Carlinville, Il. Community Unit School Dist. No. One, 352 Educ. Handicapped L. Rep. (CRR) 32 (OCR July 3, 1985) *with* Portsmouth, RI Pub. Schools, 257 Educ. Handicapped L. Rep. (CRR) 346 (OCR September 14,1982).

11. Mehlville, Mo. R-IX School Dist., 16 Educ. Handicapped L. Rep. (LRP) 465 (OCR November 29, 1989).

12. Community Unit School Dist. No. 300, 353 Educ. Handicapped L. Rep. (CRR) 296 (OCR 1989).

13. School Admin. Unit No. 19, NH, 16 Educ. Handicapped L. Rep. (LRP) 86 (OCR January 4, 1989).

14. Edinboro, Pa. Intermediate Unit No. Five, 352 Educ. Handicapped L. Rep. (CRR) 511 (OCR September 22, 1987).

15. Lake Washington, Wa. School Dist. No. 414, 257 Educ. Handicapped L. Rep. (CRR) 611 (OCR June 28, 1985).

16. York, Ill. Community High School, 352 Educ. Handicapped L. Rep. (CRR) 116 (OCR November 19, 1985).

4.3 Pre-placement Evaluations

Having identified children who may be in need of special education and related services, an evaluation must be performed. Evaluation procedures determine "whether a child is handicapped and the nature and extent of the special education and related services that the child needs. The term [evaluation] means procedures used selectively with an individual child . . . "[17]

Not surprisingly, the first evaluation must be performed before "any action" is taken with regard to the initial special education placement.[18] It is the state's responsibility to insure that all children with disabilities are identified and evaluated.[19] Once a child has been identified through pre-screening or referral, a timely evaluation must be instituted.[20] Although the statute and regulations do not establish a limit to the time between identification and evaluation, the individual states may establish absolute guidelines for the time allowed between identification and evaluation.[21] Where there is an unreasonable delay in considering a child for, and completing an evaluation, the withholding of suitable education has occurred, and LEAs may be held liable for the private placement costs.[22] Timetables have also been set by the court for implementation of evaluation procedures where a violation of the reasonable standard has been found.[23]

Section 504 requires pre-placement evaluations to be made on any child identified to an LEA as having a disability.[24] Under Section 504, an evaluation is required to be complete prior to placement.[25] Evaluations must be made in a "timely" manner, once the LEA is aware of a child's need.[26] "Timeliness" may be what is reasonable under the circumstances, or it may be measured by the maximum time allowable under LEA rules.[27] "Gross disregard" for a child's welfare may result in the LEA's liability for the cost of private placement where evaluation was not made in a timely manner.[28] Referrals for evaluation under 504 must be in writing, and evaluations must culminate in final decisions regarding the child's need for service as well as a definite placement plan.[29]

---

17. 34 C.F.R. § 300.500; *see also* 20 U.S.C. § 1415.

18. 34 C.F.R. § 300.531; 20 U.S.C. § 1412(5)(C); Dubois v. Conn. State Dep't. of Educ. 727 F.2d 44 (2d Cir. 1984).

19. *Compare* 34 C.F.R. §§ 104.35-.36 *with* 34 C.F.R. §§ 300.530-.534.

20. Kelley Inquiry 211 Educ. Handicapped L. Rep. (CRR) 240 (EHA January 16, 1981).

21. *Id.*

22. *See generally* Foster v. District of Columbia Bd. of Educ., 523 F. Supp. 1142 (D.D.C. 1981).

23. *See* Jose P. v. Ambach, 553 Educ. Handicapped L. Rep. (CRR) 298, *aff'd*, 669 F.2d 865 (2d Cir. 1982).

24. 34 C.F.R. § 104.35(a).

25. St. Claire, Mo. R-XIII School Dist., 352 Educ. Handicapped L. Rep. (CRR) 201 (OCR July 21, 1986).

26. 34 C.F.R. § 104.35(a)(b)(c).

27. North Smithfield, RI School Dist., 16 Educ. Handicapped L. Rep. (LRP) 245 (OCR September 21, 1990).

28. Foster v. District of Columbia Bd. of Educ., 553 Educ. Handicapped L. Rep. (CRR) 520 (D.D.C. 1982).

29. Allegheny, NY Central School Dist., 257 Educ. Handicapped L. Rep. (CRR) 494 (OCR March 26, 1984).

Until 1989, prescreenings were not interpreted to be evaluations unless testing or interviewing were used, and prescreenings were generally held not to require conformity with § 504 regulations for evaluations. Now however, it appears that any organized prescreening effort will be held to be a part of the evaluation process and must conform to § 504 regulations.[30]

4.4 Re-Evaluations under IDEA

After the initial pre-placement evaluation, an evaluation must take place at least every three years under IDEA. A parent or school teacher, however, may request a reevaluation, and a reevaluation should be conducted sooner than every three years "if conditions warrant" such reevaluation.[31] For example, if the parties disagree concerning placement changes, or there are perceived discrepancies in the individualized educational program, a reevaluation request would be proper. Also, for example, where only two years have elapsed, but substantive changes in standards used for the evaluation are made, a reevaluation has been held to be in order.[32]

Unlike section 504, there is no requirement under IDEA that a student be reevaluated before a significant placement change is made.[33] A decision to change placement, however, must be made by persons knowledgeable about the child, and with evaluation data in their possession.[34] No reevaluation is specifically required under IDEA regulations if services are suspended.

4.5 Re-Evaluations under § 504

Section 504 regulations have a general requirement that a reevaluation be made "periodically." A reevaluation policy consistent with IDEA regulations is one means of meeting these requirements.[35] IDEA requires reevaluation every three years or more often if the condition warrants, or if requested by parents or teachers.[36] Section 504, however, unlike IDEA also requires that each identified child be evaluated prior to any significant change in placement.[37] The United States Department of Education Office of Civil Rights has identified the following as among the circumstances that constitute a "significant" placement change:

• A change from a private to a public school[38]

---

30. *Compare* San Diego City, Ca. School Dist., 353 Educ. Handicapped L. Rep. (CRR) 236 (OCR May 17, 1989) *with* Forest Park, Mi. School Dist., 352 Educ. Handicapped L. Rep. (CRR) 182 (OCR February 28, 1986).

31. 34 C.F.R. § 300.534(b); 20 U.S.C. § 1412(5)(C).

32. Grkman v. Scanlon, 563 F. Supp. 793 (W.D. Pa. 1983).

33. Houseman, 305 Educ. Handicapped L. Rep. (CRR) 34 (OCR April 3, 1986).

34. McKenzie v. Smith, 771 F.2d 1527 (D.C. Cir. 1985).

35. 34 C.F.R. § 104.35(b).

36. 34 C.F.R. § 300.534(b).

37. 34 C.F.R. § 104.35(a); *see also* Houseman, 305 Educ. Handicapped L. Rep. (CRR) 34 (OCR April 3, 1986).

38. Humboldt, Tn. City School Dist., 352 Educ. Handicapped L. Rep. (CRR) 557 (OCR November 12, 1987).

- Transfer to a more restrictive environment[39]
- Returning a student to special education after a brief placement in regular education[40]
- Initiation of homebound education[41]
- Termination of homebound education[42]
- A change in the number of hours per week spent in regular versus special education classes[43]
- A change in status from special education to regular education[44]
- Transfers from one type of special education program to another (e.g. learning disabled to educable mentally retarded)[45]
- A transfer of a special education student to state prison[46]
- Suspension from school in excess of ten days per year[47]
- Termination of services[48]

4.6 Evaluation Standards under IDEA

Minimum standards of evaluation procedures are set forth under 34 C.F.R. § 300.532 and no single procedure or test may constitute an evaluation.[49] For example, where a hearing impaired child was evaluated and placed solely on the basis of observation, his evaluation was invalid.[50]

The extent of the evaluation performed is dependent on the suspected disability of the child. All areas related to a suspected disability must also be assessed,

---

39. Special School Dist. of St. Louis County, Mo., 352 Educ. Handicapped L. Rep. (CRR) 156 (OCR February 14, 1986).

40. Wright City, Mo. School Dist., 352 Educ. Handicapped L. Rep. (CRR) 161 (OCR February 13, 1986).

41. Southeastern Greene, Pa. School Dist. No. One, 353 Educ. Handicapped L. Rep. (CRR) 105 (OCR July 26, 1988); Russell County, Ky. School Dist., 352 Educ. Handicapped L. Rep. (CRR) 253 (OCR July 17, 1986).

42. Clermont, Oh. Northeastern Schools, 257 Educ. Handicapped L. Rep. (CRR) 577 (OCR July 23, 1984).

43. Omaha, Ne. Pub. Schools, 257 Educ. Handicapped L. Rep. (CRR) 71 (OCR December 31, 1979).

44. Dyersburg, Tn. City School Dist., 353 Educ. Handicapped L. Rep. (CRR) 164 (OCR November 4, 1988).

45. Powhattan, Ks. Unified School Dist. No. 150, 257 Educ. Handicapped L. Rep. (CRR) 32 (OCR April 6, 1979).

46. Brandywine, De. School Dist., 16 Educ. Handicapped L. Rep. (LRP) 327 (OCR December 29, 1989).

47. Pennsylvania Dep't. of Educ., 353 Educ. Handicapped L. Rep. (CRR) 115 (OCR August 12, 1988). But see Chester County (TN) School Dist., 17 Educ. Handicapped L. Rep. (LRP) 301 (OCR October 26, 1990) (10 days in-school suspension not a significant change in placement).

48. Brentwood, NY Union Free School Dist., 257 Educ. Handicapped L. Rep. (CRR) 653 (OCR April 29, 1985).

49. 34 C.F.R. § 300.532(d); see also 20 U.S.C. § 1412(5)(c). Where a test is one of three, requirements have been held to have been fulfilled. Brookhart v. Ill. State Bd. of Educ., 697 F.2d 179 (7th Cir. 1982).

50. Bonadonna v. Cooperman, 619 F. Supp. 401 (D. N.J. 1985).

"including where appropriate, health, vision, hearing, social and emotional status, general intelligence, academic performance, communicative status, and motor abilities."[51] A child, for example, with a mild disability, such as a speech impairment, may not need a full battery of assessments, however, the accessibility to additional assessments must be available if referral is later found to be needed. In fact, an assessment that is overly broad and includes tests unrelated to a suspected disability violates 34 C.F.R. § 300.532(f).[52]

Any tests or other evaluation materials must be in the native language of the child (or, where appropriate, some other means of communication). The materials must be validated for the specific purpose for which they are being used and administered by trained personnel, according to instructions prepared by the producers.

Any tests used to evaluate a child must be non-discriminatory.[53] The test must also be administered "so as best to ensure that when a test is administered to a child with impaired sensory, manual, or speaking skills, the test results accurately reflect the child's aptitude or achievement level or whatever other factors the test purports to measure ..."[54]

Observation of the child must be performed by someone other than the child's teacher.[55] The observation must take place in the child's classroom setting or if the child is not in school, then in the child's usual environment.[56]

Medical treatment is not the responsibility of the LEA, but it must pay for any medical diagnostic exams appropriate to insure a valid evaluation.[57]

"Substantial compliance" to standards has been held sufficient to avoid court ordered declaratory judgments.[58]

4.7 Evaluation Standards under § 504

Evaluation procedures outlined in § 504 provide that validated tests, administered by trained personnel, be used to assess specific disabilities on an indivi-

51. 34 C.F.R. § 300.532(f); *see also* 20 U.S.C. § 1412(5)(c).

52. Washington, Vt. Central Supervisory Union No. 32, 257 Educ. Handicapped L. Rep. (CRR) 509 (OCR February 22, 1984). Socio-cultural inventories performed on all parents of learning disabled children were ruled to be such a violation. *Id.* Psychological assessments in mentally retarded and learning disabled children have been interpreted as proper, since both conditions have social and emotional consequences. Feeley Inquiry, 211 Educ. Handicapped L. Rep. (CRR) 415 (EHA October 20, 1986).

53. 34 C.F.R. § 300.530(b); *see also* 20 U.S.C. § 1412(5)(c). The leading case in this area held that standardized I.Q. tests were racially biased against African-Americans, and that by their use, African Americans were being erroneously evaluated, so the court ordered alternative testing. Larry P. v. Riles, 793 F.2d 969 (9th Cir. 1986). *See also* Mattie T. v. Holladay, 522 F. Supp. 72 (N.D. Miss. 1978)(consent agreement entered pursuant to discriminatory violations of children under IDEA).

54. 34 C.F.R. § 300.532(c); *see also* 20 U.S.C. § 1412(5)(c).

55. 34 C.F.R. § 300.542(a).

56. 34 C.F.R. § 300.542.

57. Doe v. Board of Pub. Educ., 441 Educ. Handicapped L. Rep. (CRR) 106 (M.D. Tenn. 1988). *See* § 3.9.6.

58. Powell v. Defore, 553 Educ. Handicapped L. Rep. (CRR) 293 (M.D. Ga. 1982), *aff'd on other grounds*, 699 F.2d 1078 (11th Cir. 1983).

dualized basis, so as not to cause the disability to defeat the test results.[59] The testing method must also result in more than a single general intelligence quotient as a result.[60]

Tests used in the evaluation process must be validated for the specific purpose for which they are used and must be administered by trained personnel to conform with the producers' instructions.[61]

The tests selected for use in a § 504 evaluation must be of a non-discriminatory nature so that the results accurately reflect the child's aptitude, not his physical disability.[62] An evaluation must not be based on a single procedure.[63] A "variety of sources" must be used, and not merely I.Q. tests.[64] Indeed, I.Q. itself may not preclude a student from eligibility for special education.[65] Undue reliance on any one testing device is improper.[66]

Regulation 104.35(c) requires that students' adaptive behavior be considered in the evaluation process.[67]

4.8 Notice and Consent for Evaluation under IDEA

The LEA must provide the parents with notice of an intent to evaluate the child.[68] Consent is required for selective procedures only. Evaluation does not include tests administered to all children in a grade or class.[69]

The notice must allow a reasonable time prior to initiation of the pre-placement evaluation.[70] The notice of intent to evaluate the child must include a listing of tests that are expected to be used in the evaluation,[71] as well as the general provisions governing notice and consent.[72]

Parental consent for the pre-placement evaluation under IDEA is required.[73] Parental consent is defined as a written agreement that acknowledges the understanding of all activities sought to be performed in the evaluation process and

59. 34 C.F.R. § 104.35(b).

60. *Id.*

61. 34 C.F.R. § 104.35(b)(1).

62. 34 C.F.R. § 104.35(b)(3); California School for the Deaf, 257 Educ. Handicapped L. Rep. (CRR) 583 (OCR 1984).

63. 34 C.F.R. § 104.35(b)(2).

64. Larry P. v. Riles, 793 F.2d 969 (9th Cir. 1984).

65. Ulissi Inquiry, 18 Individuals with Disabilities Educ. L. Rep. (LRP) 683 (OSEP January 14, 1992).

66. 34 C.F.R. § 104.35(b)(2).

67. 34 C.F.R. § 104.35(c).

68. 34 C.F.R. § 300.505; *see* 20 U.S.C. § 1415(b)(1)(D).

69. Black Inquiry, 16 Educ. Handicapped L. Rep. (LRP) 1400 (OSEP August 9, 1990).

70. 34 C.F.R. § 300.504(a); *see* 20 U.S.C. § 1415(b)(1)(C), (D).

71. 34 C.F.R. § 300.505(a)(3); Gorski v. Lynchburg School Bd., 441 Educ. Handicapped L. Rep. (CRR) 415 (4th Cir. 1989).

72. See Chapter 9.

73. 34 C.F.R. § 300.504(b); *see* 20 U.S.C. § 1415(b)(1)(C), (D).

the voluntary acquiescence to these activities, subject to unilateral revocation.[74] Oral consent may never substitute for written consent.[75]

Once consent is obtained for pre-placement evaluation, it is not required for any subsequent reevaluation.[76] It does not matter that subsequent reevaluations include additional assessments, since a consent is considered to be for an evaluation as a whole and not for the individual pieces of the process.[77] Consent is a vital part of IDEA and states may amend consent requirements in only limited ways. They may, however, devise procedural steps for obtaining consent.[78]

If the parents refuse to consent to the pre-placement evaluation or revoke consent already given, the LEA may either file for a due process hearing, or initiate any state permitted procedure, such as a request for a court order.[79]

4.9 Notice and Consent for Evaluation under § 504

The Section 504 regulations' general procedural safeguards apply to the evaluation process. Although less specific than IDEA, the example given as a model of adherence is IDEA.[80] Further, notice is specifically required for evaluations under § 504.[81] Notice has been ruled to require a description of general types of tests to be used, even if the actual procedures are not known in advance.[82] Under IDEA, however, the notice need not list every test or outline qualifications of the examiners.[83]

Reevaluation must also be preceded by notice.[84]

---

74. 34 C.F.R. § 300.500(a)-(b); *see also* 20 U.S.C. § 1415.

75. Cogley, 211 Educ. Handicapped L. Rep. (CRR) 212 (EHA June 17, 1980).

76. 34 C.F.R. § 300.504(b); *see* 20 U.S.C. § 1415(b)(1)(C); Carroll v. Capalbo, 563 F. Supp. 1053 (D.R.I. 1983). A provision in the regulations states that other than for pre-placement evaluation and initial placement, "consent may not be required as a condition of any benefit to the parent or child," this initially led OSEP to conclude that a state could not require consent at other stages in the process, such as requiring consent prior to a change in placement. OSEP subsequently changed its interpretation, allowing states to require consent under other circumstances where it would not diminish parent or child rights.

77. Graham, 213 Educ. Handicapped L. Rep. (CRR) 250 (OSEP August 17, 1989).

78. 34 C.F.R. § 300.504(c); Lindsay, 211 Educ. Handicapped L. Rep. (CRR) 251 (EHA January 19, 1981).

79. 34 C.F.R. § 300.504; *see* 20 U.S.C. § 1415(b)(1)(C), (D).

80. 34 C.F.R. § 104.36. *See, e.g.,* Forest Park, Mi. School Dist., 352 Educ. Handicapped L. Rep. (CRR) 182 (OCR February 28, 1986); Tucson, Az. Unified School Dist., 257 Educ. Handicapped L. Rep. (CRR) 312 (OCR September 10, 1981). In 1987 OCR ruled that a failure to obtain parental consent prior to conducting speech and language evaluation of a child was a violation of 34 C.F.R. § 104.36. Sachem, NY Central School Dist., 352 Educ. Handicapped L. Rep. (CRR) 462 (OCR June 16, 1987).

81. 34 C.F.R. § 104.36.

82. Wisconsin Dep't. of Pub. Instruction, 352 Educ. Handicapped L. Rep. (CRR) 177 (OCR November 29, 1985).

83. Sutler and McCoy Inquiry, 18 Individuals with Disabilities Educ. L. Rep. (LRP) 307 (OSEP August 29, 1991).

84. East Stroudsburg, Pa. Area School Dist., 353 Educ. Handicapped L. Rep. (CRR) 108 (OCR August 31, 1988).

4.10 Evaluators under IDEA

"The evaluation is made by a multidisciplinary team...including at least one teacher or other specialist with knowledge in the area of suspected disability."[85] When a specific learning disability is suspected, additional team members are required to be on the team.[86] These additional team members are the child's regular teacher, or if there is no regular teacher, a teacher qualified to teach such a child, including pre-school children, and "at least one person qualified to conduct individual diagnostic examination of children, such as a school psychologist, speech-language pathologist, or remedial reading teacher."[87]

4.11 Evaluators under § 504

Section 504 requires that evaluations be made by a knowledgeable and specialized group of persons, but unlike IDEA there is nothing to indicate what kind of people must be on the evaluation team.[88]

4.12 Reporting Evaluation Results under both IDEA and § 504

Under IDEA, the results of an evaluation must be reported in a written report form.[89] Each team member must certify that the report reflects his conclusions.[90] The report must be one document, however, any team member's dissatisfaction may be presented separately.[91] Section 504 regulations require that all information obtained be documented.[92]

Failure to provide a written report may be found to be "minor" and not prejudicial when the parents have been actively involved in the process.[93]

---

85. 34 C.F.R. § 300.532(e); *see also* 20 U.S.C. 1412(5)(c).

86. 34 C.F.R. § 300.540. When determining the existence of a specific learning disability, a "severe discrepancy" must exist between a child's intellectual ability and an enumerated skill or form of expression. 34 C.F.R. § 300.541(a)(2). What constitutes a "severe discrepancy" may be defined by each state. Scovill Inquiry, 211 Educ. Handicapped L. Rep. (CRR) 14 (EHA March 3, 1978). Diagnosis of a learning disability must be made by a team judgment, and not on a prepared formula or profile, and if there is a conflict between any formula and the team's judgment, further explanation and possible further exploration may be required. O'Grady Inquiry, 211 Educ. Handicapped L. Rep. (CRR) 158 (EHA January 10, 1980).

87. 34 C.F.R. § 300.540(a)(1)-(3). Where a child has multiple diagnoses, but a specific learning disability is suspected, 34 C.F.R. § 300.540 does apply. Ehrlich Inquiry, 211 Educ. Handicapped L. Rep. (CRR) 289 (OCR December 3, 1982).

88. 34 C.F.R. § 300.532; S-1 v. Turlington, 635 F.2d 342 (5th Cir. 1981).

89. 34 C.F.R. § 300.543.

90. 34 C.F.R. § 300.543(c).

91. 34 C.F.R. § 300.543(c); McCarthy Inquiry, 211 Educ. Handicapped L. Rep. (CRR) 359 (EHA April 18, 1985).

92. 34 C.F.R. § 104.35(c)(2).

93. Hiller v. Board of Educ., 743 F. Supp. 958, 969–970 (N.D.N.Y. 1990).

4.13 Parental Participation

While there is the general requirement of consent, notice and a reasonable opportunity to attend meetings pertaining to the child and afforded to parents,[94] there is no participatory role in the evaluation mandated by explicit words of IDEA.[95] If the parent disagrees with the evaluation, however, there is the right to initiate due process procedures and seek reevaluation.[96] is conceivable that additional rights might be recognized by courts in specific circumstances. The Supreme Court, as well as lower courts, have consistently recognized that IDEA requires parental participation at all meaningful stages during the process.[97] The arbitrary refusal of an LEA to allow the parents, for example, to observe the evaluation process might well be a violation of this requirement.

Under § 504 regulations, parental participation is limited to the right of consent, notice, and initiation of due process procedures.[98]

4.14 Disputes over Evaluation

An evaluation of any child identified to the LEA as having a disability may be used to either prove or disprove the need of a special education placement, but the burden of proving, after a full evaluation, that the child is ineligible for service will be on the LEA.[99] Due process procedures allowed under IDEA regulations may be initiated at any time during the evaluation by either the LEA, the parents or a member of the evaluation team if disagreements arise.[100] If the parents do not believe the evaluation is appropriate for their child, they may seek an Independent Educational Evaluation at the LEA's expense.[101]

---

94. 34 C.F.R. § 300.345; *see also* 20 U.S.C. §§ 1412(4), § 1414(a)(4), (5).

95. Simon, 211 Educ. Handicapped L. Rep. (CRR) 436 (EHA February 6, 1987).

96. *Id.*

97. *See, e.g.* Board of Educ. of the Hendrick Hudson Cent. School Dist. v. Rowley, 458 U.S. 176, 205–206 (1982) (IDEA gives "a large measure of participation at every stage of the administrative process"); Honig v. Doe, 484 U.S. 305, 311 (1988) ("the Act establishes various procedural safeguards that guarantee parents . . . an opportunity for meaningful input into all decisions affecting their child's education . . . "); Devries v. Spillane, 853 F.2d 264, 266 (4th Cir. 1988) ("meaningful participation in all aspects").

98. *See* 34 C.F.R. § 104.36.

99. Timothy W. v. Rochester School Dist., 559 Educ. Handicapped L. Rep. (CRR) 480 (D.N.H. 1988), *rev'd. on other grounds*, 875 F.2d 954 (1st Cir. 1989).

100. McKeever, 211 Educ. Handicapped L. Rep. (CRR) 45 (EHA August 4, 1978).

101. See Chapter 6.

4.15 Identification/Evaluation Checklist-Summary

_____ LEA must establish "child find" system

_____ Preplacement evaluation required

_____ Timely evaluation following identification

_____ Reevaluation required

   _____ Every three years

   _____ Earlier if:

   _____ Conditions warrant (IDEA)

   _____ If requested by Parents (504)

   _____ If requested by teachers (504)

   _____ If there is a significant placement change (504)

_____ Evaluation Standards

   _____ No single procedure or test (IDEA & 504)

   _____ Must result in more than single intelligence quotient (504)

   _____ All areas of suspected disability must be assessed (IDEA)

   _____ Native language (IDEA)

   _____ Validated evaluation materials (IDEA & 504)

   _____ Trained personnel following instructions of producers (IDEA &504)

   _____ Administered in an individualized manner such that disability does not defeat purpose of test (IDEA & 504)

   _____ Nondiscriminatory (IDEA & 504)

   _____ Observation by someone other than child's teacher (IDEA)

   _____ Observation in classroom or usual environment (IDEA)

_____ Notice

   _____ Required for preplacement evaluation

   _____ Reasonable time prior to evaluation

   _____ Includes list of tests

   _____ Includes general provisions under IDEA governing notice and consent

   _____ Required for reevaluations

_____ Consent

   _____ Must be in writing

   _____ Must acknowledge understanding of evaluation process

   _____ Not required for subsequent evaluations

   _____ Subject to unilateral revocation by parent

_____ Evaluators

   _____ Multidisciplinary team

   _____ At least one teacher or other specialist with knowledge of area of suspected disability

_____ When specific disability is suspected also:

_____ Child's regular teacher

_____ Person qualified to conduct individual diagnostic examination

_____ Report of evaluation must be in writing

_____ Disputes over evaluation

_____ Parents may seek due process hearing

_____ Parents may seek Independent Educational Evaluation

Chapter 5

Eligibility

5.1 In General

Being an individual with a physical or mental disability does not guarantee eligibility for services under IDEA. To be eligible, the student must meet two floor requirements. The student must have a disability *and* be in need of special education as a result of the disability.[1] It is important to keep in mind that, unless a particular state has chosen to provide additional protections, the existence of either of these standards alone is insufficient. Indeed, the definition of the term of a child with a disability explicitly provides that you are eligible under the terms of the statute if "because of those impairments [the child is in] need of special education and related services."[2]

Special education is defined as "specially designed instruction, at no cost to the parent, to meet the unique needs of a child with a disability, including classroom instruction, instruction in physical education, home instruction, and instruction in hospitals and institutions."[3] Special education includes speech pathology[4] and vocational training.[5]

A recent requirement included under the umbrella of special education services is "transition services." Transition services must be included as part of the individualized education program (IEP) for students no later than the age of 16.[6] Transition services are considered appropriate for students as young as 14.[7] Transition services are those services that will promote the student's transition to life after education under IDEA. These post-school activities may include vocational training, higher education, supported employment, adult education, adult services, independent living, or community participation. The various activities that are part of the transition services are based on the students' needs, preferences and interests.[8]

---

1. 34 C.F.R. § 300.7(a); *see* 20 U.S.C. § 1401(a)(1).
2. 34 C.F.R. § 300.7; *see* 20 U.S.C. § 1401(a)(1).
3. 34 C.F.R. § 300.17(a)(1); *see* 20 U.S.C. § 1401(a)(16).
4. 34 C.F.R. § 300.17(2); *see also* 20 U.S.C. § 1401(a)(16).
5. 34 C.F.R. § 300.17(a)(3); *see also* 20 U.S.C. § 1401(a)(16).
6. 20 U.S.C. § 1401(a)(20)(D).
7. *Id.*
8. 20 U.S.C. § 1401(a)(19).

As discussed elsewhere,[9] a child eligible for special education is also entitled to related services[10] required to assist the child to receive benefit from special education. A child is not eligible for a related service if the child is not also receiving special education.[11]

5.2 Specially Designed Instruction

The statute and regulations do not define with any specificity what is meant by specially designed instruction needed to meet the unique needs of the child, other than to say that it includes vocational and physical education.[12] Issues often arise therefore concerning whether a child's particular needs are educational in nature. The three areas in which questions arise whether a service is educational or something else are: non-academic instruction; disputes over whether the services are needed for educational or medical reasons; questions of whether the child can benefit from the educational services.

5.2.1 Non-academic Instruction

IDEA and its regulations clearly indicate that vocational and physical education are included within the definition of special education.[13] Very early in the history of IDEA it was determined that education also included a wide range of subjects not commonly considered traditional education. As stated by the United States Third Circuit Court of Appeals, "the concept of education is necessarily broad with respect to persons [severely disabled] where basic self-help and social skills such as toilet training, dressing, feeding and communication are lacking, formal education begins at that point."[14] Courts have consistently made it clear that education for those with severe disabilities is broadly defined under IDEA.[15]

5.2.2 Medical v. Educational Needs

Many students with physical and mental disabilities have medical as well as educational problems. It is clear that if services are required for purely medical

9. See 3.9

10. 34 C.F.R. § 300.8; *see* 20 U.S.C. § 1401(a)(18).

11. 34 C.F.R. § 300.17, Comment 1.

12. 34 C.F.R. § 300.17(a); *see* 20 U.S.C. § 1401(a)(16).

13. 20 U.S.C. § 1401(a)(16); 34 C.F.R. § 300.17.

14. Battle v. Pennsylvania, 629 F.2d 269, 275 (3d Cir. 1981); Kruelle v. New Castle County School District, 642 F.2d 687, 693 (3d Cir. 1981).

15. *See, e.g.,* Polk v. Central Susquehanna Intermediate Unit 16, 853 F.2d 171, 176, (3d Cir. 1988) ("the physical therapy itself may form the core of a severely disabled child's special education"); DeLeon v. Susquehanna Community School Dist., 747 F.2d 149, 153 (3d Cir. 1984)("[t]he program may consist largely of 'related services' such as physical, occupational, or speech therapy"); Abrahamson v. Hershman, 701 F.2d 223, 228 (1st Cir. 1983) ("Where what is being taught is how to pay attention, talk, respond to words of warning, and dress and feed oneself, it is reasonable to find that a suitably staffed and structured residential environment providing continual training and reinforcement in those skills serves an educational service ...."); Campbell v. Talladega County Bd. of Educ., 518 F. Supp. 47, 50 (N.D. Ala. 1981) (educational program consisted of "functional" skills).

reasons, the school system is not responsible under IDEA. An emotionally disturbed child who is hospitalized solely for the purpose of psychiatric treatment is not entitled to have the psychiatric treatment paid for by the LEA. The LEA may be obligated to provide hospital-based educational programing, but the treatment portion will not be the LEA responsibility.

Quite often, however, it is impossible to separate the educational and medical problems of the student. If indeed, an emotionally disturbed child is unable to learn because the psychiatric condition interferes with the learning process, it may be impossible to separate the educational problems from the psychiatric problems. One educational goal for an emotionally disturbed child may be to develop appropriate peer relationships, but the fact that the child presently does not have those relationships may be a function of the child's psychiatric problem. Psychological or psychiatric services, therefore may be required. In some case the "unseverability of such needs is the very basis for holding that the services are an essential prerequisite for learning."[16]

The severability of the services arises quite commonly in disputes involving residential educational programs where the LEA seeks to pay only that portion of the placement which is related to educational needs. The situation can arise in several contexts, including the parents placing the child in a private program or hospital, or the state placing the child in a correctional facility. The critical question is whether the placement was for educational or non-educational reasons. If the placement is for purely non-educational reasons, the clearest example being a placement in a correctional facility, the LEA need only provide a FAPE where the child is placed. It need not pay for non-educational parts of the placement.[17]

In other words, if the LEA could have provided an appropriate program in the public school, there is no obligation to pay for the hospital or correctional facility. If the parents place a child in a hospital for purely medical reasons, the LEA is not responsible for non-educational parts of the program.[18] As stated in *Kruelle v. New Castle County School*,[19] the question is "whether full-time placement may be considered necessary for educational purposes, or whether the residential placement is a response to medical, social or emotional problems that are segregable from the learning process."[20]

Where, however, placement in a hospital or other residential program is for educational reasons, the LEA is responsible for both the educational components of the placement as well as the associated costs such as room and board. Specifically, if the service is required in order for the child to benefit from educational

16. Kruelle v. New Castle County School Dist., 642 F.2d 687, 694 (3d Cir. 1981); *see also* McKenzie v. Smith, 771 F.2d 1527, 1534 (D.C. Cir. 1985) (are the child's emotional needs "segregable from the learning process").

17. OSEP Memorandum 87-21, 202 Educ. Handicapped L. Rep. (CRR) 372, 373–374 (June 29, 1987).

18. *See* Clovis Unified School Dist. v. California Office of Administrative Hearings, 903 F.2d 635 (9th Cir. 1990) (placement in psychiatric hospital was for medical, not educational reasons); *see also* Metropolitan Government of Nashville and Davidson County v. Tennessee Dep't. of Educ., 771 S.W.2d 427 (Tn. Ct. App. 1989).

19. 642 F.2d 687 (3d Cir. 1981).

20. *Id.* at 693.

services, it is a related service and therefore must be provided by the LEA.[21] While this requirement may necessitate the provision of medical services, in no event does it appear that the school is responsible for the services of a physician.[22]

5.2.3 Ability to Benefit from Educational Services

The issue of the appropriateness of a cost-benefit analysis in determining whether a child is entitled to receive educational services is an emotional question which has received inconsistent treatment by the courts. How much benefit must a child be able to receive to be entitled to receive educational services? If we take the extreme case, what of the child in a coma? Is the child entitled to receive educational programing even if it is unclear the child will receive any educational benefit?

In *Timothy W. v. Rochester, New Hampshire School District*,[23] an eight-year-old was denied any educational program or services by the LEA, relying on the LEA's "capable of benefitting" eligibility criterion. After lengthy evaluations and hearings, the United States District Court held that because the child was not capable of benefitting from special education, the LEA was not obligated to provide special education under either state or federal law. In a thorough analysis of the statutory language, legislative history, and case law, the First Circuit reversed the district court and stated:

> The language of the Act in its entirety makes clear that a "zero-reject" policy is at the core of the Act, and that no child, regardless of the severity of his or her handicap, is to ever again be subjected to the deplorable state of affairs which existed at the time of the Act's passage, in which millions of handicapped children received inadequate education or none at all. In summary, the Act mandates an appropriate public education for all handicapped children, regardless of the level of achievement that such children might attain.[24]

Other decisions have not been as broadly written as *Timothy W.* Some opinions, for example, state that a child in a coma would be completely uneducable and therefore not eligible within the meaning of IDEA.[25] Other opinions have reached what is essentially a middle ground. In *Mathews v. Davis*,[26] for example, the district court had originally ordered a residential placement. Approximately four and one-half years later, the district court "was persuaded that, although substantial educational progress had been achieved with the program, maintenance

---

21. *See, e.g.*, Drew P. v. Clarke County School Dist., 877 F.2d 927 (11th Cir. 1989); Geis v. Board of Educ., 774 F.2d 575 (3d Cir. 1985); McKenzie v. Smith, 771 F.2d 1527 (D.C. Cir. 1985); Colin K. v. Schmidt, 715 F.2d 1 (1st Cir. 1983); Abrahamson v. Hershman, 701 F.2d 223 (1st Cir. 1983); Kruelle v. New Castle County School, 642 F.2d 687 (3d Cir. 1981); Diamond v. McKenzie, 602 F. Supp. 632 (D.D.C. 1985); Papacoda v. Connecticut, 528 F. Supp. 68 (D.C. Conn. 1981); Gladys J. v. Pearland Indep. School Dist., 520 F. Supp. 869 (S.D. Tx. 1981).

22. Irving Indep. School Dist. v. Tatro, 468 U.S. 883 (1984). See 3.9.6, 3.9.7.

23. 875 F.2d 954 (1st Cir. 1989).

24. *Id.* at 960–61.

25. Parks v. Pavkovic, 753 F.2d 1397 (7th Cir. 1985).

26. 742 F.2d 825 (4th Cir. 1984).

of the advances [the child] had made and acquisition of the few additional skills of which he was considered capable could be accomplished without a residential program ..."[27] In affirming the district court's decision, the Fourth Circuit pointed to three factors: the fact that the child had "reached the point of diminishing marginal returns and would not be able to learn much more;"[28] the residential program had become largely custodial; and experts agreed that continued educational programming "would at best yield only marginal returns and probably none at all."[29] Even given this language, however, the district court did not deny all educational services, holding only that the services did not have to take place in a residential setting.

5.3 Qualifying Conditions in General

Federal Regulations delineate the conditions which qualify a child for an individualized education program under IDEA.[30] The definitions contained in the regulations attempt to encompass any mental, physical or emotional condition which could have an adverse effect on a child's educational performance. While a complete discussion of the various disabilities is beyond the scope of this work, a brief summary of the disability from the medical perspective and its educational impact is helpful. In addition, the categories and definitions of educational disabilities are included.

The thirteen classifications which define the eligibility criteria under IDEA's regulations are most helpfully analyzed in three broad groups: physical impairments, mental, emotional and cognitive impairments, and the "catch-all" categories. The physical impairments group includes visual, auditory, speech and orthopedic impairments. The mental, emotional and cognitive impairments group includes mental retardation, specific learning disabilities, serious emotional disturbances, autism, and traumutic brain injury.[31] Finally, the regulations contain two "catch-all" categories: multiple disabilities and other health impaired.

5.3.1 Hearing Impairments

"Hearing impairments" encompass three related terms defined separately: " 'Deafness'[32] means a hearing impairment which is so severe that the child is impaired in processing linguistic information through hearing, with or without amplification, which adversely affects educational performance." " 'Deaf-blindness' means concomitant hearing and visual impairments, the combination of which causes such severe communication and other developmental and educational prob-

---

27. *Id.* at 828.

28. *Id.*

29. *Id.* at 830.

30. 34 C.F.R. § 300.7; *see* 20 U.S.C. §§ 1401(a)(1), (16).

31. It is recognized that many emotional disturbances have nothing to do with a child's actual intelligence. Mental and emotional deficits are grouped together in this instance because of their common lack of outward physical manifestations (aside from behavior) which separates them from the physical impairments.

32. 34 C.F.R. § 300.7(b)(3).

lems that they cannot be accommodated in special education programs solely for deaf or blind children."[33] " 'Hearing impairment' means a hearing impairment, whether permanent or fluctuating, which adversely affects a child's educational performance but which is not included under the definition of 'deaf' in this section."[34] The distinction drawn between deaf and hard of hearing in the regulation is artificial and somewhat meaningless in terms of causation, determination, and educational impact; thus, these terms will be analyzed generally as hearing defects.[35]

Educationally significant hearing impairments may stem from a number of causes occurring both prior to birth and during childhood.[36] Risk factors for hearing loss in neonates include inherited deafness, ear, nose, jaw and throat deformities, exposure to ototoxic drugs and chemicals,[37] prenatal infections,[38] neonatal intensive care,[39] and prematurity.[40] A child who is born with normal hearing may still be at risk for hearing loss from recurrent ear infections, childhood illness,[41] sound trauma,[42] and hearing "knock out."[43]

Children who are hearing impaired at birth may literally have an invisible disability, since many hearing losses are not associated with outward physical deformities.[44] Parents may not be aware of their child's hearing loss until it is

---

33. 34 C.F.R. § 300.7(b)(2).

34. 34 C.F.R. § 300.7(b)(4).

35. Similarly, the deaf-blind category might seem to be an odd distinction, since it concerns a combination disability which would fit under the multihandicapped label. Although there is no legislative history on point, it may be reasonable to assume that Congress chose to single out deaf-blindness because of its uniquely devastating effect on a child's educational performance.

Education of the deaf-blind child involves highly specialized training and resources, including a special language involving the touching of the hands and fingers. Although the causes of deafness and blindness are covered separately under their respective headings, the educational impact of deaf-blindness is so all-encompassing as to be beyond the scope of this work. *See* McInnes, **Deaf-Blind Infants and Children: A Developmental Guide** (1982); Kramer, **Audiological Evaluation and Aural Rehabilitation of the Deaf-Blind** (1979); Yoken, **Living with Deaf-Blindness** (1979); Freeman, **Understanding the Deaf-Blind Child** (1975). This list is by no means exhaustive.

36. Bordley, **Ear, Nose and Throat Disorders in Children** 108 (1986). Another excellent, but slightly more technical source in this area is Pappas, **Diagnosis and Treatment of Hearing Impairment in Children: A Clinical Manual** (1985).

37. Ototoxic drugs are certain diuretics, antibiotics and other chemicals which can cause hearing loss in infants through gestational or postnatal exposure. Bordley, *supra* note 36 at 123.

38. During the 1960s, mumps and rubella were the predominant causes of infant deafness; however, the development of effective vaccinations has virtually eliminated these viruses. Other congenital infections which continue to cause infant deafness today include syphillis, toxoplasmosis and other intrauterine infections. *Id.* at 126.

39. The placement of an infant in a neonatal intensive care unit is an indication of serious illness, and many illnesses in this stage of a child's life may cause hearing loss. Additionally, ototoxic drugs are often used in therapy, putting the infant at additional risk. *Id.* at 134.

40. Deafness is common in premature infants. Ten to twenty-three percent of deaf children were born prematurely. *Id.* at 134.

41. Meningitis is a common cause in sudden childhood hearing losses. *Id.* at 135.

42. Sound trauma deafness, or "boilermakers' deafness," results from prolonged exposure to loud noise, or from a single incident of acoustic trauma, such as an explosion. *Id.* at 140.

43. Hearing loss from "knock out" occurs when the ear or skull endures physical trauma. Examples include a blow to the ear, foreign bodies inserted into the ear, and skull fractures. *Id.* at 143.

44. *Id.* at 99.

manifested by delayed speech development, and then it is often tragically mistaken for mental retardation.[45]

The presence and extent of hearing loss is usually determined by a pediatric audiologist.[46] The audiologist may employ a variety of methods to determine the presence and extent of hearing loss, ranging from informal, at-home observation to formal behavioral and auditory evaluations.[47] Specialists use the results of such evaluations to classify auditory deficiency in increments of decibel loss, with each increment representing an increased level of communication impairment.[48] A child with a slight loss (27–40 decibels) may have difficulty with faint or distant speech or sounds.[49] A mild to moderate loss (41–55 decibels) impairs a child's ability to interpret conversational speech at a distance over three to five feet.[50] A child with a moderately severe loss (56–70 decibels) may hear only loud sounds at close distances, and will have difficulty in conversation.[51] A severe impairment (71–90 decibels) restricts a child's hearing to voices and sounds within one foot, often even blocking out the sound of shouted conversation.[52] Finally, a profound loss (91 or more decibels) deprives a child of most auditory awareness, forcing him to rely almost exclusively on vibrations and sight.[53]

The proper classroom setting is essential to the proper development of the hearing impaired child. When developing an IEP, the severity of the hearing loss and its impact on the child's ability to communicate and interpret should be prime considerations in the choice of special facilities.[54]

A child's educational needs will become more specialized as his level of impairment increases.[55] A child with a slight hearing loss may have difficulty with language subjects, and could benefit from vocabulary development programs, special seating, and speech therapy.[56] A mild to moderate hearing loss could cause a child to miss up to one half of classroom discussion and thus necessitate, in addition to the aids mentioned above, lip reading instruction, speech correction, and hearing aid evaluation.[57] Children with moderately severe losses require spe-

---

45. Id.; see also Mindel, **They Grow in Silence: The Deaf Child and his Family** 32 (1977).

46. After the initial testing, the pediatric audiologist may also play a valuable role in developing the child's education. See Bess & McConnell, **Audiology, Education, and the Hearing Impaired Child** 201 (1981) (chapter 9: "Audiology in the Educational Setting").

47. Mindel, *supra* note 45, at 32. For a technical explanation of the various methods of behavioral and auditory testing, see Bordley, *supra* note 36, at 151–67; **Pediatric Audiology: Current Trends** 1–124 (Jerger ed. 1984) (section on diagnostic audiometry). For a less technical, broader based assessment of auditory testing, see Bess & McConnell, *supra* note 46, at 44 (chapter 3: "Measurement of Auditory Function").

48. Bordley, *supra* note 36, at 158; Mindel, *supra* note 45, at 33.

49. Id.

50. Id.

51. Id.

52. Id.

53. Id.

54. Children with slight losses may be aided by proper classroom acoustics. See Borrild, "Classroom Acoustics," in **Auditory Management of Hearing Impaired Children** 145 (1978); see also Bess & McConnell, *supra* note 15, at 188 (chapter 8: "The Acoustic Environment").

55. Some experts believe that children with any level of hearing impairment will benefit from special education in addition to normal schooling. See Bordley, *supra* note 36, at 158.

56. Id.

57. Id.

cial classes and emphasis on communication skills, and in some cases would benefit from a full-time program for the deaf.[58] Severe and profound hearing losses impede educational performance to such a great degree that afflicted children usually receive proper instruction only in special schools for the deaf.[59]

5.3.2 Visual Impairment

" 'Visually impairment including blindness' means an impairment in vision that, even with correction, adversely affects a child's educational performance. The term includes both partial sight and blindness."[60] This broad definition of visual impairment avoids the application of labels to degrees of visual impairment.[61] Unlike hearing impairments, which despite a variety of etiologies differ only in degree, not in the type of impairment produced, there are many different types of visual impairments. For this reason, the medical community has moved away from traditional degree-based definitions of blindness and adopted functional definitions better suited to the nature of the disability.[62] The drafters of 300.7 seem to have fallen into step with this general trend.

Visual impairments may be either congenital or acquired, and their causes are varied.[63] Causes include diseases of the eye in general, trauma, or injuries to specific parts of the eye, such as the cornea, lens, and retina, damage to or disease in the optic nerve, poisoning, tumors, retrolental fibroplasia, and general hereditary defects.[64] The majority of visually impaired children have multiple disabilities,[65] and thus the visual impairment is sometimes an offshoot of another, more serious disability.

Visual impairment is determined by a pediatric ophthalmologist, neonatologist, or pediatrician who, depending on the child's age and the presence of other disabilities, will employ a battery of tests to measure distance, visual acuity, near visual acuity, and peripheral vision.[66] It is vital that eye problems be detected and correctly diagnosed at an early age in order for effective therapy to be implemented. For example, two decades ago, without early detection of visual im-

---

58. *Id.*

59. *Id.*

60. 34 C.F.R. § 300.7(b)(13); *see also* 20 U.S.C. § 1401(a)(1).

61. This approach is in contrast to the distinction drawn between "deafness," "deaf-blindness," and "hearing impairment." 34 C.F.R. § 300.7.

62. The traditional description used in most countries until this decade defined blindness as "visual acuity, in the better eye with correction, of not more than 20/200 or a defect in the visual fields so that the widest diameter of vision subtends an angle no greater than 20 degrees." **Visual Impairment in Children and Adolescents** 18 (Jan, Freeman & Scott eds. 1977).

63. *See generally* **Pediatric Ophthalmology** (Nelson ed. 1984); *see also* **Pediatric Ophthalmology** (Metz ed. 1982). This collection of essays discusses the twenty-one most common causes of visual impairment in children. Although technical, it is manageable with a medical dictionary. *See also* **Visual Impairment in Children and Adolescents,** *supra* note 62, at 38–39 (chart listing common congenital and acquired visual impairments in children).

64. **Visual Impairment in Children and Adolescents,** *supra* note 62, at 38–39; **Pediatric Opthamology,** *supra* note 4.

65. *Id.*

66. **Visual Impairment in Children and Adolescents,** *supra* note 62, at 12; *see also* Gable, **Visual Disorders in the Handicapped Child** (1984).

pairments children with congenital cataracts were referred to residential schools for the blind. Today they can be served in public school settings.[67]

Since visual testing requires comprehension and cooperation, a correct assessment may prove difficult in a child with multiple disabilities or a child below the age of four.[68] The pediatric ophthalmologist uses the data amassed through testing to determine the degree and type of visual impairment and, more important, the child's level of remaining vision or "visual efficiency."[69]

Visually impaired children may be functionally classified in three groups.[70] A child with "normal or near-normal vision" is able to perform visually related tasks without aid.[71] A child with "low vision" requires special aids to perform visually detailed work.[72] A "blind" child must rely on his other senses to accomplish tasks that sighted children accomplish primarily with sight.[73]

The educational needs of the visually impaired child will depend on the child's visual efficiency and the willingness of the child to use his remaining vision.[74] Each partially sighted child will have different needs, since there are many different types of partial sight and degrees of disability within each type.[75] A child with no residual vision, of course, will have to receive instruction in Braille.[76]

5.3.3 Orthopedic Impairments in General

An orthopedic impairment is a deformity, disease or injury of the bones or joints.[77] "Orthopedic impairment" means a severe orthopedic

> impairment which adversely affects a child's educational performance. The term includes impairments caused by congenital anomaly (e.g., clubfoot, absence of some member, etc.), impairments caused by disease (e.g., poliomyelitis, bone tuberculosis, etc.) and impairments from other causes (e.g., cerebral palsy, amputations, and fractures or burns which cause contractures). To be eligible the impairment must adversely affect educational performance. Such impairments limit a child's mobility and, depending on the severity of the impediment, may necessitate special educational facilities ranging from special access to full time special classes.[78]

---

67. **Rudolph's Pediatrics** 1879–1924 (Rudolph ed. 1991).

68. **Visual Impairment of Children and Adolescents,** *supra* note 62 at 13.

69. *Id.* at 19.

70. *Id.* at 23. There are many ways to classify visual impairment, but the functional categories seem to be the most useful in the educational arena.

71. *Id.* at 23.

72. *Id.* at 23; *see also* **Understanding Low Vision** (R. Jose ed. 1983).

73. **Visual Impairment in Children and Adolescents,** *supra* note 62, at 23.

74. Scott, Jan & Freeman, **Can't Your Child See?** 170 (1979).

75. *Id.* at 171; *see also* **Understanding Low Vision,** *supra* note 72.

76. Scott, *supra* note 74, at 171. The educational aids and teaching techniques available for the visually impaired child are so far reaching and variable that generalization in this section would not be helpful. *See* Chapman, **Visually Handicapped Children and Young People** (1978) (chapter 4: "The school years for visually handicapped children").

77. 34 C.F.R. 300.7(b)(7).

78. Children with cerebral palsy who are unable to function in a mainstream classroom setting, may require a special form of education because of the prevalence of associated defects such as deafness, seizures, and sensory impairments. *See* **Orthopaedic Aspects of Cerebral Palsy** (R. Samilson ed. 1975).

Being able to determine the existence of and the educational impact of an orthopedic impairment is easier than determining the existence of other conditions.[79] The types of issues under IDEA or § 504 regarding orthopedically impaired children deal with program accessibility.[80]

5.3.3.1 Congenital Orthopedic Disorders

Congenital orthopedic disorders are abnormal conditions which are detectable at birth. Such conditions may be caused by inherited factors, fetal exposure to drugs ingested by the mother, uterine abnormalities, and radiation.[81]

Clubfoot, or congenital talipes equinovarus, the first example of congenital anomaly provided in the regulation's definition, is a deformity of the bones of the foot.[82] Experts remain uncertain as to the causes of clubfoot, although many theories concerning genetic links, stunted embryonic development, and environmental causes have been advanced.[83] Clubfeet vary in type and severity; "conventional clubfeet" may be corrected by non-surgical methods such as corrective shoes, braces, and therapy, while other, more severe types require corrective surgery in order for the child to walk.[84] Most, if not all cases of clubfoot are treated within the first three months of the child's life,[85] and effects extending into the school years may involve his ability to participate fully in physical education classes.

"[A]bsence of some member" is the other example of congenital anomaly referred to in the definition of orthopedically impaired. This phrase refers to an amputation or "banding" of a limb prior to a child's birth, or a genetic or formative defect which causes an absence of a limb.[86] Congenital amputation may

---

79. Perhaps this is why no one has bothered to write any books on the educational impact of orthopedic impairments. Most sources on pediatric orthopedics focus on how to make the child mobile after the determination of impairment. (In the majority of cases, an orthopedic impairment may be determined by simply looking at the child). *See, e.g.*, Katz, **Common Orthopedic Problems in Children** (1981). This work is written by an orthopedist for physicians in other fields, and is a useful quick reference for the layperson as well.

80. Garfield (N.J.) School Dist., 18 Individuals With Disabilities Education Law Rep. (LRP) 545 (OCR 1991) (wheelchair users denied access to parking spaces, restrooms, entrance ramps and drinking fountains); Garaway (OH) Local School Dist., 17 Educ. Handicapped L. Rep. (LRP) 237 (OCR 1990) (carrying a mobility impaired student on and off a bus is not an acceptable means of access).

81. Cowell, "Genetic Aspects of Orthopaedic Conditions," in 1 **Pediatric Orthopaedics** 149 (Lovell & Winter eds. 1986) This two volume reference is regarded as the definitive work on pediatric orthopedics, and most citations in this section are taken from this work for this reason. However, **Pediatric Orthopaedics** is written for the orthopedic community, and is hypertechnical in places. A better overview for the layperson is provided by Katz, **Common Orthopedic Problems in Children** (1981).

82. Lovell, Price and Meehan, "The Foot," in 2 **Pediatric Orthopaedics** 901.

83. *Id.*

84. *Id.* at 904.

85. Id. at 905.

86. Cowell, *supra* note 81, at 148. "Banding" refers to the effect produced by the twining of a limb with the amniotic cords, which cuts off blood supply to the affected part and produces an abnormal band. *Id.* The banding process, carried to the extreme, causes congenital amputation. Absence of limbs may also be caused by maternal ingestion of drugs such as thalidomide during pregnancy and by hereditary or genetic defects. *Id.*

be caused by trauma experienced by the mother, which may cause constriction of the uterine environment around the fetal extremities, cutting off blood supply to the limb and eventually severing it.[87] A child born with an orthopedic congenital deformity may usually, depending on the severity of the deformity and the number of absent limbs, be fitted with a prosthesis at an early age and acquire sufficient mobility to attend a regular classroom.

5.3.3.2 Orthopedic Impairments Caused by Disease

Orthopedic impairments caused by disease affect a child's control over muscles and limbs, either through paralysis or destruction of bone and muscle tissues. IDEA's regulations offer poliomyelitis and bone tuberculosis as examples of such diseases;[88] other examples of common orthopedic diseases include arthritis, muscular dystrophy, and general bone or joint infections.[89]

Poliomyelitis, or polio, is a viral infection caused by the poliomyelitis virus.[90] Polio produces paralysis (mainly in the lower extremities) by attacking and destroying portions of the spinal cord and brain stem motor cells.[91] The development of a polio vaccine has greatly reduced the number of reported cases, and today polio occurs primarily in preschool age, unimmunized children. Polio attacks vary in severity, and recovery can range from almost total muscle recovery to complete paralysis.[92] A child's educational needs will depend on the extent of the remaining paralysis and motor impairment.

Bone tuberculosis, or tuberculous osteomyelitis, is a very rare disease which occurs most frequently in the spine and the long bones of the arms and legs.[93] Bone tuberculosis destroys bone, cartilage and joint tissues, often permanently disabling its victims. Afflicted children experience pain in their limbs and spine, shortening and deformity of limbs, weight loss and paralysis.[94] This disease is almost never seen today except as a complication of chronic pulmonary tuberculosis, a degenerative lung condition.[95]

5.3.3.3 Other Orthopedic Impairments

The final class of orthopedic impairments offered by IDEA regulations is a catchall group covering disabilities from "other causes."[96] Any orthopedic con-

---

87. *Id.*

88. 34 C.F.R. § 300.7(b)(7). The inclusion of bone tuberculosis as an example of orthopedic disease is unusual, since significant cases of bone tuberculosis are rare today. Children are, however, more frequent victims than adults. Robbins, Cotran, & Kumar, **Pathologic Basis of Disease** 1325 (3d ed. 1984).

89. *See generally* 1 **Pediatric Orthopaedics** 457, 263, and 437.

90. Drennan, "Neuromuscular Disorders," in **1 Pediatric Orthopaedics** 283.

91. *Id.* at 283–85.

92. *Id.* at 284.

93. Robbins, *supra* note 88, at 1325.

94. DeGowin & DeGowin, **Bedside Diagnostic Examination** 959 (1987).

95. Robbins, *supra* note 88, at 1325.

96. 34 C.F.R. § 300.7(b)(7).

dition which adversely affects a child's educational performance which is not covered by the previous two categories, congenital anomalies and diseases, would fall within the parameters of this group.

Cerebral palsy, the first condition listed in the regulation as an example of an orthopedic impairment stemming from "other causes,"[97] is a serious motor affliction caused by brain lesions.[98] The brain damage which causes cerebral palsy may stem from prenatal causes such as toxic pregnancy, rubella, and maternal ingestion of drugs or alcohol; perinatal causes, such as prematurity and delayed labor; and postnatal causes, including meningitis and head injury.[99]

There are three primary types of cerebral palsy, classified according to the area of the body which is most affected. Hemiplegia, the least severe type, involves one side of the body and is characterized by a limp and a tendency to favor one hand.[100] Diplegia, caused by prematurity, affects the legs and lower body more than the upper body.[101] Total involvement, the most severe type of cerebral palsy, affects the entire brain, damaging intelligence and control over all major muscle groups. Children exhibiting total involvement are unable to walk, sit, or care for themselves, and are often institutionalized.[102]

Amputations, the second example in this group, involve the surgical removal of a limb. Removal may be necessitated by a number of etiologies, including trauma to the limb (power tools, auto accidents, gunshot wounds, explosions, and railroad incidents are leading causes) and disease (malignant tumors and malformations are commonly involved).[103] When possible, pediatric amputees are fitted with prostheses which enable them to move about.[104] Educational needs could include special accesses and adaptive physical education classes.

Fractures or burns which cause contractures, the final examples in this group, deals with the more common serious injuries. The fracture or burn must cause a contracture, which is a shortening of muscle or bone, or scar tissue which produces deformity.[105] Contractures affect a child's gait and mobility, and necessitate the same types of educational considerations as do amputations and clubfoot.

5.3.4 Mental, Emotional, and Cognitive Impairments in General

Mental and emotional impairments involve a child's intelligence, aptitude, ability to learn and behavior. Many of these disabilities have no outward physical

---

97. 34 C.F.R. § 300.7(b)(7).

98. Rang, Silver, & Garza, "Cerebral Palsy," in 1 **Pediatric Orthopaedics** 345.

99. *Id.* at 346. Prematurity is currently the leading cause of cerebral palsy. *Id.*

100. *Id.* at 346.

101. *Id.*

102. *Id.; see also* **Orthopaedic Aspects of Cerebral Palsy**, (R. Samilson ed. 1975). Children with cerebral palsy of this severity are often afflicted with deafness, seizures and other disabilities. *Id.* at 41.

103. Tooms, "The Amputee," in 2 **Pediatric Orthopaedics** 979.

104. *Id.* In growing children, prostheses must be fitted and refitted frequently, and children require time to adapt to each new prosthesis. *Id.*

105. *See generally* DeGowin & DeGowin, **Bedside Diagnostic Examination** 789 (1987).

manifestations and it is often not until the child reaches school age that parents become aware of a possible problem.

5.3.4.1 Mental Retardation

The definition of mental retardation used in IDEA regulations is taken directly from the definition developed by the American Association on Mental Deficiency (AAMD). Mental retardation means "significantly subaverage general intellectual functioning existing concurrently with deficits in adaptive behavior and manifested during the developmental period, which adversely affects a child's educational performance." Similarly, the AAMD definition reads "Mental retardation refers to significantly subaverage general intellectual functioning existing concurrently with deficits in adaptive behavior and manifested during the developmental period."[106] Contrary to public belief, not all individuals with mental retardation "look" retarded, and some children with mild retardation actually progress to the fourth or fifth grade before the disability is detected.[107] Thus, mental retardation is often more prevalent in regular classroom settings than most would think, especially in poor, urban areas.[108]

One of the most common misconceptions about mental retardation is that all forms of the disability are caused by chromosomal anomalies such as Down's Syndrome, perhaps because of the visibility of Down's Syndrome characteristics.[109] However, the causes of mental retardation are as diverse and varied as the causes of any other disability. According to the AAMD, mental retardation can occur pre- or postnatally, and may stem from exposure to infection or intoxicants, trauma, metabolism or nutrition disorders, postnatal brain disease, environmental conditions, psychiatric disorders, and a wide range of other prenatal and perinatal influences, as well as chromosomal anomalies.[110] Additionally, there are some children for whom no cause for mental retardation is apparent; they simply fail to attain average mental acuity.[111]

To be classified as having mental retardation under the AAMD definition (and thus under the federal regulation) a child must have both subaverage intelligence and deficits in adaptive behavior. Subaverage intelligence is determined by standard IQ testing, and a child must score below 70 on a standardized intelligence test to meet the AAMD criterion.[112] Deficits in adaptive behavior, on the other hand, must be determined by observation, and the type of adaptive deficiency required will depend on the child's level of development.[113] For instance, a preschool child

---

106. 34 C.F.R. § 300.7(b)(5); Westling, **Introduction to Mental Retardation** 3 (1986). The Westling book is a clear, understandable source covering all aspects of mental retardation, and is highly recommended for laymen by specialists in this field.

107. Westling, *supra* note 106, at 24.

108. *See Id.*

109. Down's Syndrome produces distinctive facial characteristics such as oval, tilted eyes, squinting, and sloped skull. *See generally* Barlow, **Mental Retardation and Related Disorders** (1978) (neurological approach to mental retardation).

110. Westling, *supra* note 106, at 29.

111. *Id.*

112. Westling, *supra* note 106, at 3.

113. *Id.* at 4.

might be expected to progress beyond crawling, walking and babbling to talking and learning through experience, and failure to do so could indicate an adaptive deficit. This determination will usually be difficult only in those with IQ's over 55, since those in the lower IQ ranges will demonstrate clear adaptive deficits.[114]

The AAMD classifies levels of mental retardation by ranges of IQ scores.[115] Children with mild mental retardation score between 55 and 70 on standardized intelligence tests. Moderate mental retardation is shown by scores from 35–55. Scores from 20 to 35 are evidence of severe mental retardation, and children who score below 20 are classified as profoundly mentally retarded.[116]

Another classification system, popular with educators, groups mentally retarded persons as educable mentally retarded (EMR)(50-70), trainable mentally retarded (TMR)(25–50),and profoundly mentally retarded (PMR)(below 25).[117]

Children with mental retardation have widely varying educational needs, the range of which is dependent on the severity of the impairment. The mildly retarded generally are capable of normal academic and social development until the fourth or fifth grade, while the moderately retarded may not ever achieve more than a first grade level of academic skills.[118] The severely and profoundly retarded, however, have trouble with even the simplest daily living skills, and while sometimes trainable, require constant monitoring and attention.[119] There is much overlap in the different groups, and the specific needs will depend on individual ability. All school systems provide special programs for the mentally retarded, both in regular classrooms and in special schools for children with disabilities.[120]

5.3.4.2 Specific Learning Disabilities in General

The definition of specific learning disabilities contained in IDEA's regulations is less of a description than it is a laundry list of minor psychological disorders which prevent affected children from keeping pace with their peers despite adequate education and opportunity. " 'Specific learning disability' means a disorder in one or more of the basic psychological processes[121] involved in understanding or in using language, spoken or written, which may manifest itself in an imperfect ability to listen, think, speak, read, write, spell or to do mathematical calculations. The term includes such conditions as perceptual handicaps, brain injury, minimal

---

114. *Id.* at 5.

115. *Id.* at 23.

116. *Id.* at 24–25.

117. *Id.*

118. *Id.* at 25–26.

119. *Id.* at 27.

120. The range of programs available for the mentally retarded is all-encompassing. *See* Westling, *supra* note 106, at 175 (chapter on public school programs); **Mental Handicap Care Book**, (E. Shanley ed. 1986); **Perspectives in Mental Retardation: Social, Psychological and Educational Aspects**, (Berg ed. 1984); **Mental Retardation: A Phenomenological Approach** (Jacobs ed. 1980).

121. Kennedy Inquiry, 16 Educ. Handicapped L. Rep. (LRP) 1082 (OSEP 1990) (eligibility team is not required to identify a disorder in psychological processing but rather the disability itself manifests symptoms which result in a sever discrepancy between achievement and ability).

brain disfunction, dyslexia, and developmental aphasia . . . "[122] The definition also includes an exclusionary phrase, which specifies that the term "specific learning disability" does not include impairments from other causes covered elsewhere in the regulation, nor does it include disabilities stemming primarily from "environmental, cultural, or economic disadvantage."[123]

Federal regulations list the five most common types of conditions that produce specific learning disabilities, each of which will be discussed separately below. Although other causes exist, they involve difficulties in the realm of neuropsychology, which is beyond the scope of this book.[124]

5.3.4.3 Perceptual Disabilities

Unlike visual or hearing disorders, which limit what a child can see and hear, perceptual disorders concern a child's recognition and understanding of something after he senses it.[125] Technically, perception involves reception of a conscious impression through the senses (in this case, usually sight or sound) by which a child distinguishes objects and recognizes them by the sensations produced. The child must store in his brain an image of what he sees, so that when he is confronted with it at a later time, he can recognize it and react properly to it.[126] Children with perceptual disabilities either fail to properly store images received through sensation or, in other cases, are unable to integrate memories of past sensory experiences with immediate experience.[127] Perceptual disabilities may arise from organic causes (deficiencies in specific chemical processes within the brain itself), and from environmental causes (insufficient exposure to classes of stimuli).[128]

5.3.4.4 Brain Injury and Minimal Brain Disfunction

Minimal brain disfunction (MBD) is a term applied to children with normal or near normal intelligence who demonstrate abnormal behavior or specific learn-

---

122. 34 C.F.R. § 300.7(b)(10); *see* 20 U.S.C. 1401(a)(15). Parts of this definition seem to be standard in both education and medicine. *See, e.g.,* Johnston, **Learning Disabilities, Medicine, and Myth: A Guide to Understanding the Child and the Physician** 8 (1987). This book, in addition to containing parts of the above definition of specific learning disability, is a functionally oriented guide to symptoms exhibited by learning disabled children.

123. *Id.*

124. *See* Gaddes, **Learning Disabilities and Brain Function: A Neuropsychological Approach** (1985); **The Developing Brain and Its Disorders** (Arima, Suzuki, & Yabuuchi eds. 1985) (very technical work concerning specific etiologies of learning disabilities).

125. Gaddes, **Learning Disabilities and Brain Function: A Neuropsychological Approach** 147 (1985).

126. *Id.* at 148.

127. *See id.* at 148; *see also* Johnston, **Learning Disabilities, Medicine, and Myth: A Guide to Understanding the Child and the Physician** 26 (1987); Ohlson, **Identification of Specific Learning Disabilities** 18 (1978).

128. *See* Ohlson, *supra* note 127, at 16–18. An explanation of the specific causes of perceptual disabilities requires a working knowledge of chemistry. It is doubtful that in developing an IEP one would be concerned with the physiological aspects of perception, and should consult a specialist in the area—the applicable books are so technical that citation to them would not be useful.

ing disabilities.[129] MBD is caused by brain damage or by neurologic disfunction brought on by head trauma, pre- and postnatal diseases, delivery complications, fetal alcohol syndrome, genetic factors, and a host of other etiologies.[130] In pre-school children, the syndrome is manifested by signs of hyperactivity or lability, poor coordination and speech disorders. In school age children, the most common signs are failure in one specific academic area, language difficulties, awkwardness and emotional behavior.[131] There are no laboratory tests which can confirm a diagnosis of MBD, and thus detailed family history may become important when a disabled child is evaluated.[132]

Brain injury, which is mentioned separately in the definition, can stem from innumerable causes and produce a wide spectrum of effects, depending on severity, location, and age. Brain damage is often cited as a cause of MBD, but may also be the cause of any of the neurological disabilities defined in IDEA regulations.

5.3.4.5 Dyslexia

Dyslexia is a "disorder in children who, despite conventional classroom experience, fail to attain the language skills of reading, writing and spelling commensurate with their intellectual abilities,"[133] which involves reading comprehension, decoding, or both.[134] Dyslexia may be developmental (arising from congenital or acquired problems prior to the acquisition of reading skills) or traumatic (resulting from brain damage after the child has learned how to read).[135]

Traumatic dyslexia, which occurs primarily in adults, can be broken into several subgroups divided by the specific type of disability produced, such as alexia without agraphia (person can write, but cannot read), alexia with agraphia (person cannot read or write) and aphasic alexia (person cannot understand spoken or printed words).[136]

Developmental dyslexia is the reading disorder with which the public is most familiar. Most people with developmental dyslexia have no history of brain damage or cerebral atrophy, and although theories abound as to the causes of the disorder, no definitive answer exists.[137] Generally, people with developmental dys-

---

129. Meritt's Textbook of Neurology 357 (7th ed. 1984).

130. Id.

131. Id. at 358.

132. Id. For a more detailed assessment of minimal brain dysfunctions and their causes and determination, see Handbook of Minimal Brain Dysfunctions: A Critical View (Rie & Rie, eds. 1980) (very technical); Golden & Anderson, Learning Disabilities and Brain Dysfunction: An Introduction for Educators and Parents (1979).

133. Gaddes, Learning Disabilities and Brain Function: A Neuropsychological Approach 274 (1985). This definition was developed by the World Federation of Neurology, which also posed a second definition of Specific Developmental Dyslexia: "A disorder manifested by difficulty in learning to read despite conventional instruction, adequate intelligence, and socio-cultural opportunity. It is dependent on fundamental cognitive disabilities which are frequently of constitutional origin." Id.

134. Johnston, Learning Disabilities, Medicine, and Myth: A Guide to Understanding the Child and the Physician 8 (1987).

135. Gaddes, supra note 133, at 274.

136. Id. at 283–87.

137. See id. at 291. Since scientists do not completely understand the reading process itself, difficulties in defining a glitch in the process are to be expected.

lexia possess average to superior intelligence and are often gifted in other areas such as art, math, science, and athletics.[138] Such children simply have a processing disorder, and require intensive therapy to develop the most basic reading skills. Signs of developmental dyslexia include an inability to identify individual letters, syllables, and words.[139]

5.3.4.6 Developmental Aphasia

Aphasia is the congenital or acquired "loss or impairment of the use and/or understanding of language resulting from some type of brain injury or dysfunction."[140] Developmental aphasia[141] results from injury to or maldevelopment of the portions of the central nervous system that control language. The damage which causes developmental aphasia occurs sometime during the period between conception and the end of the first year of life.[142] Developmental aphasia may manifest itself in several different forms, including the inability to repeat spoken words, a lack of inner language functioning, and an inability to articulate words that are otherwise understood.[143] These disabilities produce a lack of cognitive and spontaneous speech and overall language retardation.[144]

5.3.4.7 Serious Emotional Disturbances

Instead of listing types of emotional disturbances, IDEA regulations create an internal definition of "serious emotional disturbance" by listing five criteria, at least one of which a child must meet to fit under this classification.[145] "Serious emotional disturbance" is defined as follows:

(i)   The term means a condition exhibiting one or more of the following characteristics over a long period of time and to a marked degree, which adversely affects educational performance:

(A) An inability to learn which cannot be explained by intellectual, sensory, or health factors;

(B) An inability to build or maintain satisfactory interpersonal relationships with peers and teachers;

(C) Inappropriate types of behavior or feelings under normal circumstances;

---

138. *Id.* at 288–89. Darwin is perhaps the most famous developmental dyslexic. *Id.*

139. *Id.* at 279.

140. Gaddes, **Learning Disabilities and Brain Function: A Neuropsychological Approach** 261 (1985).

141. 34 C.F.R. § 300.5(b)(9) specifically lists developmental aphasia; it should be noted, however, that children may also acquire aphasia between age two and puberty which will interfere with acquired language. Gaddes, *supra* note 133 at 267. Acquired aphasia may result from any of the various head traumas previously discussed.

142. *Id.* at 266.

143. *See id.* at 260–67.

144. *Id.* at 269. Although there are many functional classifications of aphasia, each specialist has a pet label for each type, and there is no standardized identification system.
For this reason, classifications are avoided in this section.

145. 34 C.F.R. § 300.5(b)(8).

(D) A general pervasive mood of unhappiness or depression; or

(E) A tendency to develop physical symptoms or fears associated with personal or school problems.

(ii) The term includes children who are schizophrenic. The term does not include children who are socially maladjusted, unless it is determined that they are seriously emotionally disturbed. Four of the criteria are broad descriptions of abnormal social and associative behavior.[146] The first criterion, however, contains the broadest language in the entire regulation, allowing children with "[a]n inability to learn which cannot be explained by intellectual, sensory, or health factors" to come within the parameters of the act as "seriously emotionally disturbed." This language could provide a shelter for parents and lawyers who find themselves at a loss to formulate a description of a child's disability for an IEP.

The only specific mental disability mentioned in the definition of serious emotional disturbance is schizophrenia. Schizophrenia is described in layperson's terms as a group of mental illnesses characterized by the disorganization and splitting of an individual's personality. There is no universally accepted medical definition of schizophrenia which covers every possible type; however, of the many definitions that exist, the easiest to comprehend was developed by Washington University in St. Louis.[147] To confirm a diagnosis of schizophrenia under the St. Louis definition, a child must have had a chronic illness of at least six months in duration, an absence of mood disorders, suffer from hallucinations, delusions, or nonsense language, have an absence of drug or alcohol use, a history of poor social interaction.[148]

Schizophrenia may be caused by physical and organic diseases of the brain, senility, brain tumors, diabetes, head injury, epilepsy, and use of hallucinogenic drugs.[149] Schizophrenia is a very serious, debilitating mental illness which must be diagnosed by a psychiatrist and treated by an experienced child psychiatrist or psychologist.[150] There are other mental disabilities of childhood and adolescence which cause symptoms which are either similar to the SED criteria or produce the behaviors which qualify under the criteria.[151] Therefore, if the disability is impacting adversely on the education the child will be eligible.

---

146. *See id.* at (9)(i)(B)-(E). There are literally hundreds of types of emotional disturbances and methods of treatment, and a sociological debate on causation rages about each one. *See generally* **Systematic Intervention with Disturbed Children** (Fine ed. 1984); **Emotional Disorders in Children and Adolescents: Medical and Psychological Approaches to Treatment** (Sholevar ed. 1980).

147. *See* Tsuang, **Schizophrenia: The Facts** 17 (1982). This is a highly readable, interesting source on schizophrenia, containing many short case studies and examples to help the reader understand the many ways which schizophrenia may manifest itself.

148. *Id.* at 17.

149. *Id.* at 15.

150. There appears to be little written on the education of schizophrenic children. Most schizophrenics are hospitalized during the chronic phase of their illness, and due to the severe symptomology may not be able to learn or attend classes.

151. **Diagnostic and Statistical Manual of Mental Disorders** (Third Edition, Revised) DSM-III-R American Psychiatric Association 1987. Some examples of additional disorders which may appear in infancy, childhood or adolescence include mood disorders, schizophreniform disorder, adjustment disorders and personality disorders.

5.3.4.8 Autism

Autism is defined in the regulations as a developmental disability significantly affecting verbal and nonverbal communication and social interaction, generally evident before age 3, that adversely affects a child's educational performance.[152] Autism is a psychological disorder characterized by perceptual and language abnormalities, an inability to relate to others, and obsessive, ritualistic behavior.[153] Autistic children tend to exhibit delayed speech, flat expressions, and signs of sensory dysfunction, and engage in self-stimulatory behaviors (e.g. rocking) which make education of any kind difficult.[154] The causes of autism are unknown, although some experts suspect a neurological connection.[155]

5.3.4.9 Traumatic Brain Injury

Traumatic brain injury is defined as an acquired injury to the brain caused by an external physical force, resulting in total or partial functional disability or psychosocial impairment, or both, that adversely affects a child's educational performance. The term applies to open or closed head injuries resulting in impairments in one or more areas, such as cognition; language; memory; attention; reasoning; abstract thinking; judgment; problem-solving; sensory, perceptual and motor abilities; psychosocial behavior; physical functions; information processing; and speech. The term does not apply to brain injuries that are congenital or degenerative, or brain injuries induced by birth trauma.[156]

5.3.5 Catch-all Categories in General

Federal regulations contain two "catch-all" categories of impairments, "multiple disabilities"[157] and "other health impaired,"[158] which are designed to provide specialized education for those children with combined disabilities and for those with chronic health problems not addressed elsewhere in the regulation.

5.3.5.1 Multiple Disabilities

The multiple disabilities category provides a special classification for those children with concomitant impairments, the combination of which so severely

---

152. 34 C.F.R. § 300.7(b)(1).

153. Kogel, Rincover, & Egel, **Educating and Understanding Autistic Children** 1 (1982).

154. Id. at 2. For an overview of the education of autistic children, see Hinerman, **Teaching Autistic Children to Communicate** (1983).

155. Koegel, *supra* note 153, at 3. One of the definitive sources in this area is **Handbook of Autism and Developmental Disorders** (Cohen & Donnellan eds. 1987). This massive volume, however, is technical enough to make it an impractical source for the layperson.

156. 34 C.F.R. § 300.7(b)(12).

157. 34 C.F.R. § 300.7(b)(6) states: " 'Multiple disabilities' means concomitant impairments (such as mental retardation-blindness, mental retardation-orthopedic impairment, the combination of which causes such severe educational problems that they cannot be accommodated in special education programs solely for one of the impairments. The term does not include deaf-blindness."

158. 34 C.F.R. § 300.7(b)(8).

affects their ability to learn that such children cannot be properly educated in regular programs designed to accommodate a single disability. The definition contains two examples, mental retardation-blindness and mental retardation-orthopedic impairment, the singular components of which have been explored elsewhere in this chapter.

5.3.5.2 Other Health Impairment

The "other health impairment" category of IDEA lists autism and eleven examples of chronic health conditions which affect a child's strength, vitality or alertness. "Other health impairment" means

> having limited strength, vitality or alertness, due to chronic or acute health problems such as a heart condition, tuberculosis, rheumatic fever, nephritis, asthma, sickle cell anemia, hemophilia, epilepsy, lead poisoning, leukemia, or diabetes, that adversely affects a child's educational performance.[159]

These conditions are briefly defined below:

• Tuberculosis: a respiratory infection which develops into a self-limited pneumonia that heals by depositing nodules of abnormal cells in the lung tissue which may calcify and reactivate at a later time. In the active stage, the disease may cause tissue destruction, shortness of breath and pneumonia.[160]

• Rheumatic fever: a condition which is believed to be caused by the body's immune response to a bacterial organism (Group A Beta hemolytic streptococcal pharyngitis). Rheumatic fever causes nodules of abnormal cells to form in the cardiac valves, which can result in valve scarring, heart dysfunction and heart failure.[161]

• Nephritis: a term referring to a group of conditions which cause an inflammatory or similar reaction in the kidneys that leads to decreased kidney function. In the chronic state, this condition can lead to kidney failure, high blood pressure, and death.[162]

• Asthma: a disease process characterized by an increased responsiveness of the airways to various stimuli, causing widespread narrowing of the airways which varies over time. Asthmatics exhibit shortness of breath associated with wheezing and an intermittent cough.[163]

• Sickle cell anemia: results from a mutation in the DNA molecule which causes red blood cells to form sickle shapes when not carrying oxygen. These cells cause congestion in the capillaries, which may lead to pain in the extremities, anemia, kidney failure, and multi-organ destruction.[164]

---

159. 34 C.F.R. § 300.7(b)(8). The language "due to chronic or acute health problems" would allow virtually any health condition which affects a child's strength and vitality to fall within this definition. In combination with the broad language in § 300.5(b)(9), it is hard to imagine a condition affecting a child's educational performance which would not be included in one of the definitions in the regulation.

160. Cecil, **Essentials of Medicine** 165 (1986).

161. *Id.* at 60.

162. *See id.* at 230.

163. *Id.* at 141–42.

164. *Id.* at 363.

• Hemophilia: an inherited bleeding disorder which is manifested by abnormal bleeding into muscles and joints with physical activity. In addition, spontaneous hemorrhage can occur as a result of physical trauma or illness.[165]

• Epilepsy: the result of disordered electrical activity within the brain which can cause generalized convulsions and loss of consciousness.[166]

• Lead poisoning: chronic poisoning resulting from absorption of small amounts of lead (such as children eating paint chips made with lead alloys). Lead poisoning may cause anemia and generalized loss of appetite.[167]

• Leukemia: a blood disease in which an abnormality within the bone marrow causes the production of abnormal types and numbers of white blood cells. The manifestations of the disease include anemia, increased susceptibility to infection and abnormal bleeding.[168]

• Diabetes: a condition characterized by elevated levels of blood glucose due to a diminished effectiveness of insulin, a chemical which aids in the transport of glucose into cells from the bloodstream. Diabetics often experience renal failure, blindness, weight loss, fatigue, increased susceptibility to infection, amputations of the lower extremities, and diabetic comas.[169]

5.3.6 Disabilities Not Mentioned Under IDEA—the Role of § 504

On occasion, questions have been raised concerning a particular condition not specifically mentioned in IDEA regulations and whether it constitutes a qualifying condition under IDEA's other health impaired language. As a general principle, it must be kept in mind that eligibility always requires an adverse affect on educational performance. Therefore, no matter how severe the disability, whether it is listed under the regulations, the provisions of IDEA will not apply if there is no adverse impact on educational performance.

The definition of who qualifies for services, however, differs between IDEA and Section 504. IDEA provides a specific list of disabilities, one or more which must exist in order to be covered by the statute.[170] Section 504 regulations provide a broad definition of qualifying conditions which includes a physical or mental impairment which substantially limits one or more major life activities.[171] In practice, therefore, § 504 may provide education rights to children with, for example, epilepsy[172] and chemical dependencies,[173] while IDEA would not. Of particular note, because of the number of children identified and recent litigation are two specific disabilities: Acquired Immune Deficiency Syndrome (AIDS) and

165. *Id.* at 401.
166. *See generally* **Meritt's Textbook of Neurology** 640–42 (7th ed. 1984).
167. *See* Robbins, Cotran, & Kumar, **Pathologic Basis of Disease** 453–55 (1984).
168. *See generally* Cecil, *supra* note 160, at 378–83.
169. *Id.* at 487–89.
170. 34 C.F.R. § 300.7; *see* 20 U.S.C. § 1401(a)(1).
171. 34 C.F.R. § 104.3(j).
172. Akers v. Bolton, 531 F. Supp. 300 (D. Kan. 1981).
173. Inquiry of Des Jardin, 213 Educ. Handicapped L. Rep. (CRR) 144 (OSEP, June 16, 1988); Inquiry by Harris, 211 Educ. Handicapped L. Rep. (CRR) 431 (OSEP, January 9, 1987).

Attention Deficit Hyperactivity Disorder (ADHD) or Attention Deficit Disorder (ADD). Each of these conditions is discussed in more detail in the following subsections.

5.3.6.1 Acquired Immune Deficiency Syndrome (AIDS)

A growing number of children are affected with Acquired Immune Deficiency Syndrome (AIDS). Studies indicate that 1.2 percent of the population under 5 years of age are infected with the Human Immuno-deficiency Virus (HIV). Three fourths of children acquire the virus across the placenta or perinatally. The rest acquire the virus through blood transfusions. There have been no known cases in which transmission has occurred in the school or day care setting.[174]

Considerable litigation is developing concerning the education of children with AIDS. The consensus appears to be that children with AIDS are not covered *per se* by IDEA, but they are covered by § 504. In determining whether the child who is HIV positive (HIV infected) has Aids Related Complex (ARC) or has AIDS is eligible courts generally focus on the connection between the disease and its impact on the educational performance of the child. If the child's ability to perform school work is affected, such as by limited strength and vitality, the child will be considered to have a qualifying disability under IDEA. Where, however, there is no showing that the disease is interfering with educational performance, the child will not be considered covered under the IDEA.[175]

In *Thomas v. Atascadero Unified School District,*[176] the United States District Court for the Central District of California held that a child infected with the AIDS virus was a protected person within the meaning of § 504. Further, the child was otherwise qualified to attend public school. Exclusion from school therefore was a violation of § 504.[177]

In *Doe v. Belleville Public School District No. 118,*[178] suit was brought under § 504 against the school system for excluding a child with AIDS. The LEA sought to dismiss the complaint on the grounds that the child's parents had failed to exhaust administrative remedies under IDEA.[179] The court held in denying a motion to dismiss that there was no requirement to exhaust the IDEA administrative remedies because the child was not covered by IDEA. The LEA argued that the child was "other health impaired"[180] and therefore covered by IDEA. The district court pointed out, however, that there are three elements to the other health impaired classification. There must be a health impairment limiting

---

174. **Comprehensive Pediatrics** 51–58 (Summit ed. 1990).

175. Doe v. Belleville Public School District No. 118, 672 F. Supp. 342 (S.D. Ill. 1987).

176. 662 F. Supp. 376 (C.D. Ca. 1987).

177. *See also* Robertson v. Granite City Community Unit School Dist. No. 9, 684 F. Supp. 1002 (S.D. Ill. 1988); Doe v. Belleville Public School Dist. No. 118, 672 F. Supp. 342 (S.D. Ill. 1987); District 27 Community School Bd. v. Board of Educ., 130 Misc. 2d 398, 502 N.Y.S.2d 325 (Sup. Ct. N.Y. Queens County, 1986).

178. 672 F. Supp. 342 (S.D. Ill. 1987).

179. It will be remembered that where IDEA provides concurrent rights, the IDEA administrative remedies must be exhausted before filing suit under § 504. 20 U.S.C. § 1415(f).

180. 34 C.F.R. § 300.7(b)(8); *see also* 20 U.S.C. § 1401(a)(1).

strength, vitality, or alertness. The impairment must adversely affect educational performance. Finally the impairment must require special education and related services. For a child who has AIDS, the AIDS does not necessarily cause an adverse educational impact. Further, at many stages of the disease there is no impairment of strength, vitality, or alertness.[181]

In the area of drug dependency there is also movement to extend IDEA type protections via § 504.[182] OSERS, interpreting IDEA and its regulations, has held that drug and alcohol addicted students are not "other health impaired" under IDEA.[183] OCR, interpreting § 504, however, has determined that these children are protected within the meaning of § 504.[184]

Perhaps counter intuitively, in the circumstance where § 504 appears to expand rights to those not covered by IDEA (for example AIDS), it seems that affirmative requirements are less likely to constitute undue burden than in circumstances where § 504 purports to provide additional benefits to those already covered by IDEA. Since the school system is already providing the services "it may be logically inferred that it would not have imposed an 'undue burden' on defendants to provide a special educational program for the plaintiff."[185] Further, if services of a particular type are already being provided to one group of people, what is being requested is a reallocation of existing resources, not an expansion of funding.[186] By the same token, these latter cases may well result in more litigation, since if there is not dual coverage with IDEA, there is no need to exhaust administrative remedies.

5.3.6.1 Attention Deficit Hyperactivity Disorder (ADHD) or Attention Deficit Disorder (ADD)

Attention Deficit Hyperactivity Disorder (ADHD) or Attention Deficit Disorder (ADD) is a common disorder which depending on your source affects approxi-

---

181. *See also* Barnes Inquiry, 211 Educ. Handicapped L. Rep. (CRR) 343 (September 27, 1984). It is also possible, of course, to have AIDS and be covered by IDEA because of an unrelated disability. *See* Parents of Child, Code No. 870901W v. Coker, 676 F. Supp. 1072 (E.D. Okla. 1987) (defendants enjoined from prosecuting state court action seeking exclusion of emotionally disturbed child with AIDS who was placed pursuant to IDEA).

Coverage of § 504 or IDEA, of course does not insure the child will be able remain in the regular classroom. *See generally*, Martinez v. School Bd., 675 F. Supp. 1574 (M.D. Fla. 1987) (preliminary injunction to keep LEA from baring student with AIDS Related Complex (ARC) denied).

182. *See also* In re Dale Shroyer, 508 Educ. Handicapped L. Rep. (CRR) 371 (SEA Ore. July 24, 1987) (violation of § 504 for failure to refer and evaluate alcoholic student).

183. Harris Inquiry, 211 Educ. Handicapped L. Rep. (CRR) 431 (EHA January 9, 1987).

184. Lake Washington (WA) School District No. 414, 257:611 (OCR 1985); *see also* Traynor v. Turnage, 485 U.S. 535, 555 (Justice Blackman concurring and dissenting 1988):

It is beyond dispute that petitioners, as alcoholics, were handicapped individuals covered by the Act. See 43 Fed. Reg. 2137 (1978) (guidelines issued by Department of Health, Education and Welfare (later the Department of Human Services) reflecting the Attorney General's specific conclusion, 43 Op. Atty Gen. No. 12, p. 2 (1977), that an alcoholic is covered by the Act) . . .

See also Rezza v. Department of Justice, 698 F. Supp. 586 (E.D. Pa. 1988) (compulsive gambling may qualify as "mental impairment").

185. Sanders, 561 F. Supp. at 1371.

186. *See generally* 1.4, 1.4.1.

mately 3 to 30 percent of the school-age population.[187] The definition of this disorder is a diagnostic category of the American Psychiatric Association.[188] This disorder affects many aspects of the child's life, at home, in school and in social situations. Inattention, impulsiveness, and hyperactivity or restlessness are the common characteristics.

There are many examples of behaviors which are manifested by the disorder. Typically at least 8 of the following behaviors must be present over the last six months, with onset before age 7: fidgeting with hands or feet, (adolescents may feel restless); difficulty remaining in a seat; easily distracted; blurts out answers to questions; difficulty with following instructions; difficulty with sustained attention; shifts from one uncompleted activity to another frequently; talks excessively; interrupts others; poor listening skills; frequently loses things; and engages in physically dangerous activities.[189] The child with ADHD may exhibit academic difficulties, conduct problems, social and peer difficulties, and problems with self-esteem.[190]

ADHD is believed to have three causes. The first theory and the most popular explanation is the biological/chemical explanation. This explanation indicates that there is a problem with the neuro-chemical transmission in regulating brain functions. The preliminary research suggests that normal amounts of neurotransmitters are not being received by the areas of the brain which control attention.[191]

The second theory postulated is the individuals interaction with the environment or a bio-environmental theory.[192] For example, ADHD behaviors may be a result of allergies to foods, food additives or inhaled substances. In addition, eating lead-based paint during a developmental stage can result in some of the specified behaviors. Exposure to alcohol or other drugs by the developing fetus can result in attentional problems. Anti convulsants or sedatives can also cause symptoms of ADHD.[193]

The last theory for explaining ADHD symptoms is an environmental theory. This theory is not well supported by research although it does support that parenting and other environmental factors can influence the emergence of symptoms rather that cause them.[194]

Recognizing that ADHD can result in significant learning problems the U.S. Department of Education issued a Joint Policy Memo addressing the importance

---

187. Silver, **Attention Deficit Hyperactivity Disorder, Guide to Diagnosis and Treatment** (1992) (using a rating scale, teachers found 10–20 percent of students while parents using the same scale found 30 percent of all students ADHD or ADD); Braswell, Bloomquist & Pederson, **ADHD, A guide To Understanding And Helping Children with Attention Deficit Hyperactivity Disorder in School Settings**, (University of Minnesota, 1991) (3–5 percent of the school age population).

188. **Diagnostic and Statistical Manual of Mental Disorders** (Third Edition, Revised) DSM-III-R American Psychiatric Association 1987.

189. *Id.* (Diagnostic Criteria for 314.01 Attention Deficit Hyperactivity Disorder).

190. Silver, *supra* note 187.

191. *Id.* at 58.

192. *Id.*

193. Braswell, Bloomquist & Pederson, **ADHD, A Guide to Understanding and Helping Children with Attention Deficit Hyperactivity Disorder in School Settings**, (University of Minnesota, 1991).

194. Silver, *supra* note 185, at 59.

of the provision of educational services to children with ADHD.[195] There are, however, few court decisions involving children with ADHD brought under either IDEA or § 504. In *Valerie J. and Michael J. v. Derry Cooperative School District*,[196] the court ruled that the IEP could not be contingent on the administration of the medication Ritalin, a drug often used as an integral part of a total treatment program for stabilize the children's symptoms.[197]

The most common source of opinions relating to these cases are a result of complaints filed with the United States Department of Education's Office of Civil Rights (OCR) in the last two years. For example, OCR issued a decision that local school divisions must evaluate students who exhibit characteristics associated with ADHD to determine whether regular or special education services were required under § 504.[198] The eligibility criteria under § 504 is different from that of the very specific conditions under IDEA. To be eligible an ADHD child would have to be found "handicapped." This means that the child has a physical or mental impairment which substantially limits one or more major life activities, has a record of impairment, or is regarded as having an impairment.[199] With ADHD children the major life activity affected is generally learning. Of course this does not mean that all ADHD children even with a record of impairment will be eligible.

Other examples of OCR rulings, in addition to failure to evaluate, include failure to properly place, failure to provide appropriate services, failure to provide proper discipline,[200] and failure to provide notice of procedural safeguards.[201]

---

195. United States Dep't. of Educ., Joint Policy Memo 18 Individuals with Disabilities L. Rep. (LRP) 118 (OSERS, OCR, Office of Elementary and Secondary Ed.) (Sept. 16 1991) (children with ADHD can be eligible under the IDEA categories of other health impaired, learning disability (LD) or serious emotional disturbance; in addition children can be found eligible under 504).

196. 771 F. Supp. 483 (D.N.H. 1991); *see also* See Ramon Valley(CA) Unified School District, 18 Individuals with Disabilities Educ. L. Rep. (LRP) 465 (OCR October 3, 1991) (school must ensure the administration of Ritalin as a related service if needed to assist a child in benefitting from his educational placement).

197. **Physician's Desk Reference**, PDR, 46 Medical Economics Data (1992).

198. Romulus Community School, 18 Individuals with Disabilities Educ. L. Rep. (LRP) 81 (OCR June 21, 1991). In *Romulus Community School*, OCR pointed out that district's procedures need to comply with 34 C.F.R. § 104.33(a) (a school must provide a FAPE to each qualified handicapped person . . .) and 104.35, (recipient must conduct a proper evaluation in order to evaluate for special education and related services). *See also* Thomason Inquiry, 18 Individuals with Disabilities Educ. L. Rep. (LRP) 536 (OSEP October 11 1991) (LEA may not refuse to evaluate a child based solely on the medical diagnosis of ADHD).

199. 34 C.F.R. 104.3(j).

200. Templeton (CA) Unified School Dist., 17 Educ. Handicapped L. Rep. 859 (CRR) (OCR March 19, 1991).

201. Prince George's County (MD) Pub. Schools, 17 Educ. Handicapped L. Rep. 875 (LRP) (OCR March 22,1991).

Chapter 6

Independent Educational Evaluations

6.1 In General

Under certain circumstances, the local education agency is required to provide at public expense an Independent Educational Evaluation (IEE) of the child. An IEE is defined as an evaluation conducted by a qualified examiner who is not employed by the agency responsible for the child's education.[1] Under IDEA, the parents may have the right to obtain an Independent Educational Evaluation (IEE) at public expense, if the parents disagree with the evaluation performed by the public agency.[2] If, however, the public agency believes its evaluation is appropriate, it may initiate a due process hearing to show that it is appropriate.[3]

In addition to disagreements with an evaluation performed by the agency, parents have been permitted reimbursement for an IEE where "special circumstances" are shown.[4] "Special circumstances" occur, for example, when the LEA acts in bad faith, such as failing to comply with the procedural safeguards of IDEA in an egregious manner. Special circumstances have also been found where a parent took action to secure services that were in dispute and were ultimately found necessary to protect the physical health of the child and which should have been provided by the school district.[5] Reimbursement has also been held proper when an LEA recommended an IEE which was subsequently used to determine the child's placement.[6]

Section 504 of the Rehabilitation Act of 1973 does not address public funding of an IEE, so parents must seek protection and reimbursement for an IEE under IDEA regulations.[7]

---

1. 34 C.F.R. § 300.503(a)(3)(i); *see also* 20 U.S.C. § 1415(b)(1)(A).

2. 34 C.F.R. § 300.503(b); *see also* 20 U.S.C. § 1415(b)(1)(A).

3. 34 C.F.R. § 300.503(b); *see also* 20 U.S.C. § 1415(b)(1)(A).

4. Akers v. Bolton, 531 F. Supp. 300 (D. Kan. 1981).

5. *Id. See generally* Anderson v. Thompson, 658 F.2d 1205 (7th Cir. 1981)

6. Hoover Schrum, Ill. School Dist. No.157, 257 Educ. Handicapped L. Rep. (CRR) 136 (OCR June 30, 1980).

7. Baltimore County, Md. Pub. Schools, 352 Educ. Handicapped L. Rep. (CRR) 352 (OCR March 18, 1987).

6.2 Notice of Availability of IEE

IDEA regulations only require that *at the request of the parent* public education agencies provide information to parents with information concerning where an IEE may be obtained.[8] The United States Department of Education, however, has held that where an LEA only provided notice of the availability of IEE when the parents requested it, after classification had already been made, there was a violation of Section 504 regulations.[9] The better practice therefore is to provide notice of the possible right to an IEE following a referral for an agency evaluation.

6.3 Standards for IEE

In general, the criteria to be used to conduct an IEE will parallel the criteria for evaluations required by the public agency. Indeed, whenever an IEE is made at public expense, agency criteria for evaluations must be met.[10] An IEE should, therefore, include a determination of specific teaching methods and instructional materials to be used. Likewise, the qualifications of the evaluators should be comparable to those required of agency evaluators.

6.4 Cost of IEE

IDEA regulations provide that the public agency either pay for the evaluation or "insure that the evaluation is otherwise provided at no cost to the parents ..."[11] For example, the public agency may be able to share this cost with another state or local agency such as a department of social services.[12]

6.5 Unilateral Action by Parent to Obtain IEE

If the parents disagree with the evaluation, they have three ways to proceed to obtain the IEE. First, of course, they may seek the agreement of the agency to pay for the IEE. Second they may unilaterally seek an evaluation and then seek reimbursement from the IEE. No approval from or notice to the LEA is required in order to permit later reimbursement for the IEE.[13] It is likely, however, that a due process hearing will result if the agency believes its evaluation is appropriate.

---

8. 34 C.F.R. § 300.503(a)(2) (emphasis added); *see also* 20 U.S.C. 1415(b)(1)(A).

9. Elmira City, NY School Dist., 352 Educ. Handicapped L. Rep. (CRR) 188 (OCR April 25, 1986) (violation of 34 C.F.R. 104.36).

10. 34 C.F.R. § 300.503(e); *see also* 20 U.S.C. § 1415(b)(1)(A); Rambo Inquiry, 16 Educ. Handicapped L. Rep. (LRP) 1078 (OSEP June 22, 1990).

11. 34 C.F.R. § 300.503(a)((3)(ii); *see also* 20 U.S.C. § 1415(b)(1)(A).

12. 34 C.F.R. § 300.301(a); *see also* 20 U.S.C. 1401(18).

13. Hudson v. Wilson, 828 F.2d 1059 (4th Cir. 1987); *see also* Thorne Inquiry, 16 Educ. Handicapped L. Rep. (LRP) 606 (OSEP Feb. 5, 1990).

The LEA is entitled to a due process hearing prior to reimbursing the costs of an IEE, and if the LEA's evaluation is found appropriate there will be no reimbursement.[14] There is no specific time limit on how long the school system has to request such a due process hearing, although it may not delay its decision for so long that the delay in requesting acts as a denial of the IEE.[15] Finally, rather than seeking an IEE and risking success in seeking reimbursement, a parent may opt to request a due process hearing. There is no specific requirement that parents wait to see if an LEA corrects the defects in its evaluation prior to taking action to seek an IEE.[16] IDEA sets no timeline for how long a parent can wait after receiving the evaluation results before seeking reimbursement for an IEE. It has, however, been interpreted as unreasonable to require payment for an IEE conducted two years after the LEAs evaluation was done.[17]

6.6 IEE at Public Expense Is Limited to One

A parent is entitled to only one publicly funded IEE for each LEA evaluation over which there is disagreement.[18]

6.7 Use of IEE

The results of any IEE that meets agency criteria must be considered by the LEA in a decision regarding the child's educational program.[19] The IEE may also be presented at any due process proceeding.[20]

6.8 IEE at Parental Expense

Parents always have the right to get an IEE at their own expense, even if due process hearings hold the LEA's evaluation appropriate.[21] As with an IEE obtained at public expense, the IEE paid for by the parent must be considered by the agency in determining the child's educational needs and may be presented as evidence in any due process proceedings.[22]

---

14. *See* Hessler v. State Bd. of Educ. of Maryland, 553 Educ. Handicapped L. Rep. (CRR) 262 (D.M.D. 1981), *aff'd.* 700 F.2d 134 (1983).

15. Smith Inquiry, 16 Educ. Handicapped L. Rep. (LRP) 1080 (OSERS June 28, 1990).

16. In an unusual 1981 decision, however, an LEA was not required to reimburse a parent for an IEE where prior notice to the LEA was not given. Norris v. Massachusetts Dept. of Educ., 529 F. Supp. 759 (D. Mass. 1981).

17. Fields Inquiry, 213 Educ. Handicapped L. Rep. (CRR) 259 (OSEP September 15, 1989).

18. Hudson v. Wilson, 828 F.2d 1059 (4th Cir. 1987); Hiller v. Board of Educ., 687 F. Supp. 735 (N.D.N.Y. 1988).

19. 34 C.F.R. § 300.503(c)(1); *see also* 20 U.S.C. § 1415(b)(1)(A).

20. 34 C.F.R. § 300.503(c)(2); *see also* 20 U.S.C. § 1415(b)(1)(A).

21. 34 C.F.R. § 300.503(c); *see also* 20 U.S.C. § 1415(b)(1)(A).

22. 34 C.F.R. § 300.503(c); *see also* 20 U.S.C. § 1415(b)(1)(A).

6.9 Hearing Officer Ordered IEE

The hearing officer may order an IEE, which must be at public expense.[23] Any IEE that duplicates an IEE ordered by a hearing officer is, however, not reimbursable.[24]

---

23. 34 C.F.R. § 300.503(d); *see also* 20 U.S.C. § 1415(b)(1)(A).
24. Williams v. Overturf, 580 F. Supp. 1365 (W.D. Wisc. 1984).

Chapter 7

Individualized Education Program

7.1 In General

The centerpiece of IDEA is the requirement that each student have an "individualized education program" (IEP).[1] The contents of the IEP are designed to provide a road map for the child's educational programming during the course of the coming year. While the IEP is not specifically required by § 504 regulations, its functional equivalent is.[2] Section 504 regulations indicate that one way to meet the special education requirements is through the IEP process of IDEA.[3]

Special education and related services must be provided in accordance with this IEP.[4] The IEP must be developed at least annually.[5] The IEP has six components:[6]

- It must contain a statement of the child's present level of educational performance;

- It must contain a statement of the annual educational goals as well as short-term objectives related to those goals;

---

1. 34 C.F.R. § 300.342; *see also* 20 U.S.C. §§ 1412(4), 1414(a)(5).

2. 34 C.F.R. § 104.33(b)(1) and (2) provides:

(1) For the purpose of this subpart, the provision of an appropriate education is the provision of regular or special education and related aids and services that (i) are designed to meet individual educational needs of handicapped persons as adequately as the needs of nonhandicapped persons are met and (ii) are based upon adherence to procedures that satisfy the requirements of Regs. 104.34, 104.35, and 104.36.

(2) Implementation of an individualized education program developed in accordance with the Education of the Handicapped Act is one means of meeting the standard established in paragraph (b)(1)(i) of this section.

3. *Id.* at 104.33(b)(2).

4. 34 C.F.R. § 300.350; *see also* 20 U.S.C. § 1414(a)(5).

5. 34 C.F.R. § 300.343(d); *see also* 20 U.S.C. §§ 1412(4), 1414(a)(5).

6. 34 C.F.R. § 300.346; *see also* 20 U.S.C. §§ 1401(19), (25), 1412(4), 1414(a)(5). *But see* Doe v. Defendant I., 898 F.2d 1186 (6th Cir. 1990) (failure to include present level of educational performance and objective criteria did not render IEP invalid where absent information was known by parents and agency).

- The IEP must contain a statement of the specific educational and related services to be provided, including the extent to which the child will be serviced in regular educational programs;
- It must contain a statement of needed transition services. These services can begin at 14 or younger if appropriate, but must begin no later than age 16. In identifying the transition services, the IEP must also include interagency responsibilities, if appropriate;
- The IEP must contain the date the services will begin as well as the expected duration of the services; and
- It must indicate "appropriate objective criteria and evaluation procedures and schedules" to allow at least an annual determination of whether the short term objectives are being met.

The IEP acts as a guide for the provision of services and insures that those services are related to identifiable educational goals and objectives. The IEP, however, does not act as a guarantee of child success, and neither the public agency or its employees are accountable under IDEA if the child fails to achieve any goals and objectives.[7]

The signature of the participants at the meeting is typically requested on the IEP document, though there is no statutory or regulatory requirement that the document actually be signed.[8] It is, however, good practice to memorialize the agreement of the parties in this manner.

7.2 Agency Responsible for IEP Development

Each public agency having responsibility to educate a child must provide for development of an IEP.[9] Typically this is the local school system where the child resides. Numerous other public agencies, however, may have responsibility for educating a child. For example, a child involuntarily committed to a mental institution or to a correctional facility may actually be educated by the particular state agency.[10]

7.3 Time Frame for Development of IEP

An initial IEP must be developed within thirty calender days following a determination that the child requires special education and related services.[11] The initial determination of need is discussed elsewhere.[12] Subsequent IEPs must be

---

7. 34 C.F.R. § 300.350; *see also* 20 U.S.C. § 1414(a)(5).
8. Peterson 211 Educ. Handicapped L. Rep. (CRR) 410 (EHA September 16, 1986).
9. 34 C.F.R. § 300.341; *see also* 20 U.S.C. §§ 1412(4), 1413(a)(4).
10. *Comment*, 34 C.F.R. § 300.341.
11. 34 C.F.R. 300.343(c); *see also* 20 U.S.C. §§ 1412(4), 1414(a)(5).
12. See chapter 4.

developed on at least an annual basis.[13] The IEP must be "implemented as soon as possible following" its development.[14]

A placement must be based on an existing IEP.[15] It is usually the case, therefore, that a change in placement will have been preceded by an IEP meeting. A student who transfers into a new school system from within the same state should be placed in a program based on the IEP developed in the previous school system, unless the parents and the school system agree to a different interim placement.[16] It is unclear whether the same is true of interstate transfers.[17] The new school system will typically call a new IEP meeting after having gained familiarity with the student's needs.

7.4 Placement Decisions and the IEP

Federal law requires all placements be based on an existing IEP.[18] The IEP is not written for a specific location.[19] The logical sequence, therefore, is to develop the IEP and then to determine placement. Deciding the placement of a child prior to development of an IEP upon which to base that placement decision constitutes a procedural violation sufficient to find that the school's placement would not provide a free appropriate education.[20] Likewise, a change in placement is improper if it will not allow implementation of the IEP.[21]

7.5 IEP Meetings

The IEP is developed at meetings involving interested parties. The public agency is responsible for initiating and conducting these meetings.[22] Participants in the meeting must include:

- a representative of the public agency, other than the child's teacher, who is qualified to supervise or provide special education;
- the child's teacher;
- one or both of the parents of the child.[23]

---

13. 34 C.F.R. § 300.343(d); *see also* 20 U.S.C. §§ 1412(4), 1414(a)(5).

14. 34 C.F.R. § 300.342(b)(2); *see also* 20 U.S.C. §§ 1412(4), 1414(a)(5).

15. 34 C.F.R. § 300.552; *see also* 20 U.S.C. § 1412(5)(B).

16. Cambell, 213 Educ. Handicapped L. Rep. (CRR) 265 (OSEP September 16, 1989). Interestingly, OCR does not interpret 504 as requiring the school to implement the existing IEP. OCR Memorandum, 307 Educ. Handicapped L. Rep. (CRR) 15 (OCR July 7, 1989).

17. *See* Nerney Inquiry, 213 Educ. Handicapped L. Rep. (CRR) 267 (OSEP September 25, 1989).

18. 34 C.F.R. § 300.552(a); *see also* 20 U.S.C. § 1412(5)(B).

19. Leonard v. McKenzie, 869 F.2d 1558 (D.C. Cir. 1989).

20. W.G. v. Target School Dist. No. 23 Bd. Of Trustees, 789 F. Supp. 1070 (D. Mont. 1991) *aff'd*, 960 F.2d 1479 (9th Cir. 1992); Spielberg v. Henrico County Pub. Schools, 853 F.2d 256 (4th Cir. 1988).

21. Angelo Inquiry, 213 Educ. Handicapped L. Rep. (CRR) 168 (EHA September 13, 1988).

22. 34 C.F.R. § 300.343(a); *see also* 20 U.S.C. §§ 1412(4), 1414(a)(5).

23. 34 C.F.R. § 300.344(a)(1)–(a)(3); *see also* 20 U.S.C. §§ 1401(19) 1412(4), 1414(a)(5).

In addition, the child may be present where appropriate,[24] as well as "[o]ther individuals at the discretion of the parent or agency."[25] The parents and school, therefore, have the right to have legal counsel at the IEP meeting.

If the IEP meeting is being held following the initial evaluation of the child, the participants in the meeting must also include a member of the evaluation team or some other person "who is knowledgeable about the evaluation procedures used with the child."[26] If the IEP meeting is to consider transition services, the public agency must also invite the student and a representative of the agency likely to be responsible for paying or providing the transition services.[27]

A recurring question is whether the parent has the right to tape or otherwise transcribe the IEP meeting. IDEA regulations are silent, and the issue remains in dispute. It seems logical, however, that since it is not prohibited, parents should be allowed to tape record IEP meetings in the absence of any harm established by the education agency.[28]

7.6 Parental Participation

The importance of parental participation in the development of the IEP cannot be underestimated. Both the letter and spirit of the IEP require parental participation at every meaningful stage of the educational process, and development of the IEP and the attendant decision is perhaps the most critical stage of that process.[29]

Central to the idea that there must be meaningful participation, of course, is the requirement that the IEP cannot be developed by the education agency prior to the IEP meeting. If the school system decides what should go into the IEP before consulting with the parents, there is a violation which itself may justify a hearing officer or judge determining that there has been a failure to provide a FAPE.[30]

While the school may not decide the contents of the IEP prior to the meeting, it is permissible for the school to develop a draft of various proposals each of

---

24. 34 C.F.R. § 300.344(a)(4); *see also* 20 U.S.C. §§ 1401(19), 1412(4), 1414(a)(5).

25. 34 C.F.R. § 300.344(a)(5); *see also* 20 U.S.C. §§ 1401(19), 1412(4), 1414(a)(5).

26. 34 C.F.R. § 300.344(b); *see also* 20 U.S.C. §§ 1401(19), 1412(4), 1414(a)(5).

27. 34 C.F.R. § 300.344(c).

28. V.W. v. Favolise, 131 F.R.D. 654 (D. Conn. 1990) (school board failed to show any authority which would prohibit parent from tape recording IEP meeting); E.H. v. Tirozzi, 735 F. Supp. 53 (D. Conn. 1990) (tape recording necessary to allow parent for whom English was second language).

29. The importance the Supreme Court attached to parental involvement in the development of the IEP was well supported in the legislative history of IDEA. As the Senate Report states, "individualized planning conferences are a way to provide parent involvement and protection to assure that appropriate services are provided to a handicapped child." S. Rep. No. 68, 94th Cong., 1st Sess. at 11–12, quoted Hendrick Hudson Dist. Bd. of Educ. v. Rowley, 458 U.S. 176, 208–209 (1981); see also Honig v. Doe, 484 U.S. 305, 311 (1988) ("the Act establishes various procedural safeguards that guarantee parents . . . an opportunity for meaningful input into all decisions affecting their child's education . . ."); DeVries v. Spillane, 853 F.2d 264, 266 (4th Cir. 1988) (parents to have "meaningful participation in all aspects"); Stemple v. Board of Educ., 623 F.2d 893, 898 (4th Cir. 1980) (parents provided with generous bill of rights).

30. Spielberg v. Henrico County Pub. Schools, 853 F.2d 256 (4th Cir. 1988).

which can then be discussed with the parents at the IEP meeting.[31] There are, of course, always difficulties of proof when the question is whether the school's "suggestion" is really its decision, or truly a proposal which can be affected by parental input.[32] Lawyers, however, have been successful in establishing premature decision-making on the part of school systems.[33]

To effectuate the central role of the parents in the IEP meeting, the educational agency is required to provide notice of the meeting to the parents,[34] indicating "the purpose, time, and location of the meeting, and who will be in attendance."[35]

The IEP meeting must be held at a mutually convenient time.[36] If neither parent can attend a meeting, the LEA must attempt an alternate form of participation such as a teleconference.[37] If both parents refuse to participate, the IEP may be held, but the LEA must have a detailed set of records establishing its attempts to schedule a mutually convenient time and place.[38] To insure meaningful participation, the LEA must take whatever steps are necessary to "insure that the parent understands the proceedings ... including arranging for an interpreter for parents with deafness or whose native language is other than English."[39]

A copy of the IEP must be provided at the request of the parent.[40]

7.7 Drafting the Document

It is important that it be kept in mind that the IEP provides an integrated approach to the child's educational programming. Each part is directed toward achieving the annual goals. IDEA distinguishes between "annual goals" and "short term instructional objectives." Goals describe what a child is expected to accomplish by the end of the next year. Objectives are measurable, intermediate steps leading to the accomplishment of the annual goal.[41] To be rational, the goals must be related to the child's present level of educational performance and, of course, the objectives must be rationally connected to the goals.

A non-educator can play an important part in drafting the present level of educational performance, the goals and objectives by 1) insuring the level of performance, goals and objectives are all rationally related to one another 2) insisting that the goals the parent believes are necessary are adequately articulated and pressing the other party to be descriptive and precise in the actual writing of the goals and objectives. It is likely that if a lawyer is involved at the IEP stage,

---

31. *See* Helmuth Inquiry, 16 Educ. Handicapped L. Rep. (CRR) 503 (OSEP January 30, 1990).

32. *See, e.g.*, Hudson v. Wilson, 828 F.2d 1059 (4th Cir. 1987).

33. Spielberg v. Henrico County Pub. Schools, 853 F.2d 256 (4th Cir. 1988).

34. 34 C.F.R. § 300.345(a)(1); *see also* 20 U.S.C. §§ 1401(19), 1412(4), 1414(a)(5).

35. 34 C.F.R. § 300.345(b); *see also* 20 U.S.C. §§ 1401(19), 1412(4), 1414(a)(5).

36. 34 C.F.R. § 300.345(a)(2); *see also* 20 U.S.C. §§ 1401(19), 1412(4), 1414(a)(5).

37. 34 C.F.R. § 300.345(c); *see also* 20 U.S.C. §§ 1401(19), 1412(4), 1414(a)(5).

38. 34 C.F.R. § 300.345(d). Examples of the appropriate records include detailed records of phone calls and visits to the parents home or place of employment, as well as copies of correspondence. *Id.*; *see also* 20 U.S.C. §§ 1401(19), 1412(4), 1414(a)(5).

39. 34 C.F.R. § 300.345(e); *see also* 20 U.S.C. §§ 1401(19), 1412(4), 1414(a)(5).

40. 34 C.F.R. § 300.345(f); *see also* 20 U.S.C. §§ 1401(19), 1412(4), 1414(a)(5).

41. 34 C.F.R. Part § 300, app. C—Notice of Interpretation II(38).

a dispute has already arisen between the parents and the school system. The school's attorney, of course, should consult with the LEA's professional staff. It may be wise for the parents' attorney to engage the services of a special educator to review the available information and advise the attorney on preparing for the IEP meeting or actually to participate in the IEP meeting.

In general, any participant should be prepared to ask the following questions in the development of goals and objectives:

- What skills and behaviors need to be addressed? What goals should the child strive for?

- What is the present level of performance? Is the present level of performance stated in objective measurable terms?

- Is there a direct relationship between the annual goals and the child's present level of performance? While the IEP does not act as a guarantee of success, goals must be reasonable.

- What intermediate objectives will allow the child to move toward the goals? Are the objectives measurable?

- Under what conditions and by whom will the child receive educational programming?

The number of goals contained within the IEP depends on the student involved. By definition it is an individual plan and the special education and related services needed by individual students will vary widely. The special education goals for a seriously emotionally disturbed child will be quite different, and perhaps more comprehensive in all areas of education, than, for example, a child with a specific learning disability.

Most children will receive not only special education and related services, but will also receive regular educational programming. While there need not be goals and objectives for regular education, the extent to which regular education is provided must be indicated in the IEP. It is important that the IEP identify where the mainstreaming will occur. For example, an IEP might provide that "Jane will be mainstreamed one and one-half hours per day in the library, cafeteria, and physical education." When a child receives regular education, the regular education teachers must be informed about the contents of the IEP.[42]

Finally, any related services must be provided for in the IEP. If the child is to receive a related service such as occupational or speech/language therapy, this must be indicated and the level of service provided must be listed (for example, "Occupational therapy, 1 hour weekly").

7.8 Drafting Example

An example may be helpful in understanding the interrelationship of the various parts of the IEP. If we assume a thirteen year-old seriously emotionally disturbed child, the present level of educational performance in each category in which she needs special education will usually be measured by standardized tests, such as the Peabody Individual Achievement Test. It might be described as follows:

---

42. Greider v. Shawnee Mission Unified School Dist. No. 512, 710 F. Supp. 296 (D. Kan. 1989).

Peabody Individual Achievement Test:

Math   G.E.   .4   (Grade Equivalent less than first grade)

Reading Recognition   G.E.   1.8

Reading Comprehension   G.E.   2.1

Spelling   G.E.   2.2

General Information   G.E.   .1

Total Test   G.E.   1.4

Expressive One Word Picture Vocabulary
      Test   A.E.   6.7 (Age Equivalent)

Language Processing Test   A.E.   6.1

Receptive One Word Picture Vocabulary Test   A.E.   6.3

Educational performance, however, must not be measured only in traditional academic subjects. The definition of education is very broad under IDEA. For some children, for example, basic self help and survival skills may need to be taught. These are sometimes referred to as activities of daily living. Our hypothetical child, for example, may need instruction in social interaction skills or self-care skills. The present level of educational performance for these areas should also be stated. For example:

Social Interaction Skills. Jane inappropriatly touches others when being introduced 80% of the time. Although Jane can play with her peer group, she oftens bosses them around.

Based on present level of educational performance, goals must be articulated. Goals are the results to be achieved and are, by their nature, more general than objectives. Objectives are the steps to be taken to meet the goals.

Taking just one area, reading skills, the goal might be "Jane will increase reading skill to G.E. 3 by the end of the year." The objectives, however, must be more specific and *measurable*. Because the objectives must be measurable, it is only logical that the present skill level of the objective also must be identified so that the measurement can be made:

Jane will identify and define basic vocabulary for functional living skills with 100% accuracy by June 15.

Skill level: 60%

Jane will be able to give synonyms, antonyms, and multiple meanings for these words with 80% accuracy and intelligibility by June 15.

Skill level: Multiple meanings subtest 8th percentile. Jane will read one story orally and silently by June 15.

Skill level: G.E. 2.1

While reading orally, Jane will be intelligible and use appropriate pitch and volume 80% of the time by June 15.

Skill level: 50%

Jane will read and explain 40 commonly seen signs with 80% accuracy by June 15.

Skill level: 65%

Jane will sequence 4 pictures with 100% accuracy by June 15.

Skill level: 10%

Jane will record a story she has created using correct sequence and grammar by June 15.

Skill level: New Skill

Jane will answer four question about the story she recorded with 75% accuracy by June 15.

Skill level: New Skill

Jane will identify main idea and facts of a second-grade story with 80% accuracy by June 15.

Skill level: New Skill

Each identified goal will in turn have a list of intermediate objectives. The actual document used will vary widely among school divisions (see Appendix), but the content should be the same: measured level of educational development, rational goals, measurable objectives.

7.9 Private Placements

Where a public agency, in order to meet its obligations under IDEA, places a child in a private facility, the public agency is responsible for developing the initial IEP upon which the placement decision is based.[43] This IEP must be developed with the participation of representatives from the private facility.[44] After development of the initial IEP, subsequent IEP meetings may, at the discretion of the public school, be initiated and conducted by the private school.[45] If the public agency allows the private facility to initiate and conduct the subsequent IEP meetings, the public agency must still insure that the parents participate in decisions concerning the IEP and agree to any changes in the program before any changes are implemented.[46]

Under all circumstances, the public agency placing the child in the private facility retains responsibility to insure compliance with the IEP requirement.[47] As discussed in detail elsewhere,[48] if the child is unilaterally placed in a private facility by the parents, the public agency still retains significant responsibilities under IDEA for providing special education and related services. One of the continuing

---

43. 34 C.F.R. § 300.348(a)(1); *see also* 20 U.S.C. 20 U.S.C. § 1413(a)(4)(B).

44. 34 C.F.R. § 300.348(a)(2); *see also* 20 U.S.C. § 1413(a)(4)(B); W.G. v. Target School Dist. No. 23 Bd. Of Trustees, _____ F. Supp. _____ , 1991 WL 333445 (D. Mont. 1991) *aff'd,* _____ F.2d _____ , 1992 WL 67214 (9th Cir. 1992).

45. 34 C.F.R. § 300.348(b)(1); *see also* 20 U.S.C. § 1413(a)(4)(B).

46. 34 C.F.R. § 300.348(b)(2). *See* McKenzie v. Smith, 771 F.2d 1527 (D.C. Cir. 1985); *see also* 20 U.S.C. § 1413(a)(4)(B).

47. 34 C.F.R. § 300.348(c); *see also* 20 U.S.C. § 1413 (a)(4)(b).

48. See § 8.10.

responsibilities is insuring the development of an IEP and insuring it implemen-tation.[49]

As stated earlier, federal law requires development of an IEP and participation of a representative of the private placement at the development of the IEP before the child is actually placed in the private facility.[50] Educational placements, how-ever, must be based on an existing IEP.[51] How do you reconcile the requirement not to decide a placement prior to development of the IEP with the requirement that the private school participate before placement in the private facility?

At least one court has simply stated that when a child is being moved from a public facility to a private facility (but not from private to a public facility) there is simply an exception to the general rule that a placement decision cannot be made prior to development of the IEP.[52]

At least two alternative reconciliations of the apparently conflicting provisions are, however, feasible. It should be kept in mind with regard to both of these interpretations, as well as the theory that there is an exception, that the overriding concern with reconciling the two provisions is to protect against a premature, unilateral decision by either the parent or the school personnel. To insure mean-ingful participation, the IEP must be developed with the parents and a placement decision must be made after that participation. To allow the placement decision to be made and then to develop an IEP to support that position would undermine the entire thrust of IDEA, allowing, for example, a school to decide to place the child in a program it already had available and then to develop an IEP to justify that placement. Instead the process must be to develop the IEP and then see if the school has the program or the capacity to develop the program to meet the IEP.

With this in mind, it is the usual case that at some point during the discussions between the parents and school officials, it becomes apparent that a private facility is required. If both the parents and the school system agree that it is likely that a private facility will be needed, or that it is at least a real possibility, it would be permissible to invite a representative of the private facility to participate in the IEP meeting.

If the parents and school do not come to an agreement to include the private parties before final development of the IEP, the option available is to develop the IEP and then make a placement decision. If the decision is that the IEP can only be implemented in a private facility, then a second IEP meeting, involving the private facility can be called.

7.10 Handling Disputes over the IEP

If the parents and LEA are unable to agree as to the contents of the IEP, the LEA will draft the document as best it can, and then each party has the oppor-

49. 34 C.F.R. § 300.341, 349; *see also* 20 U.S.C. §§ 1412 (4), 1413 (a) (4) (B).
50. 34 C.F.R. § 300.348(c); *see also* 20 U.S.C. § 1413(a)(4)(B).
51. 34 C.F.R. § 300.552. See discussion § 7.4; *see also* 20 U.S.C. § 1412(5) (B).
52. Spielberg v. Henrico County Pub. Schools, 853 F.2d 256 (4th Cir. 1988).

tunity to resolve the dispute as with other disputes, by way of the due process mechanism or one of the alternative dispute resolution procedures.[53] Because of the stay-put provision,[54] the pre-existing IEP, if there is one, remains in force during the pendency of due process proceedings. The party seeking to change the *status quo*, therefore, is the party likely to file for the due process hearing over the dispute. It is conceivable, however, that the other party might file for a due process hearing. For example, if the school system fails to abide by the stay-put provision and refuses to continue to educate the child under the pre-existing IEP, the parent may have no choice but to seek a due process hearing.[55]

Creation of new IEP by the school system during the pendency of due process proceedings instituted by the parents, does not moot the action. The court may still hear the law suit, even though the IEP has been superseded because the problem is capable of repetition, yet avoiding review.[56]

7.11 IEP Checklist

_____ The IEP must be developed at least annually.

_____ Appropriate agency responsible for IEP development

_____ Contains

_____ statement of the child's present level of educational performance;

_____ statement of the annual educational goals as well as short-term objectives related to those goals;

_____ a statement of the specific educational and related services to be provided, including the extent to which the child will be serviced in regular educational programs;

_____ Identification of transition services, including interagency responsibilities, beginning no later than age 16;

_____ the date the services will begin as well as the expected duration of the services; and

_____ "appropriate objective criteria and evaluation procedures and schedules" to allow at least an annual determination of whether the short-term objectives are being met.

---

53. Doe v. Maher, 793 F.2d 1470 (9th Cir. 1986) *aff'd on other grounds, sub nom* Honig v. Doe, 484 U.S. 305 (1988). See chapter 11 for a discussion of the due process procedure and chapter 17 for alternatives to the due process procedure.

54. See § 11.7.

55. 20 U.S.C. § 1415(e) (3); 34 C.F.R. § 300.513(a). *See* Honig v. Doe, 484 U.S. 305, 323 (1988) (change in IEP required before long term suspension); Christopher W. v. Portsmouth School Committee, 877 F.2d 1089, 1097 (1989) (change in IEP required before suspension); DeLeon v. Susquehanna Community School Dist., 747 F.2d 149, 151 n.3 (1984) (presence of related service in IEP determines whether service required by stay-put provision); Tokarcik v. Forest Hills School Dist., 665 F.2d 443, 453 (3rd Cir. 1982) (stay-put provision "at a minimum guarantees that the most recently agreed upon program cover any unresolved [disputes].").

56. DeVries v. Spillane, 853 F.2d 264 (4th Cir. 1988).

_____ Initial IEP must be developed within thirty calendar days following a determination that the child requires special education and related services.

_____ Subsequent IEPs must be developed on at least an annual basis.

_____ IEP must be "implemented as soon as possible following" its development.

_____ Placement must be based on an existing IEP,

_____ Usually a change in placement will have been preceded by an IEP meeting.

_____ Participants in the meeting must include:

_____ a representative of the public agency, other than the child's teacher, who is qualified to supervise or provide special education;

_____ the child's teacher;

_____ one or both of the parents of the child.

_____ the child may be present where appropriate,

_____ "[o]ther individuals at the discretion of the parent or agency [may be present]."

_____ In the initial IEP meeting, participants in the meeting must also include a member of the evaluation team or some other person "who is knowledgeable about the evaluation procedures used with the child."

_____ If discussing transition services, participants must include student and representative of agency responsible or paying for the transition services.

_____ Parental Notice

_____ purpose

_____ time

_____ location

_____ who will be in attendance

_____ Held at a mutually convenient time.

_____ Alternate form of participation such as a teleconference if parents can not attend.

_____ Where parents refuse, must have a detailed set of records establishing its attempts to schedule a mutually convenient time and place.

_____ Steps to "insure that the parent understands the proceedings . . . including arranging for an interpreter for parents who are deaf or whose native language is other than English.

_____ Copy of IEP provided at the request of the parent.

_____ Goals describe what a child is expected to accomplish by the end of the next year.

_____ Objectives are measurable, intermediate steps leading to the accomplishment of the annual goal.

_____ Goals related to the child's present level of educational performance.

_____ Objectives must be rationally connected to the goals.

_____ Present level of performance stated in objective terms.

_____ Direct relationship between the annual goals and the child's present level of performance.

_____ Private School IEPs

_____ Initial IEP must be developed with the participation of representatives from the private facility.

_____ Subsequent IEP, subsequent IEP meetings may, at the discretion of the public school, be initiated and conducted by the private school.

_____ Public agency must still insure that the parents participate in decisions concerning the IEP and agree to any changes in the program before any changes are implemented.

_____ Under all circumstances, the public agency placing the child in the private facility retains responsibility to insure compliance with the IEP requirement.

Chapter 8

Placement

8.1 Placement Criteria

As discussed in more detail elsewhere,[1] if the agency fails to provide an appropriate placement, the parent may unilaterally place the child and seek reimbursement from the agency.[2] Placement decisions are to be based on an existing Individual Education Program (IEP),[3] and therefore must be made after the development of the IEP. A decision to place a child prior to developing an IEP upon which to base that decision constitutes a violation of IDEA and can lead to a finding that the decision would not provide the child with a FAPE.[4]

In making the placement decision, the LEA must draw on a wide variety of information, including "aptitude and achievement tests, teacher recommendations, physical condition, social or cultural background, and adaptive behavior …"[5] The sources of information must be documented.[6]

Section 504 has equivalent criteria.[7]

8.2 Location/Least Restrictive Environment/ Mainstreaming

IDEA contains several requirements governing the location of the educational placement. The placement must be as close to home as possible,[8] and unless the IEP requires to the contrary, the child should be placed in the school where he or she would be placed were he or she not disabled.[9] There is, however, no absolute

---

1. See § 14.4.
2. *See, e.g.,* Cochran v. District of Columbia, 660 F. Supp. 314 (D.D.C. 1987) (unilateral placement by parents was justified by LEA's failure to recommend a placement and the fact that private school was existing placement).
3. 34 C.F.R. § 300.552(a)(2); *see also* 20 U.S.C. § 1412(5)(B).
4. Spielberg v. Henrico County Pub. Schools, 853 F.2d 256 (4th Cir. 1988).
5. 34 C.F.R. § 300.533(a)(1); *see* 20 U.S.C. § 1412(5)(C).
6. 34 C.F.R. § 300.533(a)(2); *see also* 20 U.S.C. § 1412(5)(C).
7. 34 C.F.R. 104.35(c).
8. 34 C.F.R. § 300.552(a)(3); *see* 20 U.S.C. § 1412(5)(B). The same requirement exists under Section 504. 34 C.F.R. 104.34(a).
9. 34 C.F.R. § 300.552(c); 20 U.S.C. 1412(5)(B).

right to have the child placed in the school closest to home. If the neighborhood school will not provide a FAPE, the agency may place the child at a more distant location.[10] Further, courts have held, however, that cost can be a factor in deciding to place a child in an otherwise appropriate placement further away from home. For example, in *Barnett v. Fairfax County School Board*,[11] the court held that "[t]he school system is not required to duplicate the Cued Speech program for [one student] merely because there exists a high school which is slightly closer to his house or one he would rather attend."[12]

Perhaps most importantly, IDEA requires that "to the maximum extent appropriate," whether the child is in a public or private facility, the placement must educate the child with children who do not have a disability.[13] The requirement of placing children with disabilities with children without to the maximum extent possible applies to non-academic and extra-curricular activities, for example, lunch and recess, as well as academic activities.[14]

Unfortunately, there has been some confusion over this requirement, perhaps generated in part by two related, though different, short-hand characterizations. Quite often, among both courts and commentators, this requirement is referred to indiscriminately as either a least restrictive environment (LRE) requirement or a mainstreaming requirement. IDEA's requirement is an LRE requirement. The child is to be educated in an environment which, given the child's individual educational needs, provides the fewest restrictions not encountered by the non-disabled student. One aspect of this LRE requirement is a presumption that this placement be with children without disabilities in regular classrooms, that is, mainstreamed. The requirement is for the least restrictive environment in which educational progress can be made.[15] Mainstreaming is a presumptive requirement under IDEA, and the agency has the burden of establishing that any mainstreamed placement will not provide a FAPE.[16]

The LRE requirement mandates that children be educated outside the regular classroom "only when the nature or severity of the disability is such that education in regular classes with the use of supplementary aids and services cannot be

---

10. DeVries v. Fairfax County School Bd., 882 F.2d 876 (4th Cir. 1989); A.W. v. Northwest R-1 School Dist., 813 F.2d 158, 163 (8th Cir.), *cert. denied*, 484 U.S. 847 (1987) (child could receive only minimal benefit from local placement; in addition, cost of hiring staff was high); Johnston v. Ann Arbor Pub. Schools, 569 F. Supp. 1502 (E.D. Mich. 1983)

11. 927 F.2d 146 (4th Cir. 1991).

12. *Id.* at 151, 153. *See also* Schuldt v. Mankato Indep. School Dist. No. 77, 937 F.2d 1357 (8th Cir. 1991)(no absolute right to place in school nearest home); A.W. v. Northwest R-1 School Dist., 813 F.2d 158, 163 (8th Cir.), *cert. denied*, 484 U.S. 847 (1987) (distance one factor); Pinkerton v. Moye, 509 F. Supp. 107 (W.D. Va. 1981) (6 miles away was acceptable because of small disabled student population).

13. 34 C.F.R. § 300.550(b)(1); *see* 20 U.S.C. §§ 1412(5)(B), 1414(a)(1)(C)(iv). The same requirement exists under Section 504. 34 C.F.R. § 104.34(a).

14. 34 C.F.R. § 300.553; *see* 20 U.S.C. § 1412(5)(B). *See e.g.* Liscio v. Woodland Hills School Dist., 734 F. Supp. 689 (W.D. Pa. 1989), *aff'd*, 902 F.2d 1561 (3d Cir. 1990). The same requirement exists under Section 504. 34 C.F.R. § 104.34(b).

15. Board of Educ. v. Diamond, 808 F.2d 987 (3d Cir. 1986).

16. Thornock v. Boise Indep. School Dist., 556 Educ. Handicapped L. Rep. (CRR) 477, 482–483 (Dist. Ct. Idaho 1985), *aff'd*, 115 Idaho 466, 767 P.2d 1241 (1988), *cert. denied*, 490 US 1068 (1989).

achieved satisfactorily."[17] In selecting the LRE, there is an affirmative obligation that consideration be given to any potential harmful effect on the child or on the quality of services he or she needs.[18] It is clear, therefore, that placement in the least restrictive environment is not an absolute right. Merely because the placement is private, or even residential, does not mean it does not meet the LRE requirements of IDEA. The LRE requirement must be viewed in light of the individual needs of the child.[19] The individual nature of these decisions cannot be overemphasized. Indeed, children with very similar situations quite often receive very different determinations.[20] Also, as with the goal of placing the child close to home, cost has been considered as a factor to balance against mainstreaming.[21]

Courts, however, do approach the decision as to when segregation is appropriate from different perspectives. The Sixth Circuit and Second Circuit have adopted a test providing great deference to the local agency. As stated by the Sixth Circuit:

> The Act does not require mainstreaming in every case but its requirement that mainstreaming be provided to the *maximum* extent appropriate indicates a strong congressional preference. The proper inquiry is whether a proposed placement is appropriate under the Act... In a case where the segregated facility is considered superior, the court should determine whether the services which make the placement superior could be feasibly provided in a non-segregated setting. If they can, the placement in the segregated school would be inappropriate under the Act.[22]

The Fifth Circuit specifically rejected this test, and articulated the test as:

> First, we ask whether education in the regular classroom, with the use of supplemental aids and services can be achieved satisfactorily for a given

---

17. 34 C.F.R. § 300.550(b)(2); 20 U.S.C. § 1412(5)(B); *see* 20 U.S.C. § 1414(a)(1)(C)(iv); Lachman v. Illinois State Bd. of Educ., 852 F.2d 290 (7th Cir.) *cert. denied* 488 U.S. 925 (1988). *See also* A.W. v. Northwest R-1 School Dist., 813 F.2d 158, 163 (8th Cir.), *cert. denied*, 484 U.S. 847 (1987); Mark v. Grant Wood Area Educ. Agency, 795 F.2d 52, 54 (8th Cir. 1986), *cert. denied*, 480 U.S. 936 (1987); Doe v. Maher, 793 F.2d 1470, 1483 (9th Cir. 1986) *aff'd. sub nom.* Honig v. Doe, 484 U.S. 305 (1988); Taylor v. Board of Educ., 649 F. Supp. 1253, 1258 (N.D.N.Y. 1986); Johnston v. Ann Arbor Pub. Schools, 569 F. Supp. 1502, 1508 (E.D. Mich. 1983)

18. 34 C.F.R. § 300.552(d); *see* 20 U.S.C. § 1412(5)(B).

19. Mark v. Grant Wood Area Educ. Agency, 795 F.2d 52 (8th Cir. 1986) (mainstreaming requirement does not always require placement in regular classroom); Geis v. Board of Educ., 774 F.2d 575 (3d Cir. 1985); Wilson v. Marana Unified School Dist., 735 F.2d 1178 (9th Cir. 1984); Taylor v. Board of Educ., 649 F. Supp. 1253 (N.D.N.Y. 1986).

20. *Compare* Bonadonna v. Cooperman, 619 F. Supp. 401 (D.N.J. 1985) (hearing impaired student should be mainstreamed where she was capable of functioning at above-average intellectual level, adjusted to regular classroom, and was learning. LEA could transport to resource program for supplemental instruction) *with* Visco v. School Dist., 684 F. Supp. 1310 (W.D. Pa. 1988) (private school for hearing impaired was least restrictive because move to public school would interrupt acquiring needed language skills).

21. A.W. v. Northwest R-1 School Dist., 813 F.2d 158 (8th Cir.), *cert. denied*, 484 U.S. 158 (1987) (citing *Roncker*, court held that cost was a legitimate factor to consider in balancing mainstreaming requirement. Court held school could place child in a state school); Roncker v. Walter, 700 F.2d 1058, 1063 (6th Cir. 1983); Pinkerton v. Moye, 509 F. Supp. 107 (W.D. Va. 1981) (close to home must be balanced against financial capacity of public agency).

22. Roncker v. Walter, 700 F.2d 1058, 1063 (6th Cir. 1983); *see also* Briggs v. Board of Educ., 882 F.2d 688 (2d Cir. 1989).

child ... If it cannot and the school intends to provide special education or
to remove the child from regular education, we ask, second, whether the
school has mainstreamed the child to the maximum extent appropriate.[23]

The Fifth Circuit Court then went on to say that various factors would inform
the decision, including, but not limited to, whether the LEA has made attempts
to accommodate the child with supplementary aids and services, whether the
child will receive educational benefit from regular education, the child's overall
experience in the mainstreamed environment, and what impact the child's presence
will have on the other children in the regular classroom.[24] The Fifth Circuit test
has been adopted by the Eleventh Circuit.[25]

The issue of impact of the disabled student's presence on the regular education
students has been an emotional topic. Two basic concerns arise. The student may
be either disruptive, may take so much attention from the instructor that the
instructor will ignore the needs of other children, or may pose a risk of physical
harm to other children. The Comment to IDEA regulations correctly points out
that where a child is "so disruptive in a regular classroom that the education of
other students is significantly impaired, the needs of the handicapped child cannot
be met in that environment. Therefore, regular placement would not be appropriate to his or her needs."[26]

Dealing with the child requiring an inordinate amount of the teacher's time
requires an inquiry into whether sufficient supplemental aids and services have
been provided. Merely because the child dominates the teacher's time is, by itself,
insufficient to remove the child from the classroom. The provision of a teaching
assistant or aide, for example, may solve the problem.[27] If, however, the time
commitment still interferes with the educational benefit others are receiving,
removal from the classroom may be appropriate.[28]

Risk of physical harm to other children has arisen mostly in the area of AIDS
and hepatitis. The general rule, whether dealing with AIDS[29] or hepatitis B,[30]
appears to be that absent a finding that a particular child poses a specific threat,
the child may not be segregated; the theoretical possibility of harm to others is
insufficient.

The LRE requirement must also be considered if the parents are placed in the
position of having to make a unilateral placement because of the agency's failure
to provide a FAPE. Where the parents unilaterally placed a child in a private
facility, a New Jersey court held the placement was appropriate and reimbursement

---

23. Daniel R.R. v. Texas Bd. of Educ., 874 F.2d 1036, 1048 (5th Cir. 1989).

24. *Id.* at 1048–50; *see also* 34 C.F.R. § 104.34(a).

25. Greer v. Rome City School Dist., 950 F.2d 688 (11th Cir. 1991) withdrawn on other grounds
956 F.2d 1025 (1992).

26. 34 C.F.R. § 300.552 cmt. (quoting 34 C.F.R. Part 104 app., para. 24); *see also* 20 U.S.C.
§ 1412(5)(B).

27. Daniel R. R. v. Texas Bd. of Educ., 874 F.2d 1036, 1049 (5th Cir. 1989).

28. *Id.* at 1049–50.

29. Martinez v. School Bd., 861 F.2d 1502 (11th Cir. 1988); Thomas v. Atascadero Unified
School Dist., 662 F. Supp. 376 (C.D. Cal. 1987); District 27 Community School Bd. of Educ. v.
Board of Educ., 130 Misc. 2d 398, 502 N.Y.S.2d 325 (N.Y. Sup. Ct. 1986).

30. Community High School Dist. 155 v. Denz, 124 Ill. App. 3d 129, 463 N.E.2d 998 (1984).

was ordered for the academic program, but not for the residential costs because the placement was not in the least restrictive environment.[31]

8.3 Annual Review of Placement Required

After the initial placement decision, the placement decision must be reviewed at least annually.[32]

8.4 Change in Placement

A placement decision must be based on an existing IEP, therefore, any change in placement must be supported by the existing IEP. If the IEP does not support a change in placement, an IEP meeting must be conducted before initiating any change.[33] Having determined that a change in placement is appropriate, before an LEA can change a placement, written notice must be given to the parents of the agency's intent to change placement.[34] The extent of the notice required is covered by the general regulatory provision on notice[35] and contains the requirement that the notice describe "the action proposed or refused by the agency, an explanation of why the agency proposes or refuses to take the action, and a description of any options the agency considered and the reasons why those options were rejected."[36] "Boilerplate language" on forms containing only general descriptions of the proposed placement without discussion of options considered for the individual child is inadequate notice.[37]

Although not required under IDEA, individual states may require parental consent prior to a change in placement.[38]

What constitutes a change in placement has been subject to some debate. Where the change does not significantly alter the educational experience of the child it has been held not to constitute a change in placement.[39]

Section 504 requires an evaluation prior to any significant change in placement.[40]

---

31. Lascari v. Board of Educ., 116 N.J. 30, 560 A.2d 1180 (1989).

32. 34 C.F.R. § 300.552(a)(1); *see* 20 U.S.C. § 1414(a)(5).

33. See 34 C.F.R. § 300.552(a)(2); *see also* 20 U.S.C. § 1412(5)(B).

34. 34 C.F.R. § 300.504(a)(1); *see* 20 U.S.C. § 1415(b)(1)(C), D *But see* Brookline School Committee v. Golden, 628 F. Supp. 113 (D. Ma. 1986) (written notice not required where parents had actual notice of intent to change placement).

35. See chapter 9.

36. 34 C.F.R. § 300.505(a)(2); *see also* 20 U.S.C. § 1415(b)(1)(D).

37. McKenzie v. Smith, 771 F.2d 1527 (D.C. Cir. 1985).

38. See 9.5.

39. Brookline School Committee v. Golden, 628 F. Supp. 113 (D. Mass. 1986) (change in day care from 2 to 3 days, with substitution of day care program on two other days not a change in placement). The United States Supreme Court has held that suspension of a child for more than 10 days constitutes a change in placement. See 10.1

40. 34 C.F.R. § 104.35(c).

8.5 Placement Decision-Makers

The placement decision "is made by a group of persons, including persons knowledgeable about the child, the meaning of the valuation data, and the placement options ..."[41] Exclusion of health care personnel from a placement decision does not violate either IDEA or § 504, since the regulations only require a qualified group of people.[42]

8.6 Extended School Day and Year

If required in order for the child to receive educational benefit, the agency must provided extended school days and an extended school year.[43]

What must be shown to justify an extended school year has been subject to some debate. In *Rettig v. Kent City School District*,[44] the court held that the parents must show that the child would suffer "significant regression of skills or knowledge."[45] This language has been interpreted as an empirical test requiring a showing of prior regression.[46]

This "empirical" approach, however, has been criticized and rejected as requiring a "Hobson's Choice" in which the parents must choose to either allow their child to regress to establish empirical data or to provide the extended school year themselves and forgo any possibility of proving regression.[47] As a result, the empirical approach has been modified by most courts to provide "where there is no such empirical data available, need may be proven by expert opinion based upon a professional individual assessment."[48]

8.7 Continuum of Placements Required

The LEA is required to "insure that a continuum of alternative placements is available to meet the needs of children with disabilities for special education and

---

41. 34 C.F.R. § 300.533(a)(3); *see also* 20 U.S.C. § 1412(5)(C); *see generally* S-1 v. Turlington, 635 F.2d 342 (5th Cir. 1981), *cert. denied*, 454 U.S. 1030 (1981). Section 504 requires the equivalent. 34 C.F.R § 104.35(a).

42. Hessler v. State Bd. of Educ. of Maryland, 553 Educ. Handicapped L. Rep. (CRR) 262 (D. Md. 1981), *aff'd*, 700 F.2d 134 (4th Cir. 1983).

43. Alamo Heights Indep. School Dist. v. State Bd. of Educ., 790 F.2d 1153 (5th Cir. 1986); Battle v. Pennsylvania, 629 F.2d 269 (3d Cir. 1980; Georgia Ass'n. of Retarded Citizens v. McDaniel, 511 F. Supp. 1263 (N.D. Ga. 1981), *aff'd*, 716 F.2d 1565 (11th Cir. 1983).

44. 539 F. Supp. 768, 778 (N.D. Ohio 1981), *aff'd in part vacated in part on other grounds*, 720 F.2d 463 (6th Cir. 1983).

45. *Id.* at 778–779.

46. *See* Cordrey v. Euckert, 917 F.2d 1460 (6th Cir. 1990).

47. Polk v. Central Susquehanna Intermed. Unit 16, 853 F.2d 171, 184 (3d Cir. 1988); Alamo Heights Indep. School Dist. v. State Bd. of Educ., 790 F.2d 1153, 1156–58 (5th Cir. 1986).

48. Cordrey, 917 F.2d at 1472; *see also* Johnson v. Independent School Dist. No. 4, 921 F.2d 1022 (10th Cir. 1990); Alamo Heights Indep. School Dist. v. State Bd. of Educ., 790 F.2d 1153, 1156–58 (5th Cir. 1986).

related services."[49] The continuum that must be available includes "instruction in regular classes, special classes, special schools, home instruction, and instruction in hospitals and institutions ... "[50] In addition, the school must insure that "supplementary services (such as resource room or itinerant instruction) be provided in conjunction with regular class placement."[51]

The continuum must be sufficient to allow the implementation of each child with a disability's IEP.[52] Because the school may be unable to meet the child's IEP goals and objectives in a publicly operated facility, the continuum of placements must include the possibility of private placements as well as public placements.[53] Further, a school must have authority to contract with out-of-state facilities in order to find an appropriate facility.[54] There is no obligation, however, to consider whether a particular private school is an appropriate placement if the public agency has an appropriate program.[55]

State and local educational agencies retain significant responsibility for children placed in private school settings. In fact, for a child placed or referred to a private school by the educational agency, the public agency remains ultimately responsible for insuring that the child receives special education and related services in conformity with the student's IEP[56] Even for children unilaterally placed in a private school, the school system retains significant responsibility for providing special education and related services.[57]

8.8 Residential School Placements

As with all placement decisions, the decision whether a child requires the structure and consistency of a residential program depends on the educational needs as defined by the IEP. Generally, a residential program is required when the structure and consistency of a 24 hour program is necessary in order for the child to learn,[58] or where the child has the inability to generalize learning across environments.[59]

As discussed elsewhere, where a child requires a residential program for medical rather than educational reasons, the educational agency is responsible only for

---

49. 34 C.F.R. § 300.551(a); *see also* 20 U.S.C. § 1412(5)(B).

50. 34 C.F.R. § 300.551(b)(1); *see also* 20 U.S.C. § 1412(5)(B).

51. 34 C.F.R. § 300.552(b)(2); *see also* 20 U.S.C. § 1412(5)(B).

52. 34 C.F.R. § 300.552(b); *see also* 20 U.S.C. § 1412(5)(B).

53. 34 C.F.R. § 300.554; *see* 20 U.S.C. § 1412(5)(B). The same requirement exists under Section 504. 34 C.F.R. § 104.33(b)(3).

54. Dubner v. Ambach, 74 A.D.2d 949, 426 N.Y.S.2d 164 (1980).

55. Hessler v. State Bd. of Educ. 700 F.2d 134 (4th Cir. 1983).

56. 34 C.F.R. § 300.401(a)(1); *see* 20 U.S.C. § 1413(a)(4)(B).

57. 34 C.F.R. § 300.451; *see* 20 U.S.C. § 1413(a)(4)(A).

58. Diamond v. McKenzie, 770 F.2d 225 (D.C. Cir. 1985); Colin K. v. Schmidt, 715 F.2d 1 (1st Cir. 1983); Abrahamson v. Hershman, 701 F.2d 223 (1st Cir. 1983); Kruelle v. New Castle County School Dist., 642 F.2d 687 (3d Cir. 1981). The same requirement exists under Section 504. 34 C.F.R. § 104.33(c)(3).

59. Board of Educ. v. Diamond, 808 F.2d 987, 992 (3d Cir. 1986).

the educational portion of the program.[60] Where, however, the social, emotional, medical and educational needs of the child are so interrelated that it is not possible to separate them, the agency will be responsible for the entire cost of the program.[61]

8.9 Private Placement by LEA in General

As part of the continuum of educational placements required to be available,[62] the LEA must include private educational programs,[63] when the LEA is unable to provide a free appropriate education within the public school system.[64]

Where the public agency places a child in a private facility, the public agency remains ultimately responsible for insuring the child receives special education and related services in conformity with the student's IEP.[65]

Where the educational authority has placed a child in a private educational setting as a means of providing the child with the required FAPE, the public agency retains responsibility for insuring the child receives special education and related services in conformity with the child's IEP.[66] The agency must also involve a representative of the private school in the development of an IEP.[67]

The public agency is responsible for insuring, in fact, that the IEP meets all the criteria that would be required were the child placed in the public school.[68] For example, the LEA must insure for parental participation in developing the IEP, and appropriate development of IEP goals and objectives.[69] This is true even if the child is placed outside the district, or even outside the state.[70]

The placing agency must also insure that the private education be provided at no cost to the parents,[71] and that the child placed has all the rights of a child

---

60. See § 5.2.2; see, e.g., Clovis Unified School Dist. v. California Office of Admin. Hearings, 903 F.2d 635 (9th Cir. 1990)(psychiatric hospitalization for medical, not educational reasons).

61. McKenzie v. Smith, 771 F.2d 1527, 1534 (D.C. Cir. 1985); Kruelle v. New Castle County School Dist., 642 F.2d 687 (3d Cir. 1981).

62. 34 C.F.R. § 300.551; see also 20 U.S.C. § 1412(5)(B).

63. 34 C.F.R. § 300.126; see 20 U.S.C. § 1412(2)(A); Abrahamson v. Hershman, 701 F.2d 223, 227 (1st Cir. 1983); Gladys J. v. Pearland Indep. School Dist., 520 F. Supp. 869, 875 (S.D. Texas 1981).

64. See, e.g., Abrahamson v. Hershman, 701 F.2d 223 (1st Cir. 1983); Hall v. Vance County Bd. of Educ., 744 F.2d 629, 635–636 (4th Cir. 1985) ("no single substantive standard can describe...Clearly, [however], Congress did not intend that a school system could discharge its duty under the EAHCA by providing a program that produces some minimal academic achievement, no matter how trivial.").

65. 34 C.F.R. § 300.401(a)(1); see 20 U.S.C. § 1413(a)(4)(B); Antkowiak v. Ambach, 838 F.2d 635 (2d Cir. 1988).

66. 34 C.F.R. § 300.401(a)(1); see 20 U.S.C. § 1413(a)(4)(B).

67. 34 C.F.R. § 300.348(a)(2); see also 20 U.S.C. § 1413(a)(4)(B).

68. 34 C.F.R. § 300.401(a)(1); see 20 U.S.C. § 1413(a)(4)(B).

69. 34 C.F.R. § 300.401 (referring to 34 C.F.R. §§ 300.340-300.350); see also 20 U.S.C. § 1413(a)(4)(B).

70. Werner Inquiry, 211 Educ. Handicapped L. Rep. (CRR) 289 (EHA, Nov. 25, 1982).

71. 34 C.F.R. § 300.401(a)(2); see also 20 U.S.C. § 1413(a)(4)(B).

who is directly served by the public agency.[72] Consistent with these obligations to privately placed students, the SEA is required to monitor LEA compliance with these requirements through such things as written reports, on-site visits and parent questionnaires.[73]

8.9.1 Requirements for Private Facilities Where LEA Places Child

Where the LEA places a child to meet its obligation to provide a free appropriate education, the private placement must meet the standards that apply to state and local educational agencies.[74] The SEA must provide private placements with applicable standards[75] and provide the private placements with an opportunity to participate in the development and revision of state standards that apply to them.[76] LEA record requirements apply to private schools.[77]

The state may limit private school placement to those schools which are state-approved.[78] Title VI prohibits placement of child in a school which is racially segregated.[79] The Establishment Clause prohibits placement by LEA in a sectarian school.[80]

8.10 Unilateral Private Placement by Parents Where LEA Offers FAPE

Even if the public agency is able to provide a free appropriate education in the public schools, the parents may choose to place the child in a private program. The state and local school systems, however, retain significant responsibility to provide special education and related services. While the LEA need not pay for the general education of the child at the private placement,[81] "[e]ach local educational agency shall provide special education and related services designed to meet the needs of private school children with disabilities residing in the jurisdiction of the agency."[82] The SEA has an obligation to insure compliance with this requirement.[83]

---

72. 34 C.F.R. § 300.401(b). The private placement must meet the standards that apply to state and local educational agencies. *Id.* § 300.401(a)(3); *see also* 20 U.S.C. § 1413(a)(4)(B).

73. 34 C.F.R. § 300.402(a). The SEA must also provide private placements with applicable standards, *id.* § 300.402(b), and provide the private placements with an opportunity to participate in the development and revision of state standards that apply to them, *id.* § 300.402(c); *see also* 20 U.S.C. § 1413(a)(4)(B).

74. 34 C.F.R. § 300.401(a)(3); *see also* 20 U.S.C. § 1413(a)(4)(B).

75. 34 C.F.R. § 300.402(b); *see also* 20 U.S.C. § 1413(a)(4)(B).

76. 34 C.F.R § 300.402(c); *see also* 20 U.S.C. § 1413(a)(4)(B).

77. 20 U.S.C § 1232(g).

78. Tucker v. Bay Shore Union Free School Dist., 873 F.2d 563 (2d Cir. 1989); Antkowiak v. Ambach, 838 F.2d 635 (2d Cir. 1988); Schimmel v. Spillane, 819 F.2d 477 (4th Cir. 1987).

79. Davis Inquiry, 211 Educ. Handicapped L. Rep. (CRR) 09 (EHA Feb. 6, 1978).

80. *See generally* Lemon v. Kurtzman, 403 U.S. 602 (1971).

81. 34 C.F.R. § 300.403(a); *see also* 20 U.S.C. §§ 1412(2)(B), 1415.

82. 34 C.F.R. § 300.452; *see also* 20 U.S.C. §§ 1413(a)(4)(A), 1414(a)(6).

83. 34 C.F.R. § 300.451(a); *see* 20 U.S.C. § 1413(a)(4)(A).

The obligation to provide special education and related services incorporates the requirements of evaluation, eligibility, IEP and the like. Where the parents make a unilateral placement *outside* the state, the home (family) residence of the child has primary responsibility for special education and related services, but funds from the out-of-state LEA *may* be expended for that child.[84] The LEA, however, is apparently not required to send its employees out of state to conduct evaluations.[85]

To the extent that a child unilaterally placed in a private school requires exclusively special education and related services, the public school may be relieved of any obligation to provide education and related services if it has an appropriate program in the public school.[86]

8.10.1 Services Required for Unilateral Private School Placements

In addition to IDEA, the Education Department General Administrative Regulations (EDGAR) impose responsibilities for special education and related service delivery to children placed in private programs.[87] These regulations, therefore, as well as the regulations promulgated under IDEA should be consulted.

Under EDGAR, public agencies must consult with private schools on matters including consideration of which children will receive benefits, how the children's needs will be identified, what benefits will be provided, how the benefits will be provided, and how the provision of services will be evaluated.[88]

The public agencies, under EDGAR, must provide a genuine opportunity for students to participate in special education programs.[89] Services need not be provided at the site of private school, unless necessary to enable the child to benefit.[90] If the educational program takes place away from the private school, the LEA must provide transportation from and back to the private school.[91] Transportation from home to the private school and back is not required.[92]

---

84. Pagano, 211 Educ. Handicapped L. Rep. (CRR) 454 (EHA July 10, 1986); Wing, 211 Educ. Handicapped L. Rep. (CRR) 414 (EHA June 6, 1986); *see also* 2.5.1.

85. Lenhoff v. Farmington Pub. Schools, 680 F. Supp. 921 (E.D. Mich. 1988).

86. Work v. McKenzie, 661 F. Supp. 225 (D.D.C. 1987).

87. 34 C.F.R. §§ 76.651–76.663; *see also* 20 U.S.C. § 1221e-(a)(1).

88. 34 C.F.R. § 76.652(a); *see also* 20 U.S.C. § 1221e-(a)(1).

89. 34 C.F.R. § 76.651(a)(1); *see also* 20 U.S.C. § 1221e-(a)(1).

90. *See, e.g.*, Silber Inquiry, 213 Educ. Handicapped L. Rep. (CRR) 110 (EHA Sept. 22, 1987) (toilet training must be provided on site of private school); School Dist. of North Platte, 507 Educ. Handicapped L. Rep. (CRR) 452 (SEA Neb. April 24, 1986) (absent establishing that the time transporting the child from parochial school to public facilities is harmful).

91. *See, e.g.*, Work v. McKenzie, 661 F. Supp. 225 (D.D.C. 1987); Cunningham Inquiry, 213 Educ. Handicapped L. Rep. (CRR) 125 (EHA 1988). *But see* Prince George's County (Md.) Pub. Schools, 352 Educ. Handicapped L. Rep. (CRR) 226 (OCR June 30, 1986) (504 does not require transportation).

92. Work v. McKenzie, 661 F. Supp. 225 (D.D.C. 1987); McNair v. Cardimmone, 676 F. Supp. 1361 (S.D. Ohio 1987), *aff'd sub nom*, McNair v. Oak Hills Local School Dist. 872 F.2d 153 (6th Cir. 1989).

The programs must be provided in a manner consistent with the number of eligible private school students and their needs.[93] The public agencies must provide comparable benefits to private school children, including quality, scope, and opportunity for participation.[94] The same benefits shall be made available to private school children as public school children where the children have the same needs and are in the same grade, age, or attendance area.[95] Mere inconvenience or cost does not alleviate the public agencies from these responsibilities. For example, public agencies have been ordered to provide toileting and writing assistance to children placed in private schools.[96]

The public agencies may not spend less on the special education and related services of private school children than on public school system children simply because they are not in the public school. EDGAR regulations also require the public agency to spend the same average amount of money on private school children if the average cost of meeting their needs is the same as public school children. If the average cost is different a different amount shall be spent.[97] In other words, the benefits provided should be based on individual needs, not on the placement of the child.

The regulations allow the public agency to hire employees of the private placement to provide the services, if the services are provided outside the employees' normal work day.[98] Further, the services may be provided at the private school site, subject to separation of church and state problems discussed below.[99]

8.11 Separation of Church and State in General

Even when public facilities are adequate to provide a child with a FAPE, some parents choose to place their child in a private institution. In many instances, the private institution selected by parents is a parochial, or church-sponsored, school.[100] While public agencies are not required to fund a unilateral private placement,[101] they do retain a significant responsibility for insuring that handicapped children in parochial schools receive special education and related services.[102] Public school authorities, therefore, may find themselves involved in ac-

---

93. 34 C.F.R. § 76.651(a)(2); *see also* 20 U.S.C. § 1221e-(a)(1).

94. 34 C.F.R. § 76.654(a); *see also* 20 U.S.C. § 1221e-(a)(1).

95. 34 C.F.R. § 76.654(b); *see also* 20 U.S.C. § 1221e-(a)(1).

96. In re Board of Educ., 506 Educ. Handicapped L. Rep. (CRR) 309 (SEA N.Y. 1984).

97. 34 C.F.R. § 76.655; *see also* 20 U.S.C. § 1221e-(a)(1).

98. 34 C.F.R. § 76.660; *see also* 20 U.S.C. § 1221e-(a)(1).

99. 34 C.F.R. § 76.659; *see also* 20 U.S.C. § 1221e-(a)(1).

100. Although parents have the right to place their children in parochial schools, it is constitutionally impermissible for public educational authorities to do so. *See, e.g.,* In re Jennifer M., 508 Educ. Handicapped L. Rep. (CRR) 259 (SEA Wash. Nov. 14, 1986). As this book goes to press the United States Supreme Court is considering many of the issues discussed in this section. Zobrest v. Catalina Foothills, 963 F.2d 1190 (9th Cir. 1992) cert. granted 113 S.Ct. 52 (1992).

101. 34 C.F.R. § 300.403(a); *see also* 20 U.S.C. §§ 1412(2)(B), 1415.

102. 34 C.F.R. §§ 300.403(a), .451-.452; *see also* 20 U.S.C. §§ 1413(a)(4)(A), 1414(a)(6). The regulations specifically provide that state educational agencies are responsible for insuring that IEPs are developed and implemented for parochial school children who receive special education or related services from a public agency. 34 C.F.R. § 300.341(b)(2); *see* 20 U.S.C. §§ 1412(4), (6); *see also* 20 U.S.C. § 1413(a)(4).

tivities which could be construed as state aid to parochial schools, including rendering public services on parochial school grounds. To be constitutional, such government aid must have a secular purpose, its primary effect may not advance nor inhibit religion, and it must not foster excessive government entanglement with religion.[103] If the special education and related services required by IDEA and provided by the local agencies do not meet these standards, then the public authorities, in fulfilling their responsibilities to children with disabilities in parochial schools, may well be running the risk of violating the establishment clause.[104]

While the Supreme Court has considered many types of state plans to aid children in parochial schools, it has never specifically addressed the constitutionality of state aid to children with disabilities in parochial schools under IDEA. However, the Court's recent decision in *Aguilar v. Felton*,[105] which involved a federal program structured similarly to IDEA,[106] provides some indication of the types of services which may be permissible under IDEA and casts serious doubts on the constitutionality of some on-site programs. The Department of Education (DOE), however, has consistently taken the position that *Felton* has no impact on the implementation of programs under IDEA, stating that it would "be presumptuous for educational authorities to extend the *Felton* decision beyond the circumstances clearly addressed by that case."[107] Whether presumptuous or not, educational authorities have continued to express concern about the permissible scope of their involvement with parochial schools, and some state agencies, purporting to follow the Court's decisions in *Felton* and its companion case, *Grand Rapids School District v. Ball*,[108] have adopted policies disallowing on-site programs under IDEA.[109] Such caution on the part of state and local school officials may be well advised. The public agency's obligation to serve handicapped children

---

103. Lemon v. Kurtzman, 403 U.S. 602, 612–13 (1971).

104. **U.S. Const.** amend. I. The amendment provides, in relevant part, "Congress shall make no law respecting an establishment of religion . . . " This prohibition applies to the states as well as the federal government. Cantwell v. Connecticut, 310 U.S. 296, 303 (1940); Everson v. Board of Educ., 330 U.S. 1 (1947).

The establishment clause of the first amendment was enacted in 1789 to guard against state-sponsored religion and the evils that the founding fathers associated with it. The concept of a state religion had been imported from England along with the first colonial charters, and had engendered the same religious intolerance and minority sect persecution that had driven many of America's initial settlers to flee England in the first place.

Lengthy, detailed treatments of the history of the establishment clause abound. See, e.g., Bradley, **Church-State Relationships in America** (1987); Cord, **Separation of Church and State: Historical Fact and Current Fiction** (1982); Levy, **The Establishment Clause: Religion and the First Amendment** (1986); Miller, **The First Liberty: Religion and the American Public** (1987)..

105. 473 U.S. 402 (1985).

106. *Felton* involved Title I of the Elementary and Secondary Educ. act of 1965, which authorized funds to be distributed to states to assist educationally deprived children from low income families. Title I, which was codified at 20 U.S.C. § 2740, has been superseded by Chapter I (containing provisions identical to those at issue in *Felton*), codified at 20 U.S.C. § 3806.

107. Letter from Secretary of Education William J. Bennett to Chief State School Officers (Sept. 12, 1985), *reprinted in* New Inquiry, 211 Educ. Handicapped L. Rep. (CRR) 372 (1985).

108. 473 U.S. 373 (1985).

109. *E.g.*, Goodall v. Stafford County School Bd. , 930 F.2d 363, 372 (4th Cir. 1991); see also Zobrest v. Catalina Foothills, 963 F.2d 1190 (9th Cir. 1992) cert. granted 113 S. Ct. 52 (1992).

in parochial schools under IDEA and EDGAR may often conflict with the Constitution's establishment clause.[110] Although the Supreme Court has not had occasion to address the possible conflicts between IDEA and the establishment clause, it has analyzed many other cases involving state aid to parochial schools. The Court's approach to "parochaid"[111] cases has evolved over the past 40 years from the neutrality rule of *Everson v. Board of Education*[112] to the trifurcated test of *Lemon v. Kurtzman*,[113] which has been applied by the Court since 1971 and which was the basis for the Court's decisions in *Grand Rapids School District v. Ball*[114] and *Aguilar v. Felton*.[115] At each step, the Court has refined and re-defined the parameters of permissible state aid to parochial schools. The evolution of the court's parochaid decisions warrants brief examination, as it provides a conceptual framework by which to analyze the implications of the *Ball* and *Felton* decisions.

The Supreme Court had addressed the issue of state aid to and regulation of parochial schools prior to 1947,[116] but it had not encountered a challenge to such state action on first amendment grounds until *Everson v. Board of Education*.[117] *Everson* involved a New Jersey statute authorizing the reimbursement of parents of public and Catholic school children for bus fares used to transport the children to and from school. The statute was challenged on first amendment grounds by taxpayers who argued that the reimbursements amounted to illegal state support of church schools.[118]

Justice Black, writing for the majority, began his treatment of the issue by indulging in a lengthy historical analysis of the establishment clause in an attempt to discern its original purpose.[119] After invoking the writings of Madison and Jefferson as further proof of the intent behind the clause,[120] the Court advanced the following definition:

---

110. *Id.*

111. This term has been used by some authors to refer to state aid to parochial schools. *See, e.g.*, Comment, *Shared Time Instruction in Parochial Schools: Stretching the Establishment Clause to its Outer Limits*, 89 **Dick. L. Rev.** 175, 175 (1984).

112. 330 U.S. 1 (1947).

113. 403 U.S. 602 (1971).

114. 473 U.S. 373 (1985).

115. 473 U.S. 402 (1985).

116. *See, e.g.*, Cochran v. Board of Educ., 281 U.S. 370 (1930) (unsuccessful due process challenge to a Louisiana statute authorizing the loan of secular textbooks to all school children, including those in parochial schools); Pierce v. Society of Sisters, 268 U.S. 510 (1925) (parents have the right to send their children to a parochial school); Meyer v. Nebraska, 262 U.S. 390 (1922) (state legislatures have a limited right to regulate private schools in the public interest under the police power).

117. 330 U.S. 1 (1947).

118. The statute was also unsuccessfully challenged on due process grounds. *See id.* at 5–8.

119. *See id.* at 8–14. The *Everson* court has been criticized by advocates of state aid to religious schools for its capsuled historical justification for its holding, despite the fact that this particular program was upheld. *See, e.g.*, Bradley, Church-State Relationships in America 2–3 (1987); Cord, Separation of Church and State: Historical Fact and Current Fiction 17 (1982). The *Everson* court, however, was not the first to entertain such historical reflection in an establishment clause opinion. *See, e.g.*, Reynolds v. United States, 98 U.S. 145 (1878).

120. The Court quotes Thomas Jefferson's "Virginia Bill for Religious Liberty" (1786) and James Madison's "Memorial and Remonstrance Against Religious Assessment" (1785). 330 U.S. at 12–13. Although these documents concerned the disestablishment of Virginia's state-sponsored church,

The "establishment of religion" clause means at least this: Neither a state nor the Federal Government can set up a church. Neither can pass laws which aid one religion, aid all religions, or prefer one religion over another... No person can be punished for entertaining or professing religious beliefs or disbeliefs, for church attendance or non-attendance. No tax in any amount, large or small, can be levied to support any religious activities or institutions, whatever they may be called, or whatever form they may adopt to teach or practice religion. Neither a state nor the Federal Government can, openly or secretly, participate in the affairs of any religious organizations or groups and *vice versa*. In the words of Jefferson, the clause against the establishment of religion by law was intended to erect a "wall of separation between church and State."[121]

Later in the opinion, these guidelines were distilled into a single, overriding concept: neutrality. The Court stated that the Establishment Clause "requires the state to be a neutral in its relations with groups of religious believers and non-believers; it does not require the state to be their adversary."[122] Using the neutrality rule, the Court concluded that since the fares of children attending parochial schools were paid directly to parents as part of a general program to help all parents transport their children safely to and from school, regardless of religion, the program did not breach the wall between church and state. To hold otherwise, the Court intimated, might prohibit the state from applying general state law benefits to all citizens without regard to their religious convictions.[123]

It is important to note that had the neutrality approach of *Everson* survived intact to the present day, there would be fewer questions about the validity of state aid to handicapped children in parochial schools under IDEA. IDEA requires states to provide special education and related services to all children, whether in public, private, or parochial schools. Under *Everson*, therefore, withholding IDEA benefits from handicapped children in parochial schools could be construed as denying the child's rights based on the religious convictions of his parents. Since *Everson*, however, the question presented by parochaid cases has not been whether public benefits should be provided to children in parochial schools, but *how* those benefits may be delivered so as not to violate the separation of church and state. This altered focus prompted the Court to begin to develop workable criteria for use in determining the validity of laws under the establishment clause, the culmination of which was the three-part test of *Lemon v. Kurtzman*.[124]

---

not the first amendment, the Court explained that the writings were equally applicable to the first amendment because of their authors' leading roles in the drafting of the amendment. *Id.* at 13 (citing *Reynolds*, 98 U.S. at 165). *But see* Bradley, *supra* note 20, at 3 (calling the Court's analogy an unexplained "historical convergence").

121. 330 U.S. 15–16 (citing *Reynolds*, 98 U.S. at 164).

122. *Id.* at 18. This type of "effect neutral" approach had been used by the Court decades before to defeat a due process challenge to a textbook loan program in Cochran v. Board of Educ., 281 U.S. 370 (1929). Defending the program's assistance to parochial school children, the Court stated that the statute's "interest is education, broadly; its method, comprehensive. Individual interests are aided only as the common interest is safeguarded." 281 U.S. at 375.

123. 330 U.S. at 16.

124. 403 U.S. 602 (1971).

Lemon v. Kurtzman[125] involved establishment clause challenges to programs enacted by Rhode Island and Pennsylvania. The Rhode Island statute authorized salary supplements for teachers of secular subjects in non-public schools. In application, the act's sole beneficiaries were 250 teachers in Catholic schools.[126] Similarly, the Pennsylvania act reimbursed private schools for teacher salaries, texts, and instructional materials in secular subjects, and the majority of schools which received funds were parochial schools.[127] The Court's analysis began with a passing nod to *Everson*, noting that Justice Black had considered the subject matter of that case on the edge of forbidden territory under the establishment clause.[128] Acknowledging that analysis was made even more difficult by the opaque language of the clause, the Court proceeded to look to past decisions for guidance and found that three criteria must be met for a state parochaid program to be constitutional. The legislation must have a secular purpose, must not have the principal or primary effect of advancing or inhibiting religion, and must not cause an excessive entanglement between government and religion.[129]

The Court invalidated both statutes, finding that the programs would foster "excessive and enduring entanglement between state and church."[130] Distinguishing the decision from *Board of Education v. Allen*,[131] the Court explained that the textbooks provided to students in that case could be monitored for religious content,[132] thus ensuring that state money was not spent to advance religion. The

125. 403 U.S. 602 (1971).

126. *Id.* at 608.

127. *Id.* at 609.

128. *Id.* at 612.

129. *Id.* at 612–13.

The Court cited Board of Educ. v. Allen, 392 U.S. 236 (1968), as the source of the secular purpose and effect neutral prongs of its test. *Allen* involved a textbook loan program for all students in grades seven to twelve, whether in public or private school. The *Allen* Court adopted a test first announced in Abingdon School Dist. v. Schempp, 374 U.S. 203 (1963), that "to withstand the strictures of the Establishment Clause there must be a secular legislative purpose and a primary effect that neither advances nor inhibits religion." *Id.* at 222. The Court upheld the program in *Allen*, noting that the *Schempp* Court's citation to *Everson*, which involved a direct aid program similar to the one challenged in *Allen*, made the otherwise difficult *Schempp* test unusually easy to apply. *Id. See Everson*, 330 U.S. 1 (1947). *But see* Norwood v. Harrison, 413 U.S. 455 (1973) (statute which made free textbooks available to students in both public and private schools, regardless of the school's policy on discrimination, held unconstitutional; discussion of inapplicability of *Everson* and *Allen*).

The Court pulled the third prong of the *Lemon* test from Walz v. Tax Commission, 397 U.S. 664 (1970), a case addressing property tax exemptions for religious organizations. After determining that the tax exemptions had a neutral legislative purpose, neither advancing nor inhibiting religion, the *Walz* Court stated that the inquiry could not end there, that there must also be a finding "that the end result— the effect—is not an excessive government entanglement with religion." *Id.* at 674.

Since *Lemon*, the Court has cautioned that the three-pronged test was meant to serve as a framework for constitutional inquiry, not as a limit to it. *See* Meek v. Pittenger, 421 U.S. 349, 358–59 (1975).

130. Lemon, 403 U.S. at 619. The court specified three criteria to be used when determining whether government entanglement with religion is excessive: (1) the purposes and character of the organizations benefitted; (2) the nature of aid provided by the state; (3) the resulting church-state relationship. Another important consideration for the Court is the way in which aid is delivered; direct subsidies seem more likely to violate the clause in the Court's eyes.

131. 392 U.S. 236 (1968).

132. Although the Pennsylvania program also included textbooks for children, the funds were

state could not, however, monitor parochial schools to guarantee that classes taught by state-subsidized teachers were devoid of impermissible religious content without "comprehensive, discriminating, and continuing state surveillance."[133] Such surveillance, said the Court, would result in excessive church-state entanglement. The Court also found that the Pennsylvania program provided funds directly to church schools, another defect which would inevitably result in excessive entanglement through the necessary administration and surveillance which accompany such arrangements.[134]

After *Lemon*, the Court proceeded to apply the three part test to numerous programs providing state aid to parochial schools.[135] While always quick to note that not all programs which confer incidental or indirect benefits on religious institutions are prohibited,[136] the Court rejected numerous aid plans for having the primary effect of advancing religion. For example, the Court struck down statutes authorizing direct money reimbursements to parochial schools for state-mandated expenditures such as testing[137] and maintenance and repair of school facilities,[138] because the statutes did not ensure that the funds would not be used to advance religious interests, such as testing religious themes or repairing buildings used for religious purposes. Similarly, statutes authorizing the purchase or loan of instructional materials and equipment for use in parochial schools were held unconstitutional.[139] The Court found that the integration of religious and

---

furnished to the parochial school for the purchase of the texts. In *Allen*, the texts were purchased by the state and loaned directly to the children.

133. Lemon, 403 U.S. at 619.

134. *Id.* at 621. However, direct funding alone does not automatically render a statute unconstitutional. Committee for Pub. Educ. v. Regan, 444 U.S. 646, 657 (1980).

135. In application, the *Lemon* test has become a two part test. The first prong of the test is quite easy to meet, since the Court accepts without question legislative pronouncements of secular purpose and has never invalidated a statute for lack of a secular legislative purpose. *See, e.g.*, Mueller v. Allen, 463 U.S. 388, 394 (1983) (accepting secular purpose of statute authorizing tax deductions for parents who send children to private and parochial schools on its face); Committee for Pub. Educ. v. Nyquist, 413 U.S. 756, 773 (1973) ("We do not question the propriety, and fully secular content, of New York's interest").

136. *See, e.g.*, Nyquist, 413 U.S. at 771; Meek v. Pittenger, 421 U.S. 349, 359 (1975).

137. Levitt v. Committee for Pub. Educ., 413 U.S. 472 (1973). The New York statute at issue in *Levitt* provided funds for both standardized testing and internally prepared tests. The Court found that most of the testing funded was of the latter type, and it was these tests with which the Court took issue, noting that "no means are available to assure that internally prepared tests are free of religious instruction." *Id.* at 480. Statutes authorizing reimbursement of parochial schools for state-mandated standardized testing, the content of which was determined by public school personnel, have been upheld by the Court. *See* Committee for Pub. Educ. v. Regan, 444 U.S. 646 (1980) (upholding the New York statute enacted in response to *Levitt*); Wolman v. Walter, 433 U.S. 229 (1977).

138. Committee for Pub. Educ. v. Nyquist, 413 U.S. 756 (1973).

139. *See* Meek v. Pittenger, 421 U.S. 329 (1975); Wolman v. Walter, 433 U.S. 229 (1977). While the program invalidated in *Meek* authorized the loan of materials and equipment directly to the parochial schools, the *Wolman* statute presented a different twist. The secular materials and equipment in *Wolman* were loaned to pupils or their parents on request and were merely stored on nonpublic school premises, an arrangement similar to many book lending programs. The Court, however, refused to distinguish *Wolman* from *Meek* on this ground, stating that "[d]espite the technical change in the legal bailee, the program in substance is the same" as the one in *Meek*, and thus still inevitably supports the religious endeavors of the school. 433 U.S. at 250 (citing *Nyquist*,

secular education in parochial schools was so great that, despite the secular nature of the equipment, aid to the educational function of these schools had the primary effect of advancing religion.[140]

The Court found violations of the excessive entanglement prong of its test as well, and also identified the crucial element of "a non-entangling aid program: the ability of the State to identify and subsidize separate secular functions carried out at the school, without on-the-site inspections being necessary to prevent diversion of the funds to sectarian purposes."[141] Thus the provision of remedial and accelerated instruction and guidance counseling on parochial school grounds was found to cause excessive entanglement between government and religion, because the state would be required to monitor teachers and counselors to insure religious neutrality.[142] The Court held that speech, hearing, and psychological diagnostic services, however, would not create excessive entanglement.[143] The services' lack of educational content removed the risk of impermissible fostering of religious views, thereby alleviating the need for the surveillance which causes entanglement.[144] Through the myriad parochaid decisions a common defect emerged in many of the plans rejected as violative of the establishment clause: a lack of state control. State programs failed the effects test when the state could not guarantee the secularity of state aid, thus creating the impermissible effect of advancing religion if the aid was used for sectarian purposes. The excessive entanglement test was violated if a program required monitoring to insure that state aid was used only for secular education, unless the nature of the aid provided by the state removed the risk of advancing religion. Yet the clause was not violated by general aid programs where benefits flowed directly from the state to the student, with little or no sectarian input or control, even if indirect benefits were conferred upon parochial schools.

For this reason, programs under IDEA did not seem to be affected by the Court's decisions in the wake of *Lemon*. State and local educational agencies made special education and related services available directly to the student, not to the parochial school as a whole. Any benefit conferred on the parochial school, therefore, was strictly incidental to the fulfillment of the rights of the child. Thus the state could theoretically guarantee the secularity of state aid provided to children under IDEA, because the state itself expended the funds for the provision

---

413 U.S. 756 (1973) for the proposition that aid to parochial schools cannot be made constitutional simply by indirect delivery).

140. *Meek*, 421 U.S. at 366; *Wolman*, 433 U.S. at 248–49.

141. Roemer v. Maryland Bd. of Pub. Works, 426 U.S. 736, 765 (1976). *Roemer* was the last in a trilogy of cases addressed by the Court in the 1970s dealing with state aid programs to religiously affiliated colleges and universities. The Court consistently held that the institutions of higher learning, unlike religiously affiliated elementary and secondary schools, were not pervasively sectarian, and thus supervision was not required to insure secularity of state funds. *See* Hunt v. McNair, 413 U.S. 734 (1973); Tilton v. Richardson, 403 U.S. 672 (1971).

142. *Meek*, 421 U.S. at 370–72. The *Meek* Court also invalidated a provision relating to speech and hearing services, but did so only because it was not severable from the other portions of the act. *Id.* at 371 n.21; *see Wolman*, 433 U.S. at 242–43 (discussing the Court's actions in *Meek* with regard to speech and hearing services).

143. *Wolman*, 433 U.S. at 244. The *Wolman* Court also upheld the provision of therapeutic services performed on non-public school grounds. *Id.* at 245.

144. *Id.*

of such aid. Monitoring of the type which would create excessive entanglement would be unnecessary. The Court's decisions in *Grand Rapids School District v. Ball* and *Aguilar v. Felton*, however, make it clear that increased state control over aid programs which affect parochial schools is often not enough to prevent a violation of the establishment clause. Indeed, *Ball* and *Felton* show that increased state control over on-site programs at parochial schools can pose additional effects and entanglement problems, some of which cannot be evaded by IDEA.

In *Grand Rapids School District v. Ball*,[145] the Court considered a first amendment challenge to Grand Rapids' Shared Time and Community Education programs. The programs were designed to enrich the core curriculum of nonpublic schools (most of which were religious schools) by providing supplementary classes at public expense. The classes were conducted by state paid teachers[146] in rooms located in and leased from the private schools. Each room leased by the school system was required to be free of religious symbols, and during supplementary class periods a sign announcing that the room was a public school classroom was posted on the door.[147]

The Court was unimpressed with Grand Rapids' efforts to protect its public classes from the religious influence of the sectarian schools, and found the programs violative of the establishment clause in three ways. First, since the teaching took place in the parochial school, the pervasive sectarian atmosphere might influence state paid teachers to subtly indoctrinate the students at public expense. Second, the symbolic union of the state and parochial schools might convey a message to the students or the public at large of state support for religion. Finally, the programs had the effect of subsidizing parochial schools by taking over their responsibility for teaching many secular subjects, thus freeing resources that could be used for religious purposes.[148]

In *Aguilar v. Felton*,[149] decided the same day as *Ball*, the Court addressed New York's implementation of Title I of the Elementary and Secondary Education Act of 1965.[150] Under the Title I program, states used federal funds to assist schools in providing special education services for educationally deprived children from low-income families by implementing programs developed by local educational agencies and approved by state agencies. A majority of the children assisted by

---

145. 473 U.S. 373 (1985).

146. The Shared Time teachers were full-time public employees, while the Community Education teachers were part-time public employees who had full-time jobs at the private school, and commenced teaching for the state at the end of the regular school day. *Id.* at 375–76.

147. The signs read in part "THE ACTIVITY IN THIS ROOM IS CONTROLLED SOLELY BY THE GRAND RAPIDS PUBLIC SCHOOL DISTRICT." *Id.* at 378 n.2.

148. *Id.* at 385, 397.

149. 473 U.S. 402 (1985). For a general criticism of *Felton* see Lines, *The Entanglement Prong of the Establishment Clause and the Needy Child in Private School: Is Distributive Justice Possible?*, 17 J. of L. & Educ. 1 (1988).

150. By the time *Felton* was decided, Title I, which had been codified at 20 U.S.C. § 2701, had been replaced by Chapter I of the Education Consolidation and Improvement Act of 1981, 20 U.S.C. § 3806. The Court noted that the "provisions concerning the participation of children in private schools under Chapter I are virtually identical to those in Title I." 473 U.S. at 404 n.1. Since the Court chose to refer to the program as Title I, for convenience sake the program will be referred to in this discussion by the same name.

the New York programs attended parochial schools.[151] In practice, the Court found the New York program very similar to the ones challenged in *Ball*: classes were taught by public school teachers during the regular school day, on parochial school premises in clearly designated classrooms devoid of religious symbols. In addition, however, New York had instituted a system for monitoring Title I classes in parochial schools in an effort to keep them free of religious content.[152]

Despite the possibility that New York's surveillance system might prevent Title I classes from being used to indoctrinate students at state expense, thus alleviating one concern presented in *Ball*, the Court held the program unconstitutional because the surveillance itself created an excessive entanglement of church and state.[153] The Court explained that the "nature of the interaction between church and state in the administration"[154] of Title I created the fatal elements of entanglement. First, the aid was "provided in a pervasively sectarian environment", making it impossible to separate and subsidize only secular functions.[155] Second, since the aid provided was in the form of teachers, a system of ongoing inspections was necessary to guarantee instructional secularity.[156]

Clearly, the concepts articulated by the Court in *Ball* and *Felton* leave states in a difficult dilemma with regard to aid to parochial school children involving on-site programs. State-paid or provided teachers in parochial schools seem to be an insurmountable stumbling block.[157] The potential for religious indoctrination of students by public teachers is ever-present because of the pervasive sectarian atmosphere of parochial schools, yet the state is forbidden to attempt to control its teachers through surveillance because such efforts would foster entanglement. Additionally, states must avoid two new effects: appearances and indirect subsidies. To avoid the appearances effect, the program must not create the appearance of church-state unity because of the danger of conveying a message of state support for religion to students or the public. Of greater significance, however, is the indirect subsidies effect. Previously, states were required to insure only that public aid was not being wrongfully diverted to sectarian purposes, thus directly subsidizing religious activity. Now states must also examine the extent and nature of the aid to insure that it has not relieved the parochial school of educational duties that it would have otherwise funded itself, thus freeing parochial school money for religious purposes.

8.11.1 Unilateral Placements and Separation of Church and State

Despite the fact that the provision of special education and related services under IDEA often involves on-site teacher instruction, the United States Depart-

---

151. 473 U.S. at 406.

152. *Id.* at 406–07.

153. *Id.* at 409.

154. *Id.*

155. *Id.* at 412.

156. *Id.*

157. The Court had previously addressed the problems presented by aid in the form of teachers in Meek v. Pittenger, 421 U.S. 349 (1975) and Lemon v. Kurtzman, 403 U.S. 602 (1971). However, the Court struck down these programs under the entanglement prong of its test, and did not directly address the effects problems inherent in its analysis until *Ball*.

ment of Education (DOE) has advised state educational authorities that the above limitations do not apply to IDEA. The DOE has "taken the position that [the *Felton*] decision does not apply to other federal programs. Therefore, there is currently no Federal prohibition on on-site services under the EHA for handicapped children."[158] The DOE has affirmed this view as recently as March, 1988.[159]

When one examines the reasoning behind the DOE's blanket statements of non-application, the defects in such a stance become clear. The DOE position was first announced in a letter from Secretary of Education William Bennett to each Chief State School Officer.[160] Secretary Bennett prefaced his analysis by noting that the Supreme Court itself had recognized the difficulty inherent in applying establishment clause decisions to "other cases presenting different facts and circumstances."[161] Therefore it would be "presumptuous," he reasoned, to extend *Felton* "beyond the circumstances clearly addressed by that case."[162] As an example of such a presumptuous extension, Bennett noted that *Felton* could not be used to prohibit the placement of Chapter 2 materials and equipment in parochial schools, since it did not address Chapter 2 materials and equipment. But he then drew an important distinction, stating that "in the case of instructional services provided on private school premises under Chapter 2, *State and local officials should carefully review these instructional services in light of the Felton decision to determine whether they are so similar to those at issue in Felton as to require modification.*"[163] Secretary Bennett then attempted to apply this distinction to IDEA, stating:

> Likewise, the *Felton* decision need not have the effect of prohibiting on-premises services to private school children in all other Federal programs. With respect to programs under . . . the Education of the Handicapped Act, for example, a prohibition of on-premises instructional services may make it impossible to provide the instructional services required [by EAHCA]. The special problems and statutory schemes for these programs were not before the Supreme Court when it decided *Felton*.[164]

This reasoning implies that instructional services under IDEA are so different from those at issue in *Felton* as to make the case inapplicable. Yet the uniqueness of instruction under IDEA did not prevent it from being "essentially the same" for purposes of delivery to parochial schools as instruction under Title I in the eyes of the DOE.[165]

---

158. Hoffman Inquiry, 211 Educ. Handicapped L. Rep. (CRR) 405 (Aug. 13, 1986).

159. Exon Inquiry, 213 Educ. Handicapped L. Rep. (CRR) 125 (Jan. 7, 1988) ("the *Felton* case has no bearing on this problem whatsoever since the has not taken the position that the prohibition against on-premises services is applicable to programs under the [EHA].").

160. Letter from Secretary of Education William J. Bennett to Chief State School Officers (Sept. 12, 1985), *reprinted in* New Inquiry, 211 Educ. Handicapped L. Rep. (CRR) 372 (Nov. 12, 1985).

161. *Id.* at 373.

162. *Id.*

163. *Id.* (emphasis added).

164. *Id.*

165. After *Felton*, the Department of Education announced that "the *Felton* decision is clear in prohibiting the provision of instructional services under [Title I] within private religious school buildings." Letter from Secretary of Education William J. Bennett to Chief State School Officers

Part of the DOE's analysis of *Felton* is correct: the decision prohibits on-site instructional services in the Title I program, and in any other program, such as chapter 2, containing instructional services similar to those at issue in *Felton*. It does not apply to non-instructional services not addressed by the Court that do not present the threats of indirect subsidization, indoctrination, symbolic union, or entanglement. The DOE's error occurs in the application of this interpretation to instructional services under IDEA, which fails to recognize the different types of services and instruction provided by IDEA. By reapplying *Ball* and *Felton* to IDEA with these differences in mind, a clearer, more logical picture of the implications of these decisions emerges.

Obviously a major concern with banning on-site instructional services is that it might make it impossible to provide the special education required by IDEA to parochial school children.[166] Such concerns, however, are perhaps over-stated. Certain on-site programs are likely to be valid while others are clearly prohibited.

Some unique aspects of IDEA stand outside the realm of *Felton*. For example, children with disabilities are entitled to both special education and related services. Related services, defined as "such developmental, corrective, and other supportive services as are required to assist a . . . child to benefit from special education,"[167] are tailored to each . . . child's special needs, and often entail little substantive content. Such highly individualized programs that can only be provided on the parochial school site are much less likely to involve effects and entanglements problems, since they are less instructional in nature and have little educational content which could be used to transmit ideological views to the child. Thus where a child requires toileting and writing assistance, for example, there is a good chance that an on-site provision would be upheld.[168]

(Sept. 12, 1985), *reprinted in* New Inquiry, 211 Educ. Handicapped L. Rep. (CRR) 372 (Nov. 12, 1985)

In 1979, however, state directors of special education received a letter from the DOE concerning the application of IDEA to children unilaterally placed in parochial or private schools. Informal Letter to State Directors of Special Education (August 24, 1979) *reprinted as* DAS Bulletin #39, 203 Educ. Handicapped L. Rep. (CRR) 07 (1979). The letter contained a review of key requirements for the implementation of IDEA, one of which stated:

> *Methods/Settings for Services*. The requirements for serving private school handicapped children under Part B are essentially the same as the requirements for serving private school educationally deprived children under Title I of the ESEA. Thus, if a State's Title I services are provided through a variety of arrangements (e.g., dual enrollment, mobile educational services, and services on private school premises) it would be legally permissible to use the same arrangements under Part B [of IDEA].

Id. The same response had also been issued in March of that year in reply to an inquiry from the Pennsylvania Catholic Conference. *See* Aschenbrenner Inquiry, 211 Educ. Handicapped L. Rep. (CRR) 110, 111 (1979).

State educational authorities, therefore, may have been seeing the logical reverse of the DOE's own parallel, that if on-site services are impermissible under Title I, they are impermissible under IDEA since the two are "essentially the same" for the purposes of delivery. However, these past comparisons were either ignored or overlooked by the DOE when it formulated the current policy on *Felton* and IDEA.

166. *See* New Inquiry, 211 Educ. Handicapped L. Rep. (CRR) 372 (1985).

167. 34 C.F.R. § 300.16; *see also* 20 U.S.C. § 1401(17).

168. *See, e.g.*, In re Board of Educ. of the City School Dist., 506 Educ. Handicapped L. Rep. (CRR) 309 (SEA N.Y. 1984). Some support for this assertion may be found in the Court's willingness

While it is true that not all services received by handicapped children under IDEA are instructional in nature, many types of handicaps, such as learning disabilities, might necessitate supplemental classes similar in form to those at issue in *Felton*. For this type of special education, the dangers pinpointed by the Court in *Ball* and *Felton* might still be present. The substantive content of such classes provides the opportunity for inadvertent student indoctrination by public school teachers, which in turn triggers the need for the type of surveillance which creates entanglement. Depending on the method and extent of implementation, such classes could present the appearance of symbolic church-state union and have the effect of indirect subsidization as well.

In one of the few reported decisions directly addressing the Establishment Clause problems, the United States Fourth Circuit Court of Appeals held that the local school system had no duty to provide a cued-speech interpreter on site at a parochial school. Provision of a publicly-paid sign language interpreter at a sectarian school would violate the establishment clause because "religion permeated every aspect of the daily curriculum... and the cued speech interpreter would be interpreting... at all times.[169]

Depending on the method and extent of delivery, on-site instructional services under IDEA could be perceived as a link between church and state in the eyes of students and the public. Such aid might indirectly subsidize the religious functions of the parochial school if the school would normally have made provision for special education and related services as part of tuition, or if class size could be reduced. Finally, teachers providing special education are just as likely inadvertently to incorporate religious teaching in their instruction, and children with disabilities are just as susceptible to influence by such indoctrination. Consequently, monitoring would be required to guarantee the secularity of state aid, resulting in entanglement problems.

Since it is difficult to imagine that the Court would ignore these dangers simply because the children involved are children covered under IDEA and not educationally disadvantaged children under Title I, the reasonable assumption for state educators to make is that such general instructional classes may not be provided on parochial school grounds under IDEA. Indeed, many school districts have already made this assumption and adopted policies against providing on-site services at parochial schools.[170]

The school district finds itself in a difficult position because its decision to discontinue on-site services at parochial schools does not negate that district's

to uphold general welfare services for children in parochial schools. *See* Wolman v. Walter, 433 U.S. 229, 242–43 (1977); *cf.* Meek v. Pittenger, 421 U.S. 349, 371 n.21 (1975).

169. Goodall v. Stafford County School Bd. , 930 F.2d 363, 372 (4th Cir. 1991); see also Zobrest v. Catalina Foothills, 963 F.2d 1190 (9th Cir. 1992) cert. granted 113 S. Ct. 52 (1992).

170. *See, e.g., See*, Board of Educ. v. Weider, 72 N.Y.2d 174, 527 N.E.2d 767, 531 N.Y.S.2d 889 (1988) (District policy against providing public services on religious school ground upheld); Wheatland Unified School Dist., 508 Educ. Handicapped L. Rep. (CRR) 310 (SEA Cal. Feb. 3, 1987) ("The school district cannot provide speech therapy on the [parochial] school site because that would be in violation of the establishment clause of the First Amendment..."); School Dist. of North Platte, 507 Educ. Handicapped L. Rep. (CRR) 452 (SEA Neb. April 24, 1986)("[I]n response to U.S. Supreme Court decisions... district concluded it could no longer offer special education services at parochial school site.").

obligation to provide special education programs for children in those schools.[171] There are, however, available options.

Direct off-site service is an obvious option. If a child requires the type of special education and related services which may not be provided on parochial school grounds, the district is obligated to provide transportation to the public site so that the student may participate.[172] In fact, the DOE has recently stated that a "general rule that services will only be offered at the public school site and that the . . . schools are not responsible for providing transportation to any private school child who is handicapped is inconsistent with the Federal regulations."[173] The local public school retains considerable flexibility in identifying the appropriate site.[174]

Felton would also appear to allow limited on-site services. On-site instructional programs should be limited in number. Where a school system has only a few children in private educational placements, monitoring of on-site programs could avoid establishment clause problems. It is conceivable that a particular school system has one or two children so placed, and therefore, the Supreme Court's concern that monitoring itself creates excessive entanglement is not justified.

Further, on-site programs limited in scope should survive attack. To the extent the program does not confer educational benefit, but is a service which allows the education to take place, it will likely be permitted. Provision of trained aides to change a catheter, or to assist a child in toileting have little educational content and hence little possibility of running contrary to *Felton*'s concerns. To the extent the assistance could involve educational content, however, it is likely to be impermissible. For example, a cued speech interpreter for a deaf student should not be provided, since the person would be interpreting material with educational content[175] as well as interpreting classes with specific religious content.

On-site programs, however, involving traditional as well as non-traditional educational content (such as education in self-help and survival skills)[176] should be prohibited in all but a few instances. Whether a child is being tutored in reading, or is being trained to make change, or even to help feed himself, the risk of establishment problems exist. Only two groups of students, therefore, in ad-

---

171. *See* 34 C.F.R. § 76.654(a); *see also* 20 U.S.C. § 1221e-(a)(1). Note that the United States Supreme Court has upheld the provision of therapeutic services, guidance, and remedial classes for parochial school children on public school grounds. Wolman v. Walter, 433 U.S. 229, 244–45 (1977).

172. Wheatland Unified School Dist., 508 Educ. Handicapped L. Rep. (CRR) 310 (SEA Ca. Feb. 3, 1987); *but see* Prince George's County Pub. Schools, 353 Educ. Handicapped L. Rep. (CRR) 226 (1986) (Office of Civil Rights letter indicating no obligation to provide transportation).

173. Exon Inquiry, 213 Educ. Handicapped L. Rep. 125, 126 (EHA Jan. 7, 1988).

174. *See* Board of Educ. v. Wieder, 72 N.Y.2d 174, 527 N.E.2d 767, 531 N.Y.S.2d 889 (1988), where a community of Hasidic Jews sought provision of special education services within the Hasidic schools or at a neutral site. The public school sought a ruling that IDEA and New York law required provision of special education only in public schools. The court held that there was neither a constitutional right to have the services performed at the private school or a neutral site, nor was the public school limited to providing services at a public school site.

175. "Cueing involves the use of handshapes with the ongoing speech to clarify the spoken language. Cueing is not intended to be a substitute for spoken language, as is sign language." Chattahoochee County Bd. of Educ. v. Tremaine S., 508 Educ. Handicapped L. Rep. (CRR) 295, 295 (SEA Ga. Jan. 26, 1987).

176. *See, e.g.,* Abrahamson v. Hershman, 701 F.2d 223 (1st Cir 1983).

dition to those merely receiving on-site related services (as opposed to educational programming) should be served on-site by the public schools. First, on-site services should be provided for children whose cognitive ability is such that their education cannot entail concepts such as church and state. Risks of the teacher imparting inappropriate content are minimal, and the small number of children involved, requiring minimal monitoring should avoid entanglement problems.[177]

Second, children who are at risk from travel involved in leaving the parochial school should be served on-site. Again, given the small number of such children, the ease of monitoring, and the inherent risks attendant to the transportation of the child, little entanglement should exist in these two instances.[178] In fact the number of such children the public system would be required to educate is made even smaller by the fact that many children with severe cognitive deficiencies require total special education, rather than a few classes or some form of related service. For these students, the issue is probably moot. To the extent that a child placed in a private school requires exclusively special education and related services, the public school is probably relieved of any obligation to provide education and related services if it has an appropriate program in the public school.[179]

Finally, as an option for providing special education, it seems likely that the public school could meet its burden by providing direct payment to the parents for services, rather than providing the money or services to the parochial school. To the extent, for example, that the child required a tutor to enable the child to receive educational benefit, the public school could provide the parents with the funds to hire the tutor themselves. Such an approach seems consistent with the United States Supreme Court's position in *Mueller v. Allen*,[180] where the Court upheld a state tax deduction for costs of tuition and related expenses at a parochial school. Any entanglement problems resulting from supervision might be minimal. In fact, in *Mueller* the tax provision also provided for state review of text books used in the parochial school.

The Supreme Court's decision in *Committee for Public Education v. Nyquist*,[181] however, makes it difficult to state categorically that *Mueller* would allow a system of direct payment to parents. *Nyquist* involved tuition reimbursement grants to parents of parochial school children. The Court held that, had the funds been given directly to the religious schools, the establishment clause would have been violated because there would be no guarantee that state aid would be used for secular purposes. The fact that the aid was given directly to the parents did not make the statute constitutional since the effect, financial support of sectarian

---

177. Many children functioning at this level, to the extent they are not in a public school program, are likely to be in private residential facilities receiving special education.

178. *Cf.* Macomb Intermediate School Dist., 401 Educ. Handicapped L. Rep. (CRR) 117 (SEA Mich. 1988) (school required to provide climate controlled bus to transport child from regular school program to special half-day special education program site).

179. Work v. McKenzie, 661 F. Supp. 225 (D.D.C. 1987).

180. 463 U.S. 388 (1983); *see also* Witters v. Washington Dep't. of Services for the Blind, 474 U.S. 481 (1986).

181. 413 U.S. 756 (1973).

schools, remained the same.[182] *Nyquist*, however, was distinguished in *Mueller* by Justice Rehnquist because aid was conferred on parochial schools only as a result of parental decision, not state action. The decision has been called "isolated" by commentators 1983.[183]

---

182. *Id.* at 780–81. The same result was reached in Sloan v. Lemon, 413 U.S. 825 (1973) (another tuition reimbursement scheme).

183. *See, e.g.,* Alley, The Supreme Court on Church and State 142 (1988).

Chapter 9

Notice and Consent

9.1 In General

Written notice and consent are required at several stages in the educational process. What follows is an overview of where notice or consent is required. Notice and consent are also discussed under particular topics, such as placement and evaluation, as appropriate.

The significance of notice as a procedural right cannot be underestimated. Failure to provide notice has been held to be sufficient to excuse exhaustion of administrative remedies.[1] Further, failure to provide notice has been held to be a sufficient procedural violation to support a finding that the agency's proposed educational program would not provide a free appropriate education (FAPE).[2] Lack of written notice, however, has been held to be not prejudicial where oral notice was given to the parents and the parents attended the Individual Education Program (IEP) meeting.[3]

9.2 Notice Concerning Identification, Evaluation, and Placement in General

Written notice is required to be given to a parent prior to an LEA proposing or refusing to change the identification, perform an evaluation, or make an educational placement of a child under IDEA regulations.[4] Section 504 regulations also provide for notice with respect to any actions regarding identification, evaluation, and educational placement of any child with a disability, and compliance with IDEA regulations is stated as one method by which § 504 regulations may be satisfied.[5]

The purpose of notice is to inform parents, and the proper time for notice is after an appropriate decision has been reached by the district, but within a

---

1. See § 13.3.
2. See § 14.7.
3. Thomas F. v. Cincinnati Bd. of Educ., 918 F.2d 618 (6th Cir. 1990).
4. 34 C.F.R. 300.504(a); *see* 20 U.S.C. § 1415(b)(1)(C).
5. 34 C.F.R. § 104.36.

reasonable time before the decision is implemented.[6] Notice must be provided within a reasonable time before institution of any change, and contain adequate information to allow a parent to raise an objection under due process procedures if desired. For example, the United States Department of Education's Office of Special Education Programs (OSEP) interpreted the notice requirement in a way that rejected a strict ten-day notice prior to an IEP meeting. Rather, OSEP indicated that ten days was a guideline for determining reasonableness.[7]

Copies of state law and regulations are not sufficient forms of notice, and parents must be given full explanations in a written form that members of the general public can understand.[8] Whenever notice is required under IDEA, it must meet several requirements. It must contain an explanation of the procedural safeguards available under the IDEA, including the availability of an Independent Educational Evaluation (IEE), and the ability to request a due process hearing.[9] The notice must describe the action taken or the decision not to take action, and describe the options considered by the agency and why other options were rejected.[10] In addition, the notice must describe each procedure, test, record or report relied upon in making its proposal or refusing to take action,[11] as well as any other factors relevant to the agency's action or inaction.[12]

In addition to the specific content just described, the actual notice must be written in language understood by the general public and provided in the native language of the parent (unless it is clearly not feasible to do so).[13] If the native language of the parent is not written, the agency must insure that there is an oral translation of the notice and that the parent understands the notice.[14]

Section 504 has a very general requirement that notice be a part of the procedural safeguards established by the educational agency "with respect to actions regarding the identification, evaluation, or educational placement ..."[15]

9.2.1 Notice of Pre-placement Evaluation

A notice of pre-placement evaluation should list the specific tests and records on which it bases its decision to conduct an evaluation.[16] In 1980, a United States Department of Education Office of Special Education Programs (OSEP) interpretation stated that listing the specific tests which the LEA intends to use in the evaluation is not required in the parental notice.[17] In 1989 OSEP however, refined its interpretation of notice requirements to include a list of anticipated tests to

---

6. Helmuth Inquiry, 16 Educ. Handicapped L. Rep. (CRR) 550 (OSEP February 23, 1990).
7. Constantian Inquiry, 17 Educ. Handicapped L. Rep. (LRP) 118 (OSEP September 6, 1990).
8. Max M. v. Thompson, 592 F. Supp. 1437 (N.D. Ill. 1984).
9. 34 C.F.R. § 300.505(a)(1); see also 20 U.S.C. § 1415(b)(1)(D).
10. 34 C.F.R. § 300.505; see also 20 U.S.C. § 1415(b)(1)(D).
11. 34 C.F.R. § 300.505(a)(3); see also 20 U.S.C. § 1415(b)(1)(D).
12. 34 C.F.R. § 300.505(a)(4); see also 20 U.S.C. § 1415(b)(1)(D).
13. 34 C.F.R. § 300.505(b); see also 20 U.S.C. § 1415(b)(1)(D).
14. 34 C.F.R. § 300.505(c). The agency must also keep written evidence that it has met these latter two requirements. Id. See also 20 U.S.C. § 1415(b)(1)(D).
15. 34 C.F.R. § 104.36.
16. Grimes Inquiry, 211 Educ. Handicapped L. Rep. (CRR) 187 (EHA March 20, 1980).
17. Id.

be used in the evaluation process.[18] The notice also does not require the identification of specific evaluators.[19]

In the case of reevaluation, the LEA must list specific tests to be used if the reevaluation was requested by one other than the parent.[20] If the reevaluation is requested by the parent, however, or is of the mandatory type required every three years, specific listings are not required.[21] Notice should, in those cases, contain a list of tests anticipated to be used in the reevaluation.[22]

The United States Department of Education Office of Civil Rights (OCR) decided in 1985 that providing a general description of the types of tests to be used was in compliance with notice requirements of Section 504.[23] OCR also ruled that "pertinent information," such as right to counsel, right to examine records, and the right to a due process hearing must also be part of any notice for the notice to be in compliance with regulations implementing § 504 during the initial identification and evaluation proceedings.[24] The identity of the § 504 coordinator must also be publicized and provided as part of notice at the initial identification and evaluation stages.[25]

9.2.2 Notice of Initial Placement

For notice of initial placement to be proper, an agency must list all the specific tests upon which it based its initial placement decision.[26] The LEA must also explain in the notice why the specific placement was chosen, as well as why other placements considered were rejected.[27]

9.2.3 Notice of Change in Placement

Notice of the intent to change placement is required.[28] "Boilerplate language" on forms containing only general descriptions of the proposed placement, without a discussion of options considered for the individual child, is inadequate notice.[29] Parents have a right to notice independent of the child's right. For example, where

---

18. Reynolds Inquiry, 213 Educ. Handicapped L. Rep. (CRR) 238 (OSEP June 12, 1989).

19. Sutler and McCoy Inquiry, 18 Individuals with Disabilities Educ. L. Rep. (LRP) 307 (OSEP August 29, 1991).

20. Grimes Inquiry, 211 Educ. Handicapped L. Rep. (CRR) 187 (EHA March 20, 1980).

21. Id.

22. Reynolds Inquiry, 213 Educ. Handicapped L. Rep. (CRR) 238 (OSEP June 12, 1990).

23. Wisconsin Department of Public Instruction, 352 Educ. Handicapped L. Rep. (CRR) 177 (OCR November 29, 1985), interpreting 34 C.F.R. § 104.36.

24. Sikeston, Mo. R-VI School Dist., 16 Educ. Handicapped L. Rep. (CRR) 351 (OCR 1990); see 34 C.F.R. § 104.36; see also Yorktown, N.Y. Cent. School Dist., 16 Educ. Handicapped L. Rep. (CRR) 108 (OCR Aug. 2, 1989); Hyde Park, N.Y. Cent. School District, 16 Educ. Handicapped L. Rep. (CRR) 182 (OCR July 14, 1989).

25. Hyde Park, N.Y. Cent. School District, 16 Educ. Handicapped L. Rep. (CRR) 182 (OCR July 14, 1989).

26. Grimes Inquiry, 211 Educ. Handicapped L. Rep. (CRR) 187 (EHA March 20, 1980).

27. New Inquiry, 211 Educ. Handicapped L. Rep. (CRR) 383 (EHA April 24, 1986).

28. 34 C.F.R. § 300.504(a)(1); see 20 U.S.C. § 1415(b)(1)(C)(i). For a discussion of other aspects of a change in placement see 8.4.

29. McKenzie v. Smith, 771 F.2d 1527 (D.C. Cir. 1985).

a student over the age of eighteen consented to a change in placement, the parents were still entitled to prior notice.[30]

What constitutes a change in placement sufficient to require notice to the parent has been the subject of considerable litigation. In general, a change in location does not constitute a change in placement if the educational program remains the same.[31] Also, a change which is superficial in nature and does not significantly affect a child's learning experience does not constitute a change in placement.[32] Where, however, a substantial change in programming will take place, a change in placement has occurred and prior notice is required.[33]

Termination of educational services also constitutes a change in placement requiring advance notice.[34] Suspension or expulsion of a student for more than ten days in duration constitutes a change in placement, and requires parental notice.[35]

9.3 Notice After Hearing Request

When a due process hearing is initiated either by the educational agency or the parents, the parents must be provided with information concerning "any free or low-cost legal and other relevant services available in the area ..."[36] This requirement would appear to include notice of the statutory provision that parents may recover attorneys' fees if they are successful.[37]

9.4 Notice to Parents Concerning Agency's Annual Program

The state educational agency has a requirement to develop an annual program, and the state must take steps to insure that parents are informed of this state obligation.[38]

---

30. Mrs. C. v. Wheaton, 916 F.2d 69 (2d Cir. 1990).

31. See Weil v. Board of Elementary & Secondary Educ., 931 F.2d 1069, cert. denied, 112 S. Ct. 306 (1991); Concerned Parents & Citizens for the Continuing Educ. at Malcolm X v. New York City Bd. of Educ., 629 F.2d 751, cert. denied, 449 U.S. 1078 (1981); Dima v. Macchiarola, 513 F. Supp. 565 (E.D.N.Y. 1981).

32. Brookline School Comm. v. Golden, 628 F. Supp. 113 (D. Mass. 1986) (change in day care from 2 to 3 days, with substitution of day care program on two other days not a change in placement).

33. See, e.g., Tilton v. Jefferson County Bd. of Educ., 705 F.2d 800 (6th Cir. 1983) (change in location and no longer providing year long education constituted change in placement).

34. See, e.g., New York Ass'n of Retarded Children v. Carey, 466 F. Supp. 479 (E.D.N.Y.), aff'd, 612 F.2d 644 (2d Cir. 1978) (exclusion of hepatitis B carrier); Richards Inquiry, 17 Educ. Handicapped L. Rep. (LRP) 288 (OSERS November 23, 1990) (graduation constitutes change in placement).

35. See Honig v. Doe, 484 U.S. 305 (1988).

36. 34 C.F.R. § 300.506(c); see 20 U.S.C. § 1415(b)(2).

37. See generally Chapter 15.

38. 34 C.F.R. § 300.561; see 20 U.S.C. §§ 1412(2)(D), 1417(c).

9.5 When Parental Consent Required

Parental consent is required under IDEA prior to initiation of a pre-placement evaluation and prior to the initial placement of a child.[39] Other than in these two instances, consent may not be required as a condition of any benefit to the child.[40] States, however, may adopt more stringent standards of notification and consent than those outlined in IDEA regulations; but an agency's more stringent standards may never serve to exclude a child from receiving a FAPE.[41]

Under both IDEA and § 504 regulations, only notice, and not consent, is required for reevaluation. Any change in placement after an initial placement has been made requires notice, but not consent.[42]

9.5.1 Content of Consent

The parent must be fully informed of all information relevant to the activity for which consent is sought.[43] Where consent is required, the parent must understand and agree to the activity in writing, and the consent must be obtained in the native language of the parent.[44] The writing must describe the activity for which consent is sought, and list any records that will be released and to whom.[45] Further, the parent must understand that the consent is voluntary and may be unilaterally revoked by the parent.[46]

The fully informed consent must include a listing of tests expected to be used if the consent is for evaluation.[47] If the consent is for initial placement, specific tests and records upon which the placement decision was made must be included to make the consent a fully informed one.[48]

Section 504 is much less specific concerning consent requirements than IDEA, merely calling for procedural safeguards during the evaluation and placement process. As a model of adherence, however, § 504 regulations cite IDEA.[49] For example, in 1987, OCR ruled that a failure to obtain parental consent prior to conducting a speech and language evaluation of a child violated § 504 regula-

---

39. 34 C.F.R. § 300.504(b)(1); *see also* 20 U.S.C. § 1415(b)(1)(C)(i), D. Selective screening procedures constitute evaluations for which consent is required. Black Inquiry, 16 Educ. Handicapped L. Rep. (LRP) 1400 (OSEP August 29, 1990).
40. 34 C.F.R. § 300.504(c); *see also* 20 U.S.C. § 1415(b)(1)(C)(i), (D).
41. 34 C.F.R. § 300.504(d); Hall v. Freeman, 700 F. Supp. 1106 (N.D. Ga. 1987); Baliles Inquiry, 213 Educ. Handicapped L. Rep. (CRR) 207 (EHA 1988).
42. Dunlap Inquiry, 211 Educ. Handicapped L. Rep. (CRR) 462 (EHA April 30, 1987); Dennelly Inquiry, 211 Educ. Handicapped L. Rep. (CRR) 349 (EHA November 21, 1984).
43. 34 C.F.R. § 300.500(a)(1); *see also* 20 U.S.C. § 1415, 1417(c).
44. 34 C.F.R. § 300.500(a)(2); *see also* 20 U.S.C. § 1415, 1417(c).
45. 34 C.F.R. § 300.500(a)(2); *see also* 20 U.S.C. § 1415, 1417(c).
46. 34 C.F.R. 300.500(a)(3); *see also* 20 U.S.C. § 1415, 1417(c).
47. Gorski v. Lynchburg School Bd., 441 Educ. Handicapped L. Rep. (CRR) 415 (4th Cir. 1989).
48. *Id.*
49. 34 C.F.R. § 104.36. See, *e.g.*, Forest Park, Mi. School Dist., 352 Educ. Handicapped L. Rep. (CRR) 182 (OCR February 28, 1986); Tucson, Az. Unified School Dist., 257 Educ. Handicapped L. Rep. (CRR) 312 (OCR September 6, 1981).

tions.[50] Placement without consent was also found to be a violation of § 504 regulations.[51]

9.5.2 Refusal to Provide Consent

Refusal to consent or revocation of consent does not lessen the obligation of the LEA to provide services to a child.[52] The agency may not terminate attempts to evaluate or place a child based on a lack of consent.[53] If parental consent cannot be obtained or is revoked, the agency may either seek a due process hearing or follow any state permitted procedure, such as seeking a court order.[54] Section 504 regulations indicate that the same procedures as under IDEA may be used to comply with § 504's own general requirement to provide due process.[55]

9.6 Notice Checklist

_____ Notice is required:

    _____ Change in identification

    _____ Perform an evaluation

    _____ Make an educational placement

_____ Reasonable time before institution of any change

_____ Adequate information to allow a parent to raise an objection under due process procedures if desired

_____ In writing

_____ Explains procedural safeguards

_____ Describes action or inaction to be taken

_____ Describes options considered

_____ Describes why other options were rejected

_____ Describes each procedure, test, record or report relied upon

_____ Describes other relevant factors

_____ Written in language understood by the general public

_____ Written in native language of the parent

---

50. Sachem, N.Y. Cent. School District, 352 Educ. Handicapped L. Rep. (CRR) 462 (OCR June 16, 1987) (interpreting 34 C.F.R. 104.36).

51. Powhattan, Ks. Unified School Dist. No. 150, 257 Educ. Handicapped L. Rep. (CRR) 32 (OCR April 6, 1979) (interpreting 34 C.F.R. § 104.36).

52. J.J. Garcia v. Board of Educ., 558 Educ. Handicapped L. Rep. (CRR) 152 (D. Conn. 1986).

53. Id.; Dyersburg, Tn. City School Dist., 353 Educ. Handicapped L. Rep. (CRR) 164 (OCR February 11, 1988).

54. 34 C.F.R. § 300.504; see Honig v. Doe, 484 U.S. 305 (1988); 20 U.S.C. § 1415(b)(1)(c), (D).

55. Tucson, Az. Unified School Dist. No. One, 257 Educ. Handicapped L. Rep. (CRR) 312 (OCR September 10, 1981); Lower Camden, N.J. County Regional School Dist. No. One, 257 Educ. Handicapped L. Rep. (CRR) 157 (OCR September 30, 1980).

9.7 Consent Checklist

_____ Parental consent required:

    _____ initiation of a pre-placement evaluation

    _____ prior to the initial placement of a child

_____ Fully informed of all information relevant to the activity

_____ Native language of the parent

_____ Parent must understand and agree to the activity

_____ In writing

_____ Describes the activity for which consent is sought

_____ Lists any records that will be released and to whom

_____ Parent understands consent is voluntary

_____ Listing of tests expected to be used if the consent is for evaluation

_____ If the consent is for initial placement, specific tests and records upon which the placement decision was made must be included to make the consent a fully informed one

_____ Due process or other state procedure filed if consent refused or revoked

Chapter 10

Discipline

10.1 In General

In general, as long as the child's educational placement does not change, the disciplinary measures available to the school are the same for students with disabilities as for other students.[1] In addition, there is often a close relationship between discipline and the educational needs of a particular student, and the Individual Education Program (IEP) may state particular modes of discipline.[2]

A significant limitation on the agency's ability to discipline the student exists if the disciple constitutes a change in placement. The Supreme Court in *Honig v. Doe*,[3] relying on the stay-put provision[4] of IDEA, held that suspensions from school for longer than 10 days constitute a change in placement and, absent agreement of the parents, this change in placement is subject to all the protections associated with other placement changes.

The Supreme Court found § 1415(e)(3) unequivocal: during pendency of proceedings initiated under IDEA, "the child *shall* remain in the current educational placement." Congress intended to strip schools of unilateral authority to exclude disabled children from school. No "dangerousness exception" is to be added to the Act. A school, however, may use normal procedures for dealing with children who endanger themselves and others. The Court listed the following alternative procedures:

- Study carrels
- Time outs[5]
- Detention
- Restriction of privileges
- Suspension up to 10 days

---

1. *See* Comment, 34 C.F.R. § 300.513 (cited with approval in Honig v. Doe, 484 U.S. 305, 325 (1988)); *see also* 20 U.S.C. § 1415(e)(3).
2. *E.g.*, Hayes v. Unified School Dist. No. 377, 877 F.2d 809 (10th Cir. 1989) ("This case is illustrative of the close relationship between the use of disciple and in-class instruction in providing a child with a 'free appropriate education' ").
3. 484 U.S. 305 (1988).
4. 20 U.S.C. § 1415(e)(3).
5. *See* Hayes v. Unified School Dist. No. 377, 877 F.2d 809 (10th Cir. 1989) (time out and in-school suspension not a change in placement).

In exceptional cases, the school systems hands are not completely tied:

> And in those cases in which the parents of a truly dangerous child adamantly refuse to permit any change in placement, the 10-day respite gives school officials an opportunity to invoke the aid of courts under § 1415(e)(2), which empowers courts to grant any appropriate relief.... The burden of proof in such cases, of course, rests with the school to demonstrate the futility or inadequacy of administrative review ... Nor do we think that § 1415(e)(3) operates to limit the equitable powers of district courts such that they cannot, in appropriate cases, temporarily enjoin a dangerous disabled child from attending school.[6]

School systems have subsequent to *Honig* been successful in seeking preliminary injunctions excluding children from school pending the administrative determination of the change in placement questions.[7] It should be kept in mind, however, that the Court in *Honig* spoke of a "temporary" injunction. Following the temporary injunction, the administrative proceedings must still be used to determine the underlying merits of the school's change in placement.[8]

In *Christopher W. v. Portsmouth School Committee*,[9] a student was frequently suspended and sought injunction against future suspensions. The court denied the relief, in part on the theory that *Honig* did not apply to his situation because the injunction sought was a permanent injunction, not a preliminary injunction pending resolution of administrative proceedings.

Several questions remained following *Honig*. First, *Honig* dealt with a child where there was an accepted connection between the disruptive behavior and the child's disability. As Justice Brennan framed the issue, "[W]e must decide whether, in the face of this statutory proscription, state or local school authorities may nevertheless unilaterally exclude disabled children from the classroom for dangerous or disruptive conduct *growing out of their disabilities*." In the absence of that connection, may the school indefinitely suspend the child receiving special education services? Courts have uniformly held that absent the causal connection there is no basis for treating the disabled child any differently than the non-disabled child.[10]

A second issue that remained after *Honig* was whether the agency must provide any alternate educational programming during the suspension. Courts are split

---

6. Honig, 484 U.S. at 327.

7. *E.g.*, Board of Educ. of Township High School Dist No. 211 v. Kirtz-Imig, 16 Educ. Handicapped L. Rep. (LRP) 17. (N.D. Ill. 1989) (court applied five factors identified in determining that preliminary injunction should issue excluding student from school pending administrative process: irreparable injury to plaintiff; lack of adequate remedy at law; likelihood of success on merits; balancing harms; public interest. Student was violent, threatening to kill students and faculty); Texas City Indep. School Dist. v. Jorstad, 752 F. Supp. 231 (S.D. Tex 1990) (psychotic behavior endangered other students); *see also* Webster Groves School Dist. v. Pulitzer Pub. Co., 898 F.2d 1371 (8th Cir. 1990) (court may exclude press from hearing seeking preliminary injunction suspending student).

8. *See id.*

9. 877 F.2d 1089 (1st Cir. 1989).

10. Doe v. Maher, 793 F.2d 1470 (9th Cir. 1986) *aff'd and modified on other* grounds *sub nom* Honig v. 484 U.S. 305 (1988); School Bd. of Prince William County v. Malone, 762 F.2d 1210 (4th Cir. 1985); S-1 v. Turlington, 635 F.2d 342 (5th Cir.) *cert. den.* 454 U.S. 1030 (1981); Doe v. Koger, 480 F. Supp. 225 (N.D. Ind. 1979).

on whether any obligation exists. The Fifth Circuit held that complete suspension of instruction is not permitted, even if there was no causal connection and the student is properly suspended.[11] The Ninth Circuit, however, has held that, at least with regard to students whose disability is not causally connected to the reason for the suspension, the school may terminate all services for a properly expelled student.[12]

The United States Department of Education Office of Special Education Programs (OSEP), interpreting IDEA, and its Office of Civil Rights (OCR), interpreting § 504 have reached contrary conclusions on the need to continue to provide educational programming. Under § 504, OCR determined that complete suspension of services is permissible if there is no causal connection, but because the Fifth Circuit's decision requiring instruction was based on an interpretation of both IDEA and § 504, OCR will not apply this policy in the Fifth Circuit.[13]

OSEP, however, has determined that even where a causal connection does not exist between the behavior and the disability, alternative educational programming must be provided.[14] OSEP and the Fifth Circuit express the better view, for both legal and educational reasons. The basic rationale for *Honig* relied on the premise that Congress intended to treat students with disabilities differently,[15] and stressed that suspension was a change in placement subject to the same requirements of all change in placements. As such, to the extent possible, the change in placement should be treated as any other change in placement; that is, the placement may change, but the student still remains eligible for special education services.

A third issue that remains after *Honig* involves the situation where the child is subjected to repeated suspensions, each of which is shorter than ten days, but over the school year actually accumulate to an amount well beyond the 10 days. The abusive example would be a series of 9 day suspensions separated by short periods. No court decisions have been reported addressing this concern, but the Office of Civil Rights, interpreting § 504, in light of *Honig*'s interpretation of IDEA, has issued a staff memorandum to its senior staff in which it states that a child who has been suspended several times during a school year for periods of 8 or 9 days would be deemed to have undergone a change in placement.[16]

A fourth issue after *Honig* relates to the procedure used to determine the causal connection. Courts have consistently held that the decision must be made by

---

11. S-1 V. Turlington, 635 F.2d 342, 348 (5th Cir. 1981); *see also* Lamont X. v. Quisenberry, 606 F. Supp. 809, 815 (S.D. Oh. 1984).

12. Doe v. Maher, 793 F.2d 1470, 1482 (9th Cir. 1986) *aff'd on other grounds sub nom* Honig v. Doe, 484 U.S. 686 (1988).

13. OCR Staff Memorandum 307 Educ. Handicapped L. Rep. (CRR) 05 (October 28, 1988).

14. New Inquiry, 213 Educ. Handicapped L. Rep. (CRR) 258 (OSERS September 15, 1989). The *New Inquiry* has been reaffirmed in subsequent opinions. *See, e.g.,* Smith, Individuals with Disabilities L. Rep. (LRP) 685 (OSERS 1992); Symkowick, 17 Educ. Handicapped L. Rep. (LRP) 469 (OSERS 1991).

15. "We think it clear...that Congress very much meant to strip schools of the *unilateral* authority they had traditionally employed to exclude disabled students, particularly emotionally disturbed students, from school." Honig, 484 U.S. at 223.

16. OCR Staff Memorandum, 307 Educ. Handicapped L. Rep. (CRR) 05 (October 28, 1988); *see also* St. Marys (Pa) Area School Dist., 16 Educ. Handicapped L. Rep. (LRP) 1156 (OCR 1990) (4 suspensions within 4 months totalling 31 days constituted change in placement).

individuals familiar with the child and knowledgeable about special education.[17] Several decisions place the responsibility specifically in the same group that makes placement decisions[18] or the IEP team.[19] Stated differently, courts consistently hold that the decision may not be made by normal disciplinary procedures.

10.2 Chemical Dependency and Suspension

As discussed elsewhere,[20] children with drug and alcohol dependencies may be eligible for special education and related services under § 504. As discussed in the previous section, OCR interpretations of § 504 impose requirements on school's similar to those imposed by IDEA as interpreted by *Honig*. The Americans with Disabilities Act, however, has amended § 504 to give broader power to school systems to discipline students currently taking illegal drugs or alcohol. Under the Americans with Disabilities Act, and the amendments made by it to The Rehabilitation Act of 1973 (§ 504), the school may discipline a student currently taking illegal drugs or alcohol in the same manner as it would discipline a student without a disability.[21] The student may be disciplined regardless of whether there is a causal connection between the disability and their behavior. Likewise, the student may be disciplined regardless of the fact that the student suffers from a disability other than current drug or alcohol abuse.[22]

10.3 Constitutional Considerations

In addition to *Honig*, the Supreme Court's decision in *Goss v. Lopez*,[23] must be considered in expulsion cases. *Goss v. Lopez* was a landmark Supreme Court decision where the United States Supreme Court held that students facing 10-day suspensions from school for disciplinary reasons have property and liberty interests under the Fourteenth Amendment's due process clause.

> Students facing temporary suspension have interests qualifying for protection of the Due Process Clause, and due process requires, in connection with a suspension of 10 days or less, that the student be given oral or written notice of the charges against him and, if he denies them, an explanation of the evidence the authorities have and an opportunity to present his side of the story.[24]

---

17. *E.g.*, Christopher W. v. Portsmouth School Committee, 877 F.2d 1089 (1st Cir. 1989).

18. Kaelin v. Grubbs, 682 F.2d 595 (6th Cir. 1982); S-1 v. Turlington, 635 F.2d 342 (5th Cir.) *cert. denied* 454 U.S. 1030 (1981); Doe v. Koger, 480 F. Supp. 225 (N.D. Ind. 1979).

19. Doe v. Maher, 793 F.2d 1470 (9th Cir. 1986) *aff'd on other grounds sub nom* Honig v. Doe, 484 U.S. 305 (1988).

20. See 5.3.6.

21. 42 U.S.C. § 12211, *amending*, 29 U.S.C. § 706(8).

22. *Id.*

23. 419 U.S. 565 (1974).

24. *Id.* at 581.

Furthermore, "[t]here need be no delay between the time 'notice' is given and the time of the hearing."[25] Generally, however, "notice and hearing should precede removal of the student from school."[26] In the context of children with disabilities, such children have a constitutional right to procedural due process independent of the due process rights provided in IDEA.

10.4 Steps to Take in Disciplinary Actions

Reading § 504 and IDEA requirements together, the following steps must be followed before disciplinary action that results in a change of placement.

• Determination by individuals familiar with the child and knowledgeable about special education (placement or IEP) whether behavior has a causal connection with the disability.

• If there is no causal connection, normal disciplinary actions may be taken. Under IDEA, however, alternate educational programming must be provided.

• If there is a causal connection, suspension may not exceed 10 days, without a change in placement having occurred.—If school seeks to suspend for longer than 10 days, absent agreement of the parents to the change, procedures for a change in placement must be followed *before the suspension for longer than 10 days can begin.*

• If the child is "truly dangerous," agency may seek preliminary injunction excluding child from school pending administrative determination of necessity to change placement.

• Under § 504 there must be a reevaluation of the child. Notice of this evaluation must be provided to the parent.

• An IEP meeting must be convened, notice of which must have been provided to the parents.

• If parent and school agree, revise IEP.

• If IEP revised, notice must be provided to parent of intent to change placement.

• Placement may then be changed.

• Under IDEA, alternate educational programming must be provided.

• If at any point in the process a disagreement occurs between the parents and the agency, a due process hearing may be initiated.

---

25. *Id.* at 582.
26. *Id.*

Chapter 11

Impartial Due Process Hearing

11.1 In General

The state education authority (SEA) is required by both IDEA[1] and § 504[2] to provide an impartial hearing to resolve disputes arising over provision of a free apropriate education (FAPE). IDEA is quite detailed in describing the nature of the required hearing. Section 504 regulations, however, do not provide specific details, merely stating the person has the right to an impartial hearing, with the parents' and their counsel's participation. Compliance with IDEA requirements will, however, meet the 504 requirements.

Under IDEA, states have the option of providing either a one-tier or two-tier due process hearing procedure. The due process hearing may be conducted by either the SEA or the LEA.[3] If the initial due process hearing is conducted by a public agency other than the SEA, aggrieved parties may appeal to the SEA for an impartial review.[4] Following the SEA decision, the aggrieved party may bring a civil action in either state or federal court.[5]

11.2 Statute of Limitations

Federal regulations do not provide for a statute of limitations for due process hearing requests.[6] Individual states do have time limits and state regulations should be checked.

11.3 Scope of Review

In general, the scope of the impartial due process hearing covers disputes over the identification, evaluation, educational placement, or provision of a FAPE.[7] A

---

1. 20 U.S.C. § 1415(b).
2. 34 C.F.R. § 104.36.
3. 34 C.F.R. § 300.506; *see also* 20 U.S.C. § 1415(b)(2).
4. 20 U.S.C. § 1415(c), (d); 34 C.F.R. § 300.510.
5. 20 U.S.C. § 1415(e)(2); 34 C.F.R. § 300.511.
6. Inquiry, 17 Educ. Handicapped L. Rep. (LRP) 355 (OSERS November 9, 1990) (no specific time limit within which district must request due process hearing after parent requests IEE).
7. 34 C.F.R. §§ 300.506(a), .504(a)(1), (2); *see also* 20 U.S.C. § 1415(b)(1)(C), (b)(2).

hearing is also appropriate to resolve disputes challenging information contained in the child's educational records.[8] These topics cover most of the disputes that arise between parents and educators concerning rights under IDEA, and each will be discussed in turn.

As stated, disputes over identification and evaluation are properly resolved by the due process procedures.[9] For example, where the school system and parents disagree over whether a child has a disability, or agree that the child has a disability but disagree over the appropriate classification of the child, a due process hearing is appropriate to resolve the dispute.[10] Failure to screen children as required,[11] and procedural violations occurring during the identification process are also subject to due process review.[12]

Prior to the initial pre-placement evaluation, IDEA requires parental consent.[13] The question has arisen whether the due process hearing is the appropriate mechanism for the school system to override a parent's refusal to give consent. The rule appears to be that the LEA may seek either a due process determination or, if allowed by state procedures, a judicial determination. The United States Department of Education's Office of Civil Rights (OCR) has cited with approval a state regulation permitting an LEA to initiate due process hearings,[14] and has specifically interpreted the Federal regulations to allow either initiation of a due process hearing or, if in accord with state procedures, filing for a court order.[15] It has, however, also been held that a due process hearing may not override the parents' lack of consent, but that the due process hearing provides the evidentiary record to override the lack of consent judicially.[16]

The better view seems to be to treat disputes over consent the same as other disputes concerning the evaluation or identification of a student. Section 300.504(c) is broad in its language that due process hearings are to resolve disputes concerning identification and evaluation. Failure to consent to an evaluation clearly raises a dispute. To allow recourse directly to court would be inconsistent with the carefully drafted and detailed administrative procedure designed to resolve disputes short of judicial intervention. Further, failure to give consent to an initial evaluation is not significantly different than failure to consent

---

8. 34 C.F.R. § 300.568; *see also* 20 U.S.C. §§ 1412(2)(D), 1417(c).

9. 34 C.F.R. § 300.506(a), 300.504(a)(1), (2); *see also* 20 U.S.C. § 1415(b)(1)(c), (b)(2).

10. De Rosa v. City of New York, 557 Educ. Handicapped L. Rep. (CRR) 279 (Sup. Ct. N.Y. 1986); Case No. 11885, 509 Educ. Handicapped L. Rep. (CRR) 169 (SEA N.Y. October 19, 1987); Case No. 86-1681E, 507 Educ. Handicapped L. Rep. (CRR) 512 (SEA Fla. June 13, 1986); Case No. 11636, 508 Educ. Handicapped L. Rep. (CRR) 101 (May 9, 1986).

11. Case No. SE-45-85, 507 Educ. Handicapped L. Rep. (CRR) 388 (SEA Ill. February 20, 1986).

12. Case No. 85-29 and 85-33, 507 Educ. Handicapped L. Rep. (CRR) 265 (SEA Wash. January 9, 1985).

13. 34 C.F.R. § 300.504; *see also* 20 U.S.C. § 1415(b)(1)(C), (D).

14. Grandview (Mo.) C-4 School Dist., 257 Educ. Handicapped L. Rep. (CRR) 158 (OCR April 30, 1980); *see also* Cogley Inquiry, 211 Educ. Handicapped L. Rep. (CRR) 212 (EHA April 30, 1980) (similar ruling from OSEP).

15. Tucson Unified School Dist. No. 1, 257 Educ. Handicapped L. Rep. (CRR) 312 (OCR September 10, 1981).

16. Case No. 41-82, 504 Educ. Handicapped L. Rep. (CRR) 214 (SEA Ill. December 16, 1982).

to a change in placement in those jurisdictions where such consent is required.[17] If the parent fails to give consent, the logical recourse is to seek a due process hearing.[18]

One of the most litigated areas under IDEA is disagreements over educational placements. Issues such as whether a child requires a residential program,[19] or whether a child belongs in a self-contained classroom rather than a regular classroom[20] are appropriate issues to be resolved through the due process hearing mechanism. There can, however, be a question whether a particular dispute involves a placement determination. For example, it has been held that merely changing the physical location of a child's program does not constitute a change in placement.[21] If there is, however, an allegation that the physical location change also resulted in program changes contrary to the requirements of the IEP, the dispute over the physical move is subject to a due process hearing.[22]

Provision of a FAPE is, of course, central to IDEA, and allegations that the LEA is failing to meet its burden are properly brought under the due process provisions. Issues such as the appropriateness of the student's IEP,[23] the need for related services,[24] the need for special transportation requirements,[25] or the need for education beyond the normal school year are among the many issues affecting the provision of a FAPE and can be resolved in the due process hearing procedure.[26]

It should be kept in mind, however, that the United States Supreme Court has determined that questions of methodology "are for resolution by the States."[27] Where the parents and school system disagree over the appropriate methodology, and both methodologies will provide educational benefit, the hearing officer must defer to the school authorities.[28] Of course, if the hearing officer finds that the proposed educational methodology does not provide educational benefit, then deference to the school is inappropriate.[29]

---

17. See 9.5.

18. *E.g.*, Spielberg v. Henrico County Pub. Schools, 853 F.2d 256 (4th Cir. 1988).

19. *See, e.g.*, Colin K. v. Schmidt, 715 F.2d 1 (1st Cir. 1983); Abrahamson v. Hershman, 701 F.2d 223 (1st Cir. 1983); Kruelle v. New Castle County School Dist., 642 F.2d 687 (3d Cir. 1981); Diamond v. McKenzie, 602 F. Supp. 632 (D.D.C. 1985); Tolland Bd. of Educ. v. Connecticut State Bd. of Educ., 556 Educ. Handicapped L. Rep. (CRR) 412 (D. Conn. 1985).

20. *See, e.g.*, Colin K. v. Schmidt, 536 F. Supp. 1375 (D.R.I. 1982), *affd.*, 715 F.2d 1 (1st Cir. 1983).

21. See 8.4, 9.2.3.

22. *Id.*

23. *E.g.* Brown v. District of Columbia Bd. of Educ., 551 Educ. Handicapped L. Rep. (CRR) 101 (D.D.C. 1978).

24. Irving Indep. School Dist. v. Tatro, 468 U.S. 883 (1984).

25. *See, e.g.*, Hurry v. Jones, 560 F. Supp. 500 (D.R.I. 1983), *affd in part rev. in part*, 734 F.2d 879 (1st Cir. 1984); Kennedy v. Bd. of Educ., 175 W. Va. 668, 337 S.E.2d 905 (W. Va. 1985).

26. Battle v. Pennsylvania, 629 F.2d 269 (3d Cir. 1980)(EHA requires extended school year); Phipps v. New Hanover County Bd. of Educ., 551 F. Supp. 732 (E.D.N.C. 1982) (extended school year required under 504).

27. Board of Educ. v. Rowley, 458 U.S. 176, 208 (1982).

28. *See* Lachman v. Illinois State Bd. of Educ., 852 F.2d 290 (7th Cir.), *cert. denied*, 488 U.S. 925 (1988); Abrahamson v. Hershman, 701 F.2d 223, 230–231 (1st Cir. 1983) ("it might be inappropriate for a district court under the rubric of statutory construction to impose a particular methodology upon a state").

29. *See generally* Lachman v. Illinois State Bd. of Educ., 852 F.2d 290 (7th Cir.), *cert. denied*,

As discussed elsewhere, the parents have the right to an Independent Educational Evaluation if they disagree with the schools evaluation *and* the school does not establish that its evaluation is appropriate.[30] The due process hearing is the appropriate forum to seek this determination.

The due process hearing is the appropriate mechanism to resolve disputes concerning allegations of procedural violations, as long as the procedural violation impacts directly on the individual student's educational program. For example, it is appropriate to seek relief in a due process hearing for allegations that the LEA has decided to place a child before development of an IEP.[31]

It has been held, however, that compliance with procedural requirements such as adhering to state timelines for developing IEPs is not a proper subject matter.[32] There are also procedural issues to which the parents are not parties. One such example would be whether the LEA or the SEA is responsible for funding the residential placement order by the hearing officer.[33]

It should be stressed, however, that if the procedural violations impact on the individual child's right to receive a FAPE, noncompliance is a proper subject matter for the due process hearing. For example, allegations that an LEA has failed to abide by a hearing officer's decision are subject to either a new due process hearing,[34] or, if preferred, direct judicial intervention, since exhaustion of administrative remedies would be futile given the LEA's refusal to abide by the administrative process.[35]

Whether a child is a resident of the particular school system can often be disputed, especially where each parent lives in a different jurisdiction. At least one SEA has held that issues of residency are not properly raised at a due process hearing, but are subject to the complaint procedure.[36] The majority view appears to reach a contrary result.[37]

Disputes concerning the contents of the records are subject to a hearing held by the public agency, under EDGAR rather than under the due process proceedings of IDEA.[38] The parents or their representatives have a right to examine all records

---

488 U.S. 925 (1988); A.W. v. Northwest R-1 School District, 813 F.2d 158, 163 (8th Cir.), *cert. denied*, 484 U.S. 847 1987); Mark A. v. Grant Wood Area Educ. Agency, 795 F.2d 52, 54 (8th Cir. 1986), *cert. denied*, 480 U.S. 936 (1987); Doe v. Maher, 793 F.2d 1470, 1483 (9th Cir. 1986) *aff'd. sub nom.* Honig v. Doe, 484 U.S. 305 (1988); Taylor v. Board of Educ., 649 F. Supp. 1253, 1258 (N.D.N.Y. 1986); Johnston v. Ann Arbor Pub. Schools, 569 F. Supp. 1502, 1508 (E.D. Mich. 1983).

30. See Chapter 6.

31. Spielberg v. Henrico County Pub. Schools, 853 F.2d 256 (4th Cir. 1988).

32. Case No. H-0197-86, 508 Educ. Handicapped L. Rep. (CRR) 158 (SEA Cal. July 14, 1986).

33. Loeffler, 211 Educ. Handicapped L. Rep. (CRR) 275 (EHA Undated); *see also* BSEA Case No. 3838, 502 Educ. Handicapped L. Rep. (CRR) 282 (SEA Mass. May 7, 1981).

34. Case No. 84-0149, 507 Educ. Handicapped L. Rep. (CRR) 160 (SEA Mass. June 12, 1985).

35. See 13.3.

36. Case No. H-0197-86, 508 Educ. Handicapped L. Rep. (CRR) 154 (SEA Mich. September 3, 1986).

37. Case No. SE 84249, 506 Educ. Handicapped L. Rep. (CRR) 371 (SEA Cal. August 6, 1984) (parent may either file a complaint or seek due process); *see generally* Pires v. Commonwealth, 78 Pa. Cmwlth. 127, 467 A.2d 79 (1983); Case No. 84-0992, 506 Educ. Handicapped L. Rep. (CRR) 344 (SEA Mass. December 5, 1984).

38. 34 C.F.R. §§ 99.22, 300.570; *see also* 20 U.S.C. §§ 1412(2)(D), 1417(c).

maintained by educational agencies relating to their child.[39] Information found to be "inaccurate, misleading, or otherwise in violation of the privacy or other rights of the child" is to be amended.[40] If the information is not found to require amendment, the parents are entitled to place in the records a statement of disagreement.[41]

11.4 Requesting the Due Process Hearing

The agency to which the due process request is directed is controlled by state law or regulation. If the impartial due process hearing is conducted by the LEA, the request will normally go to the Superintendent of Schools or person of the same job description. Neither IDEA or its supporting regulations provide any requirements concerning the content of the request, and local regulations should be consulted. In general, however, a short written request to the Superintendent, with a copy to the Special Education Director, that makes the request, identifies the child, and states the general nature of the disagreement should be sufficient. The fact that the child is not in a public school does not prohibit requesting a due process hearing, as long as the reason the child is not in the public school is related to an allegation that the LEA is failing to provide FAPE,[42] or LEA is failing to provide services required to be given students in private placements.[43]

For a discussion of who may request the due process hearing see chapter 2.

11.5 The Hearing Officer in General

IDEA regulations contain only general guidelines on the qualifications of hearing officers and are designed primarily to ensure the officer's impartiality. In fact, the regulations are written in the negative, indicating who may not be a hearing officer. Specifically, a hearing officer may not be an employee of a public agency responsible for educating the child subject to the dispute,[44] nor anyone who would have a personal or professional interest which would conflict with the obligation to remain impartial.[45]

The regulations point out that a person is not an employee simply because he or she is paid by the public agency to conduct the impartial hearing.[46] The only other specific provision of the regulations is that each public agency must keep a list, including qualifications, of persons who serve as hearing officers.[47] Parents are entitled to a copy of this list, including qualifications.[48]

---

39. See § 34 C.F.R. §§ 99.21, 300.562.
40. 34 C.F.R. § 300.569(a); see also 20 U.S.C. §§ 1412(2)(D), 1417(c).
41. 34 C.F.R. § 300.569(b); see also 20 U.S.C. §§ 1412(2)(D), 1417(c).
42. S-1 v. Turlington, 635 F.2d 342 (5th Cir. 1981).
43. See § 8.10 -8.10.1.
44. 34 C.F.R. § 300.507(a)(1); see also 20 U.S.C. § 1415(b)(2).
45. 34 C.F.R. § 300.507(a)(2); see also 20 U.S.C. § 1415(b)(2).
46. 34 C.F.R. § 300.507(b); see also 20 U.S.C. § 1415(b)(2).
47. 34 C.F.R. § 300.507(c); see also 20 U.S.C. § 1415(b)(2).
48. Matlock v. McElrath, 557 Educ. Handicapped L. Rep. (CRR) 383 (M.D. Tenn. 1986).

Parents do not have the right to participate in the selection of the hearing officer,[49] except, of course, they may challenge the selection of an improperly selected or qualified hearing officer. Interestingly, there are no provisions indicating appropriate qualifications for hearing officers. Further, there is no requirement that the hearing officers be evaluated,[50] nor are there guidelines for training the hearing officers.[51]

Any challenge to a hearing officer must be made during the administrative hearing while there is an opportunity to correct the error. For example, a challenge alleging that the hearing officer, contrary to the requirements of IDEA, is an employee of an agency responsible for educating the child, must be made during the administrative hearing.[52]

11.5.1 Hearing Officer Impartiality

IDEA requires an impartial due process hearing. Who constitutes an impartial hearing officer has been the subject of much litigation. Virtually all the reported decisions addressing impartiality deal with the ability of people with a certain status to be hearing officers, however, the actions of the hearing officer may also be grounds for claiming lack of impartiality. For example, ex parte communications between the hearing officer and a witness can affect the impartiality of the hearing officer, resulting in the decision of the officer being held invalid.[53]

IDEA specifically precludes as hearing officers employees of "such agency or unit involved in education or care of the child."[54] The regulations add that anyone having a personal or professional interest that would conflict with his or her objectivity is also disqualified.[55] Under these provisions, officers and employees of an LEA are improper hearing officers.[56] Local school board members are also improper hearing officers, at least for the LEA in which they serve,[57] as are attorneys who represent the LEA.[58]

The more difficult question involves employees or officers of one LEA acting as hearing officers for a different LEA. The United States Department of Education Office of Special Education Programs (OSEP) and its Office of Civil Rights (OCR)

---

49. Hessler v. State Bd. of Educ., 553 Educ. Handicapped L. Rep. (CRR) 262 (D. Md. 1981), *aff'd on other grounds*, 700 F.2d 134 (4th Cir. 1983).

50. *See generally* Friedlander Inquiry, 211 Educ. Handicapped L. Rep. (CRR) 463 (OCR June 11, 1987).

51. *See generally* Sinclair Inquiry, 211 Educ. Handicapped L. Rep. (CRR) 335 (OCR March 21, 1984).

52. Colin K. v. Schmidt, 715 F.2d 1 (1st Cir. 1983).

53. Hollenbeck v. Board of Educ., 699 F. Supp. 658 (N.D. Ill. 1988).

54. 20 U.S.C. § 1415(b)(2).

55. 34 C.F.R. § 300.507(a)(2); *see also* 20 U.S.C. § 1415(b)(2).

56. Mayson v. Teague, 749 F.2d 652 (11th Cir. 1984); Kotowicz v. Mississippi State Bd. of Educ., 630 F. Supp. 925 (S.D. Miss. 1986); Matlock v. McElrath, 557 Educ. Handicapped L. Rep. (CRR) 383 (M.D. Tenn. 1986).

57. *See generally* Butte (Mont.) School Dist. #1, 311 Educ. Handicapped L. Rep. (CRR) 70 (OCR July 25, 1986).

58. Allegany (N.Y.) Cent. School Dist., 257 Educ. Handicapped L. Rep. (CRR) 494 (OCR March 26, 1984).

have held that it is proper for employees of one LEA to act as hearing officers for another LEA.[59] There have also been administrative determinations to this effect.[60]

Where the SEA, however, exercises considerable control over the operations of the LEA such that employees of the LEA also constitute employees of the SEA, such crossover is improper.[61] Further, because of the potential professional conflicts that may exist, employees of LEAs under less control may also be precluded from being hearing officers.[62]

Faculty at local private universities are acceptable hearing officers,[63] as are state university employees *not* involved in formulation of state regulations and policy.[64] Where the impartial due process hearing is first held at the state level, employees of the SEA, including the head of the SEA (e.g. Secretary, Commissioner, or Superintendent of Education) is at least presumptively precluded from acting as a hearing officer.[65]

An issue of some interest is whether the LEA can challenge the impartiality of a hearing officer because they are employees of the state. At least one United States District Court, in a challenge to the use of employees of the SEA to conduct the administrative review, held that the impartial administrative review requirement (that the review officer not be an employee of an agency responsible for educating the child) is designed to benefit only the children and their parents, not the LEA. On appeal, the First Circuit indicated that it need not decide the issue, because the LEA had not properly raised its challenge to the hearing officer during the administrative hearings. The analogy to LEA's challenging local hearing officers is obvious.[66]

11.5.2 Scope of Hearing Officer's Authority

The scope of a hearing officer's authority to grant particular substantive remedies is less extensive than that of a district court judge. In certain areas, hearing

---

59. Illinois State Bd. of Educ., 257 Educ. Handicapped L. Rep. (CRR) 600 (OCR November 15, 1984).

60. Case No. 247, 508 Educ. Handicapped L. Rep. (CRR) 219 (SEA Ind. October 22, 1986 (defense attorney in another school district acceptable); Case No. 10112, 501 Educ. Handicapped L. Rep. (CRR) 319 (SEA N.Y. November 21, 1979); *but see* Case No. 80-10, 503 Educ. Handicapped L. Rep. (CRR) 336 (SEA R.I. June 13, 1980) (state law holds to contrary).

61. Mayson v. Teague, 749 F.2d 652 (11th Cir. 1984).

62. Mayson, 749 F.2d 652; Silvio v. Commonwealth, 64 Pa. Cmwlth. 192, 439 A.2d 893 (1982), *aff'd*, 500 Pa. 430, 456 A.2d 1366 (1983).

63. Case No. 291, 508 Educ. Handicapped L. Rep. (CRR) 161 (SEA Pa. July 28, 1986).

64. Mississippi Dep't. of Educ., 352 Educ. Handicapped L. Rep. (CRR) 279 (OCR July 15, 1986); *see also* Mayson, 749 F.2d 652; Silvio, 439 A.2d 893; Wisconsin Dep't of Pub. Instruction, 352 Educ. Handicapped L. Rep. (CRR) 357 (OCR November 18, 1986).

65. Robert M. v. Benton, 634 F.2d 1139 (8th Cir. 1980) (state superintendent may not be hearing officer); East Brunswick Bd. of Educ. v. New Jersey State Bd. of Educ., 554 Educ. Handicapped L. Rep. (CRR) 122 (D.N.J. 1982) (employee of SEA may not conduct hearing). For a discussion of impartiality of state level administrative review officers in general, and the impartiality of SEA employees specifically, see § 12.6.

66. Colin K. v. Schmidt, 715 F.2d 1 (1st Cir. 1983).

officers have powers that are coextensive with judicial powers. A hearing officer may, for example, order reimbursement of educational expenses incurred by parents who were forced to place a child in a private facility because of the LEA's failure to provide a FAPE.[67]

The hearing officer is generally limited to an approval or disapproval of the issue before him or her, rather than creatively formulating a solution on his or her own. Hence, the hearing officer can decide that a child in the public schools should be placed in a special day class, but the hearing officer may not require the school system to institute that special class itself. The LEA must provide the educational services, but could do so by way of private contracting.[68] Likewise, the hearing officer cannot require a specific teacher to provide related services.[69]

There is a split of opinion on whether the hearing officer is able to order a specific placement. Some authority indicates that having determined that the school's proposed placement is inappropriate, for example, the school is still left with the choice of a different appropriate placement. If the specific placement subsequently chosen is felt to be inappropriate, the parents must start the due process proceedings over to determine the appropriateness of this particular placement.[70] The better view appears to be that the hearing officer is not limited to accepting or rejecting the placement proposed by the LEA and may consider placements proposed by the parents.[71] The United States Department of Education's Office of Special Education Programs has taken the position that the hearing officer may consider alternate proposals sought by the parents.[72] The Department of Education's Office of Civil Rights has taken the position that under § 504 the hearing officer must simply accept or reject the school's proposal.[73]

While attorneys' fees can be awarded for work done in administrative proceedings, the hearing officer does not have authority to grant those fees. Suit in state or federal court, however, can be brought solely to obtain the attorneys' fees earned as a result of work done in the administrative proceedings.[74]

The only damages available under IDEA are reimbursement for educational expenses and compensatory education. The hearing officer has authority to award both of these types of damages.[75] The hearing officer does not have authority to

---

67. S-1 v. Spangler, 650 F. Supp. 1427 (M.D.N.C. 1986) *vacated on other grounds* 832 F.2d 294 (4th Cir. 1987); Van Buiten Inquiry, 211 Educ. Handicapped L. Rep. (CRR) 429A (EHA June 17, 1987).

68. Mayerson Inquiry, 211 Educ. Handicapped L. Rep. (CRR) 384 (EHA March 21, 1986).

69. Chattahoochee County Bd. of Educ. v. Tremaine S., 508 Educ. Handicapped L. Rep. (CRR) 295 (SEA Ga. January 26, 1987).

70. Davis v. District of Columbia Bd. of Educ., 530 F. Supp. 1209, 1212 (D.D.C. 1982); Hendry County School Bd. v. Kujawski, 498 So. 2d 566 (Fla Dist. Ct. 1986); *see also* District of Columbia Public Schools, 257 Educ. Handicapped L. Rep. (CRR) 208, 209 (OCR February 13, 1981).

71. Diamond v. McKenzie, 602 F. Supp. 632 (D.D.C. 1985).

72. Eig Inquiry, 211 Educ. Handicapped L. Rep. (CRR) 174 (EHA March 11, 1980).

73. *See. e.g.*, District of Columbia Pub. Schools, 257 Educ. Handicapped L. Rep. (CRR) 208 (OCR Feb. 13, 1981) (hearing officer may order residential placement, but not particular school).

74. See 15.3.

75. *See, e.g.*, Burr v. Ambach 863 F.2d 1071 (2d Cir. 1988) (compensatory education) *judgment vacated by* 492 U.S. 902 (1989).

grant other related types of damages that may be available by way of § 504 or § 1983 actions.[76]

The hearing officer has the right to order an independent educational evaluation. The hearing officer, however, cannot delegate the outcome of the due process hearing to the IEE team.[77]

11.6 Procedural Rights Related to the Hearing

IDEA and supporting regulations provide a detailed list of procedural protections available to the parties in the impartial due process hearing.[78] When either the school or the parent requests a hearing, the school is obligated to provide the parent with information concerning the availability of low cost or free legal assistance.[79] There is no obligation to provide free counsel to the parents,[80] but attorneys' fees are available to the parents if they prevail.[81]

The parties have the right to be accompanied by counsel and individuals with expertise in the area of children with disabilities.[82] This does not mean, however, that non-lawyers may necessarily be able to "represent" parents in the due process proceeding. Some states may prohibit the use of lay advocates on unauthorized practice of law grounds. Many jurisdictions, however, allow the use of lay advocates, and IDEA's provision allowing parents to be accompanied by individuals with expertise seems to indicate that Congress contemplated the use of lay advocates. There is nothing, however, that requires a hearing officer to permit lay representation by someone without knowledge of the administrative procedure.[83]

Parties also have the right to present evidence, as well as confront, cross examine, and compel attendance of witnesses.[84] The right to present evidence, as with the right to counsel, does not give the parents the right to charge the school system for the costs associated with the witnesses. These witness fees, however, may be recoverable as costs and part of attorneys' fees if the parent prevails.[85]

Introduction of evidence not disclosed at least five days prior to hearing is prohibited at due process hearings.[86] Failure to meet this deadline will preclude use of evidence at the hearing, though failure to object at the time of the hearing

---

76. Case No. H-0157-83, 505 Educ. Handicapped L. Rep. (CRR) 181 (SEA Mass August 23, 1983).

77. DuBois v. Connecticut State Bd. of Educ., 727 F.2d 44 (2d Cir. 1984); Case No. SE 45-84, 507 Educ. Handicapped L. Rep. (CRR) 111 (SEA Ill. December 14, 1984).

78. 34 C.F.R. § 300.508; see also 20 U.S.C. § 1415(d).

79. 34 C.F.R. § 300.506(c); see also 20 U.S.C. § 1415(b)(2).

80. Daniel B. v. Wisconsin Dep't. of Pub. Instruction, 581 F. Supp 585 (E.D. Wis. 1984).

81. See Chapter 15.

82. 34 C.F.R. § 300.508(a)(1); see also 20 U.S.C. § 1415(d)(1).

83. Victoria L. v. District School Bd., 741 F.2d 369 (11th Cir. 1984) (proper to prohibit non-lawyer from representing parent, but allowable to allow lay person to give advice).

84. 34 C.F.R. § 300.508(a)(2); see also 20 U.S.C. § 1415(d)(2).

85. See 15.5–15.5.1.

86. 34 C.F.R. § 300.508(a)(3); see also 20 U.S.C. § 1415(d).

will probably constitute a waiver of the rule.[87] The United States Department of Education has also taken the position that the hearing officer may exercise discretion and grant a continuance to allow 5 days to consider the evidence that was not previously disclosed.[88] Further, it should be kept in mind that the review officer has discretion to allow additional evidence at the state level review and the judge has the discretion to allow additional evidence if civil suit is filed.[89]

The parties also have the right to obtain a written or electronic verbatim record of the hearing.[90] This requirement is written in the disjunctive and courts have held that LEA cannot be required to provide a written transcription.[91] The difficulties inherent in using a tape recording for any administrative or judicial review of the due process hearing may lead to the conclusion that in certain cases, the parents might seek to have the hearing officer order a written transcription. The authority to do this, however, seems lacking.[92]

Where the LEA does not ordinarily provide a written transcript the parents may be able to convince the LEA of the value of having a written transcript, of the hearing. It is logical that if the case warrants the expense for the parents, it is probably significant enough to the school system. The parties, therefore, may be able to agree to some sharing arrangement. Where the LEA refuses to provide a written transcript, the parents may choose to hire a stenographer. In such a case, however, the parent will be liable for the cost of the stenographer. The attorneys' fee provisions will probably allow recovery of this cost should the parents ultimately prevail.[93]

While the LEA is not required to provide a written transcription, the parents have no right to prevent the taking of a transcription of a particular type. For example, the parents have no right to prevent a stenographer hired by the LEA from attending the due process hearing: "[A]ttendance of a court reporter is a reasonable and necessary means for the school district to secure its statutory right to a verbatim record."[94]

The parents are also given the right to have the child who is subject to the hearing be present and to open the hearing to the public.[95] It should be noted that these latter two rights are solely those of the parent. The LEA has no right to compel the attendance of the child, nor open the hearing to the public.

The hearing is to be held at a time and place which is reasonably convenient to the parents and child.[96] It is unclear what this standard means in practice,

---

87. *See* Case No. 228, 506 Educ. Handicapped L. Rep. (CRR) 135 (SEA Pa. March 26, 1984).

88. Steinke Inquiry, 18 Individuals with Disabilities L. Rep. (LRP) 739 (OSEP January 2, 1992)

89. *See* Nelson v. Southfield Pub. Schools, 148 Mich. App. 389, 384 N.W.2d 423 (1986). For a discussion of the ability to introduce additional testimony see 12–7, 13.1, 13.10.

90. 34 C.F.R. § 300.508(a)(4); *see also* 20 U.S.C. § 1415(d)(3).

91. Edward B. v. Paul, 814 F.2d 52 (1st Cir. 1987) (no due process or equal protection violation for failure to provide written transcript where LEA provided tape recording).

92. Roe v. Town of Westford, 110 F.R.D. 380 (D. Mass. 1980) (parent not entitled to order for written transcript on appeal since EHA allows sound recording).

93. See 15.5.2.

94. Caroline T. v. Hudson School Dist., 915 F.2d 752, 755–756 (1st Cir. 1990).

95. 34 C.F.R. § 300.508(b); *see also* 20 U.S.C. § 1415(d).

96. 34 C.F.R. § 300.512(d); *see also* 20 U.S.C. § 1415.

though a least one reported decision indicates that holding the hearing within a one hour drive of the parent's home was reasonably convenient.[97]

The parties have the right to obtain written findings and decisions of the hearing officer.[98]

11.7 Status of Child During Due Process— "Stay-Put" Provision

Unless the parties agree to the contrary, "[d]uring the pendency of any administrative or judicial proceeding...the child must remain in his or her present educational placement."[99] Therefore, if the child is not receiving special education, and the dispute involves the eligibility of the child to receive those services, the child is to remain in the regular educational program until resolution of administrative and judicial proceedings. If the child's existing program is no longer available, such as if a private school ceases operation, the public agency must provide a comparable placement during the pendency of proceedings.[100]

If the complaint involves the initial enrollment of the student in the public school, the LEA is obligated to provide at least regular educational programming during the pendency of the suit.[101] When a student transfers from one school system to another the issue arises as to whether this is an initial enrollment as contemplated under IDEA. If it constitutes an initial enrollment the LEA need provide only regular educational programming during the pendency of a complaint. It it is not an initial enrollment, that is, initial enrollment is interpreted as referring to initial enrollment in any public school, during the pendency of any dispute, the new LEA is required to continue implementation of the IEP developed by the previous school.

The United States Department of Education, interpreting IDEA, has stated the opinion that an interdistrict transfer within the state does not constitute an initial admission and therefore the new LEA is obligated to continue implementation of the preexisting IEP.[102] The Department's Office of Civil Rights, however, has taken the position that § 504 does not require the receiving school system to implement

97. Hessler v. State Bd. of Educ., 553 Educ. Handicapped L. Rep. (CRR) 262 (D. Md. 1981).

98. 34 C.F.R. § 300.508(a)(5); *see also* 20 U.S.C. § 1415(d)(4).

99. 20 U.S.C. § 1415(e)(3); 34 C.F.R. § 300.513(a). *See* Honig v. Doe, 484 U.S. 305, 323 (1988) (change in IEP required before long term suspension); Christopher W. v. Portsmouth School Committee, 877 F.2d 1089, 1097 (1st Cir. 1989) (change in IEP required before suspension); DeLeon v. Susquehanna Comm. School Dist., 747 F.2d 149, 151 n.3 (3d Cir. 1984) (presence of related service in IEP determines whether service required by stay-put provision); Tokarcik v. Forest Hills School Dist., 665 F.2d 443, 453 (3d Cir. 1982) (stay-put provision "at a minimum guarantees that the most recently agreed upon program cover any unresolved [disputes].").

100. Weil v. Board of Elementary & Secondary Educ., 931 F.2d 1069 (5th Cir. 1991).

101. 34 C.F.R. § 300.513(b); *see also* 20 U.S.C. § 1415(e)(3).

102. Campbell Inquiry, 213 Educ. Handicapped L. Rep. (CRR) 265 (EHA September 16, 1989); Rieser Inquiry, 211 Educ. Handicapped L. Rep. (CRR) 403 (EHA July 17, 1986); *see also* McCowen v. Hahn, 553 Educ. Handicapped L. Rep. (CRR) 131, 134 (N.D. Ill 1981) ("to construe 'initial admission' as anything other than the child's first admission to a public school program would render the word 'initial' superfluous").

the IEP developed by the other school system, but that § 504 does not preclude its implementation as required under IDEA.[103] Even under IDEA, the LEA is not required under the stay-put provision to continue a private placement in which the parents have unilaterally placed the child.[104]

The District of Columbia Circuit has held that this "stay-put" provision only applies during the pendency of the due process hearing, state level review, and trial court. Specifically, the stay-put requirement does not require the school system to maintain the current educational placement while the parents seek to appeal an adverse trial court determination. In *Andersen v. District of Columbia*,[105] the court held that the statute speaks only of proceedings through the trial level, not the appellate level. This interpretation, the court held, was also consistent with the Supreme Court's decision in *Honig v. Doe*[106] where the Court stated that the intent of the provision was to keep schools from unilaterally moving children, not "to limit or pre-empt the authority conferred on courts . . ."[107]

11.8 Discovery

No provision is made under IDEA or its regulations for formal discovery mechanisms, such as are found in the Federal Rules of Civil Procedure. IDEA's extensive procedural protections, including the right to have access to records, however, provide considerable means for the parents to acquire information. There is a blanket right for the parents to have access to "any education records relating to their children which are collected, maintained, or used by the agency . . ."[108] The agency is to respond to a request without unnecessary delay, but in no event more than 45 days after the request, or before any meeting regarding the IEP, identification, evaluation, or placement of the child.[109] This right includes the right to make copies,[110] and have a representative, such as an attorney, inspect and review the records.[111] The LEA may charge a fee for copying documents, but may not charge a fee to search and retrieve the documents.[112]

In addition to providing the records, the LEA must provide reasonable explanations and interpretations of the records. This requirement itself provides a fruitful source for information concerning the LEA's position.

Informal discovery is, of course, also available. Interviews with school employees should be conducted, consistent with good witness interviewing in general. Since the necessity to impeach the witness may arise, the results of the interview should

---

103. OCR Memorandum, 307 Educ. Handicapped L. Rep. (CRR) 15 (OCR July 7, 1989).
104. Joshua B. v. New Trier Township High School Dist. 203, 770 F.Supp. 431 (N.D. Ill. 1991).
105. 877 F.2d 1018 (D.C. Cir. 1989).
106. 484 U.S. 305 (1988).
107. Anderson v. District of Columbia, 441 Educ. Handicapped L. Rep. (CRR) 508, 512 (quoting Honig, 484 U.S. at 327); *see also* Manchester School Dist. v. Williamson, 17 Educ. Handicapped L. Rep. (LRP) 1 (D.N.H. 1990).
108. 34 C.F.R. § 300.562(a); *see also* 20 U.S.C. §§ 1412(2)(D), 1417(c).
109. 34 C.F.R. § 300.562(a); *see also* 20 U.S.C. §§ 1412(2)(D), 1417(c).
110. 34 C.F.R. § 300.562(b)(2); *see also* 20 U.S.C. §§ 1412(2)(D), 1417(c).
111. 34 C.F.R. § 300.562(b)(3); *see also* 20 U.S.C. §§ 1412(2)(D), 1417(c).
112. 34 C.F.R. § 300.566; *see also* 20 U.S.C. §§ 1412(2)(D), 1417(c); *see* Chapter 16.

be memorialized in some manner that can be authenticated at the due process hearing or at the court level. While a signed statement from the witness is obviously preferable, employees caught in the middle of a dispute between the parents and their employer are even more reluctant than disinterested witnesses to sign statements, especially if the interviewer is a lawyer. The presence of a nonlawyer is perhaps the easiest solution. It should be kept in mind that should a lawyer interview the witness and then have to take the stand to impeach the witness, disqualification of the lawyer is a real possibility.[113]

A common problem associated with lawyers interviewing witnesses who are employees of the school system is the position taken by the school system that all employees of the school system are opposing parties. While "all parties have a right to interview an adverse party's witness (the witness willing) in private, without the presence or consent of opposing counsel,"[114] *ex parte* communications with opposing parties, without the consent of opposing counsel is unethical.[115] In such a situation, a determination must be made as to whether or not the employee is considered an opposing party under applicable ethical interpretations.

As a general rule, when dealing with an entity with many employees, employees are considered opposing parties to the extent that they are able to "bind the corporation."[116] In the context of a dispute with the LEA, an individual school teacher, psychologist, social worker, or the like would be unable to bind the school system to a course of conduct such as settling the dispute, and therefore should not be considered a party.[117] School principals and superintendents, however, are likely to be considered parties.[118]

Local statutes and interpretations should, as always, be considered. A particular jurisdiction may have a provision which explicitly allows counsel to communicate directly with all public employees.[119]

Finally, state law may have a statute comparable to the federal Freedom of Information Act which may provide a means of acquiring relevant information.

11.9 Burden of Proof under The Act

Allocation of the burden of proof under IDEA is discussed in §§ 13.8–13.8.2.

---

113. Model Rules of Professional Conduct Rule 3.7; Model Code of Professional Responsibility, DR 5-101, 5-102.

114. IBM Corp. v. Edelstein, 526 F.2d 37, 42 (2d Cir. 1975).

115. Model Code of Professional Responsibility DR 7-104; Model Rules of Professional Conduct Rule 4.2.

116. Frey v. Department of Health and Human Services, 106 F.R.D. 32, 37 (E.D.N.Y. 1985); Wright v. Group Health Hosp., 103 Wash. 2d 192, 691 P.2d 564 (1984). *See generally* C. Wolfram, **Modern Legal Ethics** 613 (1985); Leubsdorf, *Communicating With Another Lawyer's Client: The Lawyer's Veto And The Client's Interests*, 127 U. Pa. L. Rev. 683 (1979).

117. *See generally* New York State Ass'n. for Retarded Children v. Carey, 706 F.2d 956 (2d Cir. 1983) (denial of order prohibiting plaintiffs from interviewing employees of state school for the mentally retarded).

118. It is unclear whether counsel can tell the employee-witnesses the truthful statement that they need not talk to opposing counsel. *Compare* People v. Hannon, 19 Cal. 3d 588, 138 Cal. Rptr. 885, 564 P.2d 1203 (1977) (defense lawyer not guilty of suppression) *with* State v. Martindale, 215 Kan. 667, 527 P.2d 703 (1974) (lawyer disciplined).

119. *See, e.g.*, Cal. Bus. & Prof. Code § 6076 ("This rule shall not apply to communications with a public officer, board, committee or body.").

11.10 Rules of Evidence

Rules of evidence do not apply to administrative hearings. The controlling principle is one of relevancy and reliability.[120] Objections based on technical rules of hearsay, for example, should not be sustained. Obviously once the dispute works its way into court, the rules of evidence apply. Counsel, therefore, should be particularly mindful that the due process hearing (the record of which will be reviewed by the court) provides the opportunity to introduce evidence which otherwise would be inadmissible at trial.

11.11 Conducting the Hearing

The formality of the hearing varies from jurisdiction to jurisdiction and from case to case. It is safe to say, however, that the more lawyers involved the more formal the proceeding. It is usually a good idea to seek a prehearing conference with the hearing officer to decide preliminary questions such as allocation of the burden of proof, order of presentation, whether opening statements and closing arguments will be presented and the like.

The due process hearing should be approached with the same level of preparation as a judicial proceeding. Available evidence suggests that success at the local due process hearing is critical to the ultimate outcome of the case. For example, in Virginia the local due process hearing officer is affirmed approximately 95 percent of the time by the state level review officer. The vast majority of disputes do not proceed to court. The importance of establishing your case at the local due process hearing, therefore, cannot be underestimated.

11.12 Hearing Officer's Decision

The LEA has 45 days from the date of the receipt of the request for a hearing to insure that a decision is reached and a copy of the decision has been mailed to each of the parties.[121] A hearing officer has authority to extend this deadline at the request of either party.[122] Failure to meet the deadlines is grounds for removing the hearing officer from the list of those approved to hear due process hearings.[123] Additional timelines within this 45-day requirement are often established by the various state regulations.

The hearing officer's decision must be in writing and must include findings of fact.[124] The decision of the hearing officer is final unless the hearing is appealed

---

120. McCormick, Evidence 1009–1010 (3d ed. 1984).
121. 34 C.F.R. § 300.512; *see also* 20 U.S.C. § 1415.
122. 34 C.F.R. § 300.512(c); *see also* 20 U.S.C. § 1415.
123. Virginia State Dep't. of Educ. and Prince William County Pub. Schools, 257 Educ. Handicapped L. Rep. (CRR) 648 (OCR June 28, 1985) (LEA must inform hearing officers that failure to meet 45 day timeline will prohibit their employment as hearing officers in the future).
124. 34 C.F.R. § 300.508(a)(5); *see also* 20 U.S.C. § 1415(d)(4).

to a review officer, if the state provides for a two-tier system, or to state or federal court if there is only a one tier administrative process.[125]

11.13 Due Process Hearing Checklist

_____ Statute of limitations of state

_____ Proper subject matter:

    _____ identification

    _____ evaluation

    _____ educational placement

    _____ provision of a FAPE

    _____ challenging information contained in the child's educational records

    _____ nonconsent of parents (if state law not to contrary)

    _____ obligation of LEA to pay for IEE

    _____ procedural violation impacting on educational program of child

    _____ residency

_____ Request proper agency

_____ Request proper person

_____ Standing to request:

    _____ Parent with custody or joint custody

    _____ Relative acting in capacity of parent

    _____ Other person acting in capacity of parent

    _____ Surrogate parent

    _____ School agency responsible for education

_____ Hearing officer:

    _____ meets impartiality requirements

    _____ not employed by LEA

    _____ not employed by SEA*

    _____ not employed by state to advise on educational policy

    _____ not director of special education for another jurisdiction*

    _____ not government official in jurisdiction of LEA

    _____ meets qualifications articulated by state

_____ Requested Relief:

    _____ determine whether LEA action in identification, evaluation, educational placement, provision of FAPE, or contents of student's records is appropriate

    _____ reimbursement under *Burlington*

    _____ order specific placement*

---

125. 34 C.F.R. § 300.509; *see also* 20 U.S.C. § 1415(c).

_____ find procedural violations

    _____ award compensatory education

    _____ determine whether IEE must be paid for by LEA

    _____ order related service

_____ Request subpoenas for appropriate witnesses

_____ Hearing Rights:

    _____ notified of low cost or free legal services

    _____ right to counsel

    _____ right to have others with expertise

    _____ present evidence

    _____ confront and cross examine witnesses

    _____ compel attendance of witnesses

    _____ prohibit the introduction of evidence not disclosed at least five days prior to hearing

    _____ obtain a written or electronic verbatim record of the hearing

    _____ obtain written findings and decisions

    _____ child present*

    _____ open to public*

    _____ held at a time and place which is reasonably convenient to the parents and child

_____ Timeliness:

    _____ 45 days to decide

    _____ additional state timelines

_____ "Stay-Put" Provisions Met

_____ Surrogate Parent Requirements Met

_____ Discovery Opportunities:

    _____ Access and copies of records

    _____ Explanation and Interpretation of Records

    _____ Interview Employee Witnesses

_____ Allocation of Burden of Proof Split of opinion or at parents' option.

*Split of opinion or at parents' option.

Chapter 12

Administrative Appeals

12.1 In General

If the impartial due process hearing is conducted by a public agency other than the SEA, the SEA is required to provide an administrative appeal to the SEA.[1] Any party aggrieved by the due process hearing may appeal for a state level review and the SEA shall hold an impartial review.[2] The reviewing body must:

1. examine the entire record;[3]
2. insure the procedures at the local hearing were in accord with due process requirements;[4]
3. seek additional evidence if necessary;[5]
4. at its discretion allow oral or written argument;[6]
5. make an independent decision;[7] and
6. give a written copy of the findings and decision to the parties.[8]

12.2 Notice of Appeal and Statute of Limitations

The precise person to whom the notice of appeal is sent is controlled by state law. Each state department of education has an office dealing with special education and typically the notice of appeal goes to it.[9]

IDEA is silent as to the time period in which an appeal may be made to the state level review.[10] Individual state regulations often address this issue, and thirty

---

1. 34 C.F.R. § 300.510(a); *see* 20 U.S.C. § 1415(c).
2. 34 C.F.R. § 300.510(b); *see also* 20 U.S.C. § 1415(c).
3. 34 C.F.R. § 300.510(b)(1); *see also* 20 U.S.C. § 1415(c).
4. 34 C.F.R. § 300.510(b)(2); *see also* 20 U.S.C. § 1415(c).
5. 34 C.F.R. § 300.510(b)(3); *see also* 20 U.S.C. § 1415(c), (d).
6. 34 C.F.R. § 300.510(b)(4); *see also* 20 U.S.C. § 1415(c), (d).
7. 34 C.F.R. § 300.510(b)(5); *see also* 20 U.S.C. § 1415(c).
8. 34 C.F.R. § 300.510(b)(6); *see also* 20 U.S.C. § 1415(d).
9. A list of these offices is contained in the Appendix.
10. Board of Educ. of the County of Cabell v. Dienelt, 843 F.2d 813 (4th Cir. 1988).

days is not atypical. Interestingly, at least one SEA decision exists that rejected a specific state-mandated 30 day statute of limitations. The hearing officer held that since the appeal involved issues under the federal statute, it would follow the general rule of disfavoring short state-created statutes of limitations and allow an appeal filed beyond the 30 day state statute of limitations.[11]

12.3 Timeliness

As with the local due process hearing, IDEA provides timelines under which a hearing and decision must be made in the administrative appeal. While the local due process decision must be made within 45 days of receipt of a request, a state level review must be decided within 30 days of receipt of the request for review.[12] Consistent with the requirements of the local due process hearing, a hearing officer may grant extensions at the request of either party,[13] and any hearing involving oral arguments must be held at a time and place convenient to the parents and child.[14]

State regulations will provide additional procedures and timelines as a means of insuring compliance with the 30 day requirement. For example, federal regulations are silent as to who should provide the review officer with the record.

12.4 Subject Matter/Scope of Review

The review officer under IDEA is to examine the record, insure that the due process requirements were met, seek additional evidence if necessary, allow oral or written argument at his or her discretion, and make an independent decision. IDEA, therefore, implies a de novo review. This standard would be consistent with traditional administrative procedure where one level of an administrative agency is not bound by a lower decision within that agency.[15]

A de novo review is also supported by the case law.[16] Given the United States Supreme Court's decision in *Hendrick Hudson District Board of Education v. Rowley*[17] that the courts are to give "due weight" to the administrative proceedings, the question has been raised whether the state level review must give "due weight" to the local hearing officer.[18] If due weight is considered deference, the answer should be no. Rowley's concern for giving due weight to the state ad-

---

11. Case No. 55, 506 Educ. Handicapped L. Rep. (CRR) 387 (SEA Wisc. May 24, 1985). For a discussion of statute of limitations for filing a civil action, and the policy disfavoring short, state-created time limitations, see 13.2.

12. 34 C.F.R. § 300.512(b)(1); *see also* 20 U.S.C. § 1415.

13. 34 C.F.R. § 300.512(c); *see also* 20 U.S.C. § 1415.

14. 34 C.F.R. § 300.512(d); *see also* 20 U.S.C. § 1415.

15. See 13.7.

16. *See, e.g.*, Tompkins v. Forest Grove School Dist. #115, 86 Or. App. 436, 740 P.2d 186 (1987); Independent School Dist. No. 277 v. Paultz, 552 Educ. Handicapped L. Rep. (CRR) 232 (Minn. 1980).

17. 458 U.S. 176 (1981). For a fuller discussion of *Rowley* see 3.1.

18. Rowley, 458 U.S. at 206.

ministrative proceedings was premised on a concern that the judiciary not substitute its judgment on issues of educational policy because of relative lack of expertise. Technically, there should not be the lack of expertise between the local level of review and the state level of review.[19]

On the other hand, serious consideration to the local due process hearing officer's factual conclusion should be given where the review officer relies upon the record rather than hearing the evidence firsthand. The local hearing officer was the one present to hear the testimony and judge the credibility of witnesses. Where credibility is a factor, some deference to the local hearing officer is probably sound. On issues not involving credibility, or with witnesses that the review officer has personally seen, the independent decision requirement of the Act would indicate that no deference is required.[20]

The scope of the review officer's authority is coextensive with the local hearing officer. The reviewing authority does not exceed the local officer's. For example, it would be improper for the review officer to remand the case to the local hearing officer for additional factual findings, since the review provides for the review officer to seek additional evidence.[21]

12.5 Who May Appeal—Parties Aggrieved

Clearly a parent or local educational agency which fails to achieve its goals at the local due process hearing is an aggrieved party and may institute an appeal. The question arises, however, whether the SEA, which may ultimately be responsible for the implementation, and at least part of the costs, can be considered an aggrieved party?

New York set up a system where the state was given authority to appeal from the local due process hearing, despite not being a party to the original dispute.[22] The New York law imposes the obligation on the Commissioner of Education to review and modify any decision of the local school board, to the extent deemed necessary.[23] Lower courts held that to do so, however, the Commissioner must appeal the local due process decision under provisions that apply to the appeal by the original parties.[24] If the SEA chooses not to make the appeal, it may not unilaterally modify or reject the due process decision, since the law requires the local hearing decision be final, unless appealed.[25] The propriety of this sua sponte appeal by the SEA, however, has been questioned by the Second Circuit.[26]

---

19. Community High School Dist. 155 v. Denz, 124 Ill. App. 3d 129, 463 N.E.2d 998 (1984).

20. For a complete discussion of standard of the judicial review and the impact of the court having to provide "due weight" see 13.7 through 13.7.3.

21. Birmingham and Lamphere School Dist.s v. Superintendent of Pub. Instruction for the State of Michigan, 554 Educ. Handicapped L. Rep. (CRR) 318 (6th Cir. 1982).

22. New York Educ. Law § 4404(2).

23. New York Educ. Law § 4404(2).

24. Sidney K. v. Ambach, 557 Educ. Handicapped L. Rep. (CRR) 268, 270 (Sup. Ct. N.Y. 1986).

25. Antkowiak v. Ambach, 638 F. Supp. 1564 (W.D.N.Y. 1986).

26. Antkowiak v. Ambach, 838 F.2d 635, 641 (2d Cir. 1988) (the system has also been held to be a violation of impartiality requirements because the Commissioner or his delegate was in effect acting as a review officer.

12.6 Impartiality

The Act and supporting regulations require an impartial review.[27] General issues of impartiality such as bias, prejudice or corruption are, of course contemplated within in this requirement.[28] By far the most litigated issue, however, is the question of whether employees of the SEA may be review officers. The question was complicated by language which appears contradictory to the legislative intent of Congress. IDEA states that "any party aggrieved by the findings and decision rendered in [the local due process] hearing may appeal to the State educational agency which shall conduct an impartial review of such hearing."[29] The language seems to contemplate the hearing be conducted by the SEA itself. The legislative history, however, would seem to indicate that an employee of the SEA may not conduct the review. The Senate Conference Report specifically stated:

> No hearing may be conducted by an employee of the State or local educational agency involved in the education or care of the child. The conferees have adopted this language to clarify the minimum standard of impartiality which shall apply to individuals conducting a review of the local due process hearing.[30]

The federal regulations, however, state that the impartial due process hearing officer may not be "a person who is an employee of a public agency that is involved in the education or care of the child ..."[31]

Case law is uniform in that at least lower level employees of the state department of education may not be review officers.[32] There has, however, been a split of opinion on whether the state's Secretary of Education or equivalent officer may conduct the review. The language of the court decisions range from one court holding that arguments made by lawyers from the Florida Commissioner of Education could not act as the review officer were frivolous[33] to the majority of courts which have held that individuals at the secretary level are employees of the SEA and are precluded from conducting reviews.[34] It is probably more accurate

---

27. 20 U.S.C. § 1415(c); 34 C.F.R. § 300. 510(b).

28. *See, e.g.*, Freidlander 211 Educ. Handicapped L. Rep. (CRR) 463 EHLR (OCR June 11, 1987) (review officer should not discuss substantive issues with employees of SEA).

29. 20 U.S.C. § 1415(c); 34 C.F.R. § 300.510(a).

30. Senate Conference Report, 1975 U.S. Code Cong. & Admin. News, 94th Congress, First Session, pp. 1425, 1502.

31. 34 C.F.R. § 300.507(a)(1); *see also* 20 U.S.C. § 1415(b)(2).

32. Colin K. v. Schmidt, 715 F.2d 1, 5 n. 3 (1st Cir. 1983); Grymes v. Madden, 672 F.2d 321,323 (3d Cir. 1982); Helms v. McDaniel, 657 F.2d 800, 806 n.9 (5th Cir. 1981), cert. denied 455 U.S. 946 (1982); *see also* Muth v. Central Bucks School Dist., 839 F.2d 113 (3d Cir. 1988) *reversed on other grounds sub nom.* Dellmuth v. Muth, 491 U.S. 223 (1989).

33. Victoria L. v. District School Bd. of Lee County, 741 F.2d 369, 374 (11th Cir. 1984); *see also* Brandon E. v. Wisconsin Department of Pub. Instruction, 595 F. Supp. 740, 746 (E.D. Wisc. 1984) (constitutional officer, not employee, therefore not precluded from reviewing).

34. Burr v. Ambach, 863 F.2d 1071 (2d Cir. 1988), *vacated* Sobol v. Burr, 492 U.S. 902 (1989); Muth v. Central Bucks School Dist., 839 F.2d 113 (3d Cir. 1988) *reversed on other grounds sub nom.* Dellmuth v. Muth, 491 U.S. 223 (1989); Grymes v. Madden, 672 F.2d 321, 323 (3d Cir. 1982); Helms v. McDaniel, 657 F.2d 800 (5th Cir. 1981), *cert. denied* 455 U.S. 946 (1982); Robert M. v. Benton, 634 F.2d 1139, 1142 (8th Cir. 1980); Johnson v. Lancaster-Lebanon Intermediate Unit 13, 757 F. Supp. 606, 615 (E.D. Pa. 1991); Vogel v. School Bd. of Montrose, 491 F. Supp. 989, 995 (W.D. Mo. 1980).

to say that the SEA is obligated to arrange for the review, while some other entity does the actual review.[35] This other entity may be another state agency or private individuals. Appointment of a private attorney is an acceptable way of providing for a review officer.[36]

Where the state review officer fails to meet the impartiality requirements, the trial court should vacate the review officer's decision and provide "due weight" only to the due process hearing officer.[37]

12.7 Additional Evidence Allowed

IDEA provides for an an impartial review by the state education authority with the right present additional evidence.[38] No limitation on the additional evidence is stated. Federal IDEA regulations, however, allow the reviewing body to seek additional evidence "if necessary."[39] The hearing officer has considerable discretion within which to make this decision.[40] Given the de novo nature of the state level review, it appears that review officers should be reluctant to overly restrict the presentation of evidence.

If additional evidence is taken, the protections afforded at the local due process hearing must be made available at the SEA hearing, including the right to confront and cross-examine witnesses, and the right to have five days advance disclosure of evidence.[41] The state review officer also has the discretion to allow or preclude oral or written argument.[42] Courts will review whether denial of the opportunity for either written or oral argument is an abuse of discretion.[43]

Whether to seek introduction of additional evidence is of course a highly case-specific question. It should be kept in mind, however, that the administrative process provides an opportunity not often available in litigation. The ability to introduce additional evidence may be important. Among the reasons additional evidence might be admitted include: clearing up factual ambiguities in the record, rebutting evidence that caused surprise in the due process hearing, or updating medical or educational records. This is also the last opportunity to introduce evidence under the less stringent evidentiary rules applicable to administrative hearings. Any relevant hearsay, for example, may have its last chance to be admitted.[44]

---

35. Helms v. McDaniel, 657 F.2d 800, 805, n.8 (5th Cir. 1981).

36. Missouri Department of Elementary and Secondary Educ. Inquiry, 257 Educ. Handicapped L. Rep. (CRR) 487 (OCR April 23, 1984).

37. Johnson v. Lancaster-Lebanon Intermediate Unit 13, 757 F. Supp. 606, 615 (E.D. Pa. 1991).

38. 20 U.S.C. § 1415(c), (d).

39. 34 C.F.R. § 300.510(b)(3); see also 20 U.S.C. § 1415(c), (d).

40. See Kruelle v. Biggs, 489 F. Supp. 169 (D. Del. 1980) *affirmed sub nom.* Kruelle v. New Castle County School Dist., 642 F.2d 687 (3d Cir. 1981).

41. 34 C.F.R. § 300.510(b)(3); see also 20 U.S.C. § 1415(c), (d). For a discussion of these provisions see 11.6.

42. 34 C.F.R. § 300.510(b)(4); see also 20 U.S.C. § 1415(c), (d).

43. See, e.g., Nelson v. Southfield Pub. Schools, 148 Mich. App. 389, 384 N.W.2d 423 (1986) (abuse of discretion to deny argument where opposing party has used "appeal form" to make arguments).

44. See evidentiary discussion 11.10.

The value of the review officer meeting the parents and school officials can often be overlooked. Testimony from the parents or school officials will often help personalize the cold record. Too often the LEA and parents have characterized each other in less than favorable light and allowing the hearing officer to see them adds to the credibility of the respective cases.

Whether to see oral or written argument is an individual decision. The opportunity to be present and answer legal and factual questions for the review officer, however, should not be underestimated.

12.8 Finality of Decision

The SEA decision must be a final decision, unless suit is filed in either state or federal court.[45] Hence, review systems in which following a local due process hearing a review officer heard the appeal and made recommendations to the SEA, which the SEA could accept or reject, are in violation of IDEA.[46]

12.9 Administrative Review Checklist

_____ Within statute of limitations

_____ Entire record has been forwarded to review officer

_____ Procedural allegations at local level

_____ Determine impartiality of hearing officer or selection system

_____ Identify additional evidence wish to introduce

_____ Request evidentiary hearing

_____ Request permission to file briefs and make oral argument

_____ Insure hearing officer adheres to 30 day timeline for decision

---

45. 20 U.S.C. § 1415(e)(1); 34 C.F.R. § 300.510(d).

46. *E.g.*, Helms v. McDaniel, 657 F.2d 800 (5th Cir. 1981) (Ohio scheme invalid); Monahan v. State of Nebraska, 491 F. Supp. 1074 (D. Neb. 1980); Christopher N. v. McDaniel, 569 F. Supp. 291 (N.D. Ga. 1983); *see also*, Stark v. Walter, 556 Educ. Handicapped L. Rep. (CRR) 203 (S.D. Oh. 1984); Hopkins v. Aldine Independent School Dist., 555 Educ. Handicapped L. Rep. (CRR) 412 (S.D. Tex. 1984) (improper to require appeal to local school board before appeal to SEA).

Chapter 13

Judicial Review

13.1 In General

Any party aggrieved by the final administrative proceeding under IDEA may bring a civil action in either state or federal court.[1] The action in federal court may be maintained without regard to any amount in controversy.[2] The parties, of course, may not litigate in state and federal court simultaneously and previous litigation on the same issues will constitute res judicata.[3]

IDEA provides that the trial court "shall receive the records of the administrative proceedings, shall hear additional evidence at the request of a party and, basing its decision on the preponderance of the evidence, shall grant such relief as the court determines is appropriate."[4]

13.2 Statute of Limitations

IDEA is silent on the statute of limitations for filing suit in state or federal court. The United States Supreme Court in *Wilson v. Garcia*,[5] held that when Congress fails to establish a statute of limitations, the courts should adopt the statute of limitations most analogous to the federal cause of action and which is consistent with the policies underlying the federal statute.

Courts have been inconsistent in their determinations of the appropriate statute of limitations. It should be expected that there will be different statutes of limitations periods, because the standard for determining the appropriate limitations period is state dependent. Courts, however, have not agreed on what is the basic analogous type of statute, and hence, limitations vary from 15 days to three years.

The disagreement among the courts is based on whether the analogous statute of limitations is the statute used in the more traditional judicial review of agency actions, as under the Administrative Procedure Act, or whether the analogous

---

1. 20 U.S.C. § 1415(e)(2).
2. 20 U.S.C. § 1415(e)(4)(A).
3. Coe v. Michigan Dep't. of Educ., 693 F.2d 616 (6th Cir. 1982); Scruggs v. Campbell, 630 F.2d 237 (4th Cir. 1980).
4. 20 U.S.C. § 1415(e)(2).
5. 471 U.S. 261 (1985).

statute is some other statute of limitations, such as for a personal injury action. The Administrative Procedure Act analogy results in a much shorter limitations period, usually a matter of two to four months,[6] while any analogy to a tort or similar suit may increase the period to as much as three years.[7]

A few courts have recognized different statutes of limitation for different types of actions under IDEA. For example, the Sixth Circuit Court of Appeals held that the statute of limitations for a reimbursement issue in Tennessee was three years.[8] A federal district court in Tennessee, however, subsequently held that the statute of limitations for a nonreimbursement issue was 60 days.[9]

Along a similar vein, in *Adler v. Education Department*,[10] the Second Circuit held that a four-month statute of limitations applied because an action under IDEA was analogous to administrative review. A federal district court, however, subsequently held that *Adler* did not apply when the action is for attorney's fees, because the state's three-year statute for "liability, penalty or forfeiture" was a more appropriate analogous statute.[11]

It appears that the difference of approach to the statute of limitations question bears similar attributes to the dispute over the standard of review of the due process hearing discussed in § 13.7. If, as some courts have held, the trial court's role in hearing the special education matter is to make a *de novo* determination of the issues, then a statute of limitations which treats the suit as an independent cause of action, and hence results in a longer limitations period, makes good sense. If, however, the court views the role of the trial court as fundamentally no different than its role in reviewing the typical administrative appeal, the shorter period makes sense. As indicated elsewhere, the better view is that the type of review contemplated by IDEA is fundamentally different from that of the typical

---

6. *See* Spiegler v. District of Columbia, 866 F.2d 461 (D.C. Cir. 1989) (since suit is in nature of appeal of administrative determination, shorter administrative review statute [30 days] is applicable rather than de novo law suit); Adler v. Education Dep't., 760 F.2d 454 (2d Cir. 1985) (four months); Department of Educ. v. Carl D., 695 F.2d 1154, 1158 (9th Cir. 1983) (applies Hawaii's thirty-day administrative review statute of limitations); Bow School Dist. v. Quentin W., 750 F. Supp. 546 (D.N.H. 1990) (30 days); Board of Educ. v. Halacka, 17 Educ. Handicapped L. Rep. (LRP) 788 (D. Ohio 1990) (15 days).

7. *See* Schimmel v. Spillane, 819 F.2d 477 (4th Cir. 1987) (one year statute of limitations—Virginia catch-all statute for which no other statute exists—administrative review period too short because penalize unrepresented parents and undermine federal policy); Alexopulos v. San Francisco Unified School Dist., 817 F.2d 551 (9th Cir. 1987) (in suit for failure to conduct a due process hearing, action barred by three year California statute, though court recognized that appeal from due process hearing may be different); Janzen v. Knox County Bd. of Educ., 790 F.2d 484 (6th Cir. 1986) (three years); Scokin v. Texas, 723 F.2d 432 (5th Cir. 1984) (rejected 30 day administrative appeal and adopted 2 year tort claim period); Tokarcik v. Forest Hills School Dist., 665 F.2d 443 (3d Cir. 1981), *cert. denied*, 458 U.S. 1121 (1982) (rejects thirty days, adopts two years); Lawson v. Edwardsburg Pub. School, 751 F. Supp. 1257 (W.D. Mich. 1990) (3 years); Tracey T. v. McDaniel, 610 F. Supp. 947 (N.D. Ga. 1984) (2 years for compensatory damages, same as tort law); School Bd. v. Nicely, 12 Va. App. 1051, 408 S.E.2d 545 (1991) (1 year). For a discussion of statutes of limitation in attorney's fees applications see 15.3.

8. Janzen v. Knox County Bd. of Educ., 790 F.2d 484 (6th Cir. 1986).

9. Doe v. Smith, 16 Educ. Handicapped L. Rep. (CRR) 65 (M.D. Tenn. 1988).

10. 760 F.2d 454 (2d Cir. 1985).

11. Robert D. v. Sobel, 688 F. Supp. 861 (S.D.N.Y. 1988); *but see* Vander Malle v. Ambach, 667 F. Supp. 1015 (S.D.N.Y. 1987) (using *Adler* 4 month period for reimbursement claim).

judicial review of administrative action, and therefore, the longer statutory period is more consistent with the statutory design.[12]

13.3 Exhaustion of Administrative Remedies

The right to appeal to federal or state court accrues when the parties receive notice of the final due process review decision.[13] As with more typical administrative schemes, Congress required the exhaustion of administrative remedies prior to filing an action in either state or federal court. Only the administrative remedies under IDEA, however, need be exhausted. Voluntary state dispute resolution mechanisms need not be exhausted.[14]

Congress felt sufficiently strongly about the need to exhaust administrative remedies that when, in an express rejection of the United States Supreme Court's decision in *Smith v. Robinson*, it amended IDEA to make explicit that "[n]othing in this title shall be construed to restrict or limit the rights, procedures, and remedies available under the Constitution, [§ 504], or other Federal Statutes protecting the rights of children with disabilities and youth," it also required that if relief under some other statute is also available under IDEA, administrative remedies must be exhausted.[15] In essence, Congress, recognizing that administrative remedies need not be exhausted for claims under § 504 or § 1983, did not want IDEA administrative procedures to be circumvented by resort to these statutory rights.

Exhaustion is not an inflexible doctrine, however. While time-consuming administrative procedures are not in and of themselves a basis for excusing the administrative process,[16] traditional notions which justify failing to exhaust administrative remedies also apply in the context of IDEA.

In general, exhaustion of administrative remedies is excused "where exhaustion would be futile or inadequate."[17] The most common situation in which courts have held that exhaustion would be futile is where the administrative due process procedures themselves are being attacked. For example, exhaustion is excused where the adequacy of the administrative remedy goes to the merits of the claim, such as where plaintiff brings a class action alleging failure of the state to implement administrative procedures required under IDEA.[18] Exhaustion was also

---

12. See § 13.7.2.

13. Gerasimou v. Ambach, 636 F. Supp. 1504 (E.D.N.Y. 1986).

14. Guy J. v. New Hampshire Dep't. of Educ., 131 N.H. 742, 565 A.2d 397 (1989).

15. 20 U.S.C. § 1415(f).

16. Cox v. Jenkins, 878 F.2d 414 (D.C. Cir. 1989); Howell v. Waterford Pub. Schools, 731 F. Supp. 1314 (E.D. Mich. 1990).

17. Honig v. Doe, 484 U.S. 305 (1988); *see also* Rogers v. Bennett, 873 F.2d 1387 (11th Cir. 1989) (parents required to exhaust administrative remedies absent a showing irreparable harm); Cox v. Jenkins, 878 F.2d 414 (D.C. Cir. 1989) (parents required to exhaust administrative remedies absent a showing of irreparable harm).

18. Andre H. v. Ambach, 104 F.R.D. 606 (S.D.N.Y. 1985); Diamond v. McKenzie, 602 F. Supp. 632 (D.D.C. 1985).

excused where the suit was to challenge the propriety of the administrative procedures actually implemented.[19]

A similar circumstance in which exhaustion would be futile is where the public agency fails to invoke the administrative procedures. For example, exhaustion was not required where the agency refused to appoint a due process hearing officer.[20] Exhaustion was also not required where agencies failed to provide notice of procedural safeguards,[21] where there was a failure to provide notice of a change in educational programming,[22] and where a school official allegedly forged the parent's signature on a permission form.[23] Exhaustion would also be futile where the substance of the suit is that decision makers do not have certain remedies available to them.[24] The mere fact that the administrative process is time consuming does not mean it would be futile to pursue it.[25]

The most common situation where exhaustion is excused, because the administrative procedures are inadequate, involves system-wide class action lawsuits.[26]

---

19. Monahan v. Nebraska, 491 F. Supp. 1074 (D. Neb. 1980), *aff'd in part and vacated in part*, 645 F.2d 592 (8th Cir. 1981).

20. Kerr Center Parents Ass'n. v. Charles, 897 F.2d 1463 (9th Cir. 1990); Manecke v. School Bd., 762 F.2d 912, 918 (11th Cir. 1985), *cert. denied*, 474 U.S. 1062 (1986) (exhaustion excused where school refused to initiate due process hearing at parents request).

21. Doe v. Maher, 793 F.2d 1470 (9th Cir. 1986), *aff'd sub nom* Honig v. Doe, 484 U.S. 305 (1988).

22. Abney v. District of Columbia, 849 F.2d 1491 (D.C. Cir. 1988).

23. Quackenbush v. Johnson City School Dist., 716 F.2d 141 (2d Cir. 1983), *cert. denied*, 465 U.S. 1071 (1984).

24. St. Louis Developmental Disabilities Treatment Center Parents' Ass'n. v. Mallory, 591 F. Supp. 1416 (W.D. Mo. 1984), *aff'd*, 767 F.2d 518 (8th Cir. 1985)(exhaustion excused where IEP drafters did not have the option of placing children in a regular classroom); Straube v. Florida Union Free School Dist., 778 F. Supp. 774 (S.D.N.Y. 1991) (exhaustion excused because hearing officer had no authority to place in unapproved school); *see also* Christopher W. v. Portsmouth School Comm., 877 F.2d 1089 (1st Cir. 1989) (exhaustion required where there are allegations of procedural violations under § 1415); DeVries v. Spillane, 853 F.2d 264 (4th Cir. 1988) (exhaustion excused where during pendency of action school proposed an IEP which was contrary to the IEP over which the parent filed the administrative proceeding); Armstrong v. Kline, 476 F. Supp. 583 (E.D. Pa. 1979), *remanded sub nom* Battle v. Pennsylvania, 629 F.2d 269 (3d Cir. 1980) (exhaustion excused where blanket rule prohibited educational services in excess of 180 days). Exhaustion would not be excused, however, merely because the administrative proceeding was unable to provide for attorney's fees. Buffolino v. Sachem Cent. School Dist., 729 F. Supp. 240 (E.D.N.Y. 1990).

25. Howell v. Waterford Pub. Schools, 731 F. Supp. 1314 (E.D. Mich. 1990).

26. Mrs. W. v. Tirozzi, 832 F.2d 748 (2d Cir. 1987) (hearing officer lacks authority to order system-wide relief); Hendricks v. Gilhool, 709 F. Supp. 1362 (E.D. Pa. 1989) (exhaustion excused in suit to increase state-wide classroom space); *see also* New Mexico Association for Retarded Citizens v. New Mexico, 678 F.2d 847 (10th Cir. 1982); J.G. v. Board of Educ., 648 F. Supp. 1452 (W.D.N.Y. 1986), *aff'd in part and modified in part*, 830 F.2d 444 (2d Cir. 1987) (failure to use procedures mandated by EAHCA). *But see* Association for Retarded Citizens v. Teague, 830 F.2d 158 (11th Cir. 1987) (class action for 6,000 dismissed for failure to exhaust, stating "no indication that the disposition of a few representative claims would not satisfactorily resolve plaintiff's complaint." *Id.* at 161–162. "If after a few such individualized state hearings it becomes clear that the state processes are overloaded or ineffectual, a federal court /action seeking relief under the EAHCA would then be appropriate." *Id.*); G.C. v. Coler, 673 F. Supp. 1093 (S.D. Fla. 1987) (class action for all children confined in detention center dismissed for failure to exhaust).

Often, in class action suits, exhaustion is also not required because it is § 1983[27] or § 504[28] that provides relief not available under IDEA.

In addition to situations involving futility and inadequacy, exhaustion is not required in the limited circumstances of the stay-put provision of IDEA. During the pendency of any proceedings, absent an agreement between the parents and the agency to the contrary, the child is to remain in the existing educational placement.[29] In effect, the stay-put provision provides an automatic basis for a preliminary injunction against the agency during pendency of proceedings, to require maintaining the present educational placement of the child.[30]

Finally, in a situation very similar to excusing exhaustion, where an LEA fails to appeal an adverse determination and fails to implement the hearing officer's decision, parents may seek enforcement by filing in federal court.[31] Since the due process hearing is final unless appealed, the party prevailing at the local due process hearing is in no position to appeal and therefore has exhausted administrative remedies.

13.4 Removal from State to Federal Court

Whether an action originally brought in state court may properly be removed to federal court appears to be an open question. One federal court has held that where a school system sought review of an administrative decision in a state court and in its complaint alleged only the application of state law, removal was improper.[32] The court held that state and federal law provided the same rights and protections and that plaintiff could choose whether to proceed under one or both. At least two other district courts, however, have held that removal is proper.[33]

The better view is that removal should be proper. Removal is a purely statutory right and if the action is within the court's original jurisdiction removal is proper.[34] Removal is particularly appropriate where the initial due process hearing alleged violations of IDEA. If we view the initiation of the action as being at the administrative level rather than at the court level, it is difficult to say that only state law issues are present. This is particularly the case where, as in both these district court cases, one party brought the action, but the opposing party ultimately sought review in the federal court. To allow the party seeking review to preclude removal

---

27. Mrs. W. v. Tirozzi, 832 F.2d 748 (2d Cir. 1987).

28. Doe v. Belleville Pub. School Dist. No. 118, 672 F. Supp. 342 (S.D. Ill. 1987); *see also* Sullivan v. Vallejo City Unified School Dist., 731 F. Supp. 947 (E.D. Cal. 1990) (refusal to allow service dog of student with cerebral palsy—no remedy available under EAHCA, therefore no need to exhaust).

29. 20 U.S.C. 1415(e)(3).

30. Cochran v. District of Columbia, 660 F. Supp. 314 (D.D.C. 1987); Saleh v. District of Columbia, 660 F. Supp. 212 (D.D.C. 1987).

31. Robinson v. Pinderhughes, 810 F.2d 1270 (4th Cir. 1987).

32. Amelia County School Bd. v. Virginia Bd. of Educ., 661 F. Supp. 889 (E.D. Va. 1988).

33. Boone County R-IV School Dist. v. Missouri State Bd. of Educ., 17 Educ. Handicapped L. Rep. (LRP) 946 (W.D. Mo. 1991); Olin v. Leininger, 1989 WL 165055 (N.D. Ill. 1989).

34. Grubbs v. General Elec. Corp., 405 U.S. 699 (1972).

by artful pleading would essentially deny the party initiating the administrative proceedings the opportunity to have the case heard on terms (that is, both state and federal) originally heard in the administrative proceeding.[35]

13.5   Issues Considered

The issues subject to review by the trial court are those IDEA claims raised in the administrative proceedings. The trial court may not hear any IDEA issue not raised in administrative proceeding. Otherwise the exhaustion of administrative remedies requirement would be avoided.[36]

To the extent that a matter is covered by IDEA, federal law supercedes state law. This has led several courts to make very broad statements such as "in the EHA context . . . no pendent state claim will lie,"[37] or that it is "beyond argument" that there can be no pendent state claim to provide relief.[38] These same courts, however, do recognize that where the state provides for educational standards and procedural protections in excess of those required by IDEA, the federal court has authority to assure compliance with the higher standard.[39]

The more accurate statement concerning pendent state claims, therefore, is that pendent jurisdiction of state claims is always discretionary with the court,[40] and except for the circumstance in which the services and protections under the state law are in excess of federal law, federal courts have not chosen to exercise pendent jurisdiction.[41]

Additional federal claims may be heard by the court. The 1986 amendments clearly envision the joining of federal constitutional and statutory claims by their explicit recognition that such claims are not precluded because the same claim can be made under IDEA.[42]

---

35. *See generally* Horton v. Liberty Mutual Ins. Co, 367 U.S. 348 (1961).

36. Edwards v. Cleveland Heights-University Heights Bd. Educ., 18 Individuals with Disabilities Educ. L. Rep. (LRP) 507 (6th Cir. 1991); Leonard v. McKenzie, 869 F.2d 1558 (D.C. Cir. 1989).

37. David D. v. Dartmouth School Comm., 775 F.2d 411, 422 (1st Cir. 1985).

38. Barwacz v. Michigan Dep't. of Educ., 674 F. Supp. 1296 (W.D. Mich. 1987); *see also* Town of Burlington v. Massachusetts Dep't. of Educ., 736 F.2d 773, 788 (1st Cir. 1984), *aff'd*, 471 U.S. 359 (1985) ("state law cannot provide a separate basis for relief via a pendent state claim").

39. David D. v. Dartmouth School Committee, 775 F.2d 411 (1st Cir. 1985); Town of Burlington v. Massachusetts Dep't. of Educ., 736 F.2d 773, 788 (1st Cir. 1984), *aff'd.*, 471 U.S. 369 (1985); Barwacz v. Michigan Dep't. of Educ., 681 F. Supp. 427 (W.D. Mich. 1987).

40. United Mine Workers of America v. Gibbs, 383 U.S. 715 (1966).

41. Fay v. South Colonie Cen. School Dist., 802 F.2d 21 (2d Cir. 1986) ("there is authority to hear pendent state claims, but [t]he presence of unresolved questions under New York family law regarding the rights of fathers with joint legal custody . . . should have alerted [the judge] to the fact that he need not, and therefore should not, decide the pendent claim."); Daniel B. v. Wisconsin Dep't. of Pub. Instruction, 581 F. Supp. 585 (E.D. Wisc. 1984) (urgency of need to decide educational issues precludes consideration of pendent state claims such as misrepresentation, intentional infliction of emotional distress and invasion of privacy); *see also* Burke County Bd. of Educ. v. Denton, 895 F.2d 973 (4th Cir. 1990).

42. 20 U.S.C. § 1415(f).

13.6 Discovery

Discovery under IDEA should be available to the extent of discovery in any civil matter. Discovery under Federal Rule 26(b)(1) and under most state procedural systems is limited primarily by relevancy. At least one court, relying on IDEA language that only "additional evidence" shall be submitted, has limited discovery to the type of evidence that is contemplated to be admitted in the trial.[43]

13.7 Standard of Review in General

There are fundamental differences among various courts on the standard of review to be used by the trial court. The two views can be concisely presented as whether the trial court is conducting a *de novo* review of the matter or whether it is functioning in a narrower role, as in the traditional review of administrative agency action. Section 1415(e)(2) of IDEA states in part:

> In any action brought under this paragraph, the court shall receive the records of the administrative proceedings, shall hear additional evidence at the request of a party, and, basing its decision on a preponderance of the evidence, shall grant such relief as the court determines is appropriate.[44]

This language tends to intermingle burden of proof with judicial review in a way that at least implies a complete *de novo* review by the court. The United States Supreme Court in *Hendrick Hudson District Board of Education v. Rowley*,[45] however, gave some indication that § 1415(e)(2) might not be read as allowing the district court complete *de novo* powers of review when it held:

> [T]he provision that a reviewing court base its decision on the "preponderance of the evidence" is by no means an invitation to the courts to substitute their own notions of sound educational policy for those of school authorities which they review. The very importance which Congress has attached to compliance with certain procedures in the preparation of an IEP would be frustrated if a court were simply to set decisions at nought. The fact that § 1415(e) requires the reviewing court "receive the records of the [state] (sic) administrative proceedings" carries with it the implied requirement that *due weight* shall be given to these proceedings.[46]

Clearly the Court contemplated that the administrative determination should be accorded some significant role in the judicial decision. Just what that role is remains unclear. There is the obvious question of what is due weight. Is due weight the same as deference in traditional administrative review? Also to whom is due weight to be given: the LEA, the due process hearing officers, or the SEA?

---

43. Roe v. Town of Westford, 110 F.R.D. 380 (D. Mass. 1986) (relying on *Burlington* analysis of additional evidence).
44. 20 U.S.C. § 1415(e)(2).
45. 458 U.S. 176 (1982).
46. *Id.* at 206 (emphasis added).

On the one hand, the Court in *Rowley* said "[T]he provision that a reviewing court base its decision on the 'preponderance of the evidence' is by no means an invitation to the courts to substitute their own notions of sound educational policy for those of school authorities which they review ... "[47] This language implies that due weight is to be given the LEA. On the other hand, the Supreme Court's language "that § 1415(e) requires the reviewing court 'receive the records of the [state] (sic) administrative proceedings' carries with it the implied requirement that due weight shall be given to these proceedings,"[48] implies that the due weight should be given the due process hearing officers' decisions.

13.7.1 Traditional Administrative Review

In traditional administrative settings, the judicial scope of review is controlled by at least three concerns. The first two concerns are related to the purpose in setting up the agency procedure. First, the scope of the judicial review is limited by the belief that deference should be given to agency experts.[49] Second, the scope of review is limited by the belief that courts should defer to the agency because the value of expediency will be lost. Without limited review, rather than expediting matters, the administrative proceeding becomes merely an added layer causing delay.[50] The third concern limiting review is common to all appeals, that is, a degree of deference should be given to the fact finder who has heard the evidence firsthand.[51]

These three concerns have led to what might be called a typical or traditional standard of the appropriate review of administrative determinations. This traditional approach leans heavily on the belief that a court should show significant deference to the agency. Specifically, the predominate standard of review since 1912 is that the court should determine whether the agency decision is supported by "substantial evidence."[52] Substantial evidence represents a narrow standard of review, permitting administrators greater discretion in fact-finding than, for example, that accorded to trial judges under the "clearly erroneous" standard by which trial factual determinations are reviewed.

---

47. *Id.*
48. *Id.*
49. B. Schwartz, **Administrative Law** 585 (2d ed. 1984).
50. *Id.*
51. *See* R. Pierce, S. Shapiro & P. Verkuil, **Administrative Law and Process** 358 (1985).
52. Schwartz, *supra* note 1 at 597.
What is substantial evidence is a more difficult question. *Id.* It has been pointed out, however, that "it has been generally accepted that 'substantial evidence' represents a narrower standard of review, permitting administrators greater discretion in fact-finding than accorded to trial judges under the 'clearly erroneous' standard. S. Breyer & R. Stewart, **Administrative Law and Regulatory Policy** 185 (1979). The substantial evidence test applies to formal adjudication and rule-making. Informal adjudication is tested by an 'arbitrary and capricious' standard. *Id.* 195–96; Pierce, *supra* note 3 at 360).
The quantum of evidence necessary has been variously described. It has been described as equivalent to the standard used in determining directed verdicts. Breyer at 185). In Greater Boston Television Corp. v. FCC, 444 F.2d 841, 851 (D.C. Cir. 1970) Judge Leventhal stated the court must determine whether the agency has "taken a 'hard look' at the salient problems, and has not genuinely engaged in reasoned decision-making."

The evidence to be considered in determining whether substantial evidence exists includes not just evidence favorable to the agency decision, but also evidence opposing the agency decision. Further, the agency decision to which there will be deference is to the final or review decision. For example, in a National Labor Relations Board determination, when a hearing officer reinstates an employee, but the full board reverses the hearing officer, any deference the court owes is to the full board.[53]

13.7.2 *De Novo* Review and Due Weight

As pointed out, the United States Supreme Court has stated that IDEA "carries with it the implied requirement that due weight shall be given these proceedings."[54] The immediate question is whether this requirement of due weight is the same as the deference a court traditionally gives an administrative determination. Is the review in the nature of the review of an agency determination, or is it in the nature of a de novo review?

At least one circuit has come very close to holding that the trial court is conducting a traditional administrative review. In *Karl v. Board of Education*,[55] the parents disagreed with a placement decision and requested a due process hearing. The parents wanted their mentally retarded daughter to be placed in a commercial food preparation program and the school proposed to place her in a work study program. The local due process hearing officer determined the student should be placed in the food preparation program with a student-adult ratio of nine-to-one. The school system appealed the decision to the New York State Commissioner of Education, who upheld the placement decision, but reversed the student-adult ratio requirement.

The parents then filed suit in the United States district court. The district court held that it agreed with the decision of the local hearing officer on the student-adult ratio and indicated that the court's obligation to defer to the judgment of the state educational authorities was diminished by the failure of the hearing officer and the Commissioner to agree. The Second Circuit reversed:

> we disagree with Judge Telesca's view that the federal courts need not defer to state educational authorities whenever there is some disagreement among state officers in the course of state proceedings. We believe *Rowley* requires that federal courts defer to the final decision of the state authorities, and that deference may not be eschewed merely because a decision is not unanimous or the reviewing authority disagrees with the hearing officer. There is no principle of administrative law which, in the event of a disagreement

---

53. Pierce, *supra* note 3 at 358.

Traditional judicial review of agency findings functions like appellate review of a court decision on the issue of what can be considered. The general rule is that the court is limited to the agency record. The court cannot expand or delete the evidence submitted during the agency proceedings. Schwartz, *supra* note 1 at 587.

54. Rowley, 458 U.S. at 206.

55. 736 F.2d 873 (2d Cir. 1984).

It ought at least to be clear that the standard of review is something more than an abuse of discretion standard. In *Roncker v. Walter*, 700 F.2d 1058 (6th Cir. 1983), the court reversed a district court decision which applied an abuse of discretion standard to the LEA's placement decision.

between a hearing officer and reviewing agency over demeanor evidence, obviates the need for deference to an agency's final decision where such deference is otherwise appropriate.[56]

The court's opinion evidences the strong influence of the traditional judicial approach to agency determinations. For example, the court's emphasis on deference to the final administrative determination is the classic view of administrative review. Indeed, the word deference in itself is interesting, since the United States Supreme Court in *Rowley* used the words "due weight," not deference.[57] Further, *Rowley,* contrary to the decision in *Karl,* does not even specifically state that due weight is to be given to the final administrative determination. Rather the Court left it ambiguous as to the party to whom due weight was to be given, indicating due weight was to be given to the "administrative proceedings."[58] Be that as it may, *Karl* does provide strong support for the argument that the reviewing court is to apply a substantial evidence standard.

There was a strong dissent in *Karl*:

> The majority characterizes this process as "deferential substantive review." However characterized, "deference" or "due weight" to the administrative proceedings does not mean simple subservience to the last administrator to speak, particularly when, as here, the combined expertise within the administrative system produced three different IEPs. *Rowley's* "gloss" on a clearly written statute requires only that the district judge give "due weight" to the views of the administrators; when those views conflict, it does not require him to accept the conclusion of the state's commissioner of education, nor does it relieve him of the burden of making the *de novo* determination required by congress. In ratifying the commissioner's decision, the majority has, in effect, adopted the substantial evidence standard of review that congress carefully rejected. Indeed, by semantically shifting *Rowley's* substantively oriented "reasonably calculated" standard to a procedural inquiry of whether the determination was a "reasoned calculation," the majority has effectively eliminated the substantive step of the *Rowley* analysis.[59]

Other courts, consistent with *Karl* have held that suits under IDEA are analogous to appeals from administrative agencies and are not *de novo*.[60]

The majority view is probably that the trial court's role is somewhere between *de novo* review and traditional administrative review. The First Circuit has characterized the level of review as "bounded, independent decisions—bounded by

---

56. Karl, 736 F.2d at 877; *see also* Quackenbush v. Johnson City School Dist., 716 F.2d 141 (2d Cir. 1983), in which the Second Circuit, in what is clearly a misinterpretation of *Rowley*, stated that in *Rowley*, "the Supreme Court rejected a standard of *de novo* review...." *Id.* at 146. If that were the case, there would be little function for judicial review; that conclusion would be in direct contradiction to the provision that the court base its decision on a preponderance of the evidence.

57. Rowley, 458 U.S. at 206.

58. *Id.*

59. Karl, 736 F.2d at 878–79. The court went on to state:

> ...the [the judge] properly faced up to the hopeless conflict among the administrators over Lisa's needs and carried out his statutory responsibility by making a *de novo* determination of her appropriate IEP. *Id.*

60. Spiegler v. District of Columbia, 866 F.2d 461 (D.C. Cir. 1988).

the administrative record and additional evidence, and independent by virtue of being based on a preponderance of the evidence before the court."[61] Under this view, the district court may accept or reject an administrative determination after reviewing it. "The extent of deference to be given the administrative findings of fact is an issue left to the discretion of the district court."[62] Under this view, "[f]indings by the state hearing officer must be reviewed as bearing on the federal right to an appropriate education and must receive the court's specific consideration."[63] What remains unclear under this view is what body is actually entitled to due weight. The prevailing view appears to be that due weight is not merely given to the final review officer's decision. "The court has discretion to give the administrative findings proper weight, with the concomitant obligation to consider those findings carefully and respond to the administrative resolution of issues."[64]

The approach of leaving the amount of weight given to the discretion of the trial court makes good sense. If due weight were limited to strictly educational policy questions, such as choosing the best method for educating the deaf, as opposed to factual questions of whether a particular child would benefit from one methodology or another, it would be logical to provide special consideration to the LEA, since it indeed has the expertise.

Several problems, however, exist with giving due weight to the determination of the LEA on issues other than which of two or more methodologies should be used. First, IDEA is a remedial statute and there is some lack of logic to giving special consideration to the group whose actions are sought to be remedied. Second, the language of § 1415 provides that the administrative proceedings are to be considered by the judge, and makes specific provision for the court to hear additional testimony and to make a determination by a preponderance of the evidence.[65] The ability to consider additional evidence requires the court to have the concomitant freedom to give less deference to an agency determination, since the agency will not have considered that additional evidence.

Indeed, the Fourth Circuit Court of Appeals in *School Board v. Malone*,[66] after discussing the standard of review articulated by *Rowley*, made it clear that any deference in the district court's review was to be to the state administrative proceedings and not to the school board. The court in *Malone* stated: "To give deference only to the decision of the School Board would render meaningless the entire process of administrative review."[67]

---

61. Town of Burlington v. Massachusetts Dept. of Educ., 736 F.2d 773, 791 (1st Cir. 1984), aff'd, 471 U.S. 359 (1985); *see also* Colin K. v. Schmidt, 715 F.2d 1, 5 (1st Cir. 1983); Barwacz v. Michigan Dep't. of Educ., 681 F. Supp. 427 (W.D. Mich. 1987).

62. Jefferson County Bd. of Educ. v. Breen, 853 F.2d 853 (11th Cir. 1988); *see also* G.D. v. Westmoreland School Dist., 930 F.2d 942 (1st Cir. 1991); Gregory K. v. Longview School Dist., 811 F.2d 1307 (9th Cir. 1987).

63. Town of Burlington v. Massachusetts Dept. of Educ., 736 F.2d 773, 792 (1st Cir. 1984), aff'd, 471 U.S. 369 (1985).

64. Burke County Bd. of Educ. v. Denton, 895 F.2d 973, 981 (4th Cir. 1990) (citing Burlington, 736 F.2d at 792; *see also*, Doe v. Alabama State Dep't. of Educ., 915 F.2d 651 (11th Cir. 1990).

65. Preponderance is clearly a burden of persuasion question not a standard of review question. *See generally* Jaffe, *Administrative Law: Burden of Proof and Scope of Review.*, 79 Harv. L. Rev. 914 (1966).

66. 762 F.2d 1210 (4th Cir. 1985).

67. *Id.* at 1217. *But see* Briggs v. Connecticut State Bd. of Educ., 882 F.2d 688 (2d Cir. 1989)

Limiting due weight to the final administrative decision would also be a mistake. As noted above, the Second Circuit in *Karl* gave great deference to the *final* state administrative determination.[68] The Supreme Court's language in *Rowley*, however, required that due weight should be given to the "administrative proceedings."[69] The Fourth Circuit has indicated that due weight is not limited to the review officer, but to the administrative proceedings as a whole,[70] and that the facts found by the local hearing officer concerning credibility are *prima facie* correct.[71] The Sixth Circuit, however, has held that due weight is to be accorded the final administrative decision.[72]

13.7.3 Issues Subject to Due Weight

Most courts assume, without discussion, that due weight must be provided to all issues raised in the suit. A few courts, however, appear to limit due weight to certain types of issues. Decisions made by hearing officers and judges can be placed in four different categories: purely historical fact decisions (for example, what is the age of the child, or what disability does the child have?); strictly policy questions (for example, will a developmental approach versus a behavioral approach be adopted to educate a child[73] or which of two competing methods to teach deaf children to speak is better?);[74] factual questions concerning the appropriateness of a program for a particular child (for example, does this child require a residential program versus a day program?);[75] and legal questions concerning the interpretation of the statute (for example, whether the statute contemplates provision of a particular service as part of the educational requirements imposed on the LEA).[76]

It is arguable that there should be a different level of review for each, and *Karl* could possibly be limited in its application on the grounds that what was at issue in that case was more a question of educational policy than a factual determination of, for example, whether a given program was appropriate. Parents and admin-

---

(deference is due local and state education agencies because of expertise); Doe v. Smith, 16 Educ. Handicapped L. Rep. (CRR) 65 (M.D. Tenn. 1988) (due weight to school and hearing officer).

68. *See supra* text and accompanying note 3.

69. Hendrick Hudson Dist. Bd. of Educ. v. Rowley, 458 U.S. 176, 206 (1982) (emphasis added).

70. Burke County Bd. of Educ. v. Denton, 895 F.2d 973 (4th Cir. 1990) ("the . . . argument that deference was due only to the review officer's conclusions is simply incorrect").

71. Doyle v. Arlington County Pub. School Bd., 953 F.2d 100 (4th Cir. 1991).

72. Thomas F. v. Cincinnati Bd. of Educ., 918 F.2d 618, 624 (6th Cir. 1990).

73. *See* Abrahamson v. Hershman, 701 F.2d 223, 230–231 (1st Cir. 1983):

Thus it might be inappropriate for a district court under the rubric of statutory construction to impose a particular methodology upon a state. Nevertheless, for judicial review to have any meaning, beyond mere review of state procedures, the courts must be free to construe the term "educational" so as to insure, at least, that the state IEP provides the hope of educational benefit.

74. *See generally* Rowley, 458 U.S. at 207 n.29.

75. *E.g.*, Abrahamson v. Hershman, 701 F.2d 223 (1st Cir. 1983).

76. *See* Irving Indep. School Dist. v. Tatro, 468 U.S. 883 (1984) (discussion of related services required under IDEA).

istrators agreed in *Karl* on a commercial food preparation program, but disagreed over the educational policy issue of what was appropriate staffing.[77]

Limiting due weight to matters of policy in this manner is consistent with opinions in the United States First Circuit Court of Appeals. *Doe v. Anrig,*[78] perhaps the most thoughtful case to date addressing the issue of judicial deference, involved a Down Syndrome child who had been in residential settings his entire life. In February, 1975, the LEA proposed placing the child in a non-residential school setting. The parents rejected the IEP but entered into an agreement whereby they paid for a residential component and the school paid for placement in a day school.

In 1977, on reevaluation, a new IEP proposed placing the child in a different non-residential school and provided for him to live at home with his parents. The parents rejected the IEP and sought administrative review. The Massachusetts Bureau of Special Education Appeals held that the proposed placement was appropriate but that there should be a one-year transition program. This decision was affirmed by the Department of Education's State Advisory Council for Special Education. The parents sought judicial review.

The district court found that the parents had shown by a preponderance of the evidence that the residential program was the appropriate placement. Both parties appealed the district court decision. The LEA argued that the district court failed to "grant substantial deference to the decisions of the state administrative bodies . . . "[79] The parents appealed on the issue of reimbursement. Addressing the LEA's contention, the First Circuit held:

> We disagree with [the LEA] insofar as they would limit the district court to the kind of judicial review of agency action contemplated under the Administrative Procedure Act. The statute unambiguously provides that a reviewing court may take cognizance of evidence not before the state educational agency and must base its decision on the preponderance of the evidence before it. As such, the review mechanism which the Act creates stands in sharp contrast to the usual situation where a court is confined to examining the record made before the agency [citation omitted] and to determining whether the administrative decision is supported by substantial evidence.[80]

---

77. Karl, 736 F.2d at 874.

78. 692 F.2d 800 (1st Cir. 1982). The First Circuit argument came before Rowley, but its opinion came after Rowley.

79. *Id.* at 805.

80. *Id.* at 805, *citing* Town of Burlington v. Department of Educ., 655 F.2d 428, 431 (1st Cir. 1981).

The court also rejected the contention that review was limited to whether the state had complied with procedures. This argument had been made in Rowley, the court pointed out, and was rejected:

> We find petitioners' contention unpersuasive, for Congress expressly rejected provisions that would have so severely restricted the role of reviewing courts. In substituting the current language of the statute for language that would have made state administrative findings conclusive if supported by substantial evidence, the Conference Committee explained that courts were to make 'independent decision[s] based on a preponderance of the evidence.' S. Conf. Rep. No. 94–455, *supra*, at 50 [*reprinted* in 1975 U.S. Code Cong. & Admin. News, pp. 1425, 1503]. See also 121 Cong. Rec. 37416 (1975) (remarks of Sen. Williams).

Id. mat 805, *citing* Rowley, 458 U.S. at 205.

The court then went on to indicate that "due weight" was directed toward policy considerations:

> [W]e find nothing in the record before us to suggest that "due weight" was not accorded. In addition, the Supreme Court's concern was with courts "substitut[ing] their own notions of educational *policy* for those of the school authorities" [citations omitted]. The difference here between Judge Zobel and the school authorities was not a choice of educational *policy*, but resolution of an individualized *factual* issue as to the effect of John's handicap on his ability to benefit from the proposed school setting.[81]

Then, as if to stress the point further, a footnote added:

> No contention was or is made here that the residential placement approved by the court was an option which the state would disapprove on general policy grounds.[82]

In *Abrahamson v. Hershman*,[83] the First Circuit again addressed the question of whether a child required a residential placement in order to receive a FAPE. The public school presented the parents with an IEP calling for a day program and the parents appealed to the Massachusetts Bureau of Special Education Appeals (BSEA). The BSEA hearing officer found that the student's residential needs were not educationally related and therefore not the responsibility of the school system. The parents then appealed this decision to the State Advisory Commission, which reaffirmed the hearing officer's decision. The parents then filed suit in federal district court.

The district court held that the child's residential needs were educationally related. On appeal, the school system argued that the district court had failed to give due weight to the BSEA. The Circuit Court disagreed:

> To be sure, the district court did not reach the same result as did the BSEA. But, as the Supreme Court noted in *Rowley*, while courts must give "due weight" to state administrative agencies and "be careful to avoid imposing their view of preferable educational models upon the States," . . . courts ultimately must make "independent decision[s] based on a preponderance of the evidence. . . . The court did not disagree with the state over educational policy, merely over whether the state-licensed program . . . would serve Daniel's own particular needs. Such an issue fell clearly within the scope of the question that *Rowley* left to the courts.[84]

Limiting the strong deference articulated in *Karl* to educational policy determinations makes good sense in light of the theory underlying judicial deference to administrative determinations. The history of SEAs and LEAs and the remedial nature of the legislation,[85] along with the fact that the administrative agencies to be remedied are in control of the administrative procedures,[86] makes broad deference such as suggested in *Karl* questionable.

---

81. 692 F.2d at 806.
82. *Id.* at 806 n.12.
83. 701 F.2d 223 (1st Cir 1983).
84. *Id.* at 230–231.
85. Honig v. Doe, 484 U.S. 305 (1988).
86. 20 U.S.C. § 1412(5) requires the state to establish procedural safeguards.

13.8 Burden of Proof in General

Burden of proof refers to two distinct questions: who has the burden of producing evidence on a particular issue and who has the burden of persuasion on a particular issue? Failure to produce evidence will result in a finding against the party bearing that burden. Once evidence is produced, however, there remains the separate question of whether the evidence persuades the fact finder under the applicable standard—preponderance of the evidence, clear and convincing, or beyond a reasonable doubt.[87] In determining which party has the burden of persuasion, one must take into account such things as who pled the fact, what is judicially convenient, what is fair, and what are any special policy considerations.[88]

Although the statute is explicit that the standard of proof is to be by a preponderance of the evidence, there is no specific indication which party shall bear the burdens of production and of persuasion. In the absence of this specificity, courts have reached different interpretations.[89]

13.8.1 Burden of Persuasion on Substantive Issues

There are two predominant views on who has the burden of persuasion on substantive issues. A number of courts appear to place the burden of persuasion on the party seeking to change the status quo, as measured by the initiation of the due process hearing. For example, the United States Fifth Circuit Court of Appeals confirmed this allocation of the burden in EAHCA matters in *Tatro v. Texas (Tatro II)*.[90] In *Tatro II*, the issue was whether a child's need for Clean Intermittent Catheterization fell within the requirements of IDEA. On the issue of burden of proof, the court held:

> We are convinced that the central role of the IEP in the educational scheme contemplated by the EAHCA and in the standard of review developed in *Rowley* gives rise to a presumption in favor of the educational placement established by Amber's IEP. Moreover, because the IEP is jointly developed by the school district and the parents, fairness requires that the party attacking its terms should bear the burden of showing why the educational setting established by the IEP is not appropriate.[91]

In *Doe v. Brookline School Committee*,[92] the SEA determined that the LEA's IEP was inadequate and inappropriate. Although confronted with the issue of whether the LEA must continue funding of the disputed placement, the United States First Circuit Court of Appeals clearly stated the determining factor on burden of proof:

---

87. McCormick, Evidence 947 (Cleary 3d ed. 1984).
88. *Id.* at 952.
89. See § 13.8.1.
90. 703 F.2d 823 (5th Cir. 1983).
91. *Id.* at 830.
92. 722 F.2d 910 (1st Cir. 1983).

We hold that in view of the congressional preference for maintenance of the current educational placement, a party that seeks to modify an existing educational placement, program or services must proceed by a motion for preliminary injunction. As with issues of funding interim placement,... the party seeking modification of the status quo should bear the burden of proof.[93]

Perhaps the case which is most articulate in stating that the party seeking to change the status quo has the burden is *Burger v. Murray County School District*.[94] In that case, the United States District Court was directly confronted with the issue of who had the burden of proof to establish the appropriateness or inappropriateness of the LEA's decision to remove a child from a residential placement and place him in a self-contained learning disabilities class. Citing *Tatro II*,[95] the court held that "when the suggestion is made that a child, who falls under the aegis of the EAHCA and is currently learning in what has been deemed to be an appropriate setting, be moved to a different facility, the party advocating the move should bear the burden of proving its propriety."[96]

Courts have also placed the burden of persuasion on the LEA when it is the parents who are seeking to change the status quo. In *Davis v. District of Columbia Board of Education*,[97] the parents filed for the due process hearing alleging the LEA failed to provide a placement for their child. The United States District Court, without stating reasons, held that the LEA had failed to meet its burden of proof.[98]

The second view on who has the burden of persuasion and the clear trend is to allocate the burden to the party challenging the final administrative determination.[99] This opinion is consistent with an approach that views judicial review more akin to a traditional administrative review.

---

93. *Id.* at 919; *see also* Cordrey v. Eukert, 917 F.2d 1460, 1469 (6th Cir. 1990) ("the party challenging the terms of the IEP should bear the burden of proving the educational placement ... is not appropriate."); Doe v. Defendant I, 898 F.2d 1186, 1191 (6th Cir. 1990) (citing Tatro); S1 v. Turlington, 635 F.2d 342, 348–49 (5th Cir. 1981) ("In light of the remedial purposes of these statutes [EAHCA and § 504], we find that the burden is on the local and state defendants ... Our conclusion is buttressed by the fact that in most cases, the handicapped students and their parents lack the wherewithal to know or assert their rights under either EHA or section 504."); Lang v. Braintree School Comm., 545 F. Supp. 1221 (D. Mass. 1982) (the burden of proof on the LEA in attempt to change from private to public school); Davis v. District of Columbia Bd. of Educ., 530 F. Supp. 1209 (D.D.C. 1982) (burden of proof on LEA).

94. 612 F. Supp. 434 (N.D. Ga. 1984).

95. *Id.* at 437.

96. *Id.* The Third Circuit also places the burden of proof on the LEA. In Grymes v. Madden, 672 F.2d 321 (3d Cir. 1982), the court upheld the district court award of a full tuition grant because the LEA "failed to sustain its burden of proof that an appropriate public program existed." *Id.* at 322; *see also* Silvio v. Commonwealth, 439 A.2d 893 (Commw. Ct. Pa. 1982) (burden of proof on the LEA).

97. 522 F. Supp. 1102 (D.D.C. 1981) *motion to reconsider denied*, 530 F. Supp. 1209 (D.D.C. 1982).

98. 530 F. Supp. at 1211–1212. *See also* Lang v. Braintree School Comm., 545 F. Supp. 1221, 1228 (D. Mass. 1982). At least one jurisdiction has promulgated a state regulation placing the burden of proof on the LEA. *See* Grymes v. Madden, 672 F.2d 321, 322 (3d Cir. 1982).

99. *E.g.*, Spielberg v. Henrico County Pub. Schools, 853 F.2d 256, 258 n.2 (4th Cir. 1988); Kerkam v. McKenzie, 862 F.2d 884 (D.C. Cir. 1988); Hiller v. Board of Educ., 743 F. Supp. 958

In addition to the two predominant views just stated, at least two courts have placed the burden on a particular party regardless of the status quo or prior judicial determination. One court used very broad language in allocating the burden of proof and have held the parents have the burden. In *Bales v. Clarke*,[100] the parents were advocating a change in the child's placement. The parents were also seeking reimbursement for expenses of a summer program in which they unilaterally had placed their child. The court used broad language in imposing the burden on the parents, but did not provide an analysis of why the burden was placed upon them.[101] Another court has placed the burden on the LEA regardless of the status quo, because the school has an obligation to provide an IEP, allocation to the LEA protects rights, and the burden should be placed on the party better able to meet the burden.[102]

13.8.2 Burden of Proof on Procedural Issue

There is a strong argument that the LEA should bear more responsibility for the burden of persuasion on procedural issues regardless of which party is seeking to change the status quo. As stated by the United States Supreme Court, "Congress placed every bit as much emphasis upon compliance with procedures giving parents and guardians a large measure of participation at *every* stage of the administrative process."[103] Procedural violations as a result have occupied increased importance in disputes between the LEA and the parents.[104]

In fact, the Supreme Court in *Rowley* held that judicial inquiry begins with whether "the state complied with the procedures set forth in the EAHCA."[105] The Court added that such inquiry will require a court not only "to satisfy itself that the state has adopted a state plan, policies and assurances required by the EAHCA, but also determine that the state has created an IEP . . . which conforms with the requirements of § 1401(19)."[106]

This language indicates that *Rowley* imposes an affirmative requirement that inquiry be made into procedural compliance. Since it is the LEA's responsibility to ensure the procedural rights of the parents,[107] it is arguably the LEA which

(N.N.Y. 1990); Barwacz v. Michigan Dep't. of Educ., 674 F. Supp. 1296 (W.D. Mich. 1987); Tracey T. v. McDaniel, 610 F.2d 947 (N.D. Ga. 1985); McKenzie v. Jefferson, 566 F. Supp. 404, 406 (D.D.C. 1983); Cohen v. School Bd., 450 So. 2d 1238, 1241 (Fla. App. 1984).

100. 523 F. Supp. 1366 (E.D. Va. 1981) (Judge Warriner); *see also* Cohen v. Mallory, 565 F. Supp. 701, 705–708 (W.D. Mo. 1983).

101. *See also* Cohen v. Mallory, 565 F. Supp. 701, 705–708 (W.D. Mo. 1983). For a severe criticism of *Bales* see Burger v. Murray County School Dist., 612 F. Supp. 434 (N.D. Ga. 1984).

102. Lascari v. Board of Educ., 116 N.J. 30, 560 A.2d 1180 (1989).

103. Rowley, 458 U.S. at 205 (emphasis added).

104. *See, e.g.*, Spielberg v. Henrico County Pub. Schools, 853 F.2d 256 (4th Cir. 1988) (decision to change placement prior to development of an IEP violated procedural protections); Jackson v. Franklin County School Bd., 806 F.2d 623 (5th Cir. 1986) (procedural violations sufficient to support finding that LEA has failed to provide FAPE); Hall v. Vance, 774 F.2d 629 (4th Cir. 1985) (procedural violations sufficient to support finding that LEA has failed to provide FAPE).

105. Rowley, 458 U.S. at 206.

106. *Id.* at 206–07 n.27.

107. 20 U.S.C. § 1415(a).

must carry this burden. Allocating the burden of proof to the LEA to show compliance with procedural requirements is consistent with the underlying purpose of IDEA, which was remedial in nature.[108] In *S-1 v. Turlington*,[109] a case involving student expulsion, the court stated that in "light of the remedial purposes of these statutes we find that the burden is on the local and state defendants to make this determination. Our conclusion is buttressed by the fact that in most cases, the handicapped students and their parents lack the wherewithal to know or assert their rights under either EHA or section 504."[110] Since the procedural rights of IDEA were designed to remedy a problem, it is logical that the agency sought to be remedied show that it has indeed complied.

As a further reason for allocating the burden of proof for procedural violations to the LEA, it should be kept in mind that the aids available to the parent on the substantive issues such as an IEE and access to documents, are of more limited use when it comes to procedural violations. Formal discovery procedures are not available at the administrative level, and evidence of procedural violations may not be in the student's educational records.[111] It should be pointed out, however, that the Sixth Circuit, in *Cordrey v. Euckert*,[112] held that "[a]bsent more definitive authorization or compelling justification, we decline to go beyond strict review to reverse the traditional burden of proof."

13.9 Jury Trials

Under a number of theories, IDEA claims are not subject to trial by jury. IDEA claims are not subject to a jury trial because the statute specifically provides that the court will make a determination based on a preponderance of the evidence.[113] Further, the relief available under IDEA is equitable in nature.[114]

---

108. *See* Clune & VanPelt, *A Political Method of Evaluating The Education For All Handicapped Children Act Of 1975 And Several Gaps Of Gap Analysis*, 48 Law & Contemp. Prob. 7, 12–20 (1985); Neal & Kirp, *The Allure of Legalization Reconsidered: The Case of Special Education*, 48 Law & Contemp. Prob. 63, 67–72 (1985); *see generally* S-1 v. Turlington, 635 F.2d 342, 348–349 (5th Cir. 1981)("In light of the remedial purposes of these statutes. . . . ").

109. 635 F.2d 342 (5th Cir. 1981).

110. *Id.* at 349.

111. It is conceivable, for example, that the school system, in violation of IDEA, has decided that it will not place children in residential programs. *See* Abrahamson v. Hershman, 701 F.2d 223, 227 (1st Cir. 1983). Evidence of this policy decision is most likely to exist in records other than the child's educational file.

112. 917 F.2d 1460, 1466 (6th Cir. 1990).

113. 20 U.S.C. 1415(e)(2).

114. *Compare* Guardians Ass'n v. Civil Service Comm'n, 463 U.S. 582 (1983) (no jury trial under Title VI); Great American Fed. Savings and Loan Ass'n v. Novotny, 442 U.S. 366, 372–375 (1979) (no right to a jury trial under Title VII); Doe v. Region 13 Mental Health-Mental Retardation Comm'n, 704 F.2d 1402, 1407 n.3 (5th Cir. 1983) ("The inappropriateness of trial before the jury is underscored by the apparent absence of legal damages under section 504."); Shuttleworth v. Broward County, 639 F. Supp. 654, 661 (S.D. Fla. 1986) ("Courts have generally found that there is no right to trial by jury under § 504 . . . because the remedies under the Act are essentially equitable in nature.").

An additional argument that there is no right to a jury trial under IDEA would be that judicial jurisdiction under IDEA is in the nature of a review of an administrative determination, and therefore

Suits brought under § 1983, however, are subject to trial by jury.[115] It is conceivable, therefore, that the amended IDEA may have given the option to parties to request a jury trial by bringing suit concurrently under a § 1983 claim. At least one United States District Court has provided a jury trial in a suit alleging violations of § 1983 and IDEA.[116]

13.10 Evidence

There has been little discussion in cases concerning the nature of the judicial hearing itself. IDEA states that the record of the administrative proceedings "shall" be received and that "additional evidence" "shall" be received at the request of a party. The First Circuit is one of the few courts to interpret this language:

> this clause does not authorize witnesses at trial to repeat or embellish their prior administrative hearing testimony; this would be entirely inconsistent with the usual meaning of "additional."
>
> ... [T]he Act contemplates that the source of the evidence generally will be the administrative hearing record, with some supplementation at trial. The reasons for the supplementation will vary; they may include gaps in the administrative transcript owing to mechanical failure, unavailability of a witness, an improper exclusion of evidence by the administrative agency, and evidence concerning relevant events occurring subsequent to the administrative hearing. The starting point for determining what additional evidence should be received, however, is the record of the administrative proceeding.[117]

Applying these standards, the court held that an administrative hearing witness is presumed to be foreclosed from testifying at trial. The presumption can be overcome, but the Court "must be careful not ... to change the character of the hearing from one of review to a trial *de novo*."[118]

---

raises questions for the court as opposed to a jury. *See* B. Schwartz, **Administrative Law** 71–72 (2d ed. Administrative Law 1984). The courts review under IDEA, however, is greater than the typical administrative review. The requirement that the court make an independent determination based on a preponderance of the evidence, 20 U.S.C. § 1415(e), while giving due weight to the administrative proceedings, Hendrick Hudson Cent. School Dist. v. Rowley, 458 U.S. 176, 205–206 (1982), makes the courts review close to a *de novo* hearing. *See generally* Guernsey, *When The Teachers And Parents Can't Agree, Who Really Decides? Burdens of Proof And Standards Of Review Under The Education For All Handicapped Children Act*, 36 Cleveland State L. Rev. 67, 77–86 (1988).

Although a claim may not technically be subject to trial by jury, if the parties request a jury trial and the court does not request a jury trial and the court does not on its own initiative find it improper, there is no error. *See* Doe, 704 F.2d at 1407 n.3; *see also, e.g.,* Ross v. Beaumont Hospital, 678 F. Supp. 655 (E.D. Mich. 1988) (§ 504 action tried by jury).

115. S. Nahmod, **Civil Rights and Civil Liberties Litigation** 34–35 (2d ed. 1986).

116. Dodds v. Simpson, 676 F. Supp. 1045 (D. Ore. 1987). The suit also involved claimed § 504 violations. To the extent the relief sought is equitable in nature, a jury trial is inappropriate. To the extent there are both legal issues (*e.g.*, compensatory damages) and equitable issues (*e.g.*, injunctive relief) the legal issues should first be tried by the jury and then the equitable issues tried by the court. Ross v. Bernhard, 396 U.S. 531, 537–38 (1970).

117. Town of Burlington v. Massachusetts Dep't. of Educ., 736 F.2d 773, 790 (1st Cir. 1984), *aff'd*, 471 U.S. 359 (1985).

118. *Id.* at 791.

In ruling on the motions for witnesses to testify, a court should weigh heavily the important concerns of not allowing a party to undercut the statutory role of administrative expertise, the unfairness of one party's reserving its best evidence for trial, the reason the witness did not testify at the administrative hearing, and the conservation of judicial resources.[119]

In practice, the trial court, at least outside the First Circuit, is much more likely to allow at least a brief reworking of the basic issues in the case.[120] Further, the Sixth Circuit has held that new evidence is admissible. For example, in approving the school's attempt to introduce the appropriateness of placements not raised at the administrative hearing, the court stated, "[i]t is appropriate for a court that has determined that a hearing officer failed to consider the statutorily least restrictive alternative requirement to consider less restrictive placements."[121] It appears, however, that one additional witness who may not be called in the trial is the administrative review officer.[122]

13.11 Appellate Review of Judicial Determinations

The appellate court will consider a case only under theories upon which it was tried.[123] There is, however, some disagreement as to the standard of review to which these issues will be subjected.

Traditional analysis would lead one to conclude that appellate court review of the lower court's determination would be controlled by the law-fact distinction. Trial court factual determinations are reviewable only under a clearly erroneous standard[124] whereas decisions of law are decided *de novo*.[125] Under this traditional analysis, questions such as whether IDEA requires provision of related services, whether prior to amendment IDEA contemplated an award of attorneys' fees,[126] and who under IDEA has the burden of proof are reviewed *de novo* by the appellate court.

Factual questions should, however, remain subject to the clearly erroneous standard of review required under Federal Rule of Civil Procedure 52. For ex-

---

119. *Id.*

120. *But see* Barwacz v. Michigan Dep't. of Educ., 681 F. Supp. 427 (W.D. Mich. 1987).

121. Metropolitan Gov't. v. Cook, 915 F.2d 232 (6th Cir. 1990).

122. Feller v. Board of Educ., 583 F. Supp. 1526 (D. Ct. 1984) (state review officer may not be called as a witness in subsequent trial absence allegation of bad faith or improper motive on part of officer).

123. St. Louis Developmental Disabilities Treatment Center Parents' Ass'n v. Mallory, 767 F.2d 518 (8th Cir. 1985); Alexopulos v. Riles, 784 F.2d 1408 (9th Cir. 1986).

124. *See* Jaffe, *Administrative Law: Burden of Proof and Scope of Review.*, 79 Harv. L. Rev. 914 (1966).

125. *Id.*; *see also* School Bd. v. Beasley, 238 Va. 44, 380 S.E. 2d 884 (1989) (Court of Appeals had authority to reverse trial court only if decision plainly wrong or without evidence to support it).

126. *See, e.g.,* Smith v. Robinson, 468 U.S. 992 (1984). The IDEA was recently amended to provide for the award of attorneys' fees. P.L. 99-372 (1986); 20 U.S.C. § 1415(e)(4); *see, e.g.,* Board of Educ. v. Diamond, 808 F.2d 987 (3d Cir. 1986).

ample, if it has been decided that IDEA prohibits the LEA from making a placement decision prior to development of an IEP, it is a factual conclusion whether
the LEA actually had reached the decision to place the child prior to development
of the IEP.[127]

Not all decisions, however, fall neatly into the fact or law categories. A third
category is one of mixed law and fact requiring application of a legal standard
to a particular historical fact or set of facts relating to the legal standard. Many
commentators have pointed out that there is less unanimity on the standard to
be applied to legal application decisions.[128]

Whether application of historical facts to a legal standard constitutes a factual
determination governed by the clearly erroneous standard, or a legal question
allowing de novo review, varies not simply from jurisdiction to jurisdiction, but
within jurisdictions and even within topics. An often repeated example is in the
area of negligence where the question is application of a reasonable person standard to the facts of a particular incident. Most courts have held that such an
application is a question of fact.[129] Other instances of fact application, however,
are less uniform.[130]

In the context of IDEA, most courts have held that the basic issue of whether
the LEA's proposal will provide a free and appropriate education is a factual
determination and therefore subject to the clearly erroneous standard.[131] In *Mathews v. Davis*,[132] the Fourth Circuit affirmed the decision of the district court
holding that a school system's continued funding of a residential placement was
no longer necessary. In the words of the appellate court:

> We are of the opinion the finding of the district court was not clearly er-
> roneous. FRCP 52(a). It saw some of the witnesses and heard them testify.
> It had lived with the case through a multitude of hearings, orders, etc., for

---

127. *See, e.g.*, Spielberg v. Henrico County Pub. Schools, 853 F.2d 256 (4th Cir. 1988).

128. *See, e.g.*, Weiner, *The Civil Nonjury Trial and the Law-Fact Distinction*, 55 Cal. L. Rev.
1020, 1021–1024 (1967).

129. *Id.* at 1024; *but see id.* at 1026–1031.

130. *Id.* at 1022–1024.

131. *See, e.g.*, Geis v. Board of Educ., 774 F.2d 575, 584 (3d Cir. 1985) ("The Board has referred
us to no other evidence that would tend to indicate that the district court's finding [that residential
placement was appropriate] was clearly erroneous or, indeed, even erroneous."); Cain v. Yukon Pub.
Schools, Dist. I-27, 775 F.2d 15, 20 (11th Cir. 1985) ("we cannot find clearly erroneous the district
court's determination that the response was adequate."); McKenzie v. Smith, 771 F.2d 1527, 1535
(D.C. Cir. 1985) ("although the evidence could also support a contrary conclusion, we cannot say
that the district court's factual findings were clearly erroneous."); Jackson v. Franklin County School
Bd., 765 F.2d 535, 539 (5th Cir. 1985) ("Because the district court's finding is not clearly erroneous
..."); Abrahamson v. Hershman, 701 F.2d 223, 227 (1st Cir. 1983) ("we cannot say that this
conclusion was clearly erroneous."); Colin K. v. Schmidt, 715 F.2d 1, 6 (1st Cir. 1983) ("our
responsibility [is] to uphold the court's findings unless they are clearly erroneous); Doe v. Anrig,
692 F.2d 800, 808 (1st Cir. 1982) ("The task of weighing the evidence, however, is for the trier of
fact, which here was the district court. As a reviewing court we are limited to the question of whether
the district court's finding was clearly erroneous."); Jose P. v. Ambach, 669 F.2d 865, 871 (2d Cir.
1982) (allocation of legal responsibility "was not clearly erroneous); *see also* Adams Cent. School
Dist. No. 090, Adams County v. Deist, 214 Neb. 307, _____, 334 N.W.2d 775, 782 (1983) ("We
are only to determine if the hearing officer's decision is supported by the evidence, is proper under
applicable law, and if it is arbitrary or capricious.").

132. 742 F.2d 825 (4th Cir. 1984).

a period of five years, and its sensitive, systematic and thorough treatment of the parties and issues in the case from beginning to end is a model. It was in a far better position than are we to make an adjudication as to whatever slight conflict there was in the evidence.[133]

At least one panel of a federal circuit court, however, has held that it will review *de novo* the appropriateness of a special education placement. In *Department of Education v. Katherine D.,*[134] the court stated:

We apply a de novo standard of review to the questions whether the DOE's [Department of Education] IEPs constituted a "free appropriate education" within the meaning of the EAHCA...Because those determinations require us to weigh the values underlying the statute in deciding the legal sufficiency of the DOE's offers—we must, for instance, determine the weight to be assigned the explicit congressional preference that handicapped children be educated in classrooms with their peers ...—we treat them as questions of law.[135]

---

133. *Id.* at 831; *see also* Hall v. Vance, 774 F.2d 1527 (4th Cir. 1985).

134. 727 F.2d 809 (9th Cir. 1983).

135. *Id.* at 814 n.2; *see also* Clovis Unified School Dist. v. California Office of Administrative Hearings, 903 F.2d 635 (9th Cir. 1990) (*de novo* review of whether psychiatric hospital placement was educational or medical); Gregory K. v. Longview School Dist., 811 F.2d 1307 (9th Cir. 1987) ("We review *de novo* the appropriateness of a special education placement."); *but see* Larry P. v. Riles, 793 F.2d 969, 978 (9th Cir. 1984) ("The district court made two findings that addressed this argument which appellant has not shown to be clearly erroneous."). This apparent inconsistency within the circuit on the issue of what standard to apply to a specific type of factual application is not new to the Ninth Circuit. *See* Weiner, 55 Cal. L. Rev. *supra* note 6 at 1029–30.

Chapter 14

Remedies

14.1 In General

Typically, the parties in a special education case are seeking a determination of the relative responsibilities of the parents and school system for the delivery of services to the child. The parents, for example, believe the school's proposed IEP will not provide a free appropriate education, believing different services should be provided, or the school seeks a decision determining that the level of services it is prepared to provide are sufficient under IDEA. The most common remedy sought, therefore, is in the nature of injunctive or declaratory relief. Requests for damages, reimbursement and compensatory education, however, are frequent, and under limited circumstances, may be available.

14.2 State Immunity Abrogated

Until recent amendments to IDEA, an action could not be maintained directly against the state government for a violation of IDEA. The question of whether the parents could seek reimbursement for a unilateral placement and attorney's fees from the state was addressed by the United States Supreme Court in *Dellmuth v. Muth*.[1] In *Dellmuth*, the Court held that Congress had not explicitly abrogated the state's Eleventh Amendment immunity and therefore recovery from the state was precluded. *Dellmuth* involved a lower court finding a procedural violation by the state in setting up its administrative review procedure, resulting in a determination that the child was not provided a free appropriate education, and the order of reimbursement and attorney's fees.

With the 1990 amendments to IDEA, however, the United States Congress overturned the effect of *Dellmuth* by abrogating the state's sovereign immunity. In October of 1990, Congress passed the Education of the Handicapped Act Amendments. In a section entitled "Abrogation of State Sovereign Immunity", the Amendments explicitly state that States "shall not be immune under the 11th Amendment from suit in Federal court for a violation of this chapter."[2] Only violations that "occur in whole or in part after October 30, 1990" are affected

---

1. 491 U.S. 223 (1989).
2. 20 U.S.C. § 1403.

by the abrogation amendment. Violations occurring wholly before the Amendments are not covered.[3]

The local education agency did not, even under *Dellmuth* enjoy Eleventh Amendment Immunity.[4]

Where Eleventh Amendment Immunity does not exist, most courts have held that the state does have some responsibility for the delivery of educational services to the individual. Citing the general obligation of the state agency to monitor local agencies, courts have held that state agencies could be made parties under some circumstances.[5] The United States Ninth Circuit in *Doe v. Maher*,[6] reached this conclusion based on a number of rationales including the state's general supervisory obligations under IDEA and the provision which requires the children to be educated at the state or regional level when a local agency "has one or more handicapped children who can best be served by a regional or state center …."[7] The Ninth Circuit however, stated that the breach must be significant… the child's parents or guardian must give the responsible state officials adequate notice of the local agency's noncompliance, and the state must be afforded a reasonable opportunity to compel local compliance."[8] In reviewing *Maher*, the United States Supreme Court evenly split on the question, therefore leaving standing the Ninth Circuit's decision that:

> It would seem incontrovertible that, whenever, the local agency refuses or wrongfully neglects to provide a handicapped child with a free appropriate education, the child can 'best be served' on a regional or state level.[9] However, the "state is not obligated to intervene directly in an individual case whenever the local agency falls short of its responsibilities in some small regard."[10]

---

3. 20 U.S.C. § 1407; *see generally* Joshua B. v. New Trier Township High School Dist. 203, 770 F.Supp. 431 (N.D. Ill. 1991).

4. *See* Alexopulos v. San Francisco Unified School Dist., 817 F.2d 551 (9th Cir. 1987) (Although no Eleventh Amendment bar to claim against LEA, recovery denied on other grounds); *see also* Miener v. Missouri, 673 F.2d 969 (8th Cir. 1982). *See generally* Wolterman, *Access to the Courts for the Handicapped: Does the Eleventh Amendment Bar Retroactive Relief Under Section 504 of the Rehabilitation Act of 1973?*, 53 Cin. L. Rev. 1119 (1984); Comment, *The Eleventh Amendment and State Damage Liability Under the Rehabilitation Act of 1973*, 71 Va. L. Rev. 655 (1985).

5. Doe v. Maher, 793 F.2d 1470 (9th Cir. 1986) *aff'd. sub nom* Honig v. Doe, 484 U.S. 305 (1988); Kruelle v. New Castle County School Dist., 642 F.2d 687, 696–99 (3d Cir. 1981); Georgia Association of Retarded Children v. McDaniel, 511 F. Supp. 1263 (N.D. Ga. 1981) *aff'd*, 716 F.2d 1565 (11th Cir. 1983), *vacated on other grounds* 468 U.S. 1213 (1984); San Francisco Unified School Dist. v. California, 131 Cal. App. 3d 54, 182 Cal. Rptr. 525 (1982); Woolcott v. State Bd. of Educ., 134 Mich. App. 555, 351 N.W.2d 601 (1984).

Where the action alleges a specific responsibility of the state such as for failure to insure IDEA is carried out, commissioner of education or equivalent official is a proper party, Hendricks v. Gilhool, 709 F. Supp. 1362 (E.D. Pa. 1989).

6. Doe v. Maher, 793 F.2d 1470 (9th Cir. 1986) *aff'd. sub nom* Honig v. Doe, 484 U.S. 305 (1988).

7. 20 U.S.C. 1414(3); *see* Doe v. Maher, 793 F.2d 1470 (9th Cir. 1986) *aff'd. sub nom* Honig v. Doe, 484 U.S. 305 (1988).

8. Doe v. Maher, 793 F.2d 1470 (9th Cir. 1986) *aff'd. on other grounds sub nom* Honig v. Doe, 484 U.S. 305 (1988).

9. 793 F.2d at 1492 (quoting Kruelle v. New Castle County School Dist., 642 F.2d 687, 696–99 (3d Cir. 1981)).

10. Maher, 793 F.2d at 1492, *aff'd on other grounds sub nom*. Honig v. Doe, 484 U.S. at 329;

14.2.1 Avoiding Eleventh Amendment Immunity for Pre-October 30, 1990 Actions

While there will be a natural diminution of importance of the existence of sovereign immunity as time goes by, for the next several years, the impact of *Dellmuth* will continue to be felt on violations that occurred before October 30, 1990, and attention to its effects must be kept in mind. Eleventh Amendment Immunity for IDEA and § 1983 violations may be avoided in one of two ways. Instead of suing the state, the state official may be sued in his or her "individual capacity." When sued in their individual capacity, the actions are considered not to be against the state for the purposes of seeking injunctive relief.[11] A frequently cited example involves suits against state officers seeking an injunction against maintaining segregated schools. The suit is considered a suit against individuals and not barred by the Eleventh Amendment.[12]

There are two disadvantages to suing in an individual capacity. First, in order to obtain relief, the state official must be acting in violation of state or federal law. If the officials are merely following state law and have not violated federal law, the suit will be considered one against the state and the Eleventh Amendment will apply.[13] Second, when suing in the individual capacity, there may be absolute or qualified immunity defenses. These defenses can only be raised when the person is sued in their individual capacity.[14]

A second means of avoiding the impact of the Eleventh Amendment is to bring suit in state court. The Eleventh Amendment does not apply in state courts.[15] For actions under § 1983, however, a problem still remains because the United States Supreme Court has held that the state is not a "person" for the purposes of § 1983 and therefore is not subject to suit under that statute.[16]

Finally, there is nothing inconsistent with holding that the Eleventh Amendment bars damage type claims but requires the SEA to provide direct educational services if the LEA fails to provide a free appropriate education. Prospective injunctive relief, even if it entails a considerable expenditure of money is not barred by the Eleventh Amendment.[17] Indeed this is precisely what the Ninth Circuit held in *Doe v. Maher*.[18] Courts, subsequent to *Dellmuth* and before the

---

see also Eva N. v. Brock, 741 F. Supp. 626, 634 (E.D. Ky. 1990), aff'd, 943 F.2d 51 (6th Cir. 1991) ("Nonetheless, the state, having accepted the funds of the federal government and acceded to the administrative and appellate scheme of the EAHCA, has an overriding duty to provide an appropriate IEP for every handicapped child capable of benefiting from one.").

11. Ex Parte Young, 209 U.S. 123, 159–160 (1908); *see also* Will v. Michigan State Police, 491 U.S. 58, 70, n.10 (1989).

12. Wright, Miller & Cooper, Federal Practice and Procedures 3524, (1984).

13. Pennhurst State School and Hospital v. Halderman, 465 U.S. 89 (1984).

14. *Id.*

15. Maine v. Thiboutot, 448 U.S. 1, 9, n.7 (1980).

16. Will v. Michigan State Police, 491 U.S. 58 (1989).

17. Milliken v. Bradley, 433 U.S. 267 (1977) ("the federal court may award injunctive relief that governs state official's future conduct, but not one that awards retroactive monetary relief.").

18. Maher, 793 F.2d at 1493 *aff'd. sub nom.* Honig v. Doe, 484 U.S. 305 (1988).

reversal of *Dellmuth* by Congress, held that the Eleventh Amendment does not bar prospective relief where IDEA mandates specific state agency obligations.[19]

14.3 Damages In General

Damage issues must be addressed in light of three forms of damage: reimbursement when a parent has unilaterally placed their child in a private placement and it is subsequently determined that the LEA's proposed placement was inappropriate; the provision of compensatory educational services; and general monetary awards.

14.4 Tuition Reimbursement for Unilateral Placements Where LEA Fails to Provide FAPE

A frequently litigated issue in the early years of IDEA was, given the stay-put provision and the general rule that damages are unavailable under IDEA, whether parents who unilaterally removed their children from public school programs and placed them in private placements were entitled to reimbursement even if the parents and child ultimately prevailed in establishing that the public school placement was inappropriate. Following a split among the Circuit Courts, the United States Supreme Court in *Burlington School Committee v. Massachusetts Department of Education*,[20] held that parents were entitled to reimbursement for unilateral private placements when those placements are found by the court to be necessary in order for the child to receive an appropriate education.[21] The LEA has no comparable right to reimbursement.[22] Bringing an action under § 1983 should provide not only the reimbursement costs as per *Burlington*, but also costs associated with the need to find the appropriate placement.[23]

A school system may not place a child in a sectarian school.[24] Similarly, a parent who unilaterally places a child in a sectarian school may not receive reimbursement, even if the public agency has failed to provide a FAPE.[25]

---

19. Kerr Center Parents Association v. Charles, 897 F.2d 1463 (9th 1990); Burr v. Sobel, 888 F.2d 258 (2d Cir. 1989), *reaffirming sub nom*, Burr v. Ambach, 863 F.2d 1071 (1988), *vacated sub nom*, Sobol v. Burr, 492 U.S. 902 (1989); *see also* Valerie J. v. Derry Cooperative School Dist., 16 Educ. Handicapped L. Rptr. (CRR) 1068 (D.N.H. 1990) (prospective relief available against state under IDEA).

20. 471 U.S. 359 (1985).

21. School Committee of the Town of Burlington v. Department of Educ. of Mass., 471 U.S. 359 (1985).

22. *See* Lang v. Braintree School Committee, 545 F. Supp. 1221 (D. Mass. 1982).

23. *See* Jackson v. Franklin County School Bd., 806 F.2d 623 (5th Cir. 1986); *but see* White v. California, 240 Cal. Rptr. 732, 195 Cal. App. 3d 452 (1987).

24. See 8.11.1.

25. Tucker v. Bay Shore Union Free School Dist., 873 F.2d 563 (2d Cir. 1989); Hiller v. Board of Educ., 687 F. Supp. 735 (N.D.N.Y. 1988).

Courts have held that merely because the school is unapproved does not result in the denial of reimbursement. In *Carter v. Florence County School District Four*,[26] the Court held that to deny reimbursement where an unapproved school had provided an appropriate education would "undermine the values and policies" of IDEA. Also, in *Shirk v. District of Columbia*,[27] the United States District Court held the parents were entitled to reimbursement. Where they had relied upon statements by the LEA that the school was certified, but the school became decertified during the school year in question, the parents were entitled to reimbursement. On the other hand, the school system itself has no obligation to place a child in an unapproved school when it can provide a FAPE.[28]

14.5 Compensatory Education

Compensatory educational services are services designed to provide remedial educational programming to make up for the time when the school system was responsible for providing educational services but failed to do so.[29]

Courts have split on the availability of compensatory educational services under IDEA.[30] The basic argument against compensatory educational services was that IDEA did not allow the award of retrospective monetary damages. Compensatory education, it was argued, is retrospective in nature, requires the expenditure of money, and therefore constitutes a damage award. Such damage awards were 1) not contemplated by IDEA and 2) as against state defendants, were in violation of the Eleventh Amendment.[31] In addition, it is argued that since *Rowley* did not require maximization of educational benefit, where a child has already received some educational benefit the *Rowley* standard has been met and there is no requirement for compensatory education.[32]

The early arguments in favor of compensatory educational services were 1) that what was sought was prospective relief and therefore did not constitute damages[33]

---

26. Carter v. Florence County School Dist. Four, 950 F.2d 156, 164 (4th Cir. 1991) cert. granted _____ S.Ct. _____, 1992 W.L. 68814.

27. Shirk v. District of Columbia, 756 F. Supp. 31 (D.D.C. 1991).

28. Schimmel v. Spillane, 819 F.2d 477 (4th Cir. 1987).

29. *See* Comment, *Compensatory Educational Services And The Education For All Handicapped Children Act*, 1984 Wisc. L. Rev 1469, 1473 (1984).

30. *Compare* Powell v. Defore, 699 F.2d 1078 (11th Cir. 1983) (per curiam) and Adams Central School Dist. No. 090 v. Deist, 214 Neb. 307, 334 N.W.2d 775 (1983) (no compensatory education) *with* Mrs. C. v. Wheaton, 916 F.2d 69 (2d Cir. 1990) (compensatory education permissible); Burr v. Sobel, 888 F.2d 258 (2d Cir. 1989) *reaffirming sub nom* Burr v. Ambach, 863 F.2d 1071 (1988) (compensatory education available); Jefferson County Bd. of Educ. v. Breen, 694 F. Supp. 1539 (N.D. Ala. 1987), *aff'd*, 853 F.2d 853 (11th Cir. 1988) (compensatory education available); Max M. v. Thompson, 592 F. Supp. 1450 (N.D. Ill. 1984) (compensatory education available); Campbell v. Talladega Bd. of Educ., 518 F. Supp. 47 (N.D. Ala. 1981) (compensatory education available).

31. Alexopulos v. San Francisco Unified School Dist., 817 F.2d 551 (9th Cir. 1987); Alexopulos v. Riles, 784 F.2d 1408, 1412 (9th Cir. 1986) (relying on original *Miener* opinion); Powell v. Defore, 699 F.2d 1078 (11th Cir. 1983) (per curiam); Miener v. Missouri, 673 F.2d 969, 973 (8th Cir. 1982), *rev'd*, 800 F.2d 749 (8th Cir. 1986).

32. Timms v. Metropolitan School Dist., 718 F.2d 212 (7th Cir. 1983), superceded 722 F.2d 1310 (7th Cir. 1983) (recognizing possible availability of compensatory education).

33. Timms v. Metropolitan School Dist., 722 F.2d 1310 (7th Cir. 1983) (dicta); Max M. v. Thompson, 585 F. Supp. 317 (N.D. Ill. 1984) (Max M. II).

and 2) since it was prospective in nature there was no Eleventh Amendment prohibition against state defendants.[34] Recently, for example, analogy has been made to *Burlington School Committee v. Department of Education*[35] in upholding the award of compensatory education. In *Burlington*, the United States Supreme Court held that IDEA "includes the power to reimburse parents for their expenditures on private special education for a child if the court ultimately determines that such placement, rather than a proposed IEP, is proper under the Act."[36] Rejecting the label that such payments constitute damages, the Court stated that it "merely requires the Town to belatedly pay expenses that it should have paid all along and would have borne in the first instance had it developed a proper IEP."[37] A strong argument can be made that compensatory education is likewise not damages, that it merely requires the school system to provide educational services that it would have provided all along were it meeting its requirement to provide a FAPE.[38] Whether by analogy to *Burlington*, or by way of § 1983, in circumstances where compensatory education is appropriate relief, it now appears available under § 1983, if not under IDEA.[39] In any event, if a court feels compelled to view compensatory education under IDEA as damages, recent events have called into question the inability of courts to award damages under IDEA,[40] and Eleventh Amendment sovereign immunity has been abrogated by Congress.[41]

The United States Department of Education's Office of Special Education and Rehabilitative Services has also issued an opinion interpreting IDEA as allowing compensatory education.[42]

14.5.1 Compensatory Education Beyond Age 21

A related question is whether the award of compensatory education can exceed the statutory age limits of IDEA. Can the child be awarded educational services extending beyond the twenty-second birthday? Courts have held that an award

---

34. Max M. v. Thompson, 592 F. Supp. 1450, 1461 (N. D. Ill. 1984) (Max M. IV.) (though suit dismissed against state defendants in the individual capacities because of immunity); Max M. v. Thompson, 585 F. Supp. 317 (N.D. Ill. 1984) (Max M. II); *see also* Campbell v. Talladega County Bd. of Educ., 518 F. Supp.47 (N.D. Ala. 1981) (award of compensatory education with no discussion re appropriateness under IDEA); Martin v. The School Bd. of Prince George County, 3 Va. App. 197, 348 S.E.2d 857 (1986) (dicta that compensatory education probably available).

35. 471 U.S. 359 (1985). Until the Supreme Court's decision in *Burlington*, the debate on the availability of reimbursement also was focused on whether reimbursement constituted damages. Pre-*Smith v. Robinson* cases which found IDEA to not be exclusive could avoid the problem by deciding that damages were available under § 1983 or § 504. *See, e.g.*, David H. v. Spring Branch Independent School Dist., 569 F. Supp. 1324 (S.D. Texas 1983).

36. Burlington, 471 U.S. at 369.

37. *Id.* at 370–371.

38. Jefferson County Bd. of Educ. v. Breen, 694 F. Supp. 1539 (N.D. Ala. 1987), *aff'd*, 853 F.2d 853 (11th Cir. 1988); Miener v. Missouri, 800 F.2d 749, 753 (8th Cir. 1986); White v. California, 240 Cal. Rptr. 732, 195 Cal. App. 3d 452 (1987).

39. *See* Jackson v. Franklin County School Bd., 806 F.2d 623, 631–632 (5th Cir. 1986).

40. See 14.6.

41. See 14.2.

42. Kohn Inquiry, 17 Educ. Handicapped L. Rep. (LRP) 522 (1991).

of services beyond the twenty-second birthday violates IDEA age provisions.[43] The contrary position, however, has also been upheld.[44] This latter position allowing the award of compensatory education would provide logical protection to parents who are unable to make unilateral placements pending reimbursement under *Burlington*. It is conceivable under the former view that the 20 year-old child of wealthy parents could receive education in a unilateral placement which was subsequently reimbursed after the twenty-second birthday. The child of poor parents who must await resolution of the administrative and judicial process in order to receive the educational services, however, would be precluded from receiving those same two years of educational service since the child might be twenty-two by the time the process ends.[45] The Supreme Court has repeatedly discussed the time-consuming nature of the administrative and judicial process. Indeed, the possibility of delay in receiving educational benefits was one of the factors leading the Court to its decision in *Burlington*.[46]

14.6 Monetary Damages

Until recently, the question whether general monetary damages were available under IDEA was easy to answer. As a general rule, absent egregious due process violations or endangerment of a child's health, general monetary damages were consistently held to be unavailable under IDEA.[47] Three events, however, have raised serious questions about the continued validity of these cases. Although there is sure to be continuing litigation, these three events significantly clarify whether damages are available for violations. The bottom line appears to be that by way of either IDEA, § 1983, § 504, or some combination, monetary damages are available.

The first event indicating monetary damages are probably available was recognition of the ability to bring suit under § 1983 and § 504. Damages are available under § 1983.[48] One of the first cases decided after the amendment to IDEA

---

43. *E.g.*, Alexopulos v. Riles, 784 F.2d 1408, 1411 (9th Cir. 1986); Adams Central School Dist. v. Deist, 214 Neb. 307, 334 N.W.2d 775 (1983); Natrona County School Dist. No. 1 v. McKnight, 764 P.2d 1039 (Wyo. 1988).

44. *E.g.*, Lester H. v. Gilhool, 916 F.2d 865 (3d Cir. 1990); Burr v. Sobol, 888 F.2d 258 (2d Cir. 1989) *reaffirming sub nom* Burr v. Ambach, 863 F.2d 1071 (1988); Miener v. Missouri, 800 F.2d 749, 754 (8th Cir. 1986); Campbell v. Talladega County Bd. of Educ., 518 F. Supp. 47, 56 (N.D. Ala. 1981); White v. California, 240 Cal. Rptr. 732, 195 Cal. App. 3d 452 (1987) (but holding money damages not available).

45. *See* White v. California, 240 Cal. Rptr. 732, 195 Cal. App. 3d 452 (1987).

46. Burlington, 471 U.S. at 373.

47. *E.g.* Anderson v. Thompson, 658 F.2d 1205, 1213–14 (7th Cir. 1981); Christopher N. v. McDaniel, 569 F. Supp. 291 (N.D. Ga. 1983); Johnson v. Clarke, 165 Mich. App. 366, 418 N.W.2d 466 (1987). Some courts have held that even under exceptional circumstances, damages are unavailable under IDEA. *See, e.g.,* Waterman v. Marquette—Alger Intermediate School Dist., 739 F. Supp. 361 (W.D. Mich. 1990); Smith v. Philadelphia School Dist., 679 F. Supp. 479, 484 (E.D. Pa. 1988) Sanders v. Marquette Public Schools, 561 F. Supp. 1361 (W.D. Mich. 1983); Woolcott v. State Bd. of Educ., 134 Mich. App. 555, 351 N.W.2d 601, 606 (1984).

48. *See* Carey v. Piphus, 435 U.S. 247 (1978). Damages against the state in federal court, however, are barred by the Eleventh Amendment. Edelman v. Jordan, 415 U.S. 651 (1974). To recover

allowing suit to be brought under both IDEA and § 1983 recognized the possibility of receiving monetary damages. In *Jackson v. Franklin County School Board*,[49] a student and his mother brought suit under IDEA and § 1983. In *Jackson*, the child was suspended for three days and then, as a result of delinquency charges having been brought, was sent to a state hospital for evaluation and treatment. Upon release from the hospital, the LEA indicated that the child should not return to school since there was only one month remaining and exams would soon start. Plaintiffs challenged the denial of educational services for the final month of the 1984 school year and for the first two months of the next school year, and sought monetary damages.[50]

The court held that failure of the LEA to convene a conference was a *"per se* violation of the EAHCA,"[51] and that the child's "due process rights, as contemplated by the Fourteenth Amendment and as specifically enumerated by the EAHCA, were violated by Franklin County School Officials' failure to provide notice and a hearing concerning his continued exclusion from school."[52] The court remanded the case to determine the extent to which the LEA's actions were the cause of any loss to the child and "what damages, either monetary, or in the form of remedial educational services ... would be appropriate."[53] The court, therefore, clearly recognized the right to money damages, however it did state, "although monetary relief is available, remedial educational services may be more valuable than any pecuniary damages that could be awarded."[54]

---

damages in federal court, therefore, suit must be brought against the local school district or the local educators. *See generally Id*. at 667 n.12 ("a county defendant is not necessarily a state defendant for purposes of the Eleventh Amendment"); Fay v. South Colonie Central School Dist., 802 F.2d 21 (2d Cir. 1986) (damages could not be obtained against state defendant, but damages are available against local school division); Gilliam v. Omaha, 524 F.2d 1013 (8th Cir. 1975). Damages awarded under § 1983 must be truly compensatory and not based on the abstract value or worth of the constitutional or statutory right violated. Memphis Community School Dist. v. Stachura, 477 U.S. 299 (1986). For a discussion of the ability to bring an action under 1983 for issues also covered by IDEA see 1.5.

49. 806 F.2d 623 (5th Cir. 1986); *see also* Board of Educ. v. Diamond, 808 F.2d 987, 996 (3d Cir. 1986).

50. The court seemed to assume that the provision making § 1983 and § 504 available is retroactive. *Id*. at 627–28. As it points out in a footnote, however, in response to the argument that *Smith v. Robinson* applied when the suit was originally filed

> even had Congress not amended the EAHCA, we believe James' 1983 claim was proper. The Court's holding in *Smith* was limited to equal protection claims, whereas [the child here] sought relief for a deprivation of his due process rights. ... [T]he Court explained:
>
> > [T]here is no indication that agencies should be exempt from a fee award where plaintiffs have had to resort to judicial relief to force the agencies to provide them the process they are constitutionally due.

Id. at 627–28 n.7.

51. *Id*. at 628.

52. *Id*. at 631.

53. *Id*. at 631; *see also* Fay v. South Colonie Central School Dist., 802 F.2d 21 (2d Cir. 1986) (upon appropriate proof, compensatory damages could be had for the LEA's failure to provide required notices).

54. *Id*. at 632.

It should be emphasized that for many situations there will not be monetary damages. As the

There are, however, decisions which hold that no compensatory damages are available under § 1983 for claims recognized under IDEA because 1983 is derivative of IDEA.[55] Such a holding, however, raises the question of what the congressional purpose was in providing the ability to bring suit under both IDEA and § 1983? The amended IDEA specifically provides that "[n]othing in this title shall be construed to restrict or limit the rights procedures, and remedies available under the Constitution, [Section 504], or other Federal statutes protecting the rights of handicapped children and youth ..."[56] The statute then specifically recognizes the fact that the relief may be covered under both, when it provides that "before filing for a civil action under such laws *seeking relief that is also available under this part*" administrative remedies must be exhausted under IDEA.[57] It seems logical that, as implicit in the court's holding in *Jackson* some additional protection is available. Further, to the extent a public agency argues the Congress intended to preclude a specific remedy available under § 1983 (such as damages), it has the burden of persuasion that Congress has expressly withdrawn the § 1983 remedy.[58]

The availability of damages under § 504 has not always been clear. In *Smith v. Robinson*,[59] the Court stated:

> There is some confusion among the circuits as to the availability of a damages remedy under § 504 and under the EAHCA. Without expressing an opinion on the matter, we note that courts generally agree damages are available under 504, but are available under the EAHCA only in exceptional circumstances.[60]

The Court had previously said in *Consolidated Rail Corporation v. Darrone*,[61] a § 504 action seeking back pay for being wrongfully discharged:

> Without determining the extent to which money damages are available under § 504, we think it clear that § 504 authorizes a plaintiff who alleges intentional discrimination to bring an equitable action for backpay.[62]

---

court pointed out in *Jackson*, compensatory educational services will be better suited to meet the needs of the plaintiff. *See generally*, Comment *Compensating the Handicapped: An Approach to Determining the Appropriateness of Damages for Violations of Section 504*, 1981 B.Y.U. L. Rev. 133. Also, the stay put provisions of IDEA will often protect the LEA from damages in those instance where the LEA is improperly trying to change placement. In instances of bad faith on the part of the LEA, damages had already been recognized by the courts. *See, e.g.*, Anderson v. Thompson, 658 F.2d 1205 (7th Cir. 1981); *see generally* Miener v. Missouri, 673 F.2d 969, 978 (8th Cir. 1982).

55. *See, e.g.*, Barnett v. Fairfax County School Bd., 721 F. Supp. 755 (E.D. Va. 1989), *aff'd*, 927 F.2d 146 (4th Cir. 1991).

56. 20 U.S.C. 1415(f).

57. *Id.* (emphasis added).

58. Golden Gate Transit Corp. v. City of Los Angeles, 493 U.S. 103 (1989); *see also* Wilder v. Virginia Hospital Association, 496 U.S. 498 (1990).

59. Smith v. Robinson, 468 U.S. 992 (1984).

60. Smith v. Robinson, 468 U.S. 992, 1020 n.24 (1984).

61. Consolidated Rail Corp. v. Darrone, 465 U.S. 624 (1984).

62. Consolidated Rail Corp. v. Darrone, 465 U.S. 630–631 (1984); see also Guardians Association v. Civil Service Commission, 463 U.S. 582, 607 n.27 (1983) (compensatory relief could be awarded in Title VI actions); Briggs, *Safeguarding Equality for the Handicapped: Compensatory Relief Under Section 504 of the Rehabilitation Act of 1973*, 1986 Duke L. J. 197, 208 (1986) ("Because

The second major event significantly clarifies the question of the availability of monetary damages under both IDEA and § 504. In *Franklin v. Gwinnett County Public Schools*,[63] the United States Supreme Court held that monetary damages were available in a sex discrimination action under Title IX of the Education Amendments of 1972.[64] What is significant about this case is not only that the language of Title IX is similar to § 504,[65] but that the Court explicitly stated:The general rule, therefore, is that absent clear direction to the contrary by Congress, the federal courts have the power to award any appropriate relief in a cognizable cause of action brought pursuant to a federal statute.[66] The Court's language seems clearly to lead to the conclusion that, unless Congress has indicated to the contrary, damages should be available under IDEA as well as § 504.[67]

An inquiry into whether a "clear direction to the contrary" has been made by Congress leads to the third major event indicating monetary damages are probably available. As discussed previously, in 1990 Congress overturned the Supreme Court's determination that states enjoyed Eleventh Amendment sovereign immunity.[68] As part of these 1990 amendments, IDEA was also amended to provide:

> In a suit against a State for a violation of this Act, remedies (including remedies both at law and in equity) are available for such a violation to the same extent as such remedies are available for such a violation in the suit against any public entity other than a State.[69]

Monetary damages are a traditional legal remedy, and, therefore, Congress appears to have implicitly recognized their availability under IDEA much less to have not indicated a "clear direction to the contrary."

14.7 Procedural Violation Remedy

The meaning of the phrase "free appropriate public education" was first addressed by the United States Supreme Court in *Hendrick Hudson District Board of Education v. Rowley*.[70] In *Rowley*, the Court identified both substantive and procedural components of the state's responsibilities under the Act:

> [A] court's inquiry in suits brought under § 1415(e)(2) is twofold. First has the State complied with the procedures set forth in the Act? And second, is

---

§ 505(a)(2) . . . provides that Title VI remedies are available to § 504 claimants, *Guardians* implies by analogy the existence of compensatory relief under § 504."); Flaccus, *Discrimination Legislation for the Handicapped: Much Ferment and Erosion of Coverage*, 55 Cin. L. Rev. 81, 90 (1986).

63. 112 S. Ct. 1028 (1992).

64. 20 U.S.C. §§ 1681–1688.

65. The statute provides in pertinent part that

No person in the United States shall, on the basis of sex, be excluded from participation in, be denied the benefits of, or be subjected to discrimination under any education program or activity receiving Federal financial assistance.

66. 112 S. Ct. at 1035.

67. Tanberg v. Weld County Sheriff, 787 F.Supp. 970 (D. Colo. 1992) (citing *Gwinnett County Public Schools* to support finding that monetary damages available under 504).

68. See 14.2.

69. 20 U.S.C. § 1403(b).

70. 458 U.S. 176 (1981).

the individualized educational program developed through the Act's procedures reasonably calculated to enable the child to receive educational benefits? If these requirements are met, the State has complied with the obligations imposed by Congress and the courts can require no more.[71]

The Court recognized that the procedural rights are as important as the substantive rights accorded under the Act:

> When the elaborate and highly specific procedural safeguards embodied in § 1415 are contrasted with the general and somewhat imprecise substantive admonitions contained in the Act, we think that the importance Congress attached to these procedural safeguards cannot be gainsaid. It seems to us no exaggeration to say that Congress placed every bit as much emphasis upon compliance with procedures giving parents and guardians a large measure of participation at every stage of the administrative process . . . as it did upon the measurement of the resulting IEP against a substantive standard.[72]

Given the importance Congress and the Supreme Court attached to procedural compliance, and the central requirement under the Act to provide a FAPE, it is not surprising that an increasing amount of litigation under the Act has focused on whether the school system has violated the procedural rights of the parents and if so, what remedy is available for that violation.

The procedural protections afforded by the Act are extensive. First, there are those protections afforded to both the school and to the parents for resolving disputes between them. The protections include the right to request a due process hearing,[73] a state level review,[74] and, following administrative review, the right to file suit in either state or federal court.[75]

---

71. *Id.* at 206–207.

72. Rowley, 458 U.S. at 207; *see also* Smith v. Robinson, 468 U.S. 992, 1011 (1984) (the procedures "effect Congress' intent that each child's individual educational needs be worked out through a process that . . . includes . . . detailed procedural safeguards."). On a substantive level, Congress was very general in defining a FAPE. IDEA provides that a FAPE:

> means special education and related services which (A) have been provided at public expense, under public supervision and direction, and without charge, (B) meet standards of the State educational agency, (C) include an appropriate preschool, elementary, or secondary school education in the State involved, and (D) are provided in conformity with the individualized education program. . . .

20 U.S.C. § 1401(18)(C); *see also* 34 C.F.R. § 300.8.

> The statutory definition of "special education" is: specially designed instruction, at no cost to parents or guardians, to meet the unique needs of a child with a disability, including classroom instruction, instruction in physical education, home instruction, and instruction in hospitals and institutions.

20 U.S.C. § 1401(16); 34 C.F.R. § 300.17

Regulations also indicate that "special education" includes vocational education if specially designed to meet the needs of a disabled child. 34 C.F.R. § 300.14(a)(3). Further, if "related services" have independent educational value they may constitute special education. 34 C.F.R. § 300.14(a)(2).

"Related Services" are defined as "Transportation, and such developmental, corrective, and other supportive services . . . as may be required to assist a handicapped child to benefit from special education." 20 U.S.C. § 1401(17).

Examples of related services are given in the Act as well

73. 20 U.S.C. § 1415(b)(2).

74. *Id.* § 1415(c).

Second, there are procedural requirements which insure that educational decision-making proceeds with appropriate information. These procedures include the requirement the child be identified[76] and be evaluated by a multi-disciplinary team.[77] Other protections within this category include requiring a determination of the child's eligibility for special education,[78] the development at least annually of the Individual Education Program (IEP), and re-evaluation at least every three years.[79] Congress also required multi-disciplinary and nondiscriminatory testing,[80] and to insure the parents had sufficient information available to participate in the educational decision-making, Congress provided the parents with the right to have an independent educational evaluation (IEE) at public expense.[81] The IEE, like the school system's evaluation, is to be multi-disciplinary.[82]

Perhaps most importantly, there is a third type of protection designed to insure that parents are given participation at virtually every stage of the administrative process.[83] In *Honig v. Doe*,[84] the Court stated that the procedural rights "guarantee parents both an opportunity for meaningful input into all decisions affecting their child's education, and the right to seek review of any decisions they think inappropriate."

The significant role parents are to play is reinforced throughout the Act. After an eligibility determination, an IEP is developed, with parental participation.[85] Following development of an IEP, a placement decision is made, based on the goals and objectives contained in the IEP.[86] Written notice must be provided to the parent a reasonable time before the school proposes to change the child's identification, evaluation, or educational placement, or refuses to take any of these actions[87] Parental consent is explicitly required before obtaining a preplacement evaluation or initially placing the child.[88] The role of a parent is so important, that a surrogate parent must be appointed where there is no parent or the parents' whereabouts are unknown, or when the child is a ward of the state.[89] Finally, an often potent protection for the parent is the stay-put provision previously discussed.[90]

---

74. *Id.* § 1415(c).

75. *Id.* § 1415(e)(1).

76. 20 U.S.C. § 1414(a)(1)(A); 34 C.F.R. § 300.220.

77. 20 U.S.C. § 1412(5)(C); 34 C.F.R. § 300.531.

78. 34 C.F.R. § 300.343-.345.

79. 34 C.F.R. § 300.534; *see also* 20 U.S.C. § 1412(5)(c).

80. 20 U.S.C. § 1412(5)(C); *see* 34 C.F.R. § 300.532.

81. 20 U.S.C. § 1415(b)(1)(A); *see* 34 C.F.R. § 300.503.

82. 20 U.S.C. § 1415(b)(1)(A).

83. Rowley, 458 U.S. at 207; *see also* Smith v. Robinson, 468 U.S. 992, 1011 (1984)(the procedures "effect Congress' intent that each child's individual educational needs be worked out through a process that . . . includes . . . detailed procedural safeguards.").

84. 484 U.S. 305, 311–12 (1988).

85. 20 U.S.C. § 1401(19); *see* 34 C.F.R. § 300.345.

86. 34 C.F.R. § 300.552; *see also* 20 U.S.C. §§ 1412(2)(B)(4), (5)(B), (6), 1414(a)(5); 34 C.F.R. Pt. 300, app. C, Question 42.

87. 34 C.F.R. § 300.504(a).

88. 34 C.F.R. § 300.504(b).

89. 34 C.F.R. § 300.514(a).

90. See 11.7.

Early procedural violation cases provided what appeared to be a *per se* rule that violation of the procedural rights of the parent or child resulted in the granting of substantive relief. Existing analysis of procedural violations has developed toward asking first whether a procedural violation occurred, and second whether the parents or child were prejudiced by that violation. The burden of proof appears to be on the parents to establish both the violation and the harm.

Two of the earliest procedural violation cases arose in the Fourth Circuit. In *Hall v. Vance County Board of Education*,[91] the court addressed the educational programming of a sixteen-year-old child with dyslexia. The district court ruled that the school had failed to provide a FAPE and had egregiously violated the procedural requirements of the Act.

In *Hall*, the child had difficulty in school until his parents placed him in a private educational program. Both the state level review officer and the district court found that throughout their dealings with the parents the school had consistently failed to provide the parents with notice of their procedural rights under the Act. *Hall* dealt primarily with the dispute resolution rights under the Act. While the parents and the school system had numerous contacts, the parents were never informed of their right to have the dispute resolved.[92] The Fourth Circuit held that, "[u]nder *Rowley*, these failures to meet the Act's procedural requirements are adequate grounds by themselves for holding that the school failed to provide James a FAPE before January, 1982."[93]

While *Hall* dealt with excluding parents from the dispute resolution process, *Spielberg v. Henrico County Public Schools*[94] dealt with excluding the parents from the decision-making process. *Spielberg* involved a seventeen-year-old boy with the functional skills of an eighteen-month-old child. The school system decided to change the child's educational placement from a private 12 month residential program to a nine-month regular school day program, with an abbreviated summer school program of six weeks. The district court found that the school had made this decision prior to developing an IEP upon which the decision could be based. Both the district and appellate court recognized this decision-making as a violation of federal regulations which require placement decisions to be based on an existing IEP. The appellate court wrote:

> The decision to place Jonathan at [the public school placement] before developing an IEP on which to base that placement decision violates this regulation as interpreted by the Secretary of Education. It also violates the spirit and intent of the EHA, which emphasizes parental involvement. After the fact involvement is not enough.[95]

---

91. 774 F.2d 629 (4th Cir. 1985).

92. While the court did not explicitly indicate the source of the authority to grant substantive relief, the court in discussing the nature of the procedural violation placed heavy reliance on the language in *Rowley* concerning the importance of procedural rights and in particular the importance of parental participation. Later courts have indicated that the power to award substantive relief for procedural violations "stems from the 'broad discretion' conferred on the courts to grant appropriate relief under Sec. 1415(e)(2)." Evans v. District No. 17 of Douglas County, 841 F.2d 824, 828 (8th Cir. 1988).

93. 774 F.2d at 635.

94. 853 F.2d 256 (4th Cir. 1988).

95. *Id.* at 259.

These two cases suggest, at least with regard to dispute resolution and parental participation rights, that in circumstances where there is a complete denial of procedural protection, substantive relief should be provided. Such a reading is consistent with several other early circuit court decisions. In *Jackson v. Franklin County School Board*,[96] for example, James, a sixteen-year-old child with a learning disability, functioning at a third grade level, was suspended for three days for accosting several female classmates. Delinquency charges were filed and the mother agreed to send him to a state hospital for evaluation and treatment. In early April, after a little over 2 months, he was discharged from hospital. The director of special education programs conferred with James' social worker who told his mother that it would not be a good time for the child to return to school. James, did not return to school that academic year.

In the fall, James's mother asked about his status and was told by the director of special education that James would need a new IEP before re-enrollment. The director, however, refused to develop a new IEP or discuss re-enrollment until after the delinquency matter was resolved. The mother filed a complaint with the State Department of Education, spoke to the Superintendent of Schools, and finally sought legal counsel. An IEP meeting was finally scheduled for October 31. As a result of this meeting, the school system took the position that James required a residential program. His mother believed he should be placed in the public schools.

While there was some disagreement over whether the social worker had been speaking on behalf of the mother when she stated that in April it was not a good idea to have James come back, "the burden rests squarely on the school or agency to safeguard handicapped children's rights by informing their parents of those rights."[97]

There were in effect two types of violations in *Jackson*. First, there was the failure to provide notice of the relevant procedural rights and protection. This violation was similar to the violation in *Hall*. Second, there was the failure to develop an IEP both in April and August. The court found that the failure to provide notice and a hearing concerning his exclusion from school violated James's rights under IDEA. The court also held that the school's failure to convene an IEP meeting after the April release from the state hospital "was a *per se* violation" of the IDEA.[98] Citing *Hall*, the court held that the procedural violation was sufficient to establish that the school had failed to provide a FAPE.[99] The second violation in many ways is similar to the violation in *Spielberg* in the sense that the school precluded the parents from the decision-making process by refusing to conduct an IEP meeting. Again, total exclusion from two of the three sets of protection allowed substantive recovery.

The ultimate remedy for this failure to provide procedural rights was somewhat unclear in *Jackson*. Unlike cases such as *Spielberg* where the child is already in the placement the parents are seeking,[100] or *Hall* where the parents could afford to unilaterally place the child in the desired location and then seek reimbursement, here the child was actually denied education during the relevant time period. The

---

96. 806 F.2d 623 (5th Cir. 1986).
97. *Id.* at 629.
98. *Id.* at 628.
99. *Id.* at 629.
100. *Spielberg*, 853 F.2d at 257.

court, therefore, remanded the case for a determination of whether damages or compensatory educational services were appropriate.[101]

Recent cases have been more tolerant of procedural violations. In what is perhaps the most influential decision distinguishing cases such as *Hall, Spielberg,* and *Jackson,* the Eighth Circuit dealt with the educational needs of a ten-year-old girl with cerebral palsy, mental retardation, and a severe behavioral impairment in *Evans v. District No. 17 of Douglas County.*[102] In *Evans* the parents alleged that there was a procedural violation because of a failure to provide required triennial evaluations. The district court, however, found that the failure to perform the evaluations did not deny the girl, Christine, a FAPE because there was no evidence of harm to her education.

Evans is different from *Hall, Spielberg* and *Jackson* in that there was an affirmative finding by the court that educational programming was apparently not affected by the procedural violation. The court reasoned that a triennial evaluation was ultimately scheduled before the beginning of the next school year, and that no changes would have occurred before that time anyway. The court in *Evans* also stated that the earlier cases could be distinguished perhaps on the basis that the types of procedural violations involved were by their nature more likely to result in impact on the educational programming,

Two points about *Evans* are troubling, however. The court's statement that there was no proof of harm to the child's education appears to be the first time a court explicitly required a showing of prejudice. In a sense *Evans* reconciles the cases by implying a showing of prejudice is always required and that it was obvious in the earlier cases that prejudice would occur. As significantly, the statement also seemed to place the burden of persuasion on the parents not only to show the existence of a procedural violation, but also to show that the violation caused damage.

The Eleventh Circuit has recently agreed with the *Evans* decision. In *Doe v. Alabama State Department of Education,*[103] the court held that a procedural violation was not sufficient to warrant relief. In *Doe,* the parents of a nineteen-year-old child with a manic-depressive illness sought a private residential program for their son. The school district offered in-home tutoring services and 24-hour psychiatric supervision. The district court held that the school system's educational program was appropriate, and the parents appealed.

The parents alleged numerous procedural violations. Among the allegations, the parents claimed they were not provided with the detailed notice required under IDEA and as a result, there was ineffective parental participation. The court, however, upheld the district court's finding that the parents had actual notice, despite deficiencies in the notice, and that the parents' participation had been "full and effective."[104] The court rejected the parents' argument that violation of the notice requirement was a *per se* violation of IDEA which itself constituted

---

101. The court recognized that given the Handicapped Children's Protection Act of 1986, suit could be brought concurrently under § 1983 and IDEA. While monetary damages are generally unavailable under the IDEA absent special circumstances, money damages are available under § 1983.

102. 841 F.2d 824 (8th Cir. 1988).

103. 915 F.2d 651 (11th Cir. 1990).

104. *Id.* at 662.

a failure to provide a FAPE. Citing *Evans*, the court held that "[b]ecause the notice deficiencies in this case had no impact on the Doe's full and effective participation in the IEP process and because the purpose of the procedural requirement was fully realized in this case . . . there has been no violation . . . which warrants relief."[105]

Even the Fourth Circuit, in a more recent decision, has followed *Evans*. In *Board of Education of the County of Cabell v. Dienelt*,[106] The parents of a child with a learning disability rejected the "standard" IEP suggested by his teacher and unilaterally placed him in a private school. The parents then instituted a due process proceeding. The district court found that the school did not conduct an interdisciplinary review or involve the parents in the IEP development. In a very brief opinion, citing *Rowley* and quoting *Hall*, the court held that the procedural violations constituted a failure to provide a FAPE, and upheld the reimbursement of the private placement. Exclusion of the parents in development of the IEP clearly falls within the complete denial of the decision-making rights, and therefore is consistent with the previous Fourth Circuit decisions and with *Evans* as well.[107]

There are, to be sure, a few courts which continue to hold open the question of whether a separate test of prejudice is required. In *Leonard v. McKenzie*,[108] for example, the District of Columbia Circuit Court left unanswered the question whether procedural violations were "subject to a separate test of 'prejudice,' " and held that an administrative "Foul-up" of sending an erroneous Notice of Placement, which was corrected prior to the beginning of the academic school year, did not constitute a procedural violation.[109] In *Kerkam v. McKenzie*,[110]

---

105. *Id.* (footnote omitted).

The parents also alleged that the child was suspended from school without the benefit of an IEP meeting. Such an expulsion is clearly a violation of the Act, *Honig*, 484 U.S. at 325–26 n.8, but the court held that the claim was waived in due process hearing by the parents. Doe v. Alabama, 915 F.2d at 660.

Another alleged violation of procedural requirements was the delivery of educational services without an IEP being in place. The court, however, found that this was the result of the parents' actions. *Id.* at 663.

The parents also contended that the initial classification of their son as emotionally conflicted was done without proper evaluations, and therefore the IEP was invalid because it was not based on appropriate evaluations. There was no violation, however, because the school had not evaluated the child because of his fragile emotional state. *Id.* at 664.

The final alleged procedural violation was that the school had a "generalized policy" against placing children in private programs and that this was in violation of the requirement that the school provide a continuum of educational services. Citing *Georgia Association of Retarded Citizens v. McDaniel*, 716 F.2d 1565 (11th Cir. 1983), *vacated* 468 U.S. 1213 (1984) the court recognized that if this were an inflexible policy, there would be a violation of the Act. Here, however, the school had consulted with experts and found that the public school was appropriate.

106. 843 F.2d 813 (4th Cir. 1988).

107. Finding that a failure to conduct the multidisciplinary review, however, seems more in the nature of an *Evans* problem. Given that there were both types of violations, however, Evans is not inconsistent.

108. 869 F.2d 1558, 1562 n.3 (D.C. Cir. 1989).

109. *See also* Block v. District of Columbia, 748 F. Supp. 891, 897–98 (D.D.C. 1990) where the school failed to develop an IEP for a 13 year-old student with a learning disability. Citing *Andersen*, the court stated that "assuming without deciding that 'prejudice' is a prerequisite, the Court holds that the Blocks have shown that they were seriously prejudiced and that DCPS's failure to provide

however, the District of Columbia Circuit suggested that the trial court consider the "potentially prejudicial effect" of procedural violations.[111] In *Andersen v. District of Columbia*,[112] the court went even further, citing *Evans* with approval, but, because counsel withdrew the claim, not deciding whether there was a separate requirement of prejudice.

Evans, therefore, is clearly the prevailing means by which courts will analyze procedural violations. In summary, then, the courts will not apply a *per se* analysis. Some showing of prejudice is required, and the language in *Evans* seems to indicate that the parents have the burden of persuasion on both the question of whether there was a violation to begin with and whether the violation resulted in prejudice.

The analysis of procedural violations as it has developed through *Evans* is troubling in several respects. Assuming that a *per se* rule granting substantive relief would constitute an inappropriate windfall to the parent, very little guidance is provided on what type of procedural violation will rise to the level of justifying substantive relief. *Andersen* recognized the ambiguity created by the existing analysis. The court stated that the early Fourth Circuit cases "are themselves ambiguous, as the errors were ones that the court may have viewed as inherently carrying a high probability of prejudice."[113] Citing *Evans* and *Kerkam* and recognizing that *Leonard* left open the question, the court in *Andersen* stated that "we think the plaintiffs here are wise to have abandoned their arguments" that sending an erroneous Notice of Placement which was later corrected before the beginning of the school year, constituted a procedural violation sufficient to warrant a finding that the school had failed to provide a FAPE.[114] Classifying the error as an "administrative foul-up" the court stated "that the errors are certainly far less likely to have affected the placements or the administrative decisions than those involved in *Dienelt*, *Spielberg*, and *Hall*."[115] The reference to a "foul-up" in *Andersen*, however, is, of course, conclusory and does not tell us which violations are mere technicalities.[116]

---

a complete and appropriate IEP and its delay in rectifying the problems directly affected the 1989–90 school year."

110. 862 F.2d 884 (D.C. Cir. 1988).

111. In the trial court, the defects in procedures alleged appear to have been that the hearing officer did not consider a placement proposed by the parents and defects in the proposed notice of placement. Court held that notice was defective, but that parents were aware of the reasons for the placement and were not prejudiced by the defective notice. Kerkam v. District of Columbia Bd. of Educ., 672 F. Supp. 519 (D.D.C. 1987) rev'd on other grounds 862 F.2d 884 (D.C. Cir. 1988).

112. 877 F.2d 1018 (D.C. Cir. 1989).

113. Andersen, 877 F.2d at 1021.

114. *Id.*

115. *Id.* at 1021, 1022.

116. Such conclusory statements are all too common. Doe v. Defendant I, 898 F.2d 1186 (6th Cir. 1990), for example, dealt with a child with a learning disability called dysgraphic disorder. The parents requested a delay in holding an IEP meeting prior to the child's entry into the seventh grade in order to observe the child's adjustment. An IEP was ultimately developed in November, and as a result, the school offered tutoring and testing services to the parents. The parents refused these services and obtained them privately. When the school refused to pay for these private services, the parents placed the child in a private program and requested a due process hearing. On a number of procedural challenges, the court first held that the failure to have an IEP in place at the beginning of the school year did not constitute a procedural violation. While the regulations do require the school to have an IEP in effect at the beginning of each school year, that IEP can only be implemented

Anticipating a criticism that a prejudice test would minimize the procedural importance, the court in *Evans* stated that its decision did "not in any way render the force of [IDEA] nugatory," since the parents could invoke the procedures of the Act to compel the system to provide the evaluation, or seek reimbursement for expenses incurred as a result of the violation (apparently conducting the evaluation and seeking reimbursement).[117] Despite the language in *Evans* to the contrary, that the force of the Act would not be "nugatory," focusing on prejudice may very well undermine the Act's primary purpose. Prejudice in the cases seems to focus on educational or financial harm. The Act, however, is a remedial statute. The Act was designed to correct the inappropriate behavior of the educational establishment—behavior not motivated merely by a lack of money, but by a lack of will. As the United States Supreme Court said in *Honig v. Doe*, "[a]lthough these educational failings resulted in part from funding constraints, Congress recognized that the problem reflected more than a lack of financial resources at the state and local levels."[118] As already mentioned, according to *Rowley*, the main tool used in effecting this remedy are the procedural protection. Lower courts have emphasized the procedural protection as well. The court in *Jackson*, for example, stated that the procedural safeguards are coextensive with the substantive right.[119]

As troubling as anything else in *Evans* is the language placing the burden of proof on the parents, both as to the existence of the procedural violation and

---

after appropriate IEP meetings. The parents in effect were the cause of the failure to have the IEP in effect because of their requests to delay intervention until the child's adjustment could be studied.

The parents also claimed procedural violations occurred because the IEP did not state the child's present level of educational functioning nor did it state objective criteria for determining whether the instructional objectives were being met.

Both of these items are explicitly required under both the Act and its implementing regulations. 20 U.S.C. § 1401(19); 34 C.F.R. § 300.346. The court, however, held that "to say that these technical deviations ... render appellant's IEP invalid is to exalt form over substance" since the parents and school system were all aware of the information required, but missing. Doe v. Defendant I, 898 F.2d at 1190. The court recognized that Rowley emphasized the importance of procedural safeguards, but took the position that Rowley was concerned with the process by which the IEP was developed, "rather than the myriad of technical items that must be included in the written document." Id. Because the parents fully participated in the development of the IEP, the procedural concerns expressed by the Supreme Court had been met. It appears that had the parents not been aware of the information, the court may have reached a contrary result, having stated, "[w]e underscore the fact that the information absent from the IEP was nonetheless known to the parents." Id. at 1191. See also Thomas v. Cincinnati Board of Education, 918 F.2d 618 (6th Cir. 1990), in which the school district appealed a district court's order to place an eleven-year-old severely mentally retarded and multihandicapped child in a school-based program. The parent also appealed on grounds that the district erred in not awarding compensatory education.

The student was legally blind, functioned at a one month old level, and required the use of a wheel chair and gastrostomy and tracheostomy tubes. The school district initially provided five hours per week of homebound instruction. Under a new IEP, the school district agreed to provide a school-based program. The program was not implemented, however, because of a dispute over transportation.

The parent argued that the absence of written notice was a procedural violation. The court found that actual notice was received by telephone, and therefore the violation was harmless. Technical noncompliance did not result in any substantive deprivation.

117. *Evans*, 841 F.2d at 831.
118. *Honig*, 484 U.S. at 309.
119. *Jackson*, 806 F.2d at 629.

the prejudice of the violation. Burden of proof refers to two distinct questions: who has the burden of producing evidence on a particular issue, and who has the burden of persuasion on a particular issue? Failure to produce evidence will result in a finding against the party bearing that burden. Once evidence is produced, however, there remains the separate question of whether the evidence persuades the fact finder under the applicable standard—preponderance of the evidence, clear and convincing, or beyond a reasonable doubt.[120] In determining which party has the burden of persuasion, one must take into account such things as who pled the fact, what is judicially convenient, what is fair, and are there any special policy considerations.[121]

Although the statute is explicit that the standard of proof is to be by a preponderance of the evidence, there is no specific indication which party shall bear the burdens of production and of persuasion. In the absence of this specificity, courts have reached different interpretations. The majority of courts appear to place the burden of persuasion on the party seeking to change the *status quo*, as measured by the initiation of the due process hearing.[122] The clear trend, however, is to allocate the burden to the party challenging the final administrative determination.[123]

Whatever the validity of placing the burden of persuasion on the substantive issue, there is a strong argument that the LEA should bear more responsibility for the burden of persuasion on procedural issues, regardless of which party is seeking to change the *status quo*. As stated by the United States Supreme Court,

---

120. McCormick, Evidence § 947 (Cleary 4th ed. 1992).

121. *Id.* at 952.

122. Doe v. Brookline School Committee, 722 F.2d 910, 919 (1st Cir. 1983) ("the party seeking modification of the status quo should bear the burden of proof."); Tatro v. Texas (*Tatro II*), 703 F.2d 823, 830 (5th Cir. 1983) ("We are convinced that the central role of the IEP in the educational scheme contemplated by the EAHCA and in the standard of review developed in *Rowley* gives rise to a presumption in favor of the educational placement established by Amber's IEP. Moreover, because the IEP is jointly developed by the school district and the parents, fairness requires that the party attacking its terms should bear the burden of showing why the educational setting established by the IEP is not appropriate."); *see also* S-1 v. Turlington, 635 F.2d 342, 348–49 (5th Cir. 1981) ("In light of the remedial purposes of these statutes [IDEA and § 504], we find that the burden is on the local and state defendants... Our conclusion is buttressed by the fact that in most cases, the handicapped students and their parents lack the wherewithal to know or assert their rights under either EHA or section 504."); Burger v. Murray County School Dist., 612 F. Supp. 434 (D.C. Ga. 1984) ("when the suggestion is made that a child, who falls under the aegis of the EAHCA and is currently learning in what has been deemed to be an appropriate setting, be moved to a different facility, the party advocating the move should bear the burden of proving its propriety."); Lang v. Braintree School Committee, 545 F. Supp. 1221 (D. Mass. 1982) (the burden of proof on the LEA in attempt to change from private to public school); Davis v. District of Columbia Bd. of Educ., 530 F. Supp. 1209 (D.D.C. 1982) (burden of proof on LEA); Davis v. District of Columbia Bd. of Educ., 522 F. Supp. 1102 (D.D.C. 1981) *motion to reconsider denied*, 530 F. Supp. 1209 (D.D.C. 1982); *see generally* Guernsey, *When the Teachers and Parents Can't Agree, Who Really Decides? Burdens of Proof and Standards of Review Under The Education for All Handicapped Children Act*, 36 Cleveland State Law Review 67 (1988).

123. *E.g.* Spielberg v. Henrico County Public Schools, 853 F.2d 256, 258 n.2 (4th Cir. 1988); Kerkam v. McKenzie, 862 F.2d 884 (D.C. Cir. 1988); Barwacz v. Michigan Dep't. of Educ., 674 F. Supp. 1296 (W.D. Mich. 1987); Tracey T. v. McDaniel, 610 F. Supp. 947 (N.D. Ga. 1985); McKenzie v. Jefferson, 566 F. Supp. 404, 406 (D.D.C. 1983); Cohen v. School Bd., 450 So. 2d 1238, 1241 (Fla. App. 1984).

"Congress placed every bit as much emphasis upon compliance with procedures giving parents and guardians a large measure of participation at *every* stage of the administrative process."[124] Procedural violations as a result have occupied increased importance in disputes between the LEA and the parents.[125]

In fact, the Supreme Court in *Rowley* held that judicial inquiry begins with whether "the state complied with the procedures set forth in the EAHCA."[126] The Court added that such inquiry will require a court not only "to satisfy itself that the state has adopted a state plan, policies and assurances required by the EAHCA, but also determine that the state has created an IEP...which conforms with the requirements of § 1401(19)."[127]

This language indicates that *Rowley* imposes an affirmative requirement that inquiry be made into procedural compliance. Since it is the LEA's responsibility to ensure the procedural rights of the parents,[128] it is arguably the LEA which must carry this burden. Allocating the burden of persuasion to the LEA to show compliance with procedural requirements is consistent with the underlying purpose of the Act which was remedial in nature.[129]

In *S-1 v. Turlington*,[130] a case involving student expulsion, the court stated that in "light of the remedial purposes of these statutes we find that the burden is on the local and state defendants to make this determination. Our conclusion is buttressed by the fact that in most cases, the handicapped students and their parents lack the wherewithal to know or assert their rights under either EHA or section 504."[131] Since the procedural rights of IDEA were designed to remedy a problem, it is logical that the agency from which a remedy is sought should show that it has indeed complied.

As a further reason for allocating the burden of proof for procedural violations on the LEA, it should be kept in mind that the aids available to the parent on the substantive issues such as an IEE and access to documents, are of more limited use when it comes to procedural violations. Formal discovery procedures are not available at the administrative level, and evidence of procedural violations may not be in the student's educational records.[132]

---

124. *Rowley*, 458 U.S. at 205 (emphasis added).

125. *See, e.g., Spielberg*, 853 F.2d 256 (decision to change placement prior to development of an IEP violated procedural protection); Jackson v. Franklin County School Bd., 806 F.2d 623 (5th Cir. 1986) (procedural violations sufficient to support finding that LEA has failed to provide FAPE); Hall v. Vance, 774 F.2d 629 (4th Cir. 1985) (procedural violations sufficient to support finding that LEA has failed to provide FAPE).

126. *Rowley*, 458 U.S. at 206.

127. *Id.* at 206–7 n.27.

128. 20 U.S.C. § 1415(a).

129. *See* Clune & VanPelt, *A Political Method of Evaluating The Education For All Handicapped Children Act Of 1975 And Several Gaps Of Gap Analysis*, 48 Law & Contemp. Prob. 7, 12–20 (1985); Neal & Kirp, *The Allure of Legalization Reconsidered: The Case of Special Education*, 48 Law & Contemp. Prob. 63, 67–72 (1985); *see generally* S-1 v. Turlington, 635 F.2d 342, 348–349 (5th Cir. 1981) ("In light of the remedial purposes of these statutes ...").

130. 635 F.2d 342 (5th Cir. 1981).

131. *Id.*

132. It is conceivable, for example, that the school system, in violation of IDEA, has decided that it will not place children in residential programs. *See* Abrahamson v. Hershman, 701 F.2d 223, 227 (1st Cir. 1983). Evidence of this policy decision is most likely to exist in records other than the child's educational file.

In addition, where procedural violations are such as those in *Spielberg*, for example, there is the added burden of establishing the state of mind of the school employees, and they are in a much better position to actually carry the burden on the procedural violation.[133] It should be pointed out, however, that the Sixth Circuit, in *Cordrey v. Euckert*,[134] held that "[a]bsent more definitive authorization or compelling justification, we decline to go beyond strict review to reverse the traditional burden of proof."

Evans is also troubling where it seems to say that the prejudice can be ignored if there is an alternate remedy such as correcting a defective notice. In a situation where a school system fails to provide notice, but is ultimately required to provide notice by way of a due process hearing, there is little incentive to change its inappropriate behavior in the future, especially if few parents will actually seek the alternative relief, and the *Evans* decision may render the force of the Act "nugatory."

Given the ability to bring actions under both IDEA and the Civil Rights Act, procedural violations may create a cause of action under 42 U.S.C. 1983.[135]

---

133. *See, e.g.*, Doe v. Alabama, 915 F.2d 651 (11th Cir. 1990) (illustrates the difficulty of actually proving a procedural violation).

134. 917 F.2d 1460, 1466 (6th Cir. 1990).

135. Hiller v. Board of Educ., 687 F. Supp. 735, 743–744 (N.D.N.Y. 1988). For a discussion of 42 U.S.C. § 1983 see 1.5.

Chapter 15

Attorneys' Fees and Costs

15.1 Attorneys' Fees in General

Prior to 1984, court actions brought pursuant to IDEA, also alleged violations of 42 U.S.C. § 1983 and section 504 of the Rehabilitation Act of 1973[1] in an attempt to recover attorneys' fees under §§ 1988 and 505.[2] Jurisdictions split on the availability of §§ 1988 and 505 in actions also covered by IDEA until the United States Supreme Court decided *Smith v. Robinson*.[3] In *Smith*, the Court held that the comprehensiveness of IDEA and the detail in which IDEA addressed special education evidenced Congress' intent to make IDEA the sole source for relief. The practical effect of *Smith* was to deny attorneys' fees in virtually all special education cases.

Smith was decided July 5, 1984 and on February 6, 1985, the Handicapped Children's Protection Act of 1985 was introduced in Congress. On August 5, 1986, President Reagan signed into law the Handicapped Children's Protection Act of 1986,[4] amending § 1415 of IDEA, granting courts authority to award attorneys' fees. Subsection (e)(4)(B) of the amended IDEA provides:

> In any action or proceeding brought under this subsection the court, in its discretion, may award attorneys' fees as part of the costs to the parents or guardian of a handicapped child or youth who is the prevailing party.[5]

15.2 Attorneys' Fees and Administrative Proceedings

Certainly, the primary issue that has been litigated under the attorneys' fees provision is the availability of attorney's fees for administrative actions. The statutory language, at first glance, is less than clear. In fact the language provides,

---

1. 29 U.S.C. § 794.

2. Civil Rights Attorney's Fees Awards Act of 1976, 42 U.S.C. § 1988 (1981); 29 U.S.C. § 794(a). There are additional reasons to seek relief under §§ 1983 and 504. See 1.4, 1.5.

3. 468 U.S. 2 (1984).

4. P.L. 99-372, 100 Stat. 796 (1986); 20 U.S.C. §§ 1415(e)(4) and 1415(f).

5. *Id.* § 1415(e)(4)(B). See 1.2–1.4 for a fuller discussion of the impact of *Smith* and its subsequent overturning by Congress.

"the *court*, in its discretion, may award attorneys' fees..."[6] The vast majority of courts, however, have held that attorneys' fees are recoverable for work performed during administrative proceedings.[7]

The fact that Congress intended the authority to extend to the award of fees for representation in administrative proceedings is evidenced from a reading of the amendment in its entirety. The statute clearly states "In *any action or proceeding* brought under this subsection..."[8] The disjunctive language implies an intent to distinguish between two types of proceedings. Further, in the context of placing limits on the fees, the amendment makes specific reference to "the court or administrative officer..."[9]

Legislative history also clearly evidences Congress' intent to allow awards for representation during the administrative stage. The Senate Report which accompanied the bill, in describing the bill section by section, stated:

> Section 2 provides for the award of reasonable attorney's fees to prevailing parents in EAHCA civil actions *and administrative* proceedings in certain specified circumstances.[10]

The Senate Report was explicit when it stated:

> The Committee also intends that section 2 should be interpreted consistent with fee provisions of statutes such as title VII... which authorizes courts to award fees for time spent by counsel in mandatory administrative proceedings under those statutes.[11]

The legislative history in the House of Representatives likewise makes it clear that administrative proceedings are covered by IDEA.[12]

Allowing recovery for attorneys' fees for work done at the administrative level is consistent with the award of attorneys' fees in other civil rights situations. Assuming there is ultimately a decision on the merits, attorneys' fees are recoverable under § 1988 for mandatory administrative hearings.[13] The legislative history of the amended IDEA specifically indicates Congress' intent in enacting this pro-

---

6. 20 U.S.C. § 1415(e)(4)(B) (emphasis added).

7. *See, e.g.,* Angela L. v. Pasadena Indep. School Dist., 918 F.2d 1188 (5th Cir. 1990); McSomebodies v. Burlingame Elementary School Dist., 897 F.2d 974 (9th Cir. 1989); Duane M. v. Orleans Parish School Bd., 861 F.2d 115 (5th Cir. 1988); Eggers v. Bullitt County School Dist., 854 F.2d 892 (6th Cir. 1988); Counsel v. Dow, 849 F.2d 731 (2d Cir. 1988); Williams v. Boston School Committee, 709 F. Supp. 27 (D. Mass. 1989); Burr v. Ambach, 683 F. Supp. 46 (S.D.N.Y. 1988); Prescott v. Palos Verdes Penninsula Unified School Dist., 659 F. Supp. 921 (C.D. Ca. 1987); School Bd. of the County of Prince William v. Malone, 662 F. Supp. 999 (E.D. Va. 1987); Burpee v. Manchester School Dist., 661 F. Supp. 731 (D. N.H. 1987). *But see* Rollison v. Biggs, 660 F. Supp. 875 (D. Del. 1987).

8. 20 U.S.C. § 1415(e)(4)(B).

9. *Id.* § 1415(e)(4)(D)(iii).

10. S. Rep. No. 112,99th Cong., 2d Sees. 4, *reprinted in* 1986 U.S. Code Cong. & Admin. News 1799, 1800 (emphasis added).

11. *Id.* at 14, *reprinted in* 1986 U.S. Code Cong. & Admin. News at 1804.

12. Conference Report on S. 415, Handicapped Children's Protection Act of 1986, Congressional Record—H 4841, July 24, 1986.

13. *See* North Carolina Dep't. of Transportation v. Crest Street Community Council, 479 U.S. 6 (1986).

vision was to provide that attorneys' fee awards would generally be based on the same factors as those used in granting attorney fee awards under 42 U.S.C. § 1988:

> [S]ubject to two modifications described below, determinations as to whether a parent is awarded fees and the amount of the award are governed by applicable decisions interpreting 42 U.S.C. § 1988.[14]

Further, under Titles VI[15] and VII of the Civil Rights Act of 1964[16] attorneys' fees may be recovered for work done in administrative proceedings, at least so long as there is ultimately a judicial resolution of the underlying merits of the complaint. The United States Supreme Court in *New York Gaslight Club, Inc. v. Carey*,[17] held that mandatory state employment discrimination administrative proceedings are proceedings to enforce Title VII and therefore attorneys' fees were recoverable under § 2000e-5(k) which provides "In any action or proceeding under this title the court ... may allow the prevailing party ... a reasonable attorney's fee as part of costs."[18]

Carey involved an allegation of race discrimination in employment. The respondent was denied a job as a cocktail waitress. While represented by counsel, she engaged in extensive attempts to resolve the dispute less formally than through litigation. These attempts included a state administrative hearing and appeal as well as efforts at conciliation. In addition, proceedings were conducted by the Equal Employment Opportunity Commission (EEOC). The state administrative proceedings were appealed to state court, and the EEOC's finding of reasonable cause resulted in respondent filing in United States District Court. After respondent's success in the state courts, the federal court action was withdrawn, except for the request for attorneys' fees.

The issue before the Court, therefore, was whether attorneys' fees were available under Title VII for work done in mandatory administrative proceedings. The Court, in holding that attorneys' fees were available for work in administrative proceedings, placed heavy emphasis on the language of the statute which, just as the amended IDEA states "In any action or proceeding..." [19] The Court held: "Congress' use of the broadly inclusive disjunctive phrase 'action or proceeding' indicates an intent to subject the losing party to an award of attorney's fees and costs that includes expenses incurred for administrative proceedings."[20] Further, the Court pointed out, Congress' intent was evidenced by the fact that another fee provision in the same Act used the words "any action commenced pursuant to this title." In the words of the Court, "The omission of the words 'or pro-

---

14. Conference Report on S. 415, Handicapped Children's Protection Act of 1986, Congressional Record—H 4841, 4842, July 24, 1986 (Remarks of Mr. Williams).

15. Title VI of Civil Rights Act of 1964, 42 U.S.C. § 2000d et seq. (1981).

16. Title VII of Civil Rights Act of 1964, 42 U.S.C. § 2000e et seq. (1981).

17. 447 U.S. 54 (1980). *Dictum* in Carey indicated that a suit could be brought solely to recover attorneys' fees. This *dictum*, however, was subsequently rejected by the Court in North Carolina Department of Transportation v. Crest Street Community Council, Inc. 479 U.S. 6 (1986). The Supreme Court in *Crest Street*, however, citing *Carey*, stated: "A court hearing one of the civil rights claims covered by § 1983 may still award attorney's fees for time spent on administrative proceedings to enforce the civil rights claim prior to the litigation." *Id.* 15.

18. 42 U.S.C. § 2000e-5(k).

19. *Id.*

20. 447 U.S. at 61.

ceeding' from § 204(b) is understandable, since enforcement of Title II depends solely on court actions."[21]

It would be anomalous, especially in light of the strong legislative history indicating congressional intent to allow such an award, to deny recovery under the amended IDEA while allowing recovery under Title VII.

15.2.1 What Constitutes the Administrative Proceedings?

It seems reasonably clear that attorneys' fees are available for work done in the administrative proceedings once the due process request has been filed under IDEA.[22] The question becomes how far back in the administrative process are fees taxable. Courts have been willing to award fees in situations where a due process hearing has been requested but the dispute is settled prior to the hearing.[23]

It is unclear whether actually requesting the due process hearing is necessary in order to be entitled to attorneys' fees. Are attorneys' fees available, for example, for attendance at IEP or eligibility meetings? In *Webb v. Dyer County Board of Education*,[24] the Supreme Court held that a state tenure rights hearing was not a proceeding to enforce § 1983, and therefore, attorneys' fees were not recoverable for work done for that hearing. In *Webb*, plaintiff alleged he had been discharged from his teaching position on the basis of race. For a period covering five years, plaintiff attempted to resolve the matter, through counsel, by negotiating with the school board and participating in a series of voluntary hearings with the school board. After five years of on and off hearings and negotiations, suit was filed under § 1983. In affirming the denial of attorneys' fees for work done prior to filing the law suit, the Court stressed the voluntary nature of plaintiff's actions. Unlike the administrative proceedings under Title VII for which the Court held attorneys' fees were available in *Carey*, " 'nothing in § 1983 requires that a plaintiff exhaust his administrative remedies before bringing a § 1983 suit.' "[25]

Webb would seem to draw into question the availability of attorneys' fees for work done prior to the filing of the due process hearing request. While it is clear from the above discussion that subsection (e) encompasses due process hearings and reviews, nothing in subsection (e) specifically refers to the ability to recover attorneys' fees for work done at earlier stages. While § 1415 itself does refer to a number of other steps in the educational process, including important procedural protections attaching prior to the due process hearing, these protections are contained in subsection (b), not subsection (e).

Statutory interpretation analogous to that used in *Carey* would also indicate Congressional intent to limit the attorneys' fee provision to work done beginning

---

21. *Id.*

22. See 15.2.

23. *See* Shelly C. v. Venus Independent School Dist., 878 F.2d 862 (5th Cir. 1989) *cert. denied* 493 U.S. 1024 (1990); Anderson v. Syracuse Bd. of Educ., 1989 WL 8664 (N.D.N.Y. 1989); Rossi v. Gosling, 696 F. Supp. 1079 (E.D. Va. 1988).

24. 471 U.S. 234 (1985)

25. *Id.* at 241 (quoting Smith v. Robinson, 468 U.S. 992, 1011, n.14 (1984)). Since the due process proceedings are mandatory under the IDEA, *Webb* does nothing to weaken *Carey's* application to the actions brought under the IDEA.

with the due process hearing. Subparagraph (G) of subsection (e) refers to violations of § 1415 generally. The attorneys' fees authorization, however, refers to
actions or proceedings brought only under subsection (e) of § 1415, hence evidencing Congressional intent to expand only subparagraph (G) of subsection (e)
beyond the subsection itself. Therefore, in a situation where there is clearly no
known dispute going into the IEP meeting, it could be argued that the administrative "proceedings" have not begun.

Even such a strict reading of the word proceedings, however, should recognize
that under certain factual settings, the IEP is as much a part of the proceedings
as work done at the due process hearing. This possibility was recognized in *Webb*,
where the Court stated:

> Of course, some of the services performed before a lawsuit is formally com-
> menced by filing of a complaint are performed 'on the litigation.' Most
> obvious examples are the drafting of initial pleadings and the work associated
> with the development of a theory of the case.[26]

As a general principle, it appears that work done prior to the formal due process
hearings is not compensable, unless it is performed "on the litigation." The award
of attorneys' fees is specifically for actions and proceedings under subsection (e).[27]

If a lawyer for the parents is involved at the early stages of the administrative
process, it is quite likely that a dispute has already arisen between the parents
and the LEA. For example, the parents and the LEA may have been having a
disagreement which could result in a due process hearing, and ultimately a decision in favor of the parents, concerning a student's eligibility. At the subsequent
IEP meeting, the parents might well be represented by counsel so as to insure the
development of appropriate educational goals and objectives for the child.[28] It
seems logical, given the existence of the ongoing dispute that, assuming a due
process hearing is ultimately filed, the work at the IEP meeting should be compensable, since it could be as significant as "the development of the theory of the
case."

There is an argument that regardless of the pre-existing dispute, assuming a
due process hearing is subsequently filed, attorneys' fees are available for work
done prior to the filing of the due process hearing. This more liberal reading of
subsection (e) is premised on the mandatory versus non-mandatory proceedings
distinction drawn by the Supreme Court in *Webb* and *Carey* as well as on the
basis of the language of the amended statute itself.

The language of § 1415 can be read to support the position that the administrative proceedings include pre-due process hearing components. Section 1415
is concerned with the procedural protections afforded parents under the IDEA.
Subsection (a) provides that the LEA and the state educational agency (SEA)

> shall establish and maintain procedures in accordance with subsection (b)
> through subsection (e) of this section to assure the handicapped children

---

26. Webb, 471 U.S. at 243.
27. 20 U.S.C. § 1415(e)(4)(A).
28. Parents are entitled to have counsel at IEP meetings. See 34 C.F.R. § 300.344(a)(5).

and their parents or guardians are guaranteed procedural safeguards with respect to the provision of free appropriate public education ...[29]

Subsection (b)(1) then provides "The procedures required by this section shall include, *but shall not be limited to*— "[30] It could easily be contended that the regulations requiring evaluations, eligibility determinations, IEP meetings, placement decisions based on existing IEPs and the right to independent evaluations are as derivative of § 1415(b)1)'s "not be limited to" language as §§ 1412 and 1414s' requirements of eligibility determinations and IEPs.

Indeed, requirements such as IEPs and IEEs may be as much administrative proceedings as the due process hearings. If a dispute arises it will normally have to be first addressed mandatorily in one of the early phases. This is the case simply because the due process hearing is the result of disputes occurring at these earlier stages. Subsection (b)(2) authorizes the due process hearing procedure for disputes arising under subsection (b)(1) with respect to matters "relating to identification, evaluation, or educational placement of the child, or the provision of a free appropriate public education to such child."[31] As in *Carey*, it could be argued that since the portions of the special education process occurring prior to the start of the due process hearing are mandatory, work done for those portions should be compensated.

The Supreme Court has also provided some support for including these steps as part of the administrative proceeding. In *Hendrick Hudson District Board of Education v. Rowley*,[32] the Supreme Court stated that a court's inquiry into action arising under § 1415 is twofold: "First, has the State complied with the procedures set forth in the Act? And second, is the individualized educational program reasonably calculated to enable the child to receive educational benefits?"[33] The Court also stated "When the elaborate and highly specific procedural safeguards embodied in § 1415 are contrasted with the general and somewhat imprecise substantive admonitions contained in the Act, we think that the importance Congress attached to these procedural safeguards cannot be gainsaid."[34] *Rowley* implicitly recognizes that the "not be limited to" language incorporates such procedural protections as IEP meetings with parental involvement.[35]

15.2.2 Authority of Administrative Officer to Award

If, as is likely, an award of attorneys fees can be made for the administrative level work, the question becomes whether the administrative officers are able to make the award or may only a judge? This issue was raised in a state administrative

---

29. 42 U.S.C. § 1415(a).
30. *Id.* § 1415(b)(1) (emphasis added).
31. *Id.* § 1415(b)(1)(E).
32. 458 U.S. 176 (1982).
33. *Id.* at 206–207.
34. *Id.* at 205.
35. See 34 C.F.R. § 300.344.

level hearing in *Lauren T. v. Crisp County Board of Education.*[36] In *Lauren T.*, the parent moved for award of attorney's fees and the SEA hearing officer denied the request. The SEA officer focused on subparagraph (e)(4)(B) of the amended IDEA which grants the general authority to order attorney's fees only on the court: "In any action or proceeding...the court, in its discretion, may award ..." Subparagraphs (C) through (G), the officer pointed out "provide limitations on how fees are to be awarded and calculated. Thus, only the court has the general authority to award attorneys' fees, and then only if the conditions set forth in subparagraphs C through G are met." [37] The officer did recognize that subparagraph D and its reference to an administrative officer's finding that a settlement offer was not justifiably rejected does cause ambiguity. He held, however, that subparagraph D can be read consistently with the other subparagraphs by recognizing that a hearing officer could make the factual determination, but a court would have to make the award.

> The officer also pointed to the legislative history: The committee intends that S. 415 will allow the Court but not the hearing officer, to award fees for time spent by counsel in mandatory EHA administrative proceedings.[38]

This decision makes good sense not only as being consistent with the language and legislative history of the amendment, but in practical terms as well. Hearing officers are not in a position to award fees. Many are non-lawyers,[39] and as you look at the factors that go into determining an appropriate fee, it is clearly beyond their expertise. Even for lawyers who are hearing officers, they will not have the breadth of experience to judge the relative merits.[40]

15.3 Ability to File Suit Solely for Attorneys' Fees

A determination that the administrative officers do not have authority to grant attorneys' fees should cause only minor problems to the parents, if it is also determined that a parent who prevails in the due process proceedings is able to bring a subsequent action in court solely to recover the attorneys' fees.[41] The vast majority of courts, including each United States Circuit Court of Appeals ad-

---

36. 508 Educ. Handicapped L. Rep. (CRR) 298 (Ga. SEA, Mar. 17, 1987), *see also* Oakland Unified School Dist., 508 Educ. Handicapped L. Rep. (CRR) 246 (SEA Ca., September 30, 1986); Newport-Mesa Unified School Dist., 508 Educ. Handicapped L. Rep. (CRR) 263 (SEA Ca., September 23, 1986).

37. Lauren T., 508 at 299.

38. *Id.* citing 132 Cong. Rec. H 4841, 4842 (1986) (remarks of Representative Bartlett).

39. Neither IDEA or its supporting regulations require the hearing officer be a lawyer. *See* 34 C.F.R. § 300.507; *see also* 20 U.S.C. § 1415(b)(2).

40. It is not unusual for due process hearing officers to hear no more than one special education case per year.

41. While there is certainly the added time and effort, attorneys fees and costs are available for time spent in recovering attorneys' fees. See authorities collected in Newberg, **Attorney Fee Awards** 154 (1986).

dressing the question, have held that suit may be filed solely to obtain attorneys' fees.[42]

The major hurdle to overcome in filing an action solely to recover attorneys' fees is the United States Supreme Court's decision in *North Carolina Department of Transportation v. Crest Street Community Council, Inc..*[43] In *Crest Street,* rejecting, dicta in *New York Gaslight Club v. Carey,*[44] the Court held that an action solely to recover attorneys' fees could not be brought under § 1988. The Court focused on the specific language of § 1988 which speaks to recovery of attorneys' fees in an action or proceeding to enforce specific rights. Since an action solely to recover attorneys' fees was not to enforce those rights, attorneys' fees could not be awarded. The Court also stated that this interpretation of the statute was consistent with the legislative history of § 1988.

Crest Street and § 1988 can be readily distinguished from IDEA. The language of § 1988 and § 1415(e) is very similar. Both statutes refer to "action or proceeding," but § 1988 goes on to state "to enforce a provision of [certain civil rights acts]." Unlike § 1415, § 1988 explicitly refers to actions to enforce specific statutes. Section 1415 is not as narrow.[45]

The United States Supreme Court in *Crest Street* had pointed out that the legislative history of § 1988 "supports the plain import of the statutory language" not to allow separate action for attorney's fees.[46] Contrasting the legislative history under § 1415(e) with that of § 1988, shows particular emphasis in the House and Senate Reports that attorney's fees be available for prevailing parties at the administrative hearing level.[47]

If suit can be brought solely to recover attorneys' fees, what is the statute of limitations on bringing that suit? One possibility is a statute of limitations which is the same as applies to the appeal of the underlying merits. There is, however, no consensus on the statute of limitations for filing suit on the merits following the due process proceedings.[48]

---

42. *See* Johnson v. Bismarck Pub. School Dist., 949 F.2d 1000 (8th Cir. 1991); Angela L. v. Pasadena Indep. School Dist., 918 F.2d 1188 (5th Cir. 1990); Moore v. Dist. of Columbia, 907 F.2d 165 (D.C. Cir. 1990)(en banc); McSomebodies v. Burlingame Elementary School, 897 F.2d 974 (9th Cir. 1989) (as supplemented March 2, 1990); Mitten v. Muscogee County School Dist., 877 F.2d 932 (11th Cir. 1989); Duane M. v. Orleans Parish School Bd., 861 F.2d 115 (5th Cir. 1988); Eggers v. Bullitt County School Dist., 854 F.2d 892 (6th Cir. 1988); Turton v. Crisp County School Dist., 688 F. Supp. 1535 (M.D. Ga. 1988); Keay v. Bismarck R-V School Dist., 1987 WL 16882 (E.D. Mo. 1987); Mathern v. Cambell County Children's Center, 674 F. Supp. 816 (D. Wyo. 1987).

43. 479 U.S. 6 (1986).

44. 447 U.S. 54 (1980).

45. *See* Moore v. District of Columbia, 907 F.2d 165 (D.C. Cir. 1990) (en banc); McSomebodies v. Burlingame Elementary School, 897 F.2d 974 (9th Cir. 1989) (as supplemented March 2, 1990); Mitten v. Muscogee County School Dist., 877 F.2d 932 (11th Cir. 1989); Duane M. v. Orleans Parish School Bd., 861 F.2d 115 (5th Cir. 1988); Eggers v. Bullitt County School Dist., 854 F.2d 892 (6th Cir. 1988).

46. Crest Street, 479 U.S. at 12.

47. *See* Moore v. District of Columbia, 907 F.2d 165 (D.C. Cir. 1990) (en banc); McSomebodies v. Burlingame Elementary School, 897 F.2d 974 (9th Cir. 1989) (as supplemented March 2, 1990); Mitten v. Muscogee County School Dist., 877 F.2d 932 (11th Cir. 1989); Duane M. v. Orleans Parish School Bd., 861 F.2d 115 (5th Cir. 1988); Eggers v. Bullitt County School Dist., 854 F.2d 892 (6th Cir. 1988).

48. *E.g.,* Schimmel v. Spillane, 819 F.2d 477 (4th Cir. 1987) (one year); Janzen v. Knox County

It could be argued, of course, that a suit solely for attorneys' fees is in the nature of a fee application and that any local rule such as one requiring filing within 10, or within 14 days as required by Federal Rule of Appellate Procedure 39(a) should apply. Courts, however, have rejected this approach adopting more liberal time periods consistent with the remedial nature of the legislation, read any statute of limitations liberally.[49]

15.4 Lay Advocates/Paralegals

It is not unusual for lay advocates or paralegals to represent parents during the administrative stage of the process up to and including the due process hearing.[50] The availability of attorneys' fees for that work may well depend on the relationship the advocate has with an attorney.

As a general matter, the cases establish that fees for paralegals and law clerks are taxable as attorneys' fees.[51] These cases, however, typically involve time spent by paralegals at the direction of a lawyer and represent work that would have to have been done by the lawyer representing the client already. This general rule should apply under the amended IDEA as well.[52] Whether an advocate unsupervised by a lawyer is entitled to attorneys' fees is more problematic. Section 1988 has been interpreted as not authorizing the award of attorneys' fees for non-lawyer advocates.[53] The one reported IDEA decision to date addressing the issue agreed that attorneys' fees were unavailable for lay advocates handling administrative due process hearings. Drawing an analogy to § 1988, and pointing to the omission of reference to lay advocates in the amendment, the court held Congress did not intend to allow recovery.[54] For those offices which employ non

---

Bd. of Educ., 790 F.2d 484 (6th Cir. 1986) (three years); Adler v. Education Dep't., 760 F.2d 454 (2d Cir. 1985) (four months); Scokin v. Texas, 723 F.2d 432 (5th Cir. 1984) (two years); Department of Educ. v. Carl D., 695 F.2d 1154 (9th Cir. 1983) (30 days); Tokarcik v. Forest Hills School Dist., 665 F.2d 443 (3d Cir. 1981) (two years). For a discussion of statutes of limitation in general, *see* 11.2, 12.2, 13.2.

49. *See* Max M. v. New Trier High School Dist., 859 F.2d 1297 (7th Cir. 1988) (request one year after enactment of attorneys' fees provision was within discretion of court where LEA not prejudiced); James v. Nashua School Dist., 720 F. Supp. 1053 (D.N.H. 1989) (3 year personal injury action statute of limitations applies); Robert D. v. Sobel, 688 F. Supp. 861, 864 (S.D.N.Y. 1988) (three year statute); Michael M. v. Board of Educ. of New York City School Dist., 686 F. Supp. 995, 1002 (E.D.N.Y. 1988) (three year statute); School Bd. of Prince William County v. Malone, 662 F. Supp. 999 (E.D. Va. 1987) (three months was not an unreasonable period of time to expect the defendants to learn about the amendment to IDEA and file a request).

50. Congress recognized the likelihood of nonlawyers being active in due process hearings. 20 U.S.C. § 1415(d)(1).

51. Newberg, **Attorney Fee Awards** 118 (1986); *see, e.g.*, Vaughns v. Board of Educ., 770 F.2d 1244 (4th Cir. 1985) ($35–$50 for law clerk/paralegal work in a 1988 school discrimination case); *but see* Bill Rivers Trailers Inc. v. Miller, 489 So. 2d 1139 (Fla. Ct. App. 1986) (no recovery for time spent by nonlawyer assistant).

52. *See generally* Muth v. Smith, 646 F. Supp. 280 (E.D. Pa. 1986) (court denied law clerk fees for failure to establish time, implicit recognition that fees awardable if properly established).

53. *E.g.*, Pitts v. Vaugn, 679 F.2d 311 (3d Cir. 1982) (pro se non-lawyer advocate); Peniman v. Cartwright, 550 F. Supp. 1302 (S.D. Iowa 1982) (1988 does not allow award for "jailhouse lawyers").

54. Arons v. New Jersey State Bd. of Educ., 842 F.2d 58 (E.D. Pa. 1988).

lawyers to handle part or all of the administrative process it would be wise to reevaluate the lines of authority to ensure that the work was adequately supervised and directed by lawyers so as to create a more traditional paralegal-lawyer relationship

15.5 Costs as Well as Attorneys' Fees—in General

The amended IDEA also contemplates the award of other costs associated with the administrative and judicial proceedings. As indicated above, 20 U.S.C. § 1415(e)(4)(B) granted the court authority to award attorney's fees *"as part of the costs*[55]

Awarding costs in federal court is generally governed by Federal Rule of Civil Procedure 54(d)[56] and 28 U.S.C. § 1920.[57] Section 1920 allows the court to award 1) fees of the clerk and marshal; 2) fees for the court reporter for necessary parts of the transcript; 3) fees for witnesses and printing; 4) fees for copies of necessary papers; 5) docket fees; and 6) costs of interpretation.

15.5.1 Expert Fees and Expenses

Perhaps the single largest expense associated with litgation in special eduction is expert testimony. In many instances, the LEA has paid for an IEE prior to the due process hearing,[58] but the parent still confronts the costs and travel of the expert testifying at trial as well as any additional expert testimony.

Witness fees are taxable under 54(d) and are specifically enumerated under 28 U.S.C. § 1920. To what extent expert fees above statutory witness fees are taxable was recently resolved by the United States Supreme Court.

In *Crawford Fitting Co. v. J.T. Gibbons, Inc.,*[59] the United States Supreme Court held that when a prevailing party seeks reimbursement for expert witness fees, the party is bound by the statutory limit set by Congress. *Crawford Fitting* involved two consolidated cases; one alleging violations of the antitrust laws; the other alleged racial discrimination in violation of Title VII and 42 U.S.C. § 1981. The Supreme Court held that if district courts had the discretion under Federal Rule of Civil Procedure 54(d) to pay more than the statutory witness fee, such discretion would be directly contrary to congressional intent in establishing the

---

55. 20 U.S.C. § 1415(e)(4)(B) (emphasis added).

56. Fed. R. Civ. Proc. 54(d) provides "costs shall be allowed as of course to the prevailing party unless the court otherwise directs …")

57. 28 U.S.C. § 1920.

58. 20 U.S.C. § 1415(b)(1)(A) provides as part of the procedural protections of the parents, the right to obtain an independent educational evaluation. 34 C.F.R. § 300.503(b) provides: "A parent has the right to an independent educational evaluation at public expense if the parent disagrees with an evaluation obtained by the public agency. However, the public agency may initiate a [due process] hearing … to show that its evaluation is appropriate …"

59. 482 U.S. 437 (1987).

witness fee.[60] Therefore, absent explicit statutory authority to the contrary, a trial court is limited to the award of costs as provided in § 1920.

More recently the United States Supreme Court has held that the limitations in *Crawford Fitting* were applicable to actions brought under § 1988. In *West Virginia University Hospitals, Inc. v. Casey*,[61] the Court held with regard to 42 U.S.C. § 1988 that

> The record of statutory usage demonstrates convincingly that attorney's fees and expert fees are regarded as separate elements of litigation cost. While some fee-shifting provisions, like § 1988, refer only to "attorney's fees," *see, e.g.*, Civil Rights Act of 1964, 42 U.S.C. § 2000e-5(k), many others explicitly shift expert witness fees as well as attorney's fees.[62]

The Court then went on to state that

> None of the categories of expenses listed in § 1920 can reasonably be read to include fees for services rendered by an expert employed by a party in a nontestimonial advisory capacity.[63]

The Court also reiterated that to overcome the limitations of § 1920 there must be "contract or explicit statutory authority to the contrary."[64]

The legislative history may indicate that Congress intended that the amended IDEA be contrary to the limits imposed by § 1920. The legislative history of the amended IDEA is explicit in indicating Congressional intent to include expenses associated with experts as costs:

> The conferees intend that the term 'attorneys' fees as part of the 'costs' include reasonable expenses and fees of expert witnesses and the reasonable costs of any test or evaluation which is found to be necessary for the preparation of the parent or guardian's case in the action or proceeding, as well as traditional costs incurred in the course of litigating a case.[65]

There is, however, authority that interprets *Casey* as applying to actions under IDEA. In *Aranow v. District of Columbia*,[66] the court applied *Casey* and held that the parents in a special education action were entitled to reimbursement for only the statutory witness fee and transportation cost of their expert, reimbursement that totaled $49.

15.5.2 Transcripts

IDEA requires the recording of the due process hearing[67] and in many jurisdictions this is done by recording rather than stenographically. In either event, a

---

60. *Id.* Witness fees are provided for in 28 U.S.C. § 1821.

61. 111 S.Ct. 1138 (1991).

62. *Id.* at 1140.

63. *Id.*

64. *Id.* at 1141.

65. H.R. Conf. Rep. No. 687, 99th Cong., 2d Sess. 5, *reprinted in* 1986 U.S. Code Cong. & Admin. News 1808.

66. 780 F. Supp. 46 (D.D.C. 1992).

67. 20 U.S.C. § 1415(d)(3).

stenographic copy of the due process proceedings is at least helpful, if not crucial to the parent's preparation of the judicial action, as well as to the court's understanding of the due process hearing.

Costs of a stenographic transcription of the due process hearing would seem to be covered under § 1920 "Fees of the court reporter for all or any part of the stenographic transcript necessarily obtained for use in the case ... "[68] Since the due process hearing is part of the record in the judicial action,[69] recovery of its cost seems appropriate.

15.5.3 Discovery and Miscellaneous Expenses

Discovery expenses can also be a significant factor once judicial action has been instituted. Actions related to interrogatories, requests to admit and the like are for the most part covered by the attorneys' fees provisions. Depositions, however, involve non-attorney costs. Generally, if depositions are introduced in evidence, the costs are taxable.[70] Depositions which "simply are investigative or preparatory in character, rather than for the presentation of the case, typically are not taxable."[71]

Many related expenses associated with the litigation, including long distance phone calls, postage and attorneys' traveling expenses are not taxable as costs.[72] In an IDEA decision which predates the attorneys' fee amendment, *Yaris v. Special School District of St. Louis County*,[73] plaintiffs sought costs for "1) depositions; 2) transcripts; 3) experts; 4) expenses of plaintiffs' counsel; 5) copying; 6) court costs; 7) postage; 8) long distance telephone calls; and miscellaneous."[74] Expenses for depositions, experts[75] and copying were disallowed because of insufficient documentation. Expenses of plaintiffs' counsel, postage, phone calls and miscellaneous expenses were disallowed "because said items are not taxable as costs."[76]

Yaris was reargued after the attorneys' fees amendment and the court allowed the expenses it had earlier refused to award on the theory that reasonable expenses were allowed as part of attorneys' fees.[77] Statutory fee provisions, such as § 1988, which provide attorneys' fees as part of costs, have usually been interpreted to allow reimbursement of reasonable expenses of litigation, including these miscellaneous items.[78] Unlike expert witness fees, however, there are no legislative

---

68. 20 U.S.C. § 1415(d)(3).

69. *See* 20. U.S.C. § 1415(e)(2).

70. Wright, Miller, Kane, **Federal Practice and Procedure** § 2676 (1983).

71. *Id.* at 345.

72. Wright, *supra* note 1, at § 2677.

73. 604 F. Supp. 914 (E.D. Mo. 1985) aff'd. 780 F.2d 724 (8th Cir. 1986).

74. *Id.* at 915.

75. *Id.* The court also pointed out that although the it has the discretion to grant them, experts' fees are permitted only in the "exceptional case" *Id.*, citing Paschall v. Kansas City Star Co., 695 F.2d 322, 338–39 (8th Cir. 1982). This part of the opinion, of course, is contrary to the legislative history of IDEA as later amended. See 1.2–1.4.

76. Yaris, 604 F. Supp. at 915.

77. Yaris, 661 F. Supp. 996, 1003 n.9 (E.D. Mo. May 29, 1987) *citing* Northcross v. Board of Educ., 611 F.2d 624, 639 (6th Cir. 1979) (attorneys' fees includes expenses under 42 U.S.C. § 1988).

78. *See* authorities collected in Newberg, **Attorney Fee Awards** 70–72 (1986).

history references concerning to payment of miscellaneous expenses under IDEA. The question is, therefore, again presented whether the Supreme Court under *Crawford Fitting* would consider the amended IDEA and § 1988 to be explicit statutory authority allowing the award of these expenses. *Yaris*, having been redecided two weeks before *Crawford Fitting*, did not address the issue.

15.6 When Is a Parent a Prevailing Party?

Subsection (e) provides for the award of attorneys' fees to the parents or guardians who are the prevailing party. When a party prevails is likely to be a matter of considerable litigation, especially in light of the need to confront both substantive and procedural issues in each action arising under IDEA.

The United States Supreme Court has addressed the issue of the effect of partial success in *Hensley v. Eckerhart*,[79] a case arising under 42 U.S.C. § 1988 and it said:

> Where a plaintiff has obtained excellent results, his attorney should recover a fully compensatory fee ... In these circumstances the fee award should not be reduced simply because plaintiff failed to prevail on every contention raised in the lawsuit ... Litigants in good faith may raise alternative legal grounds for a desired outcome, and the court's rejection of *or failure to reach certain grounds* is not sufficient reason for reducing a fee. *The result is what matters.*[80]

Courts have fairly consistently held, consistent with *Hensley* that partial success does not preclude an award of attorneys' fees, but that an award may be reduced for unsuccessful claims.[81]

The result of the action, of course must be against the part from whom fees are sought. Where in a consent decree, the state agency has agreed to provide services, for example, but the local agency has not so agreed, the local agency is not obligated.[82]

15.6.1 Procedural and Substantive Violations

Given the Supreme Court's language in *Hendrick Hudson District Board of Education v. Rowley*,[83] that a court's inquiry into an action arising under § 1415 is twofold, procedural and substantive, it is not surprising that a large number of cases are now being brought alleging procedural violations of IDEA. Courts, in turn, are responding to the language that "[w]hen the elaborate and highly

---

79. 461 U.S. 424 (1983).

80. *Id.* at 436 (emphasis added). *See also* Angela L. v. Pasadena Indep. School Dist., 918 F.2d 1188 (5th Cir. 1990).

81. Barlow/Gresham Union High School Dist No. 2 v. Mitchell, 940 F.2d 1280 (9th Cir. 1991).

82. Counsel v. Dow, 849 F.2d 731 (2d Cir. 1988) (settlement obligated only the state, and, therefore, parents were not prevailing parties requiring local agency to pay fees).

83. 458 U.S. 176 (1982).

specific procedural safeguards embodied in § 1415 are contrasted with the general and somewhat imprecise substantive admonitions contained in the Act, we think that the importance Congress attached to these procedural safeguards cannot be gainsaid."[84] The issue then arises under the attorneys' fees amendment as to what happens when the parent prevails on one of these two prongs, but loses on the other.

The problem can arise in a number of different contexts. The United States Supreme Court's language that it is the results that matter is particularly helpful in organizing the analysis. Take, for example, a dispute in which the parents allege that the LEA's proposed placement will not provide a FAPE for their child and also that the LEA failed to provide the parents with notice of their procedural rights as required by IDEA.[85]

In such a case, the parents are asserting one position, the inability of the LEA to provide a FAPE. They happen to assert two grounds for that position, one substantive, one procedural, but since the apparent remedy for violation of procedural protections is the same as for an inappropriate finding on the substantive issue, that is, that the LEA is unable to provide a FAPE, recovery of attorneys' fees should be available for all work done regardless of whether the court decides that the parents have not "prevailed" on one of their contentions. If the parents win on procedural violations, but lose on the substantive position, the result is the same, a finding that the LEA was not proposing a FAPE.

To encourage the court to accept this reasoning, it is incumbent on the parents' counsel to have a consistent theory of the case and consistently argue the inter-relation of the issues. It must be made clear to the court that there is only one issue in the case; whether the LEA's proposed or existing action can provide a FAPE. There are then two "alternative legal grounds for a desired outcome."[86]

There are, however, situations where procedural violations and the substantive merits are so distinct that they are indeed independent, requested outcomes and failure to succeed on one should preclude attorneys' fees for work done seeking the particular outcome. For example, the Third Circuit held that where the parents established the state agency had set up an improper procedure for hearing appeals, but that the parents had not prevailed on the independent question of whether the IEP was appropriate, the parents were entitled to attorneys' fees only on the substantive question.[87]

Likewise, a case could arise where the parties agree that a residential program is required, but the LEA contends the residential program in which the parents

---

84. Rowley, 458 U.S. at 205.

85. See, e.g., Hall v. Vance County Bd. of Educ., 774 F.2d 629 (4th Cir. 1985).

86. A procedural violation may also force the parents to defend a substantive issue they would otherwise not have to defend. If the LEA has violated the procedural protections requiring the parents (or the LEA) to file for a due process hearing, the due process hearing should address the procedural and substantive violations. Had the LEA not violated the procedural protections; for example had they provided the IEE, there may have been no need for the Plaintiffs to incur any costs in responding to the underlying substantive allegations. Attorneys' fees, therefore, should be awarded for both the procedural violation and work done in defending on the merits.

87. Muth v. Central Bucks School Dist., 839 F.2d 113 (3d Cir. 1988) rev. on other grounds sub nom. Muth v. Dellmuth, 491 U.S. 223 (1989).

have placed the child is inappropriate.[88] It is also conceivable, for example, that the procedural protections afforded the parents were violated by the LEA's failure to pay for the IEE. If the parents prevail on the procedural issue, but lose on the substantive issue attorneys' fees should be awarded only for work done on the issue on which they were successful. The procedural violation was clearly distinct and unrelated to the decision of the parents to place the child in the inappropriate placement and therefore recovery should be had only for prevailing on the procedural issue.

15.6.2 Prevailing on Part of the Substantive or Part of the Procedural Claims

A more difficult issue is likely to arise when the specifics of the IEP or the particular placement are in issue. For example, suppose the issue is whether an emotionally disturbed child needs a residential program and then whether a specific residential program is the appropriate program. If we assume the child is presently in a residential setting already and the LEA alleges 1) the child does not need a residential program and 2) if he does, the particular program in which he is presently placed is too restrictive, we can see the difficulty of allocating attorneys' fees for partial success. If the final decision is that a residential program is necessary, but that the existing program is more restrictive than needed, what portion of the attorneys' fees will be taxable?

Focusing on the result obtained, the parents have clearly not prevailed on a major separate issue and it would seem logical to deny them relief. It then becomes incumbent on the parents' attorney to establish that portion of his time which was spent on each issue. *Hensley* has made it clear that "A reduced fee award is appropriate if the relief, however significant, is limited in comparison to the litigation as a whole... [W]here the plaintiff achieved only limited success, the district court should award only that amount of fees that is reasonable in relation to the results obtained."[89] It is particularly clear that plaintiffs' counsel has the burden of establishing which hours were expended on which issues.[90]

15.7 Setting the Fee

The amended IDEA requires that any award of attorneys' fees be reasonable and based on the prevailing rates in the community for the kind and quality of services furnished.[91] This is the general standard applied by courts in most statutory fee awards.[92] The court in all likelihood will use the same approach under the amended IDEA as in the determination of the prevailing rate generally used

---

88. *See generally* Schimmel v. Spillane, 819 F.2d 477 (4th Cir. 1987).
89. Hensley, 461 U.S. at 437.
90. *Id.* n.12.
91. 20 U.S.C. § 1415(e)(4)(C).
92. *See, e.g.,* Blum v. Stenson, 465 U.S. 886, 895 (1984).

in statutory fee awards.[93] These standards include the awarding of fees for efforts taken to prevail in fee award disputes.[94]

Numerous cases have discussed the factors to consider in determining the prevailing rate. As pointed out in *Sun Publishing Company v. Mecklenburg News, Inc.*,[95]

> The general principles governing the amount of statutory fee awards are well developed in this circuit ... The Court of Appeals for the Fourth Circuit has further specified the appropriate approach to attorneys' fee determinations in *Anderson v. Morris*, 658 F.2d 246 (4th Cir. 1981). The basic approach is to multiply the customary hourly rate for the services rendered by the number of hours reasonably expended; the product of these two is the so-called "lodestar" figure. The lodestar is then adjusted on the basis of enumerated other factors.[96]

The "enumerated other factors" have been generally recognized as those identified in *Johnson v. Georgia Highway Express, Inc.*[97] and cited with approval by the United States Supreme Court in *Hensley v. Eckerhart*:[98] time and labor required; amount involved and results obtained; experience, reputation and ability of the attorney; skill necessary to perform the legal service; customary fee in the community; nature and length of the professional relationship; novelty and difficulty of issues or undesirability of the case; awards on similar cases; whether the fee is fixed or contingent; time limitations imposed by the client or circumstances; preclusion of other employment.

The amended IDEA does indicate these factors are likely to be used at least to reduce attorneys' fees. Section 1415(e)(4)(F) provides:

(F) Whenever the court finds that —

> . . .

> (ii) the amount of the attorneys' fees otherwise authorized to be awarded unreasonably exceeds the hourly rate prevailing in the community for similar services by attorneys of reasonably comparable skill, experience, and reputation; or

> (iii) the time spent and legal services furnished were excessive considering the nature of the action or proceeding, the court shall reduce, accordingly, the amount of the attorneys' fees awarded under this subsection.[99]

By definition, of course, the lodestar is first determined by reference to rates prevailing in the community in which the action or proceeding arose. Some

---

93. *See* Medford v. The District of Columbia, 559 Educ. Handicapped L. Rep. (CRR) 468 (D.C. 1988) (fee set by appropriate rate, appropriate hours, level of success, documentation of hours); Kristi W. v. Graham Independent School Dist., 663 F. Supp. 86 (N.D. Tex. 1987) (number of hours and information concerning the kind and quality of services).

94. Angela L. v. Pasadena Indep. School Dist., 918 F.2d 1188 (5th Cir. 1990).

95. 594 F. Supp. 1512 (E.D. Va. 1984).

96. *Id.* at 1517.

97. 488 F.2d 714 (5th Cir. 1974).

98. 461 U.S. 424, 431 n.3 (1983).

99. 20 U.S.C. § 1415(e)(4)(F).

important general guidelines, however, that may be of help are clear from some recent litigation. For example, it is clear that simply because the parents' attorney is young or works for legal aid there is no need to reduce the fee award. In *City of Riverside v. Rivera*,[100] a case in which $125 per hour was awarded to two recent law school graduates, the United States Supreme Court cited with approval the language found in *Johnson v. Georgia Highway Express, Inc.*,[101] that "[i]f a young attorney demonstrates the skill and ability, he should not be penalized for only recently being admitted to the bar."[102]

The attorney must be sure to maintain adequate records to establish hours spent. These will typically be the actual time sheets kept by the attorney.[103] Further, affidavits by attorneys' familiar with special education litigation which attest to the reasonableness of the time spent may be helpful. The attorney must also be prepared to establish the prevailing rate within the community.[104] Establishing the prevailing rate may be done in a number of ways including affidavits of practicing attorneys, where permitted by the court or actual testimony. One piece of evidence that has proved particularly useful to parents in establishing that rate is surveying attorneys who represent local school divisions to find out how much they charge the school system for representing it in special education cases. If the state has a freedom of information statute, the information is quite easy to obtain.

15.7.1 No Bonus or Multiplier

One exception to treating the award of attorneys' fees under the amended IDEA the same as under § 1988 is in the area of the ability of the court to grant "upward enhancement." Given the imprecise nature of considering the various factors to determine prevailing rate, many courts are awarding upward adjustments or multipliers for various factors such as efficiency, economy, delay in fee payment, or contingency of success.[105] Such multipliers were specifically approved under some circumstances by the United States Supreme Court in *Blum v. Stenson*.[106]

---

100. 477 U.S. 561 (1986).

101. 488 F.2d 714 (5th Cir. 1974).

102. *Id.* at 718–719. *See also* Blum v. Stenson, 465 U.S. 886 (1984) ($95 to $105 per hour awarded to second and third year associates). Blum also set out the general requirement that plaintiffs must establish by "sufficient evidence" the rate in the prevailing community. *Id.* n.11.

103. *See* Behavior Research Institute v. Ambach, 535 N.Y.S.2d 465, 144 A.D.2d 872 (1988) (attorney narrative insufficient, required production of time sheets).

104. *See* Williams v. Boston School Committee, 709 F. Supp. 27 (D. Mass. 1989) (where there is an absence of evidence concerning prevailing rate in the community, court had discretion to reduce fee request); *see also* Nadeau v. Helgemoe, 581 F.2d 275, 279 (1st Cir. 1978) (" 'As for the future, we would not view with sympathy any claim that a district court abused its discretion in awarding unreasonably low attorney's fees in a suit in which plaintiffs were only partially successful if counsel's records do not provide a proper basis for determining how much time was spent on particular claims.' ").

105. Newberg, **Attorney Fee Awards** 163 (1986).

106. 465 U.S. 886, 896–902 (1984).

The amended IDEA specifically states "No bonus or multiplier may be used in calculating the fees under this subsection."[107] As will be discussed later, however, under some very limited circumstances, including those in which the school system has violated the procedural protections of § 1415, the functional equivalent of a multiplier may well be authorized.[108]

15.8 Fees or Costs Subsequent to Time of Written Offer

The amended IDEA precludes the award of attorneys' fees and costs for services performed subsequent to a written offer of settlement made to a parent within the time requirements of Federal Rule of Civil Procedure 68 if 1) the offer is not accepted within ten days, and 2) the relief finally obtained is not more favorable to the parents than the settlement.[109] The statute then, however, goes on to provide that an award may be made after a failure to accept, if the parent "was substantially justified in rejecting the settlement offer."[110]

The provision is interesting in its obvious difference to Rule 68. Federal Rule 68 provides that if an offer of settlement is made more than 10 days prior to trial, and the settlement offer is rejected, "[i]f the judgment finally obtained by the offeree is not more favorable than the offer, the offeree must pay the costs incurred after the making of the offer."[111]

The amended IDEA is different from Rule 68 in that it is negative in its impact, whereas rule 68 is positive, that is, the former denies the parent recovery of costs, while the latter requires the payment of the other party's costs. It is, of course, possible that both Rule 68 and IDEA provision would apply to the same case. By its terms, an administrative officer may determine that the result has not been more favorable to the parent. As such, under the amended IDEA, if an offer of settlement were made by the LEA more than 10 days prior to the due process hearing and the ultimate result was not more favorable, the parent would be precluded from recovering fees and related costs, but would not be required to pay the fees and related costs of the LEA incurred in the due process proceedings. Once the judicial proceeding was brought, however, the parents would become liable for the fees and costs of the LEA should they not obtain a more favorable result.

The question then becomes would the parent be responsible for the costs and fees incurred in the administrative process? If so, the risk of incurring this additional obligation would provide a major disincentive for filing in federal court.

---

107. 20 U.S.C. § 1415(e)(4)(C).

108. See 15.9.

109. Fed. R. Civ. Proc. 68.

110. 20 U.S.C. § 1415(e)(4)(E).

111. Fed. R. Civ. Pro. 68. This language has been interpreted by the United States Supreme Court in 1988 cases as requiring the payment of attorneys' fees as well, since § 1988 includes attorneys' fees as part of costs. Marek v. Chesny, 473 U.S. 1 (1985). In Marek, the Court held the term "costs" in Rule 68 was to include attorneys' fees. The Court held that since § 1988 defined attorneys' fees as part of costs, Rule 68 precluded plaintiffs from recovering attorneys' fees incurred after the settlement offer.

Indeed, in many cases, the LEA would be wise to make a very modest offer of settlement very early in the process, since not only might this preclude parents from claiming attorneys' fees, but it might ultimately allow shifting of LEA fees and costs in the administrative as well as judicial proceeding to the parents should the dispute end up in court.[112]

15.8.1 Justified Rejection of the Offer

Merely engaging in settlement discussions does not immunize the public agency from liability for attorneys' fees no matter how vigorous the attempt to settle.[113] Interesting questions arise as to what would be a substantial justification for rejecting an offer? A proposed amendment to Rule 68, which was ultimately not sent to Congress, provides some useful guidance. Rather than limiting the sanction under Rule 68 to costs, the amended Rule would have provided:

> If . . . the court determines that an offer was rejected unreasonably, resulting in unreasonable delay and needless increase in the cost of the litigation, it may impose an appropriate sanction upon the offeree. In making this determination the court shall consider all of the relevant circumstances at the time of the rejection, including (1) subject of the offer, (2) the closeness of the questions of fact and law, (3) whether the offeror had unreasonably refused to furnish information necessary to evaluate the reasonableness of the offer, (4) whether the suit was in the nature of a "test case," presenting questions of far-reaching importance affecting non-parties, (5) the relief that might reasonably have been expected if the claimant should prevail, and (6) the amount of additional delay, cost, and expense the offeror reasonably could be expected to incur if the litigation should be prolonged.[114]

The six circumstances used as examples in the proposed amendment are useful for determining whether the rejection by the parent under the amended IDEA was also reasonable. For example, it would appear reasonable to reject an offer made so early in the process that there was insufficient time to determine the facts. An offer made prior to an IEE, for example, might justifiably be rejected, since prior to the IEE the only available expert evaluations might be those controlled by the LEA.[115]

Further, it might be reasonable to reject a settlement offer at the administrative level because, absent formal discovery mechanisms in the due process hearing,

---

112. The Supreme Court in Marek v. Chesny, 473 U.S. 1 (1985) focused on the narrow question of whether plaintiffs were precluded from recovering their attorneys' fees following a Rule 68 offer and rejection. Defendants in Marek had not appealed that portion of the district court decision which held that the costs plaintiffs had to pay did *not* include defendants' post-offer attorneys' fees

113. *See* Laura I. v. Clausen, 676 F. Supp. 717, 720 (M.D. La. 1988).

114. Fed. R. Civ. Proc. 68 (Official Proposed Rule), 105 S. Ct. LXXIX (1985); *see generally* Comment, *Current Federal Rule of Civil Procedure 68 and Official Proposed Changes: Important Impacts on Attorney's Fee Awards*, 31 S.D. L. Rev. 209 (1985).

115. *See generally* Hyden v. Wilson County Bd. of Educ., 714 F. Supp. 290 (M.D. Tenn. 1989) ("counsel should have *promptly* informed the Board of any objection to the offer, so that negotiations could continue. He [counsel] might not have wished to accept this particular olive branch, but it does not follow that he was 'substantially justified' in answering with cannon fire").

information may be severely limited.[116] Once discovery is available, rejecting the same offer might be unreasonable.

It should be noted that reliance on the above-mentioned factors would also protect against the LEA making an unreasonably low settlement offer in a non-frivolous dispute simply in an attempt to take advantage of the potential cost shifting under Rule 68 once suit is filed. As pointed out in the Committee Note to the proposed Rule 68:

> The court has sufficient authority [under the proposed rule] to prevent the rule from being used by a party who makes an offer in bad faith. The purpose is to prevent a defendant offeror from taking unfair advantage of a claimant-offeree by making a reckless offer; for example, offering to settle a non-frivolous claim for an amount so small in relation to the merits of the claim that the offeror should know the offeree certainly will decline to accept it.[117]

15.9 Procedural Violations or Undue Protraction by LEA

As indicated above, the amended IDEA requires the reduction of attorneys' fees under circumstances where the parents have unduly protracted the final resolution; the amount of fees unreasonably exceeds the hourly rate prevailing in the community; or the time spent or the legal services performed were excessive. The amended IDEA, however, also provides:

> The provisions [authorizing the reduction of attorneys' fees] shall not apply in any action or proceeding if the court finds the State or local educational agency unreasonably protracted the final resolution of the action or there was a violation of this section.[118]

This provision appears to be a clear response to recurring criticisms parents have had concerning the advantage to the school system of delaying the process. Since the child's current placement must remain, pending resolution of the administrative and judicial process, it is often in the LEA's interest to delay the process, since as often as not, the dispute arises over the attempt of the parents' child to acquire special education services not presently being provided.[119]

---

116. IDEA provides no discovery provisions other than the right to access the student's educational records. 34 C.F.R. § 300.502.

117. Fed. R. Civ. Proc. 68 (Official Proposed Rule), 105 S. Ct. LXXXII (1985). The justified rejection language in the amended IDEA was at least in part a reaction to the United States Supreme Court decision in Marek v. Chesney, 473 U.S. 1 (1985). The legislative history to the amended IDEA provides:

> The conferees intend that this provision clarify the application of the Marek v. Chesney decision [to this amendment]. One exception is made to the applicability of the . . . decision. When the parent or guardian is substantially justified in rejecting the settlement offer . . . the decision would not apply.

Joint Explanatory Statement of the Committee of the Conference, Rep. No. 687, 99th Cong., 2d Sess. 5, *reprinted in* 1986 U.S. Code Cong. & Admin. News 1809.

118. 20 U.S.C. § 1415(e)(4)(G).

119. 20 U.S.C. § 1415(e)(3) provides that "During the pendency of any proceedings conducted pursuant to this section . . . the child shall remain in the then current educational placement . . ."

Further, reference to procedural violations appears in response to the emphasis IDEA has placed on the importance of the procedural requirements. This importance as already mentioned was recognized by the Supreme Court in *Hendrick Hudson District Board of Education v. Rowley*.[120] In fact, the Court in *Rowley* stated:

> Adequate compliance with the procedures [will] in most cases assure much if not all of what Congress wished in the way of substantive content in an IEP.[121]

The practical import of the prohibition in the amended IDEA against reduction of attorneys' fees may well be to negate the "no bonus or multiplier" provision in the amended IDEA in certain circumstances. The law appears to state that even when the parents unreasonably protract the resolution (with the likely result that billable hours have increased), and the parents ask for attorneys' fees beyond those prevailing in the community or for hours that were excessive, the fees shall be awarded in full if the LEA protracted the process or violated § 1415. This prohibition against reduction looks suspiciously like a bonus for having had to cope with the inappropriate behavior of the LEA.

The first question that comes to mind is whether the prohibition against reduction provides carte blanche for the parents to request excessive attorneys' fees. There are implicit limits on what could be asked for. Indeed, ethical provisions would prohibit a lawyer seeking inflated hours, or alleging tasks that were not actually done.[122] If, however, the tasks were actually done and the hours were actually worked, then the court would seem to be prohibited from reducing the fee requested.

It is likely, however, that this provision will be read with a rule of reason in mind. Indeed, the fact that awarding attorneys' fees is discretionary to begin with would seem to allow the court to place some type of reasonable restraints on requested fees. Thus, for example, when the prevailing rate in the community ranges between $90 and $150, the court should be justified in refusing to award fees at an hourly rate of $200. However, if the requesting attorney in our example normally charges $90 per hour, but establishes procedural violations and requests $150, the court ought not reduce the fee, since it is within the range of what attorneys charge in that jurisdiction for work under IDEA.

There, of course, will be factual disputes over whether the LEA has "unreasonably protracted the final resolution." An interesting legal question, however, is what constitutes a violation of § 1415? Section 1415 refers specifically to a limited number of procedural safeguards. These are the parental right to examine records and obtain an IEE,[123] the requirement to protect the rights of children when the parents are unknown,[124] the requirement of written prior notice when the LEA proposes to initiate or change or refuses to initiate or change the iden-

---

120. 458 U.S. 176 (1982).

121. Rowley, 458 U.S. at 206.

122. ABA Model Code of Professional Responsibility DR 7–102 and ABA Model Rules of Professional Responsibility 4.1 both provide that a lawyer shall not make a knowingly false statement of law or fact.

123. 20 U.S.C. § 1415(b)(1)(A).

124. *Id.* § 1415(b)(1)(B).

tification, evaluation, or educational placement of the child,[125] an opportunity to present complaints, the right to request a due process hearing,[126] as well as specific protections accorded in that hearing,[127] and finally, the right to judicial review.[128]

What happens, however, if there is a violation of other procedural protections. For example, what happens if, contrary to regulations under IDEA, the LEA makes a placement decision prior to development of an IEP[129] or an IEP is developed without parental participation?[130] Are these procedural violations a violation of § 1415?

Technically, it could be said that the regulations controlling IEP development, eligibility hearings, placement decisions and the like are derivative of §§ 1412– 1414,[131] not of § 1415, and therefore violation of these protections would not be a violation which would prohibit a reduction in the fees requested. But it is also quite logical to say that these procedural protections are also derivative of the language of § 1415(b)(1) that provides: "The procedures required by this section shall include, *but not be limited to* ..."[132]

Additional statutory support for this position is found in subsection (b)(2), which authorizes the due process hearings for disputes arising under procedures outside the specifically delineated protections of § 1415 with respect to matters "relating to identification, evaluation, or educational placement of the child, or the provision of a free appropriate public education to such child."[133] Since subsection (e) incorporates due process proceedings, and due process proceedings are designed to protect procedural rights more fully articulated outside § 1415, it is arguable that a violation of subsection (e) in turn includes a violation of rights "relating to identification, evaluation, or educational placement of the child, or the provision of a free appropriate public education to such child."[134]

An expansive reading of procedural violations is also consistent with the legislative intent of the original IDEA, as recognized by the United States Supreme Court in *Rowley* as well as in *Smith v. Robinson*,[135] where the Supreme Court

125. *Id.* § 1415(b)(1)(C) and (D).

126. *Id.* § 1415(b)(2).

127. *Id.* § 1415(d).

128. *Id.* § 1415(e).

129. 34 C.F.R. § 300.552(a)(2)(placement to be based on IEP); *see also* 20 U.S.C. § 1412(5)(B).

130. 34 C.F.R. § 300.345.

131. 20 U.S.C. §§ 1412, 1414.

132. *Id.* § 1415(b)(1) (emphasis added). Section 1415(b)(1)(C) provides that the LEA shall provide "written prior notice to the parents or guardian of the child whenever such agency ... proposes to initiate or change ... the identification, evaluation, or educational placement of the child or the provision of a free appropriate public education to the child ..." This duty to provide notice also supports an expanded view of § 1415 violations. For example, if the placement decision was made before the IEP was developed, the parents never received notice that the decision process was *to begin*. In other words, the notice provision of § 1415 was violated because there was never any notice of the process which led to the pre-decision.

133. 20 U.S.C. §§ 1415(b)(1)(E), (b)(2). These protections are more fully articulated in §§ 1412– 1414.

134. 20 U.S.C. § 1415(b)(1)(E).

135. 468 U.S. 992 (1984).

further stressed the importance of faithful compliance with the procedural mechanism of IDEA. In *Smith*, the Court stated that the procedures:

> effect Congress' intent that each child's individual educational needs be worked out through a process that... includes... detailed procedural safeguards.[136]

It is precisely the procedural protections inherent in the IEP and placement process where the individual educational needs of the child are met. Hence, the Supreme Court was equating procedural safeguards with the provisions in the entire IDEA, not simply § 1415. It would make little sense to read the amended IDEA as providing less importance to the procedural protections which Congress and the Court recognized as paramount.

15.10 Retroactive Application

The amended IDEA provides that the attorneys' fees provisions shall have retroactive application:

> The amendment made by [amending subsection 20 U.S.C. § 1415(e)(4) of this section] shall apply with respect to actions or proceedings brought under section 615(e) of the Education for All Handicapped Children Act [subsection (e) of § 1415] after July 3, 1984, and actions or proceedings brought prior to July 4, 1984... which were pending on July 4, 1984.[137]

Constitutional challenges have been made to the retroactive application of the statute. Specifically, it has been argued that retroactive application violates the spending clause of the United States Constitution in that it attaches a retroactive condition and that when Congress attaches conditions they "must be clearly expressed and prospective in nature since the states cannot be expected to predict the future actions of Congress."[138] It has also been argued that retroactive application to cases which have already been decided on the merits violates the doctrine of separation of powers, since it would allow the nullification of a final court order.[139] Every court addressing the constitutional arguments to date has held the retroactivity provision to be constitutional.[140]

---

136. *Id.* at 1011.

137. Handicapped Children's Protection Act of 1986, P.L. 99-372, § 5, 100 Stat. 796, 798 (1986).

138. Gittins, Challenging Attorney's Fees Under the Education for the Handicapped Act, Inquiry & Analysis 1, 4 (November 1986).

139. *Id.* 4–5.

140. *See, e.g.,* Counsel v. Dow, 849 F.2d 731 (2d Cir. 1988); Tonya K. v. Chicago Bd. of Educ., 847 F. 2d 1243, 1246–47 (7th Cir. 1988); School Bd. of the County of Prince William v. Malone, 662 F. Supp. 999 (E.D. Va. 1987); *see also* Rollison v. Biggs, 656 F. Supp. 1204 (D. Del. 1987) vacated on other grounds 660 F. Supp. 875 (D. Del. 1987); Cappello v. District of Columbia Bd. of Educ., 669 F. Supp. 14 (D.D.C. 1987); Moore v. District of Columbia, 674 F. Supp. 901 (D.C. 1987) *aff'd.* 907 F.2d 165 (D.C. Cir. 1990). For cases recognizing the retroactive application of the amendment, but not addressing the constitutional claims see Taylor v. Board of Educ. of Copake-Taconic Hills Central School Dist., 649 F. Supp. 1253 (N.D.N.Y. 1986) (recognition of right to recover attorneys' fees since suit filed after July 3, 1984); Silano v. Tirozzi, 651 F. Supp. 1021 (D. Conn. 1987) (recognition of right to recover attorneys' fees since suit pending on July 4, 1984); Board of Educ. of the East Windsor Regional School Dist. v. Diamond, 808 F.2d 987 (3d Cir. 1986) (recognition of right to recover attorneys' fees since suit pending on July 4, 1984).

15.11 Waiver of Attorneys' Fees

The fact that a dispute under the amended IDEA has been settled rather than litigated should not itself affect the availability of attorneys' fees. *J.G. v. Board of Education of the Rochester City School District*,[141] was the first significant decision under the new attorneys' fee act. In *J.G.*, plaintiffs had filed a class action suit against both the LEA and the SEA alleging a violation of IDEA. A consent decree was then entered resolving the merits between plaintiffs and the LEA. The plaintiffs then filed a motion to dismiss the SEA and requested attorneys' fees. The motion to dismiss was granted, but the motion for attorneys' fees was denied. The denial of attorneys' fees was appealed. Before the appeal was heard, the attorneys' fee provisions were signed by President Reagan. The parties agreed to withdraw the appeal and resubmit the question to the district court.

The court held that the fact that the plaintiffs prevailed by settlement did not preclude an award of fees. The court drew the clear analogy between actions arising under the amended IDEA and those brought under § 1988 where the United States Supreme Court has held that "the fact that [plaintiff] prevailed through settlement rather than through litigation does not weaken her claim to fees."[142] Subsequent decisions have consistently held that prevailing by settlement prior to the hearing entitles the party to attorneys' fees.[143]

Where the settlement agreement is silent as to attorneys' fees but refers to a settlement including "costs incurred to date," the court must not only inquire as to the fairness of awarding attorneys' fees, but also as to whether costs are to include attorneys' fees. Although there is some split of authority, it is likely a court would find that such a settlement agreement waives attorneys' fees.[144] The proposed amendment to Rule 68, which was not sent to Congress, would have made it clear that for settlement purposes "costs" include attorneys' fees.[145] Where the agreement is silent on the award of attorney's fees, and the parties are aware that attorney's fees are an issue, the court should grant reasonable attorney's fees.[146]

Since attorneys' fees can be waived, it seems logical that LEAs will attempt to insert a waiver of attorneys' fees provision into settlement offers to parents. The ability of the district court to enforce such a waiver was addressed by the United States Supreme Court in *Evans v. Jeff D.*[147] In *Evans*, the parties had entered into

---

141. 648 F. Supp. 1452 (W.D.N.Y. 1986), *modified on other grounds*, 830 F.2d 444 (2d Cir. 1988). Interestingly, the Second Circuit modified *J.G.* in part by awarding attorneys' fees under the Civil Rights Act §§ 1983, 1988 saying that this would avoid the question of whether attorneys' fees were available to litigants who, under one of the recognized exceptions, filed suit directly in district court by-passing the administrative process of IDEA.

142. *Id.* at 1458 citing Maher v. Gagne, 448 U.S. 122, 129 (1980).

143. *See, e.g.*, Barlow/Gresham Union High Dist. No. 2 v. Mitchell, 940 F.2d 1280 (9th Cir. 1991); Angela L. v. Pasadena Indep. School Dist., 918 F.2d 1188 (5th Cir. 1990); Field v. Haddonfield Bd. of Educ., 769 F. Supp. 1313 (D.N.J. 1991).

144. *See* authorities collected in Fed. R. Civ. Proc. 68 (Official Proposed Rule), 105 S. Ct. LXXXI (1985).

145. *Id.* at LXXXIII.

146. *See generally* Barlow/Gresham Union High School Dist. No. 2 v. Mitchell, 940 F.2d 1280 (9th Cir. 1991).

147. 475 U.S. 717 (1986).

an agreement in a class action suit. The agreement was then submitted for court approval. The agreement provided for a waiver of the attorneys' fees. Plaintiffs' lawyer asked for approval of the agreement except for the fee waiver provision. The district court denied this.

The issue on appeal was "whether the District Court had a duty to reject the proposed settlement because it included a waiver of statutorily authorized attorney's fees." [148] The United States Supreme Court held that the district court had the discretion to approve a settlement which included the waiver provision.

It should be kept in mind that *Evans* also recognizes the discretion of the trial court to reject fee waivers. *Evans* seems to stress the need to look at the circumstances of the particular case. For example, the Solicitor General, in his argument in *Evans*, had suggested that fee waivers should not be approved when the defendant acts vindictively or where the defendant has no reasonable defense. [149]

Finally, with regard to waiver provisions, a waiver may be a justifiable reason to reject a settlement offer under the amended IDEA. To the extent the proposed settlement does not provide adequate recovery to the parents because they will have to bear their own attorneys' fees, the settlement may reasonably be unacceptable. [150]

---

148. *Id*. at 1537.

149. *Id*. at 1544. Bar organizations in several jurisdictions have also been successful in promulgating ethical opinions which make entering into waiver agreements unethical. *See* Note, *The Ethics of Fee Waivers: Negotiation of Statutory Fees In Civil Rights Cases*, 5 Yale Law & Policy. Rev Law & Policy, 157–58 (1986).

150. *But see* Marek, 673 U.S. at 6–7: "If defendants are not allowed to make lump sum offers that would, if accepted, represent their total liability, they would understandably be reluctant to make settlement offers."

Chapter 16

Records

16.1 In General

Student records are subject to at least four sets of federal government regulations: IDEA, § 504, EDGAR,[1] and the Family Educational Rights And Privacy Act (FERPA or the Buckley Amendments).[2] IDEA requirements are consistent with and go beyond the requirements of the other provisions. For example, § 504 regulations provide only a general requirement that the agency "shall establish and implement . . . a system of procedural safeguards that includes an opportunity for the parents or guardian of the person to examine relevant records . . . "[3] IDEA as well as Part H, Infants and Toddlers' regulations specifically reference FERPA regulations.[4] For purposes of special education, therefore, compliance with IDEA will ordinarily provide compliance with the other regulations.

IDEA contains broad parental rights for access to educational records of the child: "The parents of a child with a disability shall be afforded . . . an opportunity to inspect and review all education records with respect to . . . [t]he identification, evaluation, and educational placement of the child, and . . . [t]he provision of a free appropriate public education to the child."[5] The right to access includes all records "relating to their children which are collected, maintained, or used by the agency . . . "[6]

The agency is responsible for responding to a request to inspect documents "without unnecessary delay and before any meeting regarding an IEP or any hearing relating to the identification, evaluation, or placement of the child, and in no case more than 45 days after the request has been made."[7]

The right to inspect the records includes the right to have explanations and interpretations of the records, the right to have copies of the record if failure to

---

1. 34 C.F.R. § 75.734.
2. 20 U.S.C. § 1232. A violation of FERPA may be maintained in an action under § 1983. Fay v. South Colonie Central School Dist., 802 F.2d 21 (2d Cir. 1986). Section 1983 actions may be maintained in addition to IDEA claims. See chapter 1.
3. 34 C.F.R. § 104.36.
4. *See, e.g.,* 34 C.F.R. § 300.560(a)(4); *see also* 20 U.S.C. §§ 1412(2)(D), 1417(c).
5. 34 C.F.R. § 300.502; *see* 20 U.S.C. § 1415(b)(1)(A).
6. 34 C.F.R. § 300.562; *see also* 20 U.S.C. §§ 1415(b)(1)(A), 1417(c)
7. 34 C.F.R. § 300.562(a); *see also* 20 U.S.C. §§ 1412(2)(D), 1417(c).

have copies would prevent the parent from reviewing the records, and the right to have a representative review the records.[8]

The agency is required to maintain records of all parties obtaining access to the educational records of the child.[9]

If the records contain information related to a child of another parent, the inspecting parent has the right to review only their own child's portion.[10]

The agency must, at the parents request list the types, and locations of all educational records of the child.[11]

Fees for copying the records may be charged the parent, if the fee does not preclude the review by the parent. In no event may a fee be charged for search or retrieval of the records.[12]

Any parent who believes the education records contain information that is "inaccurate or misleading or violates the privacy or other rights of the child" may request that the information be changed.[13] The agency must then review the information and within a reasonable time inform the parent whether the information will be changed.[14] If after a review of the information the agency refuses to change the records, the parents may seek a hearing to challenge the information.[15] The parents must be given notice of the right to this hearing when they are informed by the agency that the agency will not change the record.[16]

A finding from the hearing that the information is inaccurate or misleading or violates the privacy or other rights of the child will result in amending the records. If, however, there is a finding that the records are not inaccurate or misleading or violate the privacy or other rights of the child the parent still has the option of placing an explanation in the child's record which will become a part of the child's educational record and must be disclosed whenever the contested information is disclosed.[17]

The hearing required to determine whether the records are inaccurate or misleading or violates the privacy or other rights of the child is *not* held in accord with the requirements of IDEA due process hearings. Rather the hearing is held in accordance with the Family Educational Rights And Privacy Act (FERPA).[18] The hearing under FERPA must, at a minimum,

- be held within a reasonable period of time;
- provide the parent or eligible child notice of the date, time, and place of the hearing within a reasonable period of time.

---

8. 34 C.F.R. § 300.562(b); *see also* 20 U.S.C. §§ 1412(2)(D), 1417(c).
9. 34 C.F.R. § 300.563; *see also* 20 U.S.C. §§ 1412(2)(D), 1417(c).
10. 34 C.F.R. § 300.564; *see also* 20 U.S.C. §§ 1412(2)(D), 1417(c).
11. 34 C.F.R. § 300.565; *see also* 20 U.S.C. §§ 1412(2)(D), 1417(c).
12. 34 C.F.R. § 300.566; *see also* 20 U.S.C. §§ 1412(2)(D), 1417(c).
13. 34 C.F.R. § 300.567(a); *see also* 20 U.S.C. §§ 1412(2)(D), 1417(c).
14. 34 C.F.R. § 300.567(b); *see also* 20 U.S.C. §§ 1412(2)(D), 1417(c).
15. 34 C.F.R. § 300.567(c), .568; *see also* 20 U.S.C. §§ 1412(2)(D), 1417(c).
16. 34 C.F.R. § 300.567(c); *see also* 20 U.S.C. §§ 1412(2)(D), 1417(c).
17. 34 C.F.R. § 300.569; *see also* 20 U.S.C. §§ 1412(2)(D), 1417(c).
18. 34 C.F.R. § 300.570; *see also* 20 U.S.C. §§ 1412(2)(D), 1417(c). FERPA regulations are contained in 34 C.F.R. part 99.

- must be conducted by an individual who has no interest in the outcome of the hearing, but it may be an employee of the agency.

- there must be an opportunity to present evidence relevant to the issue of whether the records are inaccurate or misleading or violate the privacy or other rights of the child.

- the decision of the agency must be in writing, and it must be based only on the evidence present, and it must include a summary of the evidence and a reason for its decision.[19]

16.2 Safeguards

The agency is under an obligation to provide significant safeguards protecting the confidentiality of the students records. Parental consent is required before any information "personally identifiable"[20] is disclosed to anyone "other than officials of participating agencies"[21] or used in a meeting contemplated under IDEA. IDEA, however, effectively defines officials of participating agencies as those to whom disclosure may be made without consent under FERPA.

Under FERPA, disclosure without the consent of the parents or child 18 or over, may be made only if it is:

- to school officials, including teachers;
- to officials of another school in which the child intends to enroll;
- to state, federal and accrediting authorities for auditing or evaluating educational programming requirements;
- to agencies or organizations involved in developing, validating or improving tests, instruction or programming;
- the disclosure is in connection with the students application for financial aid;
- the disclosure is by court order;
- the information is necessary because of a health or safety emergency;
- the information is "directory information."[22]

Additional safeguards available to the parents include informing the parents when personally identifiable information is no longer necessary to be maintained, and destroying this information at the request of the parent. The student's name, address, phone number, classes attended, grade, attendance record, years and grade level completed, however, may be kept indefinitely.[23]

---

19. 34 C.F.R. § 99.22; *see also* 20 U.S.C. § 1232g(a)(2).

20. *See generally* Child v. Spillane, 866 F.2d 691 (4th Cir. 1989) (per curiam) (a school's policy of general notification to parents that a student with AIDS was enrolled in the public school, there was not violation of FERPA because there was no personally identifiable information).

21. 34 C.F.R. § 300.571(a)(1); *see also* 20 U.S.C. §§ 1412(2)(D), 1417(c); *but see* Howey Inquiry, 17 Individuals with Disabilities Law Rep. (LRP) 701 (ED 1991) (An educational agency's policy of disclosing legal invoices to the public "likely" violates disclosure of confidential information).

22. 34 C.F.R. § 99.31; *see also* 20 U.S.C. § 1232g(b)(1)(D).

23. 34 C.F.R. § 300.573; *see also* 20 U.S.C. §§ 1412(2)(D), 1417(c).

Chapter 17

Monitoring and Compliance

17.1 State Monitoring and Compliance

Each State Education Agency (SEA) is responsible for insuring that all educational programs for children with disabilities are in compliance with IDEA.[1] Federal Regulations originally promulgated under the IDEA were explicit in requiring adoption of procedures for reviewing, investigating and acting on allegations of violations of IDEA.[2] These regulations were superceded by the Education Division General Administration Regulations (EDGAR); general regulations applying to most grants and applicants of the United States Department of Education (DOE).[3] Coming full circle, the EDGAR regulations have in turn been superceded by recent amendments to DOE regulations. The state complaint procedure must:

- Provide for receiving and resolving complaints against the SEA or LEA.[4]
- Review an appeal from an LEA complaint decision.
- Provide for conducting an independent on-site investigation.[5]
- 60 day time limit to investigate and resolve the complaint.[6]
- An extension of time only under exceptional circumstances.[7]
- The right to request the Secretary of DOE to review the final decision of the SEA.[8]
- The complaint must include a statement that the SEA or LEA has violated the statute or regulations, and must provide facts upon which the allegation is based.[9]
- Review all relevant information and issue a written decision[10]

It has also been held that the complaint procedure must have an enforcement

---

1. 20 U.S.C. § 1412(6); 34 C.F.R. § 300.600.
2. 34 C.F.R. § 300.602 (repealed).
3. 34 C.F.R. § 76.780.
4. 34 C.F.R. § 300.660.
5. 34 C.F.R. § 300.661(a)(1).
6. 34 C.F.R. § 300.661(a).
7. 34 C.F.R. § 300.661(b).
8. 34 C.F.R. § 300.661(d).
9. 34 C.F.R. § 300.662.
10. 34 C.F.R. § 300.661(a)3−(a)(4).

mechanism.[11] SEAs have, as a result of complaints, withdrawn Part B funding from LEAs.[12] Prior to withdrawing funds, the SEA must provide the LEA with a hearing.[13] Given the SEAs overriding responsibility, courts have held that a school system's failure to provide educational services, requires the SEA to directly provide those services.[14]

Federal regulations do not state a statute of limitations requirement for complaints to the SEA. Individual states, however, have promulgated time frames in which complaints must be made.

The scope of subject matter coverage is violations of state or federal laws or regulations.[15] It has been held that this precludes raising in a complaint any issue that can be resolved in a due process hearing.[16] Some state regulations make this explicit.[17] Most states, however, will not make such a distinction and the general rule would be that the only issue exclusively within the authority of the due process hearing is the appropriateness of a specific educational program for an individual child.

17.1.1 State Complaint Checklist

_____ Jurisdiction

　　　_____ LEA violation of statute or regulation, or

　　　_____ SEA violation of statute or regulation, or

　　　_____ Appeal from LEA complaint procedure.

_____ State mandated statute of limitations met.

_____ Complaint states LEA or SEA has violated law or regulation.

_____ Complaint alleges facts which indicate violation of law or regulation.

_____ Investigation and Resolution.

　　　_____ 60 day time limit.

　　　_____ May involve on-site investigation.

　　　_____ Extension of time only under exceptional circumstances.

_____ Appeal to Secretary of DOE.

_____ Enforcement mechanism.

Exhaustion of this remedy is _not_ required before judicial action sought.

---

11. Illinois Sate Bd. of Educ., 257 Educ. Handicapped L. Rep. (CRR) 573 (OCR August 16, 1984).

12. _See_, Wilson v. McDonald, 558 Educ. Handicapped L. Rep. (CRR) 364 (E.D. Ky. 1987).

13. 34 C.F.R. § 76.783.

14. Doe v. Maher, 793 F.2d 1470 (9th Cir. 1986) _aff'd. sub nom_ Honig v. Doe, 484 U.S. 305 (1988); _see also_ Wilson v. McDonald, 558 Educ. Handicapped L. Rep. (CRR) 364 (E.D. Ky. 1987) (LEA's failure to implement hearing decision requires SEA to provide direct educational services).

15. 34 C.F.R. § 76.780(a)(1).

16. _E.g._, Wilson v. School Dist. No. 1, 556 Educ. Handicapped L. Rep. (CRR) 235 (Or. Ct. of App. 1984); _see also_ Johnson Inquiry, 18 Individuals with Disabilities Educ. Rep. 589 (LRP) (OSERS June 28, 1991) (when a complaint and a due process hearing are filed simultaneously the SEA must review complaints not covered by the hearing decision).

17. Oregon Administrative Regulations 581-01-010(1).

17.2 Office of Special Education Programs

The Office of Special Education Programs of the Department of Education (OSEP) was authorized by § 1402 of IDEA and "shall be the principal agency in the Department for administering and carrying out [IDEA]"[18] In addition to general administrative activities, the Department of Education (DOE) was given specific enforcement powers. Specifically, DOE has authority to withhold funds where 1) "there has been a failure to comply substantially with any provision of section 1412 or section 1413 ...:[19] The DOE also has this authority concerning violations of the state plan.[20]

In the representation of an individual parent or child, the first of these powers is most significant since it provides a mechanism, other than the formal due process hearing, which may bring different, perhaps even greater power to pressure the LEA or SEA to fulfill its obligations under IDEA. Sections 1412 and 1413, respectively, articulate the requirements the states must meet in order to be eligible for funding under IDEA and the details to be contained in the State plan. These two sections require, among other things, the provisions contained in the regulations concerning items such as identification, evaluation, FAPE, and the various procedural protections.

On a practical level, a complaint to OSEP concerning the actions of an LEA operates as filing a complaint with the SEA, since it is the normal practice of OSEP to refer complaints of this type to the individual state SEA's. The SEA is then required to investigate the complaint and report back to OSEP within 60 days concerning findings and resolution.[21] If the complaint is about an SEA, OSEP will investigate the SEA to determine if there is noncompliance. If there is a finding of noncompliance, OSEP will order corrective action.[22]

OSEP, upon a finding of noncompliance has several options, including withholding funds, canceling a grant, reviewing a state plan, and seeking a cease and desist order from the Education Appeals Board[23] or referring the matter to the Justice Department.[24]

17.3 Office for Civil Rights

The Office for Civil Rights of the Department of Education has responsibility for monitoring state compliance with the provisions of § 504. In furtherance of this requirement, OCR publishes a number of documents useful to the lawyer representing the school, child or parent.

---

18. 20 U.S.C. § 1402(a).

19. 20 U.S.C. § 1416(a)(1).

20. 20 U.S.C. § 1416(a)(2).

21. Trible Inquiry, 211 Educ. Handicapped L. Rep. (CRR) 395, 397 (EHA July 23, 1986). This 60 days is the 60 day time frame required of complaints under the SEA complaint procedure required by 34 C.F.R. § 300.661(a).

22. Trible Inquiry, 211 Educ. Handicapped L. Rep. (CRR) 395, 397 (EHA July 23, 1986).

23. 34 C.F.R. § 76.901(3). See 34 C.F.R. §§ 78.31–78.34.

24. Trible Inquiry, 211 Educ. Handicapped L. Rep. (CRR) 395, 397 (EHA July 23, 1986).

First, it publishes formal policy interpretations. Second, there are informal policy interpretations which are generally written in response to specific inquiries concerning OCR's interpretation of § 504. Finally, there are two types of letters related specifically to the compliance requirements imposed on OCR. There are Compliance Letters of Finding, generally letters which summarize matters as a result of inspections conducted of institutions being monitored by the DOE. There are also Complaint Letters of Finding which are responses to complaints concerning LEAs and SEAs received from individuals or groups.

While none of these documents has the force of law, they should be persuasive authority concerning the interpretation of the regulations promulgated under § 504, since an agency is given deference in the interpretation of its own regulations.

As implied by the existence of complaint letters, OCR will investigate certain complaints against an LEA or SEA which alleges a violation of § 504. OCR has discretion as to whether to investigate an individual complaint. The stated policy of the Office of Civil Rights, however, is that as long as the procedural requirements of the law are met it will not investigate individual placement or other educational decisions unless there are extraordinary circumstances, with an emphasis on cases excluding a child from services or cases evidencing pattern and practice.[25]

In 1983, OCR was placed under a court order to comply with specified time lines to conduct its compliance review. In *Adams v. Bell*,[26] the court ordered DOE to implement the following procedures for investigating complaints:

1. Notify the complainant within 15 calendar days in writing whether the complaint is complete.

2. A complete complaint is one that:

   a. identifies the complainant by name and address

   b. generally identifies or describes those injured

   c. identifies the institution or individual who has allegedly discriminated "in sufficient detail to inform the Office of Civil Rights" what occurred, when it occurred and to permit the commencement of an investigation.

   d. to be complete the complaint does not need to allege the law or laws that were violated.

3. If the complaint is complete, the DOE has 15 days in which to inform the complainant

   a. whether the DOE has jurisdiction over the complaint.

---

25. 34 C.F.R. Part 104, app. A.; San Francisco (CA) Unified School Dist. 17 Educ. Handicapped Law Rep. 487 (LRP) (OCR, November 21, 1990) (OCR investigations found multiple FAPE violations including failure to ensure educational placements with non-handicapped to the maximum extent appropriate, failure to place children in non-public schools in a timely manner, failure to conduct the triennial evaluations in a timely manner and failure to evaluate the data of the reevaluations, placing unqualified teachers in special education classes, and failure to ensure that children receive necessary mental health services; Los Angeles City Unified School Dist., 257 Educ. Handicapped L. Rep. (CRR) 06 (OCR December 15, 1978); Office of Standards, Policy and Research, Policy Memorandum I/4/8 *digested in* 133 Educ. Handicapped L. Rep. (CRR) 08 (December 6, 1979).

26. 48 Fed. Reg. 15,509 (D.C.D. 1983).

b. whether the complaint is frivolous

c. of the time frames, procedures and the laws affecting processing of the complaint

d. whether an on-site investigation will take place.

4. If the complaint is not complete, the DOE shall inform the complainant in what manner the complaint is incomplete. The complainant will then have 60 days in which to provide the information to complete the complaint.[27] Following provision of this additional information, the DOE has 15 days in which to respond as if the complaint were correctly filed originally.[28]

5. Within 15 days of the completed complaint, the DOE will notify the institution against whom the complaint was made of the same information provided the complainant.

6. During the investigation, DOE shall:

a. investigate all allegations in the complaint

b. interview the complainant

c. contact information from the institution and gather information from it and relevant witnesses

d. afford all parties a full opportunity to present evidence.

DOE has 105 calendar days from the date of a completed complaint in which to makes its determination.

7. At any point when the DOE anticipates even a partial adverse finding to the complainant, DOE will give notice to the complainant and an opportunity to respond to the evidence relied upon by the DOE.

8. If the DOE finds no violation it will inform the complainant and the institution in writing. This notice will address allegations providing an analysis of the information upon which the conclusion was made.

9. If there is a finding of noncompliance, DOE will seek voluntary compliance. If voluntary compliance is ineffective, administrative or judicial remedies are available. DOE has 195 days from the date of filing a complete complaint in which to seek voluntary compliance. If after 195 days voluntary compliance was not effective, DOE has no later than 225 days following the complete complaint in which to seek administrative or other remedies.

10. Time frames may be tolled if, among other things

a. witnesses are unavailable because of an extended absence (for example, summer vacation)

b. court order

c. pending litigation on the same issues.

Although the OCR is no longer under the court order in *Adams v. Bell*, it continues to impose these requirements on itself.

---

27. For good cause, the Assistant Secretary for Civil Rights may reopen a complaint that is completed after this 60 day deadline.

28. The complainant will also be notified that the institution or individual against whom the complaint was filed may not retaliate against the complainant.

If voluntary means are ineffective OCR can seek compliance through withdrawal of funding or referral to the Justice Department with a recommendation to file suit. A § 504 violation can result in termination of all federal funds to the affected program, whereas the EHA violation would only affect Part B funds. Termination of funding has been ordered.[29] Before federal funds are withheld, however, a formal administrative hearing must be held.[30] The results of this hearing may then be reviewed by the Secretary of DOE in certain cases where important reasons are found for doing so.[31] The OCR and DOE decisions are subject to judicial review.[32]

OCR complaints are handled by one of its ten regional offices. A list of those offices is found in the Appendix. Complaints must be made within 180 days of the alleged discriminatory action.[33] Given the reluctance of OCR to review individual complaints concerning educational issues, the best use of OCR would be to seek systemic changes in the manner in which LEAs are conducting its responsibilities under § 504 and its regulations. This is particularly appropriate for violations of procedures. A reading of OCR Complaint Letters of Findings shows that by far the most common complaint investigated as the result of third party complaint are violations of procedural issues such as failure of LEA and SEAs to monitor time lines appropriately,[34] failure to provide impartial hearing officers,[35] or substantive issues that represent a pattern and practice such as standard policies limiting educational rights,[36] or where the parties have agreed to the appropriate educational benefit and the LEA withdraws the benefit.[37]

There is no obligation to exhaust administrative remedies under § 504 in order to preserve the complaint for judicial review. To the extent that the same complaint is covered by the EHA, the administrative remedies under that act must be complied with.

17.3.1 OCR Complaint Checklist

Filing the Complaint

_____ 180 day statute of limitations met

_____ Appropriate Regional Office

---

29. Freeman v. Cavazos, 939 F.2d 1527 (11th Cir.1991) (court refused to order a stay of funding for failure to cooperate with an OCR investigation); In re Mo. State Dep't. of Elementary and Secondary Educ., 311 Educ. Handicapped L. Rep. (CRR) 98 (OCR April 13, 1987).

30. 34 C.F.R. § 100.8(c).

31. 34 C.F.R. § 101.10(e).

32. 34 C.F.R. § 100.11.

33. 34 C.F.R. § 104.61, incorporating 100.7(b).

34. Virginia State Dep't. of Educ. and Prince William County Pub. Schools, 257 Educ. Handicapped L. Rep. (CRR) 648 (OCR June 28, 1985).

35. Allegany (N.Y.) Central School Dist., 257 Educ. Handicapped L. Rep. (CRR) 494 (OCR March 26, 1984).

36. Robbinsdale (Minn.) Pub. School Dist., 257 Educ. Handicapped L. Rep. (CRR) 304 (OCR April 19, 1981) (violation of 504 regulations to offer home training only after three week absence from school).

37. San Diego Unified School Dist., 352 Educ. Handicapped L. Rep. (CRR) 257 (OCR 1986) (students denied adaptive physical education as required by IEP).

_____ Complaint complete

_____ Complainants name and address

_____ Identifies or describes those injured

_____ Identifies the institution or individual who has allegedly discriminated

_____ Indicates what happened and when it happened in sufficient detail to allow commencement of an investigation

_____ allegation that § 504 and supporting regulations were violated[38]

If Complaint Was Complete

Notice to Complainant

_____ 15 days in which to inform the complainant

_____ whether the DOE has jurisdiction over the complaint

_____ whether the complaint is frivolous

_____ of the time frames, procedures and the laws affecting processing of the complaint

_____ whether an on-site investigation will take place.

Notice to the Institution

_____ whether the DOE has jurisdiction over the complaint.

_____ whether the complaint is frivolous

_____ of the time frames, procedures and the laws affecting processing of the complaint

_____ whether an on-site investigation will take place

If Complaint Was Incomplete

_____ 15 days notice of manner in which the complaint is incomplete

_____ 60 days in which to provide the information to complete the complaint

OCR Investigation

_____ investigate all allegations

_____ interview the complainant

_____ gather information from institution

_____ gather information from relevant witnesses

_____ afford all parties a full opportunity to present evidence

_____ 105 calendar days from the dated of a complete complaint in which to makes its determination

OCR Decision

_____ Notice to complainant of anticipated finding in favor of institution

_____ Opportunity to respond to the evidence relied upon by the DOE for anticipated decision

_____ Notice of finding to complainant and the institution in writing

_____ Notice of decision addresses allegations providing an analysis of the information upon which the conclusion was made

---

38. Not required but clearly helpful.

OCR Enforcement

_____ If there is a finding of noncompliance, DOE will seek voluntary compliance within 195 days of completed complaint

_____ If after 195 days voluntary compliance was not effective, DOE has no later than 225 days following the complete complaint in which to seek administrative or other remedies

Time frame Tolled

_____ witnesses are unavailable because of an extended absence (e.g. summer vacation)

_____ court order

_____ pending litigation on the same issues.

Exhaustion of this remedy is _not_ required before judicial action sought.

17.4   Coordination of OCR and OSEP

The overlapping responsibilities of OCR and OSEP for monitoring and investigation of educational issues does lead to the possibility of inconsistent positions within the DOE. To limit this possibility, the two offices have developed a memorandum of understanding which outlines their effort to coordinate and communicate with each other.[39] Of particular importance is the agreement that "[w]hen policy is being formulated, by either OCR or OSERS, on any issue concerning the provision of a free appropriate education, every effort will be made to consult on the issue prior to issuance of the policy."[40] Each has also agreed to refer cases involving the others area of coverage to each other.[41]

17.5   Mediation

Several jurisdictions, both on the state[42] and local level,[43] have implemented mediation programs for complaints arising under the IDEA. True mediation involves the use of a neutral third party to help the parents and the LEA arrive at their own solution to the disagreement. Comments to the IDEA regulations recognize the value of mediation, but point out "mediation may not be used to deny or delay a parent's rights under this subpart."[44] The Office for Civil Rights has also made it clear that mandatory mediation is inconsistent with the proce-

---

39. Revised Memorandum of Understanding, August 20, 1987, published in 202 Educ. Handicapped L. Rep. (CRR) 395 (August 20, 1987).

40. _Id._ at 396.

41. _Id._

42. _E.g._, Mass. Chapter 766 State Regulations at Chapter 4, Section 400 cited in 352 Educ. Handicapped L. Rep. (CRR) 313, 315 (OCR Nov. 7, 1986).

43. _See_ West Hartford Bd. of Educ., 352 Educ. Handicapped L. Rep. (CRR) 300 (OCR Oct. 23 1986).

44. 34 C.F.R. § 300.506 cmt.; _see also_ 20 U.S.C. § 1415(b)(2).

dural requirements of the § 504 regulations.[45] Despite this warning, on occasion LEAs have been called to task for making mediation a mandatory step.

17.6 Choosing Dispute Resolution Process

The clear advantage to following any of the above complaint procedures is twofold. First, of course, for some problems, a complaint may be the only means short of litigation that is available to resolve the issue. The due process hearings provided for under IDEA cover disputes over the identification, evaluation, educational placement, or provision of a FAPE.[46] A hearing is also appropriate to resolve disputes challenging information contained in the child's educational records.[47] These topics cover most of the disputes that arise between parents and educators concerning rights under IDEA, but not all of the disputes.[48] Not all complaints can be resolved, therefore by way of the due process mechanism. Second, allowing the state or federal offices to do the investigation may save the client considerable expense since the investigation and compliance mechanism is controlled and paid for by the office. It is possible that the complaint investigation will provide valuable information for use in the subsequent due process hearings.[49] A negative result of the complaint process is not res judicata, therefore the due process mechanism under IDEA will still be an option after exhaustion of the complaint process.[50] An agreement between the parties resolving the complaint should not, however, be overturned absent a showing that "the complaint resolution process did not address and resolve the questions presented in the hearing."[51]

The disadvantages are that the lawyer does not exercise the control over the investigation that he or she might have. The complaint is controlled by the respective governmental office, and any investigation or hearing such as is done by OCR will not make counsel an active participant. Further, should a negative result occur, though it is not res judicata, its precedential impact on a subsequent hearing officer could be damaging.

Finally it should be kept in mind that these complaint mechanisms are not mandatory and the parents need not exhaust them, unlike the due process pro-

---

45. Missouri Dep't. of Elementary and Secondary Educ., 352 Educ. Handicapped L. Rep. (CRR) 397 (OCR Jan. 22, 1987) (mandatory informal administrative review prior to impartial hearing violates regulations); Massachusetts Dep't. of Educ., 352 Educ. Handicapped L. Rep. (CRR) 313 (OCR Nov. 7, 1986) (mediation process improperly characterized as mandatory); West Hartford Bd. of Educ., 352 Educ. Handicapped L. Rep. (CRR) 300 (OCR Oct. 23 1986) (violation of 34 C.F.R. § 104.36 by failure to inform parents that mediation was not mandatory).

46. 34 C.F.R. §§ 300.506(a); 300.504(a)(1), (2); *see also* 20 U.S.C. § 1415(b)(2).

47. 34 C.F.R. § 300.568.

48. See 11.5.2.

49. Johnson Inquiry, 18 Individuals with Disabilities L. Rep. (LRP 589) (OSERS June 28, 1991) (Due process and complaints are separate proceedings. Generally the hearing officer's decision prevails over the complaint investigation of the same issue. The findings of an SEA complaint can be used as subsequent evidence in a Due Process proceeding); *see also* Case No. SE-10-85, 507 Educ. Handicapped L. Rep. (CRR) 188 (SEA Ill. April 19, 1985) (records and resolution admissible in subsequent due process hearing).

50. *Id.*

51. *Id.* at 188.

cedures under the EHA which must be exhausted. Further, it is unlikely that attorneys' fees will be awarded for time spent on the non-mandatory complaint mechanism.

Joint filing of due process and complaint procedures will not provide any additional immediate substantive benefit, since OCR, as well as most states will stay the investigation pending the litigation. OSERS recently issued a policy letter holding that when a parent simultaneously files a due process request and an SEA complaint, the SEA may suspend its investigation portion of the complaint which is also subject matter of the due process hearing in order to avoid conflicting decisions.[52] However, filing of the complaint concurrently with the due process hearing may be wise in order to toll the statute of limitations for the complaint process. If it is possible that the due process hearing may not resolve all contested issues, it will be necessary to seek relief under the complaint procedures. Failure to file the complaint during the pendency of the due process litigation may, therefore, allow the statute of limitations to run.

---

52. Johnson Inquiry, 18 Individuals with Disabilities L. Rep. (LRP) 589 (OSERS June 28, 1991).

Chapter 18

Infants and Toddlers

18.1 Introduction to Infants and Toddlers with Disabilities Act

The need for early intervention services for infants and toddlers with disabilities (or those who have the potential for developing disabilities) has been apparent for a number of years. For example, infant survival rates have increased greatly over the last thirty years. In 1960, according to the National Center for Health Statistics, twenty-eight percent of low birth weight babies were still alive at age one. In 1980, the number had increased to fifty percent.[1] As the number of children who survive increases, there are an increasing number of children who have disabilities.[2] Low birth weight infants, as an example, often need the services of a neonatal intensive care unit and can have complications which put them at risk of delayed development.[3] Studies indicate that special education services are required two and one half more times more frequently for low birth weight children than for normal birth weight children.[4]

Not only are early intervention services needed, they are effective. In 1990, the results of a study in the Journal of the American Medical Association indicated that there were significant improvements in intelligence scores, fewer behavior problems, and improved health for children who receive early educational services after birth.[5] In addition, studies show children make gains in physical, cognitive, communicative and psychosocial development because of the early intervention services they receive.[6]

Studies such as these played a significant role in motivating Congressional enactment in October of 1986 of legislation focusing on infants and toddlers with disabilities. The legislation, Public Law 99-457, Part H, entitled the Infants and Toddlers with Disabilities Act (ITDA) (now a subchapter of IDEA)[7] was enacted

---

1. R. Weiner & J. Koppleman, **From Birth to Five** 15 (1987); *see also* R. Weiner & M. Hume, *and Education for All—Public Policy and Handicapped Children* 101–102 (1987).

2. Wang, *Implementing the State of the Art and Integration Mandates of P.L.-142*, in Policy Implementation and P.L. 99-457 (J. Gallagher, P. Trohanis & R. Cliffords ed. 1989).

3. *Id.* One child in twenty is in a neonatal intensive care unit due to low birth weight.

4. *Id.*

5. Karasik, "The Right Way to Educate the Handicapped," Washington Post, Jan. 18, 1992 at A21.

6. Wang, *supra* note 2 at 50.

7. 20 U.S.C. § 1471.

to satisfy a need to identify and provide services to a specified population of infants and toddlers through a multiagency approach.[8]

Like IDEA, states receive federal funding if they agree to abide by ITDA's terms.[9] ITDA requires provision of coordinated, multiagency, multidisciplinary services necessary to "enhance" the development of infants and toddlers with disabilities. In addition to enhanced development, the law seeks to minimize potential for developmental delay of children;[10] eventually to reduce the need for special education and related services, and thereby reduce the cost of education for these children;[11] to decrease the need for institutionalization and to "maximize" their potential for independent living in society;[12] to work with families to assist them in meeting their children's needs;[13] and to assist the state and localities in meeting the needs of populations which are often under represented, for example, children living in poverty.[14]

Prior to the 1986 amendments, only a small number of states mandated the provision of services for children with disabilities from birth.[15] IDEA, as proposed in 1975, included a requirement to serve children beginning at age three. A compromise which deleted the age three requirement gave states discretion over whether to serve this preschool population.[16] As a result many children who had or were at risk of having a disability were not receiving adequate services during the years critical to their development.[17]

The states and territories that choose to participate in ITDA's coordinated, comprehensive, multidisciplinary interagency approach for the delivery of early intervention services have specific statutory requirements to meet.[18] Although there are exceptions,[19] by the fifth year of participation a state must have a system

---

8. OSEP Policy Memorandum 90-14, (March 20, 1990) (memorandum provides a discussion of Part H regarding entitlement and eligibility, fiscal responsibility, monitoring requirements, and timelines).

9. A state application for funds requests both general and specific information in addition to specifically identified assurances. 20 U.S.C. § 1478; 34 C.F.R. §§ 303.140–146 and 303.120–127.

10. 20 U.S.C. § 1471(1).

11. 20 U.S.C. § 1471(2).

12. 20 U.S.C. § 1471(3).

13. 20 U.S.C. § 1471(4).

14. 20 U.S.C. § 1471(a)(5).

15. R. Weiner & J. Koppleman, *From Birth to Five* (1987); *see also* 132 Cong. Rec. § 13504 (1986).

As of 1988, the states and territories mandating special education to all children with disabilities from birth were Iowa, Maryland, Michigan, Minnesota, Nebraska, America Samoa, Guam, and Puerto Rico. Virginia mandated services from age two. The remaining states mandated services from age three and older. R. Weiner & J. Kopplemand, *supra* note 1 at 105.

IDEA provided a disincentive for states to service disabled children who were younger or older than the traditional school age. IDEA limited the number of disabled children a state could count for federal funding purposes to 12 percent. S. Rep. No. 315, 99th Cong., 1st Sess., at 5 (1986) [hereinafter S. Rep. No. 315].

16. R. Weiner & M. Hume, *and Education for All—Public Policy and Handicapped Children* (1987).

17. Gallagher, *The Implementation of Social Policy* in Policy Implementation and P.L. 99-457 (J. Gallagher, P Trohanis & R. Clifford ed. 1989).

18. 20 U.S.C. §§ 1474, 1475.

19. 20 U.S.C. § 1475(d).

whereby fourteen statutorily defined components must be in place to receive funding. The components include community, regional and statewide services.

Early intervention services under ITDA are defined as special education, related services, free public education or education under ITDA itself.[20] An early intervention program means the total effort that a state engages in to meet the needs of eligible families and children.[21] To implement its program, states must first define the population of infants and children it plans to serve. The regulations contain three definitions of developmental delay, two of which are required to be included in the identified population for states to receive funds under the early intervention program. The state has an obligation to define the term developmentally delayed.[22] States also need to identify the various procedures and the criteria used for determining the level of functioning.[23] The term developmental delay is used in ITDA because of the difficulty of properly diagnosing disabilities in infants and toddlers as well as to prevent labelling a child. While some children are easy to diagnose others have numerous symptoms based on the rapidly fluctuating development.[24] Therefore, the use of the word is a means to serving children without labelling them.

The term developmental delay can include those children who are already experiencing developmental delays, for example deaf or blind, have a diagnosed physical or mental condition that has a high probability of developmental delay and, at the states discretion, children who are at risk of having substantial delays if services are not provided can be included.[25] Children considered to have a high probability of developing a delay include those children with known etiologies and developmental consequences, for example Down's syndrome or fetal alcohol syndrome.[26] Children who are at risk, eligible only at the state's discretion include known biological factors that put children at risk. Examples of children at risk include low birth weight infants or infants who experience respiratory distress or brain hemorrhage.[27]

Once the terms of eligibility are defined, states are required to include additional specific components in their statewide system. The other major components include

- timetables ensuring appropriate early intervention to all infants and toddlers with disabilities before the state's fifth year of participation (there are, however, exceptions and waivers which may be granted);[28]

---

20. 20 U.S.C. §§ 1401–1418, 1420, 1483; 34 C.F.R. § 303.4(b)(1)(2).

21. 20 U.S.C. § 1471; 34 C.F.R. § 303.11.

22. 20 U.S.C. § 1472(1), 1476(b)(1); 34 C.F.R. § 303.300.

23. 20 U.S.C. § 1476(b)(1); 34 C.F.R. § 303.300(b), (c).

24. R. Weiner & Koppleman, *supra* note 1 at 16.

25. 20 U.S.C. § 1472(1); 34 C.F.R. § 303.16(a), (b).

26. *Id.* at Note 1.

27. *Id.* at Note 2.

28. Rehabilitation Act Amendments of 1991, PL 102-52 § 675(e). *See* Congressional Record, May 20, 1991. These amendments allow states two one-year requests for extended participation in Part H due to the realization of budget constraints who are unable to meet fourth and fifth year requirements; *see also* OSEP Policy memorandum 92-12, 18 Individuals with Disabilities Law Rep. (CRR) 599 (December 13, 1991).

- a timely, comprehensive multidisciplinary evaluation of each disabled infant and toddler's functioning;
- an individualized family service plan (IFSP) including case management services;
- a comprehensive child find system;
- a public awareness program;
- a central directory of services, resources, experts research, and demonstration projects in the state;
- a comprehensive system of personnel development;
- a single line of responsibility in the lead agency to carry out the general administration and supervision of the program. For example, this may include the assignment of financial responsibility and the method for resolution of interagency disputes or disputes among service providers;
- a policy regarding contracting or making arrangements with service providers;
- a procedure for securing timely reimbursement of funds;
- a system of procedural safeguards;
- developing policies and procedures regarding personnel standards; and
- a system for compiling data regarding the numbers of infants and toddlers in need of services, and the numbers and types of services provided. [29]

18.2 Relationship to Other Laws in General

Just as with IDEA, when dealing with ITDA, several other statutes and regulations need to be considered. For example, EDGAR,[30] FERPA,[31] and IDEA[32] regulations pertaining to confidentiality of information need to be considered. Care should be taken, however, in applying these regulations since there is often a need to transfer definitions from one set of regulations to the other. For example, when dealing with ITDA, a state educational agency means the lead agency. The lead agency will not always be the state educational agency. For example, the lead agency could be any agency designated by the Governor as long as it has responsibility for administering the ITDA.[33] Examples of lead agencies include mental health, social services or health agencies, generally those which have already provided services to infants and toddlers.[34]

---

29. 20 U.S.C. §§ 1476(b)(1), 1418(b)(1); *see also* OSEP Policy Memorandum 92-2, 18 Individuals with Disabilities Law Rep. (LRP) 246 (OSEP October 10,1991). This OSEP memorandum discusses instructions for ease of collection as well. For example, recognizing that the distinction between a child service and a family service is often artificial, a family service is defined as a service which is provided when the child is not present.

30. See 1.6.

31. See 1.7, Chapter 16.

32. 34 C.F.R. § 303.4(a)(1).

33. 34 C.F.R. § 303.500.

34. McNulty, *Leadership & Policy Strategies for Interagency Planning: Meeting the Early Childhood Mandate*, in Policy Implementation and P.L.457 (J. Gallagher, P., Trohanis & R. Clifford, eds. 1989).

18.3 Funds

For implementation of the IFSP and other requirements of the ITDA, Congress provided funds to be used for planning, developing, and implementing the state-wide system; for providing direct services not otherwise provided from other public or private sources; for expanding and improving existing services; and for providing a free and appropriate public education to children with disabilities at their third birthday to the beginning of the following school year.[35] Congress, however, put restrictions on the use of the money. The funds may not be used for services that otherwise would be paid for from some other public or private sources, except where it would be necessary to prevent a delay in receiving services. In addition, payment must be pending from the appropriate source.[36] The state may not reduce the benefits available to eligible children under either Title V of the Social Security Act, SSA, or title XIX under the SSA regarding Medicaid payments.[37]

18.4 Eligibility

Three groups of infants and toddlers are potentially eligible for services under the ITDA. The first group includes infants and toddlers, age birth to two, who need early intervention services because of "developmental delays" as measured in specific areas.[38] The areas of delay can be in the area of cognitive or physical development including vision and hearing, language and speech or communication development, psycho-social or social-emotional development and adaptive development or self-help skills.[39]

The second group of infants and toddlers who are eligible include those children who have been diagnosed with a physical or mental disability that has a " high "probability" of resulting in a developmental delay.[40] Lastly, a state may choose to serve those infants and toddlers who are at risk of having "substantial" developmental delays if services are not provided.[41]

18.5 Identification and Assessment

Each state early intervention system must establish procedures by which children who may be in need of services are identified, located and evaluated. Effective referral efforts are to be included in this child find system. This may include tracking high risk birth conditions.[42]

---

35. 20 U.S.C. § 1479.
36. 20 U.S.C. § 1481(a); 34 C.F.R. § 303.527(a), (b).
37. 20 U.S.C. § 1481(b); 34 C.F.R. § 303.527(c).
38. 20 U.S.C. § 1472(1)(A).
39. 20 U.S.C. § 1472(1)(A); 34 C.F.R. § 300.300(a).
40. 20 U.S.C. § 1472(1); 34 C.F.R. § 303.16(a)(2).
41. 34 C.F.R. § 303.16(b).
42. 20 U.S.C. § 1475(b)(5); 34 C.F.R § 303.321.

The identification and assessment process begins by a referral to the lead agency. After a child is referred, the state agency must complete the evaluation process to determine eligibility. If the child is eligible, an individualized family service plan (IFSP) meeting must be conducted within 45 days of the initial referral.[43]

ITDA has defined both evaluations and assessments, although the distinction is not clear. For example, ITDA has defined evaluations as the procedures used to determine whether a child is eligible for early intervention services.[44] Assessments are defined as the ongoing procedures for identifying the unique needs of the child, the family's strengths and needs related to the child and the nature and extent of services needed. The evaluations and assessments draw conclusions about the level of the child's developmental functioning. These evaluations and assessments are to be conducted by trained personnel, based on informed clinical judgments and should include a review of pertinent health/medical records.[45] With the parent's consent, the family must also be assessed to determine its strengths and needs as they relate to the developmental enhancement of the child. A personal interview, conducted by trained personnel, is held to obtain this information. The results of this interview is then, with parental permission, incorporated into the IFSP as the strengths and needs which are viewed as enhancing the child's development.[46]

The evaluations and assessments must be conducted by non-discriminatory procedures. The minimum requirements in conducting the evaluation and assessment are that they are administered in the parents' native language unless not feasible, that they do not discriminate based on race or culture,[47] that more than one criterion is used for determining eligibility, and that only qualified personnel administer them.[48]

18.6 Individualized Family Service Plan

Just as the individual education program (IEP) is the centerpiece of IDEA, the individual family service plan (IFSP) is the centerpiece of ITDA. It serves as the road map for the provision of services. The early intervention services must be provided in accordance with this IFSP.[49] The services must be evaluated at least annually,[50] and reviewed every six months or more frequently if requested or need warrants a review.[51] The IFSP has eight components. It must contain:[52]

- a statement of the child's present level of skills in the areas of physical development, cognitive, speech-language, and social-emotional development

---

43. 34 C.F.R. § 303.321(e).
44. 34 C.F.R. § 303.322(1).
45. 34 C.F.R. § 303.323(c).
46. 34 C.F.R. § 303.323(d).
47. 34 C.F.R. § 300.323(b); see No Name Inquiry, 18 Individuals with Disabilities Law Rep. (LRP) 741, (January 10,1992) (tests cannot be culturally or racially biased; local norms may be used).
48. 20 U.S.C. §§ 1476(b)(3), 1477(a)(1), (d)(2), (d)(3); 34 C.F.R. § 303.323.
49. 20 U.S.C. § 1477; 34 C.F.R. § 303.340(b).
50. 20 U.S.C. § 1477; 34 C.F.R. § 303.342.
51. 20 U.S.C. § 1477(b); 34 C.F.R. § 303.342(b).
52. 20 U.S.C. § 1477(d); 34 C.F.R. § 303.344.

as well as in and self-help areas. The determination of the level of skills must be based on objective criteria;

- information in collaboration and agreement with the family about the family's strengths and needs for enhancing the child's development;

- a statement of the major "outcomes to be achieved. The procedures, criteria, and time lines used to determine achievement of outcomes must also be included.

- The IFSP must contain a statement of the early intervention services necessary to meet the unique needs of the child and family. The frequency, intensity, method of delivery and location of delivery of the services and method of payment if required must also be included;

- other appropriate services which the child may need but are not required such as the medical-health services listed previously;

- the date the services will begin as well the expected duration of the services;

- the name of the qualified case manger must also be included; and

- the steps necessary to ensure appropriate transition to other services or programs which may be required when the child reaches the age of three years old.

It is also important that the document delineate the services which are to be provided, those actions required by the case manager and those actions which are the responsibility of the parents. The IFSP must include these required components, but in order to avoid a detailed repetition of service requirements, documents containing the various information may be attached.[53]

The IFSP acts as a guide for the provision of services but does not act as a guarantee of the child's success. Neither the public agencies nor personnel involved in the delivery of services are accountable if the child does not achieve the outcomes in the IFSP.[54]

Informed written consent must be obtained prior to the delivery of any services in the IFSP.[55] The parents and appropriate personnel jointly develop the IFSP based on the input from the multidisciplinary evaluation and assessments to include the services necessary to enhance the development of the child.[56] The parents have a right to attend the initial and subsequent IFSP meetings. Other participants who are required to attend are the case manager, a person who has conducted an evaluation or assessment, and appropriate service providers. In addition, at the request of the parents, other family members and advocates may attend. For those persons required to attend and who are unable to, alternative arrangements must be made in order that they have input.[57] If it is evident that services are needed before the evaluation process is complete they can only be provided if the parents agree and an interim IFSP is developed.[58]

---

53. 34 C.F.R. § 303.344, Note 3.
54. 34 C.F.R. § 303.346.
55. 20 U.S.C. § 1477(e).
56. 20 U.S.C. § 1477; 34 C.F.R. § 303.340.
57. 34 C.F.R. § 303.343.
58. 34 C.F.R. § 303.345.

18.7 Early Intervention Services

Early intervention services are defined as services to meet the developmental need of infants and toddlers with a disability in the areas of delay. The services are designed to meet the needs of delay and are selected in collaboration with the parents and provided under public supervision, by qualified personnel. The services must be provided in conformity with an individualized family service plan (IFSP), meet state standards, and be provided at no cost to the parent, unless payment is required by law.[59]

Early intervention services include family training, counseling, and home visits; special instruction; speech-language pathology and audiology; occupational and physical therapy; psychological services; case management services; medical diagnosis and evaluation; early identification, screening, and assessment services; necessary health services so that the infant and toddler can benefit from other early intervention services; social work services, nursing services, nutrition services, vision services, assistive technology services; and transportation services.[60]

These services must be provided in the environments where children without disabilities normally participate.[61] In addition, the role of the service providers is included in the regulations. This includes consultation with the parents; training the parents and others; and participating in the multidisciplinary assessment and developing goals and objectives in the IFSP.[62]

The subsections that follow provide a more comprehensive list of the services required under the ITDA. This list is not exhaustive and may include other services.

18.7.1 Audiology Services

Audiology services are required under ITDA. Federal regulations provide that audiology means identification of and determining the range, nature and degree of loss, referral for habilitation or rehabilitation, auditory training, aural rehabilitation, speech reading and listening device orientation and training, prevention of hearing loss services, and providing services for amplification.[63]

18.7.2 Case Management Services

One of the unique concepts of ITDA is the requirement that each eligible family and child have a case manager. The responsibilities of the case manager include assisting the family in obtaining services, coordinating the delivery of the identified

---

59. 20 U.S.C. § 1472(2)(B); 34 C.F.R. § 303.12(a)(1)-(4). *See* 34 C.F.R. § 303.521. Fees may not be charged for child find, evaluations and assessments, case management, administrative and coordinative activities related to the IFSP process, and implementation of procedural safeguards. *See also* Inquiry of Eaton 18 Individuals with Disabilities Law Rep. (LRP) 183 (October 29, 1990) (discussing child find obligations impermissible fee charges).
60. 20 U.S.C. § 1472(2)(E); 34 C.F.R. § 303.12(d)(1)–(13).
61. 20 U.S.C. § 1472(2)(G).
62. 34 C.F.R. § 303.12(c)(1)–(3).
63. 34 C.F.R. § 303.12(1).

services,[64] facilitating the timely delivery of the services,[65] and continuously seeking the services necessary to benefit the child.[66] The case manager also assists in protecting the child's and parent's rights.[67]

The regulations further delineate specific case management activities. These responsibilities include performing assessments and evaluations, delivering services, and coordinating with the medical and health personnel.[68]

The case manager also facilitates the individual family service plan process and the transition plan to pre-school services.[69] Lastly the case manager has the responsibility to work with the family in identifying service providers and informing the family of available advocacy services.[70]

18.7.3 Family Training, Counseling, and Home Visits

Family training, counseling, and home visits are, where needed, required under ITDA. These services are to be provided by "qualified" personnel and are intended to assist the family to understand the "special" needs of the child and to assist with the enhancement of the child's development.[71] Qualified personnel, including professionals representing various disciplines, are required to meet state approved or other recognized certification, licensing, registration or comparable requirements required by the state.[72] In addition, states must establish policies and procedures related to the personnel standards.[73]

18.7.4 Health Services

Health services where needed are required under ITDA. Health services are those services which help a child benefit from other services they might be receiving at the time.[74] These services include intermittent catheterization, (a procedure used to drain urine from the bladder), tracheotomy care (which may include suctioning or cleaning an artificial airway), tube feeding, changing dressings and changing ostomy bags (bags used to collect bodily wastes).[75] Health services also include consultation by physicians with other service providers.[76]

Several services are specifically excluded from the definition of health services under ITDA. These services include "medical-health" services such as surgical

---

64. 34 C.F.R. § 303.6 (a)(3)(i)–(ii).
65. 34 C.F.R. § 303.6(a)(3)(iii).
66. 34 C.F.R. § 303.6(a)(3)(iv).
67. 34 C.F.R. § 303.6(a).
68. 34 C.F.R. § 303.6(b)(1), (4), (6).
69. 34 C.F.R. § 303.6(b)(2), (7).
70. 34 C.F.R. § 303.6(b)(3), (5).
71. 34 C.F.R. § 303.12(3).
72. 20 U.S.C. § 1472(2); 34 C.F.R. § 303.21.
73. 34 C.F.R. § 303.361.
74. 34 C.F.R. § 303.14(a).
75. 34 C.F.R. §§ 303.12(4), 303.14(b)(1), 303.14(b)(2).
76. 34 C.F.R. § 303.14(b)(2).

services and services that are purely medical in nature, for example prescribing medications. Also excluded are those devices used to treat or control a medical condition. Well baby services such as immunizations are also excluded.[77]

Although these medical-health services need not be provided, they should be included in the IFSP to the extent appropriate. The IFSP should also contain the sources available for payment of these other medical-health services.[78] Identification of these other services assists the case manager and the family to understand what other services they should be accessing.

18.7.5 Medical Services for Diagnosis or Evaluation

Medical services for diagnosis or evaluation are available under ITDA. These services must be provided by a physician to determine whether a developmental delay exists and whether the child needs early intervention services.[79]

18.7.6 Nursing Services

Nursing services must also be available under ITDA. Nursing services are those activities and services used to assess health status, to identify the child's and family's response to actual or potential health problems, to provide direct care in order to prevent, promote or restore health and to administer medications and any other regimens prescribed by physicians.[80]

18.7.7 Nutrition Services

Nutrition services are also available services under ITDA. Nutrition services includes conducting assessments and developing appropriate plans based on the assessments. These services also include making appropriate referrals to allow the nutritional goals for the child to be carried out.[81]

18.7.8 Occupational Therapy

Occupational services designed to improve the functional ability of a child in the performance of various skills are included in the required available services. The required services relate to the areas of self-help, adaptive behavior, sensory, motor and postural development.[82] These skills, which are to be performed in all settings, include identification, assessment and intervention, which includes the required adaption of the environment to promote the acquisition of the skills.[83]

---

77. 34 C.F.R. § 303.14(c)(1)–(3).
78. 34 C.F.R. §§ 303.344(e), 303.13(c) and Note.
79. 34. C.F.R. § 303.12(5).
80. 34 C.F.R. § 303.12(6).
81. 34 C.F.R. § 303.12(7)(i)–(iii).
82. 34 C.F.R. § 303.12(8).
83. 34 C.F.R. § 303.12(8)(i)–(iii).

18.7.9 Physical Therapy

Physical therapy is a service available under ITDA. The definition of physical therapy includes screening activities to identify movement problems and services to prevent or alleviate movement dysfunction and movement problems.[84]

18.7.10 Psychological Services

ITDA requires that psychological services be available if needed. Psychological services includes administering tests; interpreting results; assessing child and family behavior, providing psychological services including family counseling, and providing consultation and training on child development.[85]

18.7.11 Social Work Services

Required social services that must be available if needed include visiting the home to assess the environmental context,[86] conducting a psycho-social assessment within the family structure,[87] providing counseling and social skill building activities within the family,[88] and working on the identified problems.[89]

18.7.12 Special Instruction

Special instruction is required under ITDA and is defined as designing learning activities to assist in promoting the acquisition of skills in the various developmental areas,[90] developing curriculum,[91] and assisting the family with skill development of the child.[92]

18.7.13 Speech-Language Pathology

Speech-language services are required under ITDA and focus on the identification of children with delays and disorders in communication skills,[93] referral for habilitation or rehabilitation services,[94] and provision of those identified services.[95]

---

84. 34 C.F.R. § 303.12(9)(i)–(iii).
85. 34 C.F.R. § 303.14(10)(i)–(iv).
86. 34 C.F.R. § 303.12(11)(i).
87. 34 C.F.R. § 303.12(2).
88. 34 C.F.R. § 303.12(11)(iii).
89. 34 C.F.R. § 303.12(11)(iv).
90. 34 C.F.R. § 303.12(12)(i).
91. 34 C.F.R. § 303.12(12)(ii).
92. 34 C.F.R. § 303.12(12)(iii).
93. 34 C.F.R. § 303.12(13)(i).
94. 34 C.F.R. § 303.12(13)(ii).
95. 34 C.F.R. § 303.12(13)(iii).

18.7.14 Transportation

ITDA requires transportation services. Transportation costs are defined as the cost of travel and the related cost necessary to enable a child to obtain early intervention services.[96]

18.7.15 Personnel

The people qualified to provide early intervention services are defined in both the statute and regulations. They include a wide variety of professional service providers, including audiologists, nurses, pediatricians, orientation and mobility specialists, family therapists and special educators.[97]

18.8 Procedural Safeguards

Parents are entitled to certain procedural safeguards under ITDA. The lead agency has the responsibility to develop and implement the procedural safeguards. The agency may follow those safeguards used that have been developed under IDEA.[98] The safeguards, however, must include that the parents cannot be charged fees for costs associated with a due process hearing or other procedural safeguards.[99] In addition, the following safeguards are the minimum requirements to which parents or guardians are entitled:[100]

- Timely resolution of complaints by parents. A written decision must be rendered and sent to the parents not later than 30 days;
- Confidentiality of personally identifiable information;
- The right to accept or decline services without jeopardizing the receipt of other early intervention services;
- The opportunity to inspect records;
- The right to the appointment of a surrogate parent if the parents or guardians whereabouts are unknown, if they are unavailable or if the child is a ward of the state;
- Written prior notice whenever the service provider or state agency proposes to initiate or change or refuses to initiate or change the identification, evaluation, placement or the provision of the services;
- Notice provided in the parents or guardians native language;
- The continuation of services during the pendency of a dispute unless there is another agreement. If the parents are applying for initial services then the child shall receive those services not in dispute.[101]

---

96. 34 C.F.R. § 303.23; *see also* 34 C.F.R. § 303.12(14).
97. 20 U.S.C. § 1472(F); 34 C.F.R. § 303.12(e).
98. 20 U.S.C § 1480; 34 C.F.R. § 303.400.
99. 20 U.S.C. § 1472(2); 34 C.F.R. § 303.521(b)(4)(ii); *see* Kemmer Inquiry, 18 Individuals with Disabilities Law Rep. (LRP) 624 (October 25, 1991). The Kemmer Inquiry also indicates that the attorney's fees provisions are not applicable to Part H.
100. 20 U.S.C. §§ 1480(1)–(8); 34 C.F.R. §§ 303.420–423, 460(a).
101. 20 U.S.C. §§ 1480(d)(1)–(7).

18.9 Comparison of IDEA and ITDA

The ITDA, differs from IDEA in three distinct ways. First, ITDA has included more extensive definitions of qualifying conditions which makes the concept of eligibility more comprehensive. Second, the ITDA enlarges the role of the family members. Third, the services under ITDA are provided through coordinated interagency efforts rather than through one agency.

ITDA recognizes that early intervention is not limited to education alone, but rather it includes a combination of services designed to meet the needs of infants and toddlers across a range of domains.[102] ITDA, therefore, reflects the need to provide services in conjunction with multiple agencies. It also serves to strengthen some of the weaker aspects of IDEA.

One main difference is the age and criteria for eligibility. ITDA serves eligible birth to two population. IDEA serves children and youth from ages 3–21.

Children with disabilities under IDEA must be identified under one of the many categories of handicapping conditions and be in need of special education and related services.[103] These impairments must "adversely" affect their educational performance as well. Under ITDA the categorization as disabled is not necessary. Rather there are three potential groups who could qualify for early intervention services based on a state's definition of developmental delay.[104] This tends to avoid the labelling which may later lead to problems with self-esteem and discrimination in providing services.

Another major difference between IDEA and ITDA is the role of the family. The family's role is expanded in ITDA beyond the parental input required by IDEA. While Congress believed that parental input would be an important means for catching inappropriate programs and placements, in general, parental involvement is low under IDEA.[105] A significant number of parents do not attend all of the IEP conferences, and, of those parents who do attend, there is little significant input from the parents.[106] ITDA moves beyond this problem area by requiring the family to become an integral part of the process. The IFSP includes the family's strengths and needs in relationship to the child's development, the outcomes expected to be achieved by the parents, and the services necessary to meet the unique needs of both the child and family.[107]

The role of the parents in the IFSP was modified as a response to the role parents assume at an IEP meeting. A primary factor contributing to the modification of the parental role was the House Committee report which found "overwhelming testimony affirming the family as the primary learning environment for children under six years of age pointing out the critical need for parents and professionals to function in a collaborative fashion."[108]

---

102. 132 Cong. Rec 13504 (1986) (Senator Stafford).

103. 20 U.S.C. § 1401(a)(1).

104. See 18.4.

105. Clune & Pelt, *A Political Method of Evaluating the Education for All Handicapped Act of 1975 & the Several Gaps of Gap Analysis*, 48 Law & Contemp. Probs. 5, 31 (1985).

106. *Id.*

107. 20 U.S.C. § 1477(d)(2)–(4).

108. H.R. Rep. No. 860, 99th Cong., at 62 (1986).

The role of agencies is also different between IDEA and ITDA. Under IDEA, one agency, the state education agency, has ultimate responsibility, although other agencies may actually provide services.[109] Under ITDA, the lead agency may be any designated agency assuming major responsibility for administering the program. In addition, under ITDA, a state Interagency Coordinating Council, ICC, assists the lead agency in the development and implementation of its statewide system.[110]

Some responsibilities of the ICC include defining contracting and reimbursement responsibilities between the agencies, ensuring the coordinated delivery of services to all children with disabilities and their families, and assisting the lead agency in the resolution of disputes.[111] Thus, while IDEA obligates the education agency, ITDA places the responsibility in multiple agencies with the lead agency having extensive input from the ICC. Practically speaking this means that the educational agency has responsibility for developing, implementing and financing the IEP.[112] Under ITDA there is a greater interdependence of both public and private agencies.

The multiagency approach has several advantages. One is the wide spectrum of services which can be provided.[113] Further, interagency coordination maximizes use of community resources,[114] reduces duplication of services,[115] balances the influence of a variety of agencies,[116] and balances funding.[117] There are several other relevant comparisons. Following is a chart.

---

109. 20 U.S.C. § 1412(6).
110. 34 C.F.R. § 303.650(1).
111. 20 U.S.C. § 1482(e).
112. H.R. Rep. No. 860, 99th Cong., at 94 (1986).
113. *Id.* at 121 (testimony of Charlotte Jones Fraas, Specialist in Education).
114. *Id.* at 295.
115. *Id.*
116. *Id.* at 153.
117. *Id.*

Comparison of IDEA and ITDA

	IDEA	ITDA
Definition of Parent	Yes	Same
Surrogates	Yes	Same
Lead Agency	Education	Governor designated & ICC
Interagency Agreements	No	Yes
Cost for Services Required Functions	None	None but State Law may require it for specific services
Personnel Qualifications	Yes	Same
Funding Statute	Yes	Yes
Child Find	Yes	Same
Evaluations		
Multidisciplinary	Yes	Same
Non discriminatory	Yes	Same
Reevaluations	Yes	Same
Ages of eligibility	3-21	0-2
Handicapping conditions	11 categories	developmental delay
Types of Services	Fewer	More, e.g., Nursing, Nutrition
Educational Plan	IEP Student focus Annual Review	IFSP Family focus Annual & 6 months
Notice	Yes	Same
Consent	Yes	Same
Parental Participation	Yes	Yes, more involvement
Procedural Protections	Yes	Same
Responsible Agency	SEA, LEA	Lead
Examination of Records	Yes	Same
Confidentiality of Information	Yes	Same
Complaint to SEA/Lead Agency	Yes	Yes
Complaint	Written procedures	Same
Time Lines	60 days	Same can use IDEAs
Due Process hearing	Yes	Yes, can use same system
Due Process Hearing Time Line	45 days review	30 days
Status of Child Pending Dispute Resolution	Stay-put	Same
Judicial Action Following Hearing	Yes	Same
Attorney's Fees	Yes	No

Appendix 1 Note to Non-lawyers

The Individuals with Disabilities Education Act is a Federal statute. Each state in turn has adopted statutes implementing special education requirements. As a general matter, a state may provide more protection or insure additional rights not required by IDEA. States may not, however, offer fewer services, protections, or rights. For this reason, and because this book is intended as an overview of the law that applies in all jurisdictions, we have focused on the federal statute and on federal cases.

This book is not intended to act as a substitute for legal counsel. On the other hand, it is clearly hoped that it will provide practical information necessary for day-to-day use by educational professionals as well as lawyers. Many of the footnotes will be most useful for lawyers wishing to conduct further legal research. For non-lawyers, we offer the following, brief explanation of the legal citations. Court cases cited are primarily in federal court.

U.S.C.   United States Code. Federal statutes.

C.F.R.   Code of Federal Regulations. Regulations promulgated by federal agencies pursuant to authority Congress has granted in the U.S.C. In this work we will be citing regulations developed by the United States Department of Education.

F. Supp.   Federal Supplement. This is the reporter service publishing United States District Court opinions. The United States District Court is the general trial court in the federal system. Not all decisions of the District Court are actually printed. In fact, the percentage of decisions printed is quite low. Each state has at least one United States District Court. Most states have several, each covering a particular geographic area. Virginia, for example, has two: the Eastern District and the Western District. New Hampshire, on the other hand, has one.

F.2d   Federal Reporter, Second. This reporter reprints United States Circuit Court of Appeals opinions. Appeals from the District Courts go to a Circuit Court of Appeal covering a particular region within the country. The Fourth Circuit Court, for example, hears appeals from United States district courts in Maryland, North Carolina, Virginia, West Virginia, and South Carolina. This structure of appellate courts means that the various appellate courts can reach directly contrary results on the same issue. It is not unusual for Circuit Courts to disagree on an interpretation of the law. When this happens, district courts will apply the law as interpreted by the Circuit Court to which appeals from that district go.

U.S.   United States Reporter. This reporter reprints opinions of the Supreme Court of the United States. The United States Supreme Court, as a general matter, does not have to hear education cases on appeal from the Circuit Courts. A party wishing to appeal beyond the Circuit Court must seek a discretionary grant of a writ of certiorari. The court actually reviews very few cases. Among the reasons that the Court will grant a writ of certiorari is that the Circuit Courts have reached differing opinions on a particular issue.

Educ.   Handicapped L. Rep. (CRR) (renamed Individuals with Disabilities Educ.

L. Rep. in 1991) This reporter specializes in reporting cases dealing with special education issues. This service reports cases cited in other reporters as well as other useful information, including cases not reported in the previous mentioned reporters, opinions of OSEP, OSERS, and OCR; and selected state administrative decisions. It also contains the complete text of IDEA and its regulations.

Appendix 2 State Educational Agency Addresses

Coordinator
Alabama Program for Exceptional
Children & Youth
50 N. Ripley Street
Montgomery, AL 36130-3901
(205) 242-8114

Administrator
Office of Special Services
Alaska Department of Education
P.O. Box F
Juneau, AK 99811
(907) 465-2970

Director
Special Education
Department of Education
Pago Pago, American Samoa 96799
(684) 633-1323

Assistant Commissioner
Special Education Section
Department of Education
1535 W. Jefferson
Phoenix, AZ 85007-3280
(602) 542-3183

Associate Director
Special Education Section
Arkansas Department of Education
Education Bldg., Room 105-C
#4 Capitol Mall
Little Rock, AR 72201
(501) 682-4221

Assistant Superintendent & Director,
Special Education
Specialized Programs Branch
Special Education Division
California Department of Eduction
721 Capitol Mall
Sacramento, CA 95814
(916) 323-4768

Executive Director
Special Education Services Unit
Colorado Department of Education
201 E. Colfax
Denver, CO 80203
(303) 866-6694

Bureau Chief
Bureau of Special Education and
  Pupil Personnel Services
Connecticut Department of Education
25 Industrial Park Road
Middletown, CT 06457
(203) 638-4265

State Director
Exceptional Children/
  Special Programs Division
Department of Public Instruction
P. O. Box 1402
Dover, DE 19903
(302) 736-5471

Assistant Superintendent
Division of Special Education &
  Pupil Personnel Services
District of Columbia Public Schools
Webster Administration Building
10th & H Streets, N.W.
Washington, DC 20001
(202) 724-4018

Chief
Branch of Except. Ed., BIA
Room 4646, MIB/CODE 523
1951 Constitution Avenue, N.W.
Washington, DC 20245
(202) 343-6675

State Director
Bureau of Education for
  Exceptional Students
Florida Department of Education
Knott Building
Tallahassee, FL 32399
(904) 488-1570

Director
Program for Exceptional Children
Georgia Department of Education
1970 Twin Towers East
205 Butler Street
Atlanta, GA 30334-1601
(404) 626-2425

Associate Superintendent
Special Education Division
Department of Education
P.O. Box DE
Agana, GUAM 96910
(671) 472-8901

Administrator
Special Education Section
State Department of Education
3430 Leahi Avenue
Honolulu, HI 96815
(808) 737-3720

Supervisor
Special Education
State Department of Education
650 W. State Street
Boise, ID 83720-00001
(208) 334-3940

Assistant Super.
Special Education
Illinois State Board of Education
Mail Code E-216
100 North First Street
Springfield, IL 62777-0001
(217) 782-6601

State Director
Division of Special Education
Indiana Department of Education
229 State House
Indianapolis, IN 46204
(327) 232-0570

Special Ed. Director
Division of Special Education
Iowa Department of Public Instruction
Grimes State Office Building
Des Moines, IA 50319-0146
(515) 281-3176

Director
Special Education
Kansas Department of Education
120 E. Tenth Street
Topeka, KS 66612
(913) 296-4945

State Director
Kentucky Dept .of Education
Office of Education for
  Exceptional Children
Capitol Plaza Tower, Room 820
Frankfort, KY 40601
(502) 564-4970

State Director
Special Education Services
Louisiana Department of Education
P. O. Box 94064, 9th Floor
Baton Rouge, LA 70804-9064
(504) 342-3633

Director
Division of Special Education
Maine Department of Educational and
  Cultural Services
Station #23
August, ME 04333
(207) 289-5953

State Director
Division of Special Education
Maryland State Department
  of Education
200 W. Baltimore Street
Baltimore, MD 21201-2595
(301) 333-2400

State Director
Division of Special Education
Massachusetts Department of
Education
1385 Hancock Street, 3rd Floor
Quincy, MA 02169-5183
(617) 770-7468

State Director
Special Education Services
Michigan Department of Education
P. O. Box 30008
Lansing, MI 48909-7508
(517) 373-9433

Manager
Special Education Section
Department of Education
812 Capitol Square Bldg.
550 Cedar Street
St. Paul, MN 55101-2233
(612) 296-1793

Bureau Director
Bureau of Special Services
State Department of Education
P. O. Box 771
Jackson, MS 39205-0771
(601) 359-3490

Coordinator
 of Special Education
Department of Elementary &
 Secondary Education
P. O. Box 480
Jefferson City, MO 65102
(314) 751-1909

State Director
Special Education Division
Office of Public Instruction
State Capitol, Room 106
Helena, MT 59620
(406) 444-4429

Director
Special Education
Nebraska Department of Education
Box 94987
Lincoln, NE 68509-4987
(402) 471-2471

Director
Special Education
Nevada Department of Education
Capitol Complex
400 W. King Street
Carson City, NV 89710-0004
(701) 885-3140

Director
Special Education Bureau
New Hampshire Department
 of Education
101 Pleasant Street
Concord, NH 03301-3860
(603) 271-3741

Director
Division of Special Education
New Jersey Department of Education
P. O. Box CN 500
225 W. State Street
Trenton, NJ 08625-0001
(609) 633-6833

State Director
Special Education
State Department of Education
300 Don Gaspar Avenue
Santa Fe, NM 87501-2786
(505) 827-6541

Director
New York State Department of
Education
Office of Education of Children
 with Handicapped Conditions
Education Building Annex, Room 1073
Albany, NY 12234-0001
(518) 474-5548

Director
Division of Exceptional Children
North Carolina State Department of
  Public Instruction
Education Bldg., Room 442
116 W. Edenton
Raleigh, NC 27603-1712
(919) 733-3921

Director
Special Education
Department of Public Instruction
600 E. Boulevard
Bismark, ND 58505-0440
(701) 224-2277

Director
Ohio Department of Education
Division of Special Education
933 High Street
Worthington, OH 43085-4017
(614) 466-2650

State Director
Special Education Division
State Department of Education
Oliver Hodge Memorial Bldg., Room
215
Oklahoma City, OK 73105-4599
(405) 521-3351

Associate Superintendent
Special Education and
  Student Services Division
Oregon Department of Education
700 Pringle Parkway, S.E.
Salem, OR 97310-0290
(503) 378-3591

State Director
Bureau of Special Education
Pennsylvania Department of Education
333 Market Street
Harrisburg, PA 17126-0333
(717) 783-6913

Assistant Secretary of
  Special Education
Department of Education
P.O. Box 759
Hato Rey, PR 00919-0759
(809) 765-8059

Coordinator
Special Ed. Program Services Unit
R.I. Department of Education
Roger Williams Bldg., Room 209
22 Hayes Street
Providence, RI 02908-5025
(401) 277-3505

Director
Office of Programs for Handicapped
South   Carolina   Department   of
Education
100 Executive Center Drive, A-24
Columbia, SC 29201
(803) 737-8710

State Director
Section for Special Education
State of South Dakota Department
  of Education
Richard F. Kneip Bldg.
700 N. Illinois Street
Pierre, SD 57501-2293
(605) 773-3315

Assistant Commissioner
Special Education Programs
Tennessee Department of Education
132 Cordell Hull Bldg.
Nashville, TN 37219
(615) 741-2851

Director
Special Education Programs
Texas Education Agency
William B. Travis Bldg., Room 5-120
1701 N. Congress
Austin, TX 78701-2486
(512) 463-9414

Coordinator of Special Education
Utah State Office of Education
250 E. 500 South
Salt Lake City, UT 84111-3204
(801) 538-7706

State Director
Division of Special Education
Vermont Department of Education
State Office Bldg.
120 State Street
Montpelier, VT 05602-3403
(802) 828-3141

Special Education
Department of Education
P.O. Box 6640
Charlotte Amalie, St. Thomas
Virgin Islands 00801
(809) 776-5802

Division Chief
Early Childhood, Pre & Early
Adolescent, Adolescent, and Regional
Services in Special Education
Virginia Department of Education
P.O. Box 6Q
Richmond, VA 23216-2060
(804) 225-2402

Director
Special Education Section
Superintendent of Public Instruction
Old Capitol Bldg.
Olympia, WA 98504-0001
(206) 753-6733

Director
Office of Special Education
West Virginia Department of
   Education
Bldg., #6, Room B-304
Capitol Complex
Charleston, WV 25305
(304) 348-2696

Assistant State Superintendent
Division of Handicapped Children
   and Pupil Services
Department of Public Instruction
125 S. Webster
P.O. Box 7841
Madison, WI 53707-7841
(608) 266-1649

State Director
Wyoming Department of Education
Hathaway Bldg., 2nd Floor
2300 Capitol Avenue
Cheyenne, WY 82002-0050
(307) 777-7414

Bureau of Exceptional Education
Office of Indian Education Programs
Bureau of Indian Affairs
18th & C Street, N.W., Room 4642
Washington, D.C. 20245
(202) 343-4071

Special Education Coordinator
Department of Education
P.O. Box 3, Majuro
Marshall Islands 96960

Special Education Coordinator
P.O. Box 278
Koror, Belau 96940

Federal Education Program Specialist
National Government
Federated States of Micronesia
Kolonia, Pohnpei 96941

Appendix 3 United States Department of Education Addresses

Office of Special Education Programs
330 "C" Street, S.W.
Mary Switzer Building
Washington, D.C. 20202
(202) 732-1007

Office for Civil Rights
330 Independence Avenue, S.W.
Washington, D.C. 20201
(202) 732-1213

Regional Offices
Office for Civil Rights

REGION I.

Connecticut, Maine, Massachusetts,
New Hampshire, Rhode Island, Vermont

Director
Office for Civil Rights
Room 222, J. W. McCormack
 Post Office and Courthouse
Boston, MA   02109
(617) 223-9662

REGION II.

New York, New Jersey, Puerto Rico,
Virgin Islands

Director
Office for Civil Rights
Federal Building
26 Federal Plaza, 33rd Floor
New York, NY   10278
(212) 264-5180

REGION III.

Delaware, District of Columbia,
Maryland, Pennsylvania, Virginia, West
Virginia

Director
Office for Civil Rights
Gateway Building, 6th Floor
3535 Market Street, Room 6300
Philadelphia, PA   19104-3326
(215) 596-6772

REGION IV.

Alabama, Florida, Georgia, Kentucky,
Mississippi, North Carolina, South
Carolina, Tennessee

Director
Office for Civil Rights
101 Marietta Street, N.W.
27th Floor
Atlanta, GA   30323
(404) 331-2954

REGION V.

Illinois, Indiana, Minnesota, Michigan,
Ohio, Wisconsin

Director
Office for Civil Rights
401 South State Street
Chicago, IL   60605
(312) 886-3456

REGION VI.

Arkansas, Louisiana, New Mexico,
Oklahoma, Texas

Director
Office for Civil Rights
1200 Main Tower Building
Room 1935
Dallas, TX 75202
(214) 767-3959

REGION VII.

Iowa, Kansas, Missouri, Nebraska

Director
Office for Civil Rights
10220 N. Executive Hills Blvd.,
8th Floor
Kansas City, MO 64153
(816) 891-8026

REGION VIII.

Colorado, Montana, North Dakota,
South Dakota, Utah, Wyoming

Director
Office for Civil Rights
Federal Office Building, Room 1185
1961 Stout Street
Denver, CO 80294
(303) 844-5695

REGION IX.

Arizona, California, Hawaii, Nevada,
Guam, American Samoa, Trust
Territory of Pacific Islands, Wake Island

Director
Office for Civil Rights
221 Main Street, 10th Floor
San Francisco, CA 94103
(415) 227-8040

REGION X.

Alaska, Idaho, Oregon, Washington

Director
Office for Civil Rights
2901 Third Avenue, M/S 106
Seattle, WA 98101
(206) 442-1636

Appendix 4 Forms

PRIOR NOTICE

The _____, _____
                    (Division)   (County/City)
Public Schools offer many special programs and services. In order to better meet the educational needs of your child,

_____,
                    (Name of child)

a formal evaluation is needed. *All components of the evaluation are available at no cost to the parent.* The purpose of the evaluation is as follows:

1. ___   (Initial evaluation) This evaluation is to determine the eligibility of your child for special education and related services. Before we can begin formal initial evaluation we must have your written permission to give the evaluation(s) checked below.

2. ___   (Triennial evaluation) This evaluation is to be conducted every three years to see if your child continues to be eligible for special education and related services. Although your written permission is not required, notice is being given to you that we will begin the formal evaluation(s) checked below.

3. ___   (Other) This evaluation is being conducted because the division needs additional information regarding your child and the disability. Although your written permission is not required, notice is being given to you that we will begin the evaluation(s) checked below.

            Attached you will find a copy of procedural safeguards which explain your rights pertaining to the proposed action(s).

___   EDUCATIONAL: Describe the evaluation procedures/tests

___   MEDICAL: Describe the evaluation procedures/tests

___   SOCIAL HISTORY: Describe the evaluation procedures/tests

___   PSYCHOLOGICAL: Describe the evaluation procedures/tests

___   DEVELOPMENTAL: Describe the evaluation procedures/tests

___   SPEECH AND LANGUAGE: Describe the evaluation procedures/tests

___ OTHER RECOMMENDED EVALUATIONS, I.E., audiological, vision, occupational therapy, physical therapy, psychiatric, hearing screening or other assessment components as appropriate (specified below).

_____

_____

_____

_____

These evaluations are given as examples of those which may need to be conducted. The law requires that the child be assessed in all areas of suspected disability.

_____

Signature of School Official

_____

Title

___/___/___
Month Day Year

CONSENT

I give permission for _____,
(Division)

_____
(City, County)

Public Schools to proceed with the evaluation of my child in order to determine

whether or not_____
(Child's Name)
is eligible for special education and related services. I have received a copy of the procedural safeguards, they have been explained to me, and I understand these rights.

_____

Signature(s) of Parent(s)/Guardian(s) or Surrogate

___/___/___
Month Day Year

I DO NOT give permission for _____,
(Division)

_____
(City, County)

Public Schools to proceed with the evaluation of my child in order to determine

whether or not _____
(Child's Name)

is eligible for special education and related services. I have received a copy of the procedural safeguards, they have been explained to me, and I understand these rights.

_____

Signature(s) of Parent(s)/Guardian(s) or Surrogate

___/___/___
Month Day Year

NOTICE OF PROCEDURAL SAFEGUARDS

As a parent(s)/guardian(s) or surrogate parent of a child with a disability or a child who is suspected of having a disability, you should know and understand the procedural safeguards that are in effect to protect your rights and those of your child.

Your child has the right to a free appropriate public education (FAPE) in the least restrictive environment (your child is to be educated with children without disabilities to the maximum extent appropriate). Special education and related services, including all evaluations needed for a comprehensive assessment are provided at no cost to parent(s).

RIGHTS IN ASSESSMENT

1. You must give written permission before your child is given preplacement evaluation for the first time.

2. You must be informed of the nature of tests and evaluations utilized by the school division to assess your child.

3. You have the right to have your child assessed in a non-discriminatory manner, thus tests and evaluations must not be either culturally or racially biased and must be validated for the specific purpose for which they are used.

4. You have the right to have your child evaluated in all areas of the suspected disability by a multidisciplinary team, one of whom is knowledgeable in the area of suspected disability.

5. You have the right to an independent educational evaluation or evaluation of your child at public expense if you disagree with the evaluation conducted by the school division. The school division may also initiate a due process hearing to show that its evaluation is appropriate. If the final decision is that the evaluation is appropriate, the parent still has the right to an independent evaluation, but not at public expense.

6. If you obtain an independent evaluation at your own expense the school division must consider it in developing the IEP.

RIGHTS TO PRIOR NOTICE AND CONSENT

1. The parent of a child with a disability must be given written notice before the school division proposes (or refuses) to initiate or change the identification, evaluation, or educational placement of the child.

2. Consent is required for the preplacement evaluation and the initial placement.

RIGHTS TO PARTICIPATION

1. The parent is assured of the opportunity for participation in all conferences regarding the development of an Individualized Education Program (IEP).

2. The parent has a right to receive a copy of the written IEP at no cost.

RIGHTS IN RECORDS

1. You have the right to have your child's evaluations and reports treated in a confidential manner.

2. Your written permission is needed before any confidential information is released to other agencies.

3. You have the right to inspect and review your child's educational records upon request and the school must comply without unnecessary delay and in no case more than 45 days after your request.

4. You have the right to request that information contained in these records be changed or removed if you believe that the information is inaccurate, misleading, or in violation of your child's right to privacy. If a disagreement occurs when information in your child's records is challenged, you have the right to a hearing.

RIGHTS IN THE IMPARTIAL DUE PROCESS HEARING

1. The parent of a child determined or believed to have a disability shall have the right to initiate a hearing, as does the school division, on matters relating to identification, evaluation or educational placement of the child or the provision of a free appropriate public education to the child. Information may be requested as to whom you should address your request for a hearing.

2. You have the right to:

   a. Receive the names of any low cost legal and other relevant services and agencies available.
   b. Bring your own attorney or other persons with knowledge or training about disabled children.
   c. Present evidence, compel attendance of witnesses and examine and cross examine witnesses.
   d. Have the child present at the hearing.
   e. Open the hearing to the public.
   f. Prohibit the introduction of evidence not disclosed 5 days before the hearing.
   g. Obtain a written or electronic verbatim recording of the hearing.
   h. Receive a written copy of the decision.

i.   Appeal the decision of the local hearing officer by either party in a dual level state to the state educational agency who shall conduct an impartial review of the hearing according to state procedures.

j.   Bring a civil action in the appropriate court upon completion of all administrative procedures if you are the aggrieved party.

k.   Have the hearing completed in forty-five (45) calendar days and when the hearing decision is appealed, the review is to be completed in thirty (30) calendar days.

l.   During any administrative or judicial proceedings regarding an appeal, unless the local school division and the parent agrees otherwise, the student shall remain in his/her present educational placement.

m.   Attorney's Fees—if you are the prevailing party. These fees will not be awarded if you reject a settlement offer from the school division and do not obtain better relief in a subsequent hearing or court action. Other limitations may also apply.

3.   Before or during the time that parents seek relief in due process hearings or court action, they may exhaust their school division's mediation/ appeal mechanisms. These procedures may not, however, delay the administrative process or deny your rights.

RIGHTS IN PLACEMENT

1.   Information must come from a variety of sources which is documented and considered carefully.

2.   Placement must be made by a group of persons who have knowledge of the child, the evaluation data and the placement options.

3.   Placement must be made in the least restrictive environment with age appropriate peers.

4.   Placement must be based on the IEP.

5.   If you, on your own and without the agreement of the IEP committee decide to children with disabilities, the school division will not be responsible for the cost of the placement, if it *is proven* by the due process procedure that the school division's proposed placement *does* provide a free appropriate public education in the least restrictive environment for your child.

FOR ADDITIONAL INFORMATION PLEASE CONTACT YOUR SCHOOL DIVISION AND REQUEST/REFER TO **any material related to the rights of disabled students and their parents under state law, Section 504, and IDEA.**

ELIGIBILITY COMMITTEE SUMMARY OF DELIBERATIONS

( ) Initial
( ) Triennial
( ) Transfer
( ) Other_

Name of Student _____
                    Last   First   Middle

Date of Birth __/__/__ School _____ Grade _____

Student ID No./SS No. ___/___/___

Name of Parent(s)/Guardian(s) or Surrogate _____
                                                              Last   First   MI

Address _____
              Number & Street   City/County   Zip

Home Telephone No. _____ Work Telephone No. _____

Eligibility Committee Meeting held _____/_____/_____
                                            Month   Day   Year

EVIDENCE OF DELIBERATIONS: The following reports (as appropriate) were presented by school division personnel representing the disciplines providing the evaluation components. All evidence was carefully considered. The major points of discussion were:

A. Classroom Observation: (required for suspected LD but recommended for all)

    Date: _____

    _____

    _____

    _____

B. Educational: Date: _____

    _____

    _____

Name of Student _____

C. Medical: Date:_____

_____

_____

_____

D. Psychological: Date: _____

_____

_____

_____

E. Social History: Date: _____

_____

_____

F. Speech and Language: Date: _____

_____

_____

_____

G. Hearing Test: Date: _____

_____

_____

_____

H. Other Reports: _____

_____

_____

The student is eligible for special education and related services: Yes ____ No _

Identified Handicapping Condition(s) (Complete addendum if LD):

_____

_____

Essential deliberations supporting the findings of the committee:

_____

_____

_____

_____

ADDENDUM TO ELIGIBILITY COMMITTEE
SUMMARY OF DELIBERATIONS FOR LEARNING DISABLED STUDENT

Name of Student: _____
                           Last   First   Middle

Student ID/SS No. _____

I.   The above named student was determined to have a specific learning disability. Basis for making the determination:

_____

_____

II.   Relevant behavior noted during the observation and the relationship of that behavior to the student's academic functioning:

_____

_____

_____

III. Educationally relevant medical findings:

_____

_____

_____

_____

IV. Does this information indicate that there is a severe discrepancy between achievement and ability which is not correctable without special education and related services? If yes, describe:

_____

_____

_____

Name of Student _____

V. What are the effects of any environmental, cultural, or economic disadvantage as determined by the team?

_____

_____

_____

_____

Support Conclusions and Recommendations

Signatures of Committee Members   *Position*   *Date (M/D/Y)*

_____   _____   _____

_____   _____   _____

_____   _____   _____

_____   _____   _____

Oppose Conclusions and Recommendations

(Each dissenting member will attach a statement reflecting their conclusions)

Signatures of Committee Members   *Position*   *Date (M/D/Y)*

_____   _____   _____

_____   _____   _____

_____   _____   _____

_____   _____   _____

Others in Attendance: _____

_____

PARENT(S)/GUARDIAN(S) OR SURROGATE LETTER OF INITIAL ELIGIBILITY AND IEP

(Date)

[Address]

Dear _____: (Name of Parent(s))

On _____ (date), our Eligibility Committee met to discuss results of the formal evaluation concerning _____(Child's name). We have determined that your child has the following disabilities

_____

and is eligible for special education and related services.

Before we are permitted to proceed with developing a program for your child, we must have your written permission, and request your involvement in the writing of an Individualized Education Program (IEP). A meeting has been scheduled as follows:

Date:_____   Time: _____

Location: _____

Participants: _____

_____

_____

If this time is not convenient for you, please contact your child's teacher, _____ (Telephone Number), or principal, _____ (Telephone Number), to discuss another time.

Attached is a copy of the procedural safeguards. If you would like to discuss this matter, please call me at _____.

I look forward to meeting with you.

Sincerely yours,

_____
Title

PARENT(S)/GUARDIAN(S) OR SURROGATE LETTER OF INELIGIBILITY

(Date)

[Address]

Dear _____ : (Parent(s) Name)

On _____ (date), our Eligibility Committee met to discuss results of the formal evaluation concerning _____(Child's name). We determined, after a careful review and discussion of all the information, that your child is not eligible for special education services at this time. We would be happy to discuss the results of the evaluation with you.

We want to inform you that you have the right to appeal our decision. You have already received a copy of the procedural safeguards. If you would like to discuss this or receive another copy of the procedural safeguards, please call me at _____.

Sincerely yours,

_____
Title

CONFIDENTIAL

SPECIAL EDUCATION INDIVIDUALIZED EDUCATION PROGRAM

LEA _____

SCHOOL _____

GRADE _____

Name of Student _____

Date of Birth ___/___/_____   Age _____

Student ID/SS No. _____

Parent(s)/Guardian(s) or Surrogate:

Name _____
     Last   First   Middle

Telephone _____ (Home) _____ (Work)

Address _____
     Number & Street   City / County   Zip Code

Most Recent Eligibility   ____ / ____ / ____ IEP Meeting ____ / ____ / ____

Triennial Date ____/ ____/ ___

Disability/Disabilities _____

Beginning Date: ____ / ____ / ___   Ending Date: ____ / ____ / ___

PRESENT LEVEL OF EDUCATIONAL PERFORMANCE
Summary of Data/Strengths and Weaknesses
to include academic, social, emotional, motor,
communication, cognition, and behavior.
(Explain in narrative, test scores alone are insufficient)

_____

_____

_____

_____

_____

_____

CONFIDENTIAL

Name of Student _____

LEA _____

Services Provided (Type and Intensity of Service)

Special Education Related	Frequency & Duration (Per Week)	Date to Begin	Anticipation Completion	Environment Location/ Provider
_____	_____	_____	_____	_____
_____	_____	_____	_____	_____
_____	_____	_____	_____	_____
_____	_____	_____	_____	_____
_____	_____	_____	_____	_____

* *

Transportation: General___ Special___ (Describe special trans.)

_____

_____

Extent of Participation with Students Without Disabilities:

Subject and/or Activity   Frequency and Duration (per week)

Physical Education:

_____   _____

_____   _____

Vocational Education:

_____   _____

_____   _____

Other:

_____   _____

_____   _____

Student will participate in _name of specialty program i.e. competency test._

____ Yes ____ No

If yes list accommodations needed.

_____

Does the program described above ensure the required hours of instruction or training per day? ____ YES   _____ NO

CONFIDENTIAL

INSTRUCTIONAL SECTIONS
(Use Additional Sheets, if Necessary)
Relate to Present Level of Educational Performance

Name of Student _____   LEA_____

Student ID/SS No. _____

Area of Instruction _____

Annual Goal _____

Short Term Objectives	Evaluation Criteria	Evaluation Procedures	Evaluation Schedule	Date Completed
1. _____	_____	_____	_____	_____
2. _____	_____	_____	_____	_____
3. _____	_____	_____	_____	_____
4. _____	_____	_____	_____	_____
_____	_____	_____	_____	_____

(Additional objectives and sheets may be added as needed.)

CONFIDENTIAL

JUSTIFICATION FORM

Least restrictive environment has been addressed in placement decision for

_____

Date of Birth ____ / ____ / ____

Student ID/SS No. _____

Check the following items YES or NO. A written explanation for items marked No must be provided.

		YES	NO
1.	The school the student would normally attend, without disability, is the recommended placement or is the placement. Placement is as close as possible to the student's home.	___	___
2.	The student is educated in the regular class with the use of supplementary aids and services.	___	___
3.	The student is educated in special education class in the regular school building.	___	___
4.	The placement providing educational services required to meet the student's IEP goals is appropriate taking into account the potential harmful effects to the student.	___	___
5.	The student is educated with chronologically age-appropriate peers (age appropriate to school and class).	___	___
6.	The student will participate in a regular physical education program with non-disabled, chronologically age-appropriate peers.	___	___

YES   NO

7.   The student is educationally integrated with nondisabled chronologically age-appropriate peers.   ———— ————

8.   The placement in a more restrictive environment is based on the individualized needs of the student.   ———— ————

After considering all the options on the continuum below, select the appropriate placement and provide a written explanation for the placement chosen, to include why the lesser restrictive placements are not appropriate.

Direct instruction and/or consultative services within the regular class.   ————

Regular class with instruction in the resource room.   ————

Self-contained class with full-time academic instruction in regular public school facility; non-academic instruction with peers.   ————

Self-contained class with full-time academic and non-academic instruction in regular public school facility.   ————

Separate day school.   ————

Private day school for disabled.   ————

Public and/or private residential facility.   ————

Homebound.   ————

Hospital.   ————

Homebound instruction for pre-school age students with disabilities.   ————

Placement Justification: _____

_____

_____

CONFIDENTIAL

Signature of Participants	Position	Date
_____	_____	___ / ___ / ___ Mo. Day Yr.
_____	_____	___ / ___ / ___ Mo. Day Yr.
_____	_____	___ / ___ / ___ Mo. Day Yr.
_____	_____	___ / ___ / ___ Mo. Day Yr.

I give permission for my child, _____,
to be enrolled in this initial special education program described in this Individualized Education Program (IEP). I understand the contents of this document and I have been informed of my due process rights. I understand that I have the right to review my child's records and to request a change in the IEP at anytime. I also understand that I have the right to refuse this placement and to have my child continue in his/her present placement pending exhaustion of due process procedures. I have received a copy of the IEP.

___/___/___
Month Day Year

_____
Signature of Parent(s)/Guardian(s) or Surrogate

I do not give permission for my child, _____, to be enrolled in this initial special education program described in the Individualized Education Program. I understand that I have the right to review his/her records and to request another placement. I understand that the action described above will not take place without my permission or until due process procedures have been exhausted. I understand that if my decision is appealed, I will be notified of my due process rights in this procedure. I have received a copy of the IEP.

___/___/___
Month Day Year

_____
Signature of Parent(s)/Guardian(s) or Surrogate

Permission is required for initial placement only.

I E P INSTRUCTIONS

1. *Triennial Date*
   Indicate <u>month/day/year</u>.

2. *Disability or Disabilities*
   Spell out the label for each handicapping condition such as Learning Disabled, Emotionally Disturbed. Do not use initials.

3. *Frequency and Duration*
   Frequency is defined as number of times per time period such as two times per week or once per month. Duration is the length of each session such as 15 minutes, 30 minutes.

4. *Environment/Location/Provider*
   Environment is defined as the type of class such as resource or self-contained. Location is where the service is provided such as Lakeview Middle School. Provider is the person who will provide the instruction such as LD teacher-Miss Doe; Instructional Aide-Mr. Sloe.

5. *Extent of Participation with Students Without Disabilities*
   Indicate both academic and nonacademic activities including school sponsored activities, games, lifetime sports, band, lunch, recess . . . as appropriate.

6. *Justification Form*
   The written explanation for negative responses (1-8) must describe the modifications considered or attempted and the criteria used to determine that the child's IEP goals cannot be achieved in this situation. This would include factors considered potentially harmful and the criteria used to determine that the child's IEP goals cannot be achieved. Explanation cannot be based on such criteria as: availability of educational or related services, availability of space, category of disabling condition, or administrative conveniences.

REQUEST FOR DUE PROCESS HEARING

DATE

Address of Superintendent
or Other Designated Official

      Re: [Student Name]

Dear

      As attorney for [Student's Name] and his/her parents, [Parents' Names], a due process hearing is requested under 20 U.S.C. § 1415, 29 U.S.C. § 794, and the supporting regulations of each (34 C.F.R. Parts 104 and 300), as well as [State Special Education Law] and supporting state regulations. The due process hearing is requested to consider issues related to the failure of [Education Agency] to [list complaint, e.g., provide educational services consistent with IEP] as required by law.

Sincerely,

cc: Director of Special Education

REQUEST FOR ADMINISTRATIVE APPEAL

DATE

Address of State Education Agency
Official Responsible for Appointing
Hearing Officers

      Re: _____ v. _____

Dear _____:

      [Name of Appealing Party] hereby appeals the decision of the Hearing Officer in the above referenced case with respect to the determination that [Insert Complaint With Hearing Officer's Decision, e.g. the Public School's proposed placement is not appropriate to meet the educational needs of _____].

Sincerely,

cc: [Attorney for Opposing Side]

COMPLAINT

UNITED STATES DISTRICT COURT
DISTRICT OF -----

JONATHAN SMITH, a minor, by
his parents, Howard and Susan
Smith, as his next friend;
HOWARD SMITH; SUSAN SMITH,
 	
                    Plaintiffs,
 	
v.
 	
COLUMBIA COUNTY PUBLIC SCHOOLS,
ADAM DOE, Superintendent, in his
individual and official capacity,
 	
                    Defendants.
	)
	)
	)
	)
	)
	)
	)
	)
	)
	)
	)
	)
	)
	)
	)
		CA 86-0304-R

COMPLAINT

1. Jurisdiction is conferred upon this court by 28 U.S.C. § 1331 and 20 U.S.C. § 1415. The action arises as the result of violations of 20 U.S.C. § 1401 et seq., 29 U.S.C. § 794, and 42 U.S.C. § 1983.

2. Defendant is organized and exists under the laws of the State of _____ and is the local educational agency responsible under 20 U.S.C. § 1411(d) for the educational program of plaintiff Jonathan.

3. Defendant receives federal financial assistance.

4. Plaintiff has exhausted all administrative procedures required to allow filing this action.

COUNT I

5. [Insert facts which set forth a claim for relief].

6. As a result of these actions, defendants have violated the plaintiffs rights under the Individuals with Disabilities Education Act, 20 U.S.C. §§ 1401 et seq., state special education statutes [insert state statutory citation] and supporting state and federal regulations.

COUNT II

7.   Plaintiff realleges each allegation contained in paragraphs 1 through __.

8.   [Allege any additional facts necessary to set forth claim for relief under Count II].

9.   As a result of these actions, defendants have violated the Civil Rights of plaintiff under § 42 U.S.C. § 1983.

COUNT III

10.   Plaintiff realleges each allegation contained in paragraphs 1 through __.

11.   [Allege any additional facts necessary to set forth claim for relief under Count II].

12.   As a result of these actions, defendants have violated Section 504 of the Rehabilitation Act of 1973, 29 U.S.C. § 794, and supporting federal regulations, 34 C.F.R. Part 104.

WHEREFORE, Plaintiffs pray this Court:

1.   Assume jurisdiction of this case;

2.   Order transfer to this Court of the transcript, documents, memoranda, and briefs used by the administrative review officer;

3.   Find that Defendant's proposed placement of Jonathan is not reasonably calculated to provide educational benefit as required by 20 U.S.C. § 1401 *et seq.*, 29 U.S.C. § 794, [State Special Education Statute] and supporting federal and state regulations.

4.   Find that the actions of Defendant has violated Plaintiffs' rights under 42 U.S.C. § 1983;

5.   Award plaintiff's attorneys' fees and costs under 20 U.S.C. § 1415; 29 U.S.C. § 794a(b), 42 U.S.C. § 1988.

By Their Attorney

_____

Name
Address

MOTION FOR ALLOWANCE OF ATTORNEY'S FEES AND COSTS

UNITED STATES DISTRICT COURT
DISTRICT OF ------

JONATHAN SMITH, a minor, by his parents, Howard and Susan Smith, as his next friend; HOWARD SMITH; SUSAN SMITH, Plaintiffs, v. COLUMBIA COUNTY PUBLIC SCHOOLS, ADAM DOE, Superintendent, in his individual and official capacity, Defendants.	))))))))))))))))	CA 86-0304-R

MOTION FOR ALLOWANCE OF ATTORNEY'S FEES AND COSTS

Comes now the plaintiffs and respectfully move this court for an order allowing attorney's fees and costs in favor of the plaintiffs.

In support of this motion, plaintiffs attach:

1. an affidavit of plaintiffs' counsel itemizing the time and services expended in the above matter as well as costs incurred by plaintiffs (Appendix 1);

2. an affidavit of Frank Jones, Esq., indicating his standard charge for representing parents in proceedings under the Individuals with Disabilities Education Act (IDEA) (Appendix 2); and

3. letters obtained under the Freedom Information Act which indicate what school systems within the geographic area of Columbia County are paying lawyers for representing the school system in proceedings under the IDEA (Appendix 3).

Based on the attachments, plaintiffs request that their attorney be awarded $_____ in attorney's fees and that they be awarded $_____ as costs of the above captioned proceeding for a total of $_____.

_____

Attorney for Plaintiffs
Address

CERTIFICATE

I hereby certify that a true copy of the original Motion for Allowance of Attorney's Fees and Costs, along with supporting affidavits, memorandum and attachments were mailed the _____ day of _____, 19__, to [Opposing Counsel], Esq., at [Address].

_____

UNITED STATES DISTRICT COURT
DISTRICT OF _____

Appendix 1

JONATHAN SMITH, a minor, by
his parents, Howard and Susan
Smith, as his next friend;
HOWARD SMITH; SUSAN SMITH,
 	
                     Plaintiffs,
 	
v.
 	
COLUMBIA COUNTY PUBLIC SCHOOLS,
ADAM DOE, Superintendent, in his
individual and official capacity,
 	
                  Defendants.
	)
	)
	)
	)
	)
	) CA 86-0304-R
	)
	)
	)
	)
	)
	)
	)
	)
	)

AFFIDAVIT OF [Attorney's Name]

[Attorney's Name], being duly sworn, deposes and says:

1. I am an attorney at law duly licensed to practice in the State of _____ and in the United States District Court for the District of _____. I am the attorney representing the plaintiffs in the above entitled action. I was first admitted to the bar in _____ I was admitted to the bar of _____ in _____.

2. I began representing the plaintiffs in this matter on _____, 19___.

3. The following is an itemization of the work performed by me in the above captioned proceeding:

Itemization Of Time
Based On Contemporaneous Records

Date	Work Performed	Time/hours
	19___	
May 10	Initial Client Interview	2.1

[insert remainder of date/work/time]

_____

4. The total hours spent by me representing the Plaintiffs, based on the itemizations in paragraph 3 is 392.95

5. The costs incurred by Plaintiffs in this action are itemized as follows:

Expert witness fees & expenses
Due Process Hearing $3862.37

    * * *

                                                              _____

Total $_____

6.   I routinely charge $____ per hour for client representation.

_____
Attorney for Plaintiff

This day, _____ personally appeared before me, a Notary Public, and made oath and affirmed that the matters contained in the foregoing Affidavit are true to the best of his knowledge and belief.

Given under my hand this _____ day of _____, 19__.

_____

My Commission expires: _____

UNITED STATES DISTRICT COURT
DISTRICT OF _____

Appendix 2

JONATHAN SMITH, a minor, by his parents, Howard and Susan Smith, as his next friend; HOWARD SMITH; SUSAN SMITH,	)))))	
Plaintiffs,	)	CA 86-0304-R
v.	))	
COLUMBIA COUNTY PUBLIC SCHOOLS, ADAM DOE, Superintendent, in his individual and official capacity,	))))	
Defendants.	))	

AFFIDAVIT OF FRANK M. JONES, ESQ.

Frank M. Jones, being duly sworn, deposes and says:

1. I am an attorney at law duly licensed to practice in the State of _____ and in the United States District Court for the District of _____.

2. I am presently associated with the firm of Jones and Associates, [address].

3. Jones and Associates routinely represents parents from the in proceedings and actions arising under P.L. 94-142.

4. I presently bill parents $_____ per hour for representation in proceedings under P.L. 94-142.

_____
Frank M. Jones

This day, Frank M. Jones personally appeared before me, a Notary Public, and made oath and affirmed that the matters contained in the foregoing Affidavit are true to the best of his knowledge and belief.

Given under my hand this _____ day of _____, 19___.

_____

My Commission expires: _____

304

In The
United States Court Of Appeals
Fourth Circuit

JONATHAN SMITH, a minor, by)
his parents, Howard and Susan)
Smith, as his next friend;)
HOWARD SMITH; SUSAN SMITH,)
)
             Plaintiffs,)   CA 86-0304
v.)   Cross Appeal 87-3643
)
COLUMBIA COUNTY PUBLIC SCHOOLS,)
ADAM DOE, Superintendent, in his)
individual and official capacity,)
)
            Defendants.)
_____)

MOTION FOR ALLOWANCE OF ATTORNEY'S FEES

Appellees/Cross Appellants, Jonathan, Howard and Susan Smith, respectfully move this court for an order allowing attorney's fees in their favor under 20 U.S.C. § 1415(e)(4)(B).

In support of this motion, the Smiths attach:

1. an affidavit of the Smiths' counsel itemizing the time and services expended in the above matter as (Appendix 1);

2. an affidavit of Frank Jones, Esq., indicating his standard charge for representing parents in proceedings under the Individuals with Disabilities Education Act (IDEA) (Appendix 2); and

3. letters obtained under the [insert state] Freedom of Information Act which indicate what school systems within the geographic area of ---------- are paying lawyers for representing the school system in proceedings under the IDEA (Appendix 3).

4. a memorandum of law in support of this motion.

Based on the attachments, the Smiths request that they be awarded $_____ in attorney's fees.

_____

Attorney for Appellees
[Name and Address]

CERTIFICATE

I hereby certify that a true copy of the original Motion for Allowance of Attorney's Fees and Costs, along with supporting affidavits, memorandum and attachments were mailed the _____ day of _____, 19__, to [Opposing Counsel], Esq., at [Address].

_____

[ATTACH AFFIDAVITS]

SETTLEMENT AGREEMENT

THIS AGREEMENT is made this ___ day of ____, 199_, by and between the School Board of _____ ("School Board") and _____ ("Parents") individually and on behalf of _____.

A dispute has arisen between the School Board and Parents over the provision of a free appropriate public education to ____ under P.L. 94-142, the Individuals with Disabilities Education Act (IDEA); Section 504 of the Rehabilitation Act of 1973; and 42 U.S.C. § 1983. The parents requested a due process hearing. The School Board and Parents now wish to resolve all issues in dispute which gave rise to the due process hearing;

It is, therefore, agreed as follows:

1. [Describe the nature of the agreement]

2. The Parents rescind their objection to the current IEP. The Parents will sign the proposed IEP, which is attached, indicating their agreement.

3. The Parents will dismiss the Due Process Hearing requested to resolve the issues addressed by this Agreement.

5. The School Board will pay $_____ for all attorney's fees and costs incurred by virtue of this dispute. The check will be made payable to _____.

6. By signing this Agreement, the Parents, for good and valuable consideration, do hereby release the _____ School Board from all claims, actions, causes of action, demands, rights, damages, costs, expenses and compensation whatsoever, on account of or in any way resulting from the provision of educational services in accordance with the Individual Education Plan for _____ for the 19__ - 19__ academic school year.

Agreed this ___ day of _____, 19__.

/s/ _____

/s/ _____
PARENTS

/s/ _____
SCHOOL BOARD OF

_____

Table of Cases

Index